OPERATION KRONSTADT

OPERATION KRONSTADT

The True Story of Honor, Espionage,
and the Rescue of Britain's Greatest Spy,
The Man with a Hundred Faces

HARRY FERGUSON

THE OVERLOOK PRESS
NEW YORK

This edition first published in the United States in 2009 by

The Overlook Press, Peter Mayer Publishers, Inc.
141 Wooster Street
New York, NY 10012
www.overlookpress.com

Cataloging-in-Publication Data is available from the Library of Congress

Printed in the United States of America
FIRST EDITION
1 3 5 7 9 8 6 4 2
ISBN 978-1-59020-229-6

For

Benny

If only we'd had one more bullet . . .

'*The spy is the greatest of soldiers. If he is the most detested by the enemy, it is only because he is the most feared.*' King George V

Contents

Author's Note

As a former MI6 officer, it seems incredible to me that the story of Cromie, Dukes and Agar has ever been forgotten. It is as heroically British as the Great Escape or the defence of Rorke's Drift and yet if you were to stop people in the street today, not one in a thousand would have heard of them. These men very nearly changed the course of the history of Western Europe and therefore of the world. If their reports had been listened to and their daring actions supported there is a good chance that the Bolsheviks would have lost the Civil War and the Soviet Union might never have existed.

I rediscovered this story whilst researching the history of MI6 for a television documentary. I had been aware of the bare outline of the tale for many years but it was only as I began to study the original sources that I discovered the fascinating details of the mission. Originally I thought that this would be perfect operation to celebrate the centenary of MI6. As you will see, our actions were so clumsy (and sometimes, reprehensible) that this has not turned out to be the case. And yet, given the Service's poor performance in recent years, perhaps it is a good thing if some of the mystique which has prevented proper consideration of the Service's numerous faults is brushed aside, even if only for a short while.

In fact I was concerned that this tale presents a rather too negative, if accurate, picture of MI6. I have always enjoyed a productive relationship with my former employers and I did not want to be seen to be unduly knocking the Service. In view of this, I have consulted representatives of the Service and discussed this issue with them. They are content for the record to stand in its current form.

If you enjoy this story I hope you will take time to read the endnotes. A lot of detail which was taken out of the story at the drafting stage has been placed there. I believe it adds considerably to the background and if you find this story interesting, it is well worth browsing through.

Similarly, I am sure that there is a great deal more information in family memories, photographs and other records which I was not able to uncover during my research. If anyone has information relating to the characters or events in this book then they are warmly encouraged to write to me care of the publishers.

Finally, as young Secret Intelligence Service trainees we all used to receive regular lectures on the history of the Service and its most exciting operations. Take it from me, in the annals of the Service there is no more thrilling story than that of Paul Dukes.

This was the sort of spy we all wanted to be . . .

H.F.
February 2008

[N.B. I have used the term MI6 to refer to the Secret Intelligence Service (SIS) throughout this work as I believe the general reader will be more comfortable with the term. I apologise in advance to those who will doubtless point out that the latter is the technically correct term.]

Acknowledgements

One of the great pleasures in writing this book has been contacting the following historians, enthusiasts and family members who have been unfailingly helpful and friendly. Each one of them has contributed at least a small part to the jigsaw which makes up this story and if there are any mistakes remaining they are most definitely mine.

There are no surviving members of the crews of the Coastal Motor Boats and many technical details about their operation have been lost, so in the first place I would like to thank Captain Stephen R. New, maritime historian and expert on the history of the motor torpedo boat. He gave unstintingly of his time and knowledge as well as allowing me to consult his unpublished MA dissertation. I would also like to thank: Commander Rodney Agar RN (retired), for his memories of his uncle; Phil Tomaselli, already well known to researchers in the history of espionage, who supplied the final part of the jigsaw by finding Paul Dukes's private diaries; Dr John Fisher of UWE, Bristol and author of *Gentleman Spies*; Frances Welch, author of *The Romanovs & Mr Gibbes*; Sergey Gavrilov for his research in Finland and Russia into Peter Sokolov; Ann Trevor for her research in US archives; the Head of Security Department and several old friends at the Secret Intelligence Service; Francis M Newton, Jean Cowell, Daphne Porter, Lizzie Sanders and Roz Acland, who all contributed valiantly to my search for Laura Cade; Vin Callcut for sharing the memories of his father, CMB Motor Mechanic Horace G. Callcut; Peter and Christopher Hampsheir for their knowledge of the Hampsheir family; Nigel Watts for his knowledge of the Armistead family; Professor Paul Dukes, recently retired Professor of Russian History at the University of Aberdeen (sadly – and astonishingly – no relation); Dr Letas Palmaitis for his knowledge of the Ingrian people; author and historian Phillip Knightley; Roy Dean and Gerald Blackburn of the HMS Dorsetshire Association; Alina Rennie and Alan Howe of Caterham School; John Roycroft for his thoughts on Paul Dukes; the staff of the Tourist Offices in Bridgwater, Somerset and Maldon, Essex; the staff and trustees of the following institutions: the National Archives at Kew; the Department of Documents and the Photograph Archive at the Imperial War Museum at Lambeth; the National Portrait Gallery, London; the Caird Library at the National Maritime Museum, Greenwich; the British Library Newspaper Archive at Colindale; the Hoover Institution Archive at Stanford University, California. UK material which is not under private copyright is unpublished Crown-copyright material and is reproduced by kind permission of the Controller of H.M. Stationery Office. I am also grateful to the following publishers for permission to quote from their works: Cassell (*The Story of ST-25* and *The Unending Quest*), Evans Brothers (*Footprints in the Sea*) and Hodder and Stoughton (*Baltic Episode*). The publisher has undertaken every effort to trace copyright holders. If any copyright holder believes that they have not been consulted they are urged to contact the publisher directly.

Finally, my thanks to a few special people: Helen Hawken, my absolute favourite television producer, who first suggested that this story might be suitable for a book; Tony Whittome, James Nightingale and everyone at Hutchinson for their enthusiasm and all their hard work; my agent Julian Alexander for his continuing faith in defiance of all the evidence; and last, but not least, my six wonderful children and my long-suffering secretary Rita – I still await a decent cup of coffee from one of them.

H.F.
February 2008

Illustrations

Kronstadt Harbour
HMS *Vindictive*
Bill Bremner arrives at Biorko Sound with CMB79
Two 55-ft CMBs reach attack speed
Richard Marshall
The wreck of CMB7
Agar salutes CMB4, 1967
Paul Dukes on the eve of his knighthood (*National Portrait Gallery*)

Unless otherwise attributed, all photographs are courtesy of the
Imperial War Museum, London

Prologue

The place: Petrograd (formerly St Petersburg, the capital of Russia).
The time: Saturday, 31 August 1918. The First World War was almost over. The Russian Revolution of November 1917 was almost one year old.

In a first-floor office of the British Embassy four men were deep in conversation. A squeal of brakes as several large vehicles arrived in the courtyard outside caused one of the men to look up suspiciously.

Captain Francis Cromie of the British Naval Intelligence Department (NID) was the de facto chief of all British intelligence operations in northern Russia. Cromie was 36, a tall and distinguished officer, always immaculately dressed and a well-known figure in the city to his friends and his enemies alike. It was shortly after four o'clock. Together with Harold Hall, an MI6 officer, Cromie had just begun a meeting with two of the leading British agents in the city, whose names were Steckelmann and Sabir. Cromie had called the meeting to discuss launching a military coup that would almost certainly overthrow the tottering regime of the Bolsheviks and return Russia to Tsarist rule. But Cromie knew that the Cheka, the Bolshevik secret police, were closing in on him. His flat had been ransacked whilst he was at the Embassy a few weeks earlier and so he had moved to a 'safe house'. However, someone must have talked because, only two days before, the Cheka had raided this second flat in the middle of the night. Cromie had only narrowly evaded capture by escaping over the roof in his pyjamas as they came charging up the stairs. On the previous evening, his assistant, Commander Andrew Le Page, had disappeared while walking to the Embassy and Cromie was sure that the Cheka had kidnapped him. Cheka surveillance officers could be seen watching the Embassy from parked vehicles and from alleyways across the street. They made no attempt to hide. Their purpose was to increase the sense of oppression and isolation within the Embassy.

Tension in the city was at its height now. Only the day before, on 30 August, Moses Uritsky, the chief of the Petrograd Cheka, had been assassinated by a Russian military cadet named Leonid Kanegisser as the official was about to enter the elevator to his office. Uritsky had been the second most powerful man in the city after Grigory Zinoviev, the leader of the Petrograd Soviet, so this was seen as a blow, not just against the Cheka but against the entire Bolshevik leadership. Kanegisser had fled the scene of the shooting but had been caught nearby in a disused building formerly known as the English Club. The Club actually had nothing to do with Britain officially, but just the name was enough to convince the Cheka and many Bolshevik supporters that the British secret service must be behind Uritsky's assassination. They had already widely penetrated British intelligence operations in the city and knew that there were plans to overthrow Bolshevik rule and to capture or assassinate both Vladimir Lenin and Leon Trotsky. This seemed as if it might be the first stage in that scheme.

In the evening of the same day a young woman named Fania Kaplan had fired two shots at the Bolshevik leader, Lenin, as he was leaving a rally at the Michelson factory in Moscow. One bullet had hit him in the chest, puncturing his left upper lung and the other had ripped through his neck, missing the jugular vein by less than half an inch. Gravely wounded, Lenin was thought unlikely to live. As a result of this second attack in a single day, the Cheka and their supporters were now almost uncontrollable in their demands to clear out the 'nests of conspirators' in foreign embassies. Cromie knew that it would not be long before the Bolshevik leadership let them off the leash and they would arrive at his door. There was only one hope: if he could launch the coup before they got to him, then the situation might be saved. But it was a matter of hours not days and that was why this emergency meeting with his chief agents was so important.

Cromie stood up and crossed quickly to the net curtains of the large sash window that overlooked the courtyard. He muttered something under his breath.

Harold Hall looked up. Although the planned coup was an NID operation he had been called to the meeting to represent the interests of MI6. His station chief, Commander Ernest Boyce RN, was working elsewhere in the Embassy. Suddenly the sounds of crashing doors and shouting began to filter up from the floor below where the Embassy staff were still working. Most of the shouting was in Russian. Women began screaming.

'There are trucks outside,' said Cromie urgently. 'Patrol boats have moved up the canal in front of the Embassy building and have their guns trained on us.'

Steckelmann and Sabir glanced at each other in apparent horror. If they were discovered in the Embassy it would certainly mean torture and then a firing squad. Hall watched as Cromie pulled a revolver from his pocket. He had clearly been expecting trouble. He had already destroyed any sensitive papers which were held in the Embassy so he was not worried about that, but he would never give up any of his agents without a fight. Cromie flicked the revolver's chamber open to check that the gun was fully loaded. As he did so, Hall crossed the room and opened the door into the passage. They could both see a Chekist officer with a revolver advancing towards them. Hall quickly slammed the door shut. Cromie strode across the room, grasped the handle and then turned to Hall:

'Remain here and keep the door after me.'

He swung the heavy door open and immediately came face to face with the startled officer. Cromie shoved the barrel of his revolver into the man's chest before the Chekist had a chance to aim his own weapon and then forced him to step away.

'Get back, you swine!' barked Cromie and he pushed his way through the door, before slamming it shut behind him to prevent the officer seeing who was inside.

Shortly afterwards Hall heard the sound of a shot. He turned back to the two agents, trying to think of words to reassure them. He had no weapon of his own and was not sure what he was going to do if the Cheka forced their way past Cromie. But although Sabir and Steckelmann had drawn their pistols they now showed no signs of panic. In fact they looked remarkably relaxed. A horrible suspicion began to form in Hall's mind: these men were Chekist agents. He remembered that Sabir had gone outside for a few minutes while they were waiting for Cromie to arrive, supposedly to check on his 'detectives' who were keeping watch. He wondered if Sabir had actually left to give the Cheka the all-clear for the raid to go ahead. Outside the room a ferocious barrage of shooting began.

Moments earlier, Cromie had fired a single shot to make the Chekist drop his pistol. Cromie had then forced him to walk slowly backwards along the corridor towards the top of the Embassy's sweeping grand staircase. He could now make out the shouting of Cheka guards in the main Embassy rooms downstairs, together with the screams and angry protests of the Embassy staff. But they could not have got far. If he could force them back through the main entrance, then the staff might be able to barricade the heavy mahogany doors long enough for Cromie to get his agents to safety.

Arriving at the top of the staircase, Cromie took in the sight of the main entrance hall. At first it was hard to make out exactly what had happened. Because of the fuel shortage caused by conditions in Petrograd there were only a few lights burning in the Embassy. But Cromie soon realised that the Embassy doors were wide open and the main hall was full of ten or more Chekist officers. One or two of them glanced up at the two men who had appeared at the head of the stairs. Cromie's gaze came to rest on the uniform of a Cheka Commissar, a well-known local firebrand called Geller who was barking orders from the centre of the hall and who had been itching for the chance to get at Cromie for months. Cromie realised that there were now so many troops in the Embassy that there was no chance of clearing them out. For a moment he lowered his pistol, at a loss what to do.

Seeing his men looking at the top of the stairs, the Commissar stopped shouting orders, turned and looked up. Geller's stare met Cromie's and for a moment all activity in the hall stopped . . .

. . . and then all hell broke loose.

Glancing over his shoulder, the soldier whom Cromie had taken prisoner turned and shouted for help. Several of the Cheka officers in the hallway raised their pistols and opened fire, barely taking time to aim. Bullets smashed into the marble balustrade of the staircase and ricocheted around the two men. Several bullets struck the unfortunate Cheka officer in front of Cromie and he slumped gurgling onto the top steps. Cromie returned fire and pulled the body of the dying soldier in front of him for cover. Grasping the collar of the man's uniform, Cromie fired his weapon and hit a soldier in the hall below who staggered backwards into one of the offices.

In the hallway, Cromie's return fire had caused panic among the

Cheka officers who were diving for cover in all directions, some of them running back out of the main door of the Embassy, others fleeing into the ground-floor offices. Caught in the middle of the hall, Geller struggled with the flap of his holster and finally managed to drag his gun clear. Cromie fired again as he scrambled back up the stairs and the bullet ricocheted near Geller's head. Geller returned fire wildly as he dived sideways, hitting one of his own men in the back.

Cromie knew that he was in a desperate position. The badly wounded Chekist he was trying to use for cover struggled from his grip and staggered away up the last few stairs. Cromie now had nowhere left to go except up or down – the balustrade of the staircase offered him no protection at all. From the cover of the doorways below, the Chekists now began to take better aim and it would only be a matter of moments before one of them hit Cromie. More Bolshevik troops were also starting to pour in through the doorway. Cromie knew now that there was no chance of retaking the entrance to the Embassy. He had to get back and warn his agents to get out any way they could. Glancing back over his shoulder, Cromie tried to judge the distance to the corner of the upper hallway. He would have to make a run for it.

As Cromie stood up to make his move, some of the Chekists tried to rush the staircase. Cromie opened fire, forcing them back. Bullets thudded into the wall of the staircase, scattering fragments of plaster all around him, but miraculously none of the bullets hit him. Geller screamed at his men to force their way up the staircase and just for a moment it looked as if Cromie was going to make it.

But what Cromie did not know was that in the moments it had taken him to work out what was happening and leave Le Page's office some Chekists had charged straight up the staircase and were busy looting offices further down the corridor. When they heard shooting break out on the staircase several of them crept back cautiously along the corridor to find out what was going on. Sadly for Cromie, it was just as he made his move that they arrived. One of them knelt at the corner of the corridor and took careful aim. His first shot hit Cromie in the back of the head.

Cromie lurched upwards and his finger reflexively closed on the trigger squeezing off a final shot which went wild. Another of the troops behind him fired and he was hit in the head a second time, the bullet lodging in the centre of his forehead.

It did not matter. From the moment the first shot hit him, Cromie was already dead. His body slumped forwards and rolled brokenly down the Embassy staircase. His revolver skittered away from his hand. His body came to rest about three stairs up from the bottom of the flight and, as the echoes of the shooting died away, for a moment there was silence.

It was Geller who broke the spell. He shouted at his men to continue the search. As Cheka troops stormed up the staircase, Cromie's body was kicked aside and rolled the rest of the way to the bottom. Two of the soldiers hauled his corpse to a place just under a window by the main doors and searched his pockets. They took all his personal papers, his money and his pocket watch, but they left a baby's glove which he had been carrying. No one has ever found out why it was there.

His body remained under the window near the door as the thirty or so Embassy staff, including Boyce and Hall, were lined up and led out of the building with their hands on their heads. They were to be loaded into the trucks and taken to Cheka headquarters at No. 2 Gorohovaya Street for interrogation. The staff recognised the body of Cromie and several of the Embassy secretaries burst into tears at the sight of his corpse, which had been trampled by the Bolshevik troops. The Embassy chaplain, Reverend Lombard, tried to get to the body to administer the last rites, but he was clubbed with rifle butts and thrown back into the line.

And that was the end of the head of British intelligence in Russia. Cromie had held the organisation together at a time when the country was in chaos, but there were to be no medals for him. After a swift autopsy, embarrassed Soviet officials had his body buried in a grave (the location of which has since been lost) provided by the Dutch Legation and in London he was soon forgotten, never receiving the Victoria Cross which many felt he deserved, not just for his single-handed defence of the Embassy but also for his many brave actions in Russia over the preceding ten months.

But at least Geller did not escape retribution. Just over a year later, on 10 December 1920, he was to die in front of the rifles of the same men he had led against Cromie, executed by a Cheka firing squad on suspicion of conspiring against the Revolution.

The assassination of Uritsky, the attempted assassination of Lenin and the murder of Francis Cromie marked the beginning of a period of Russian history known as the Red Terror. On

1 September, *Krasnaya Gazeta*, the official newspaper of the Red Army, issued a demand for retribution: 'Without mercy, without sparing, we will kill our enemies in scores of hundreds. Let them be thousands, let them drown themselves in their own blood. For the blood of Lenin and Uritsky ... let there be floods of blood of the bourgeois – more blood, as much as possible!' Two days later, *Izvestia*, the Bolshevik Party newspaper, printed a telegram from one of the then lesser-known Bolshevik leaders named Josef Stalin. He demanded 'open, mass, systematic terror.' On 5 September the Bolshevik Commissars for Justice and Internal Affairs issued a joint statement: the infamous Decree on the Red Terror. It stated: '... in the given situation it is absolutely essential to safeguard the rear by means of terror; ... it is essential to protect the Soviet Republic against its class enemies by isolating these in concentration camps; all persons involved in White Guard organisations, plots and insurrections are to be shot; ...' As one historian has since remarked, it was an open licence for the Cheka to kill.

Martial law was imposed throughout the country. As the Cheka were unleashed, suspects were rounded up, tortured and summarily executed. In Petrograd alone official statistics show that over 6,000 people were killed, but the true figure was almost certainly far higher and will never be known for sure.

But the Red Terror served its purpose. The population were cowed and all over Russia the remainder of the British spy networks that Cromie had so patiently built up closed down as agents either fled the country or went underground.

Boyce and Hall were released from captivity, exchanged along with the other British Embassy prisoners a month later. Other agents made their own way back. There was now no British secret agent left in Bolshevik Russia. But as all these men headed westward for the safety of continental Europe, just one man was struggling through the snowy landscape of the Russo-Finnish border in the opposite direction. His mission: to set up a new British intelligence organisation.

He had no support.

He had no weapons.

He had no training.

He was a concert pianist and his code name was ST-25.

I

The Man with the Punch-like Chin

In Parliament Square in London, Big Ben struck a quarter past eleven.

Just a short distance away, Lieutenant 'Gus' Agar RN was becoming increasingly uneasy. He had been standing for some time in front of the large oak desk in an attic room just off Whitehall watching a thickset elderly man in civilian clothes read through an official-looking file of papers. The old man had not even acknowledged his presence yet and Gus had no idea why he had been summoned so urgently from his weekend leave on that morning in May 1919. He certainly did not know the identity of this strange individual with his horn-rimmed spectacles and comically jutting chin – rather like the Mr Punch character in a seaside puppet show.

But as Gus stood there feeling awkward, it gradually dawned on him that he had met this strange man somewhere before. He remembered being briefly introduced to an elderly naval captain just a few weeks ago by his commanding officer at their base on Osea Island in Essex. The old officer had walked with a pronounced limp and had used a silver-topped cane to support himself. Gus had assumed that the visit had simply been some routine naval inspection and the meeting had been so brief that he could not even recall the officer's name. But although the old man was now out of uniform and wearing a grey three-piece suit, this was definitely the same person. Gus could see the walking stick leaning in a corner of the room behind the desk.

As the old man continued to read, Gus took the opportunity to glance around the room. His commanding officer at HMS Osea had ordered him to report to the Admiralty that morning where he would have a meeting with a Commander Goff of the Naval

Intelligence Department about 'Special Service'. However, once he had finally found the commander's office amidst the warren of passages at the Admiralty, Gus had been surprised to be taken back out of the building and then on a deliberately confusing route through the side streets of Whitehall. They had entered another building which housed, amongst other things, the Royal Automobile Club and had taken the lift to the top floor. They had then taken the stairs to the roof where they proceeded to walk up and down through a disorientating maze of temporary offices and gantries. Finally the pair had arrived at the ante-room of this office where, after a brief word with the Commander, an attractive secretary had ushered Gus straight inside. Since then he had been left to wait with nothing to do but watch this old man reading through the file slowly and methodically. He wondered why on earth he was there.

At long last, the grey-haired officer removed his spectacles and slipped a gold rimmed monocle into his right eye. He looked up for a moment. Then, dramatically slapping the desk hard with his hand, he suddenly addressed Gus for the first time:

'Sit down, my boy – I think you will do!'

The greatest rescue operation in the history of the British Secret Intelligence Service had begun.

Augustus Willington Shelton Agar was the youngest of thirteen children. He had been born in 1890 and was orphaned by the age of twelve. His mother, who was Austrian, had died shortly after his birth and his father, an Irish tea planter based in Sri Lanka, died of cholera during a business trip to China in 1902. 'Gus' (as he was understandably known to his family and friends) had been sent away to boarding school in England at the age of eight and in 1904, at the suggestion of his beloved eldest brother Shelton, Gus had joined the Royal Navy as an officer cadet. He was to remain with the Navy for the next forty years.

By 1919 Gus was skipper of one of the fastest pieces of naval weaponry in the world. Officially it was designated simply as a 'Coastal Motor Boat' or 'CMB'. Unofficially it was known as a 'skimmer'. Developed in great secrecy in 1916, the skimmers were the brainchild of three young naval officers which had been transformed into reality by the boat builder Sir John Isaac Thornycroft. The skimmers possessed revolutionary hydroplane hulls which enabled most of the craft to leave the water and to

almost literally fly above the waves. They could achieve speeds of
up to forty-five knots, fast even by today's standards but
astonishing for 1919. Gus's boat was forty feet in length and carried
a crew of three: captain, gunner and engineer. It was armed with
twin Lewis machine guns and a single torpedo which weighed three-
quarters of a ton and contained a charge capable of sinking a
battleship. Some later CMBs were fifty-five feet long and could
carry two torpedoes. However, the CMBs also had an Achilles heel:
they were constructed with a skin of thin plywood in order to make
them as light as possible and there was little room in their tiny hulls
for anything other than weapons, ammunition, the massive engines
and their fuel tanks. One shot, even landing close to a CMB, could
blow the entire boat to smithereens. Sheer breathtaking speed was
a skimmer's only defence.

Following their successful development and deployment, a flotilla
of CMBs had been formed by the Royal Navy for special duties in
1918. They had been intended for a secret mission in the Baltic
aimed at the destruction of the German High Seas Fleet. The unit
had the pick of all the best young officers in the Royal Navy. Each
of them was desperate for command of one of these craft with the
speed and freedom of a fighter plane, plus the punch to put a capital
ship out of commission. Only the best had been selected for the
intensive training that the mission required. They spent their time
roaring up and down the English Channel, sinking small enemy
craft and generally making things unpleasant for the Germans. They
had already achieved their first major combat honour when they
helped in the operation to sink blockships in the approaches to
Zeebrugge harbour on St George's Day, 1918.

But before their plan to attack the German High Seas Fleet could
be put into effect, the war had come to an end. The unit now kicked
its heels on a dreary base on Osea Island in Essex at the mouth of
the river Blackwater. Some CMBs had been sent abroad on other
duties but for the rest of the flotilla there was nothing to do except
watch the rain pelt steadily onto the mudflats that ringed the island
and dream about the Wrens who were billeted in the neighbouring
facility. Occasionally, a few officers were granted leave in London,
a chance to see a West End show and sink a few drinks, but that was
as exciting as it got.

Gus Agar felt particularly hard done by. In 1913 he had qualified
as a fighter pilot for the Royal Naval Air Service, but there had been

a shortage of aircraft so he had been forced to give that up. In 1916 he had missed the Battle of Jutland, the only major naval battle of the Great War, because the battleship on which he was serving was too slow to join the British fleet in time. Finally, he had been tricked into joining the CMB flotilla at Osea simply because they needed a torpedo and mining specialist. Now, with the war over, it seemed that any chance of glory had gone for ever.

It was then that he was abruptly summoned from his few days' leave and ordered to report to London immediately.

The elderly gentleman behind the desk was Captain Mansfield Cumming RN, the head of MI1C, the foreign section of the British Secret Service Bureau, the organisation which we know today as the Secret Intelligence Service (SIS) or, more commonly, as MI6. Gus later described this meeting as '... like one of those strange and vivid dreams where every detail stands out with startling and unforgettable clearness. It seemed to me as if I was living in a George Henty short story specially written for the *Boys' Own Paper* of my childhood days in the nineties, but in which I was to play a part.'

It is hardly surprising that the meeting had a dreamlike quality for Gus because Mansfield Cumming appears to us today like an intelligence-service chief straight out of the pages of a cheap thriller. Within Whitehall he was known simply as 'C', a tradition which has persisted to this day for every head of MI6. His office was secreted amidst a warren of passages and temporary offices which had been built high amongst the rooftops around Whitehall. Looking through the dormer windows of Cumming's office, Gus would have gazed across the plane trees of Victoria Embankment to the grey waters of the River Thames. The room itself was like an alchemist's laboratory: one table was covered with parts of various intriguing machines, another with bottles of chemicals and apparatus for creating secret inks (one of Cumming's personal favourites was an invisible ink made from his own semen). Another table was littered with detailed maps of far-off parts of the world and along one wall there stood a row of telephones ready to connect Cumming with the various parts of his mysterious organisation. Most of these were links to different rooms in the rooftop labyrinth, but we know that one connected him directly to the Director of Naval Intelligence at the Admiralty.

Cumming loved gadgets of any kind and carried a sword stick whenever he travelled abroad on missions. He was always eager to obtain an example of any invention which might be useful for espionage. He kept a fully equipped workshop both at his headquarters in London and at his home in the village of Burlesdon, Hampshire. His other great passion was speed, an urge which was so strong in him that Gus later referred to it as a 'mania' having been driven across London by Cumming on a terrifying journey. In his early life Cumming rode fast horses and was a keen huntsman. But following a bad fall in which he broke both his arms he turned to the brand new sport of motor racing, taking part in many semi-professional races on the Continent such as the Paris-Madrid rally of 1903. He described his 50 h.p. Wolseley motor car as 'almost human – far more so than many folk of my acquaintance.' Meanwhile, at sea, he owned a series of fast motor boats which he raced. They had names such as: *Commander, Communicator, Competitor* and *Comely*. He even took to the air in his quest for speed and exciting new machinery: he became a founder member of the Royal Aero Club in 1906, just three years after the Wright brothers' first flight, and like Gus he had qualified as a pilot – in 1913, at the grand old age of fifty-four.

Cumming's other great weakness was women. According to the playwright Edward Knoblock, who was an MI6 officer during the Great War, Cumming kept a book of erotica (*Le Nu au Salon*) in a secret drawer in his desk which he liked to show to selected officers. He would then extol the virtues of 'the female form divine'. This disclosure was considered a singular, if rather weird, honour. At lunchtimes Cumming would often take off in his Rolls-Royce (swerving onto the wrong side of traffic islands for the sheer excitement of it) and drive along Regent Street just so that he could 'have a look at the girls'. He used his position as head of the Secret Service to employ a succession of pretty private secretaries. Many visitors to his office commented on them. He selected these young women for their looks and it is hardly surprising that those who knew him well described him as 'a notorious womaniser'.

There was one other thing which was distinctive about Mansfield Cumming – his wooden leg. Cumming's only child, Alastair, had been killed on 2 October 1914, shortly after the outbreak of war. Alastair had been attached to the Intelligence Corps in France and Cumming had stopped off to visit him – he often visited France for meetings in the first few months of the war. They had been speeding through woodland near Meaux in Cumming's Rolls-Royce when a tyre suddenly burst and the car span out of control. It careered into a tree and was wrecked. Alastair was thrown some distance from the car whilst Cumming was trapped under the wreckage by his right leg. Hearing his dying son's fading cries for help, Cumming used his penknife to saw through the remains of his shattered limb and then hauled himself across the ground to lay his coat across Alastair. But it was no good. A few hours later, Cumming was found unconscious next to the body of his dead son. A large portrait of Alastair in military uniform dominated one wall of the office. Early press reports stated that Cumming was driving at the time of the accident, although later writers have said that Alastair was at the wheel. In any case, there is some evidence that Cumming's wife never forgave him for the loss of her beloved son.

If Cumming felt that he was to blame for the crash, he never discussed it with anyone and although he had walked with a wooden leg ever since that day he did not let it slow him down. In keeping with his mildly eccentric character he travelled around the corridors of MI6 on a child's scooter which had been specially imported for him from America. He had also developed a habit of suddenly driving a paperknife into the wooden leg during meetings to test the nerve of prospective agents. On one occasion he even used it as a club to attack Vernon Kell, the head of MI5, during an interdepartmental argument.

Over the course of the next hour this rather bizarre character presented Gus with a seemingly intractable problem. The primary post-war intelligence target for MI6 was the former Russian empire which had been suffering under the rule of Vladimir Lenin and the Bolsheviks since their coup in November 1917. The country was locked in a bloody civil war between the Bolsheviks (known as the 'Reds' from the colour of their banners) and a loose coalition of former Tsarists and nationalists supported by the West (known as the 'Whites' from the colour of the flag of the former Russian empire). The struggle was delicately balanced and it was unclear if the Bolshevik government would survive. If they did not, it was equally unclear which of the many contenders would rule in their place. At one point it had even seemed possible that the new government might be formed by an MI6 officer: Lieutenant Sidney Reilly, a Russian Jew and conman, who had begun to organise a daring coup. But his plans had been ruined following the attempted assassination of Lenin in August of that year. The Bolsheviks had retaliated with a period of brutal reprisals known as the 'Red Terror'. Thousands of their political opponents were simply rounded up and shot – including most of those who would have supported Reilly's scheme. Reilly and every other British intelligence officer in Russia had been forced to flee the country in order to avoid capture.

The entire future of the Russian empire was now at stake. All that was required to seize control was determined action. But the governments of Western Europe and the United States dithered, knowing that although they could send armies to ensure that the victors were favourable to them, their electorates would be reluctant to undertake another conflict so soon after the horrors and losses of the Great War. If Western governments were to make the right decision, then accurate intelligence was vital – yet all the Western embassies in Russia had been closed in February 1919. This meant that the task of providing all this badly needed information fell upon the intelligence services and, with Britain as the dominant power in Western Europe, on MI6 in particular. Despite this desperate need for intelligence, conditions in the country were now so dangerous that MI6 had only one agent there. A man who would be known to Gus only by his code name: ST-25. The ST designation was because all Russian operations were run out of MI6's regional headquarters at Stockholm in Sweden.

Gus was told that ST-25 was based in Petrograd, which, until a few months before, had been the capital of Russia. From there he had been producing vital information including copies of key documents right from the heart of the Bolshevik government. But now communications with him had broken down completely. ST-25 had been using a system of couriers crossing the northern border between Russia and Finland on foot and ST-25 himself had left Russia twice during his mission using this route. But on the second journey he had barely escaped with his life and the border was now so closely guarded by the Bolsheviks that it was almost impossible for couriers to get through. It was believed that his two most recent couriers had been captured and shot. The only other route out by land was to the south through the Baltic republics of Estonia and Latvia. But this area was now being fought over by the Red and White armies and security was even tighter than in the north as the

Cheka, the dreaded Bolshevik secret police, hunted for deserters and infiltrators.

There was only one other possibility – an idea so apparently preposterous that it had been rejected until now. Petrograd lay at the head of the Gulf of Finland, an approach guarded by the guns of the massive island fortress of Kronstadt. This factor alone would make the Gulf a difficult proposition, but there were also fifteen sea fortresses running in a line from Kronstadt island to both the northern and southern coasts in order to ensure that the approach was completely controlled. These sea fortresses were so close to one another that by day Gus's boat would be seen and by night there wasn't an inch of water that wasn't covered by their searchlights. The fortresses to the north of Kronstadt island were linked by a hidden breakwater just three feet below the surface, making it impassable to most vessels. There was no breakwater between the forts to the south of Kronstadt but, apart from a narrow deepwater channel, the area was guarded by extensive minefields. There was also the threat of loose mines in the area – contrary to international conventions, the Bolsheviks had disabled the safety devices that were supposed to deactivate them if they broke free of their moorings. These were a hazard to most shipping, but to a vessel the size of a skimmer they would be instantly fatal. The southern approach was also guarded by the fortress of Krasnaya Gorka on the mainland and then there was the nearby seaplane base at Oranienbaum. Submarines, motor patrol boats and aircraft constantly patrolled the entire area.

But the problems did not end there. The only likely base from which Gus could operate would be in Finland, but that country had only just survived a Communist uprising of its own and would certainly not compromise its neutrality by cooperating in this kind of venture. Cumming had agents in Finland who were trying to secure the necessary permissions, but former German agents were working against them and it might be necessary for Gus to work in complete secrecy.

Even if Gus could come up with a workable plan, he would have to move fast. The area lay near the line of the Arctic Circle and was approaching the period known as 'the White Nights', when the sun barely sank below the horizon and there would be no cover of darkness.

The only hope for ST-25 was if a route could be found through the defences. Speed seemed like Gus's greatest hope of breaking through, but they both knew that this created a problem: when a CMB reached top speed the noise of the engines was deafening. The crews could barely hear themselves speak on the boat. The gunners on the sea fortresses would hear them coming from miles away.

All that Cumming could offer was a way to get Gus, his crew and two CMBs to Finland secretly. They would travel via Sweden, disguised as representatives of a boat-building firm seeking to interest potential customers in former British military motor boats as pleasure craft. All the details of how to reach ST-25 once they were in Finland would have to be worked out by Gus and his team.

The mission was a very tall order indeed, especially for a young naval lieutenant who had never before had his own command. Cumming asked Gus what he thought of the idea and then, without even giving Gus a chance to reply, said, 'I won't ask you to take it on, for I know you will.' As if to emphasise the danger, Cumming then asked Gus if he was married or engaged. When Gus confirmed that he was not, Cumming told him that any crew member he selected must also be unmarried and without ties of any kind. He pointed out that if they were caught by the Bolsheviks there would be nothing that MI6 could do to protect them. As spies, they would almost certainly be shot. But Cumming could see that Gus was uneasy about this and relented a little. He agreed that the crews could keep uniform caps and jackets on the boats for use in an emergency. It was not much, but it might save their lives.

Finally, Cumming emphasised that time was all-important. He gave Gus just forty-eight hours to come up with a plan to penetrate the Petrograd defences.

And with that the interview ended.

Closing the door quietly behind him, Gus recalled later that he stood feeling dizzy, hardly able to believe what he had just been through. It was at this point that Dorothy Henslowe, Cumming's personal secretary, spoke to him from the neighbouring office:

'You look rather bewildered. Come in here and have a cigarette.'

Dorothy was to be secretary to both Cumming and his successor, Admiral 'Quex' Sinclair. She was Cumming's confidante and, although Gus did not know it, there was a rumour that she was also his mistress. Any papers that Cumming saw went through her office. It is strange, considering that the British secret service did not employ any women as intelligence officers until the Second World

War, that this woman probably knew more about MI6 than any other person in the world. She clearly knew exactly why Gus was there. When both cigarettes were lit, she asked:

'Well, what are you going to do about it?'

Gus leaned against her desk and was silent for a while. Although he had wished for a mission like this for such a long time, it had finally turned up at just the wrong moment. He was in the middle of setting up a flat with 'Dor', the woman he planned to marry. What would she think if he went trotting off to Finland on a secret mission for several months? Then again, she knew what the life of a naval officer could mean and it was not as if they were married yet.

'Of course I'm going,' Gus replied eventually. 'Who wouldn't? I have no responsibilities and besides, the war is over – where else would I see action? This is a chance. Maybe a great chance.'

Gus later recalled that Dorothy smiled thoughtfully at this:

'Yes. I can see you haven't had enough. Some of us have, though.' There was a long pause as she gazed reflectively out of the window for a while. He wondered who she had lost in the dreadful conflict that had just ended. But then she turned back to him and added: 'And yet if I were a man, I think I would do the same. I believe I envy you.'

Perhaps Gus thought then about the fortresses, the minefields, the searchlights, the seaplanes, the submarines, the patrol boats and the hidden breakwater. He almost certainly thought about the lone figure of Cumming's mysterious agent struggling through the snow, the Bolshevik secret police closing in behind him. A desperate man on a vital mission, praying for a rescue that might never come.

Whoever ST-25 was, Gus had just forty-eight hours to work out how to save his life.

2

The secret that 'C' couldn't tell

If Cumming had stood at the windows of his office and watched Gus Agar hurry away across Whitehall Place to catch the afternoon train back to Maldon, he must have thought about how much this brave young officer could never know. The mission that Cumming had outlined was dangerous, almost impossible and that meant there was already far too much weight on such young shoulders. Cumming could not afford to tell Gus that in reality he would be racing to Finland to save not just one agent but quite possibly the entire future of the British Secret Intelligence Service.

Today we think of MI6 as a powerful Whitehall organisation with a budget measured in millions of pounds and intelligence stations in every corner of the world, staffed by hundreds of well-trained men and women. But MI6 in 1919 was very different. For a start it was only ten years old. In 1909, a series of spy scares in leading newspapers had led to a nationwide sense of panic and in response the Government had ordered a review of Britain's intelligence organisations. As part of that review it had been agreed to set up a 'Secret Service Bureau' (SSB), but this was not the significant force we have come to know today.

It would be staffed by just two men: Commander Mansfield Cumming representing the Navy and Captain Vernon Kell for the Army. (There was, of course, no Royal Air Force at that date.) One of the officers would be responsible for searching for German spies within the UK and the British Empire (in other words about a third of the globe), the other would have responsibility for gathering intelligence in the rest of the world – principally continental Europe.

Kell and Cumming were very different men. Kell was 36 years old, a talented linguist who spoke fluent French and German as well as having a working knowledge of Russian and Chinese. He had served in posts around the world, worked for military intelligence at a senior level for many years and was considered by his peers to have a brilliant career ahead of him. On the other hand, Mansfield Cumming was an officer whose career had stagnated so much that he had taken twelve years out of the Navy to be an estate manager in Ireland. He had little experience of working abroad and only spoke a little French. Since his return to duty in 1898, he had spent ten years stuck in a dead-end post devising a boom defence system for the harbour at Southampton. He was now aged 50. He had still not reached the key naval rank of captain and, after a thoroughly unremarkable career, there seemed to be little in store for him except retirement.

These were the two men that the Army and the Navy put forward to be the representatives of the Secret Service Bureau. With Whitehall's talent for screwing up even the simplest of decisions they put Kell, the man with years of international experience, in charge of counter-espionage operations. Cumming, the man who had not travelled further than short hops across the Channel in the past twenty years, was put in charge of foreign intelligence-gathering. Cumming was so uninterested in this new post that he very nearly refused it altogether and only accepted the appointment provided he could continue on a part-time basis with his boom defence work.

This may seem a little odd, but the Foreign Section of the SSB had not been envisioned as an intelligence network covering the globe as it does now. The Military Intelligence Directorate of the War Office (MID) and Naval Intelligence Department of the Admiralty (NID) already had that job well in hand. The NID had a series of 'coast watchers' established at important points in Europe and selected ports elsewhere. Together with intelligence officers on every British warship, they monitored all naval movements by potential enemies. The NID also secretly sponsored voyages by selected agents who would, whilst supposedly on a holiday cruise or scientific exped-ition, map and photograph naval fortifications and important coastal sites. For the army, the MID also ran agents to places where it required information. Suitable army officers were dispatched on 'walking holidays' which just happened to pass new fortifications and other points of interest. Lord Baden-Powell, who later founded the Boy Scout movement, was one such officer and he has left us a detailed account of his methods. Of course, Germany and other nations were doing exactly the same thing and in the pre-war years spies from both sides had been arrested while doing just this sort of work. But it was seen by all nations as simply one of the duties of a military officer – rather like their duty to escape from a POW camp – and those caught were usually let off with a small fine or the lightest of prison sentences.

With all this intelligence already available, Cumming's foreign section had been established with only one aim in mind. There was another source of intelligence besides these established military methods. Certain dubious individuals offered key intelligence in return for money. There were in Europe professional bureaux of spies, usually retired police detectives but more often conmen. For considerable sums, these individuals and bureaux offered to provide intelligence reports as required. Of course, many of these reports were bogus and the 'bureaux' simply scams, but sometimes they did produce valuable information. Whilst coast watching and walking holidays were seen as honourable spying activites, dealing with these men was seen as dirty work, beneath the contempt of a serving British officer. So it was agreed that what was needed was an individual whose activities could be denied. *He* would go to clandestine meetings in seedy hotels; *he* would haggle over money with people who were in effect criminals; most importantly, *he* could be disowned if he embarrassed the British government. That was the new job that Cumming was being offered, not to run the worldwide multimillion-pound empire we see today. It is hardly surprising that he was less than enthusiastic.

From the start Cumming was isolated and sidelined by the Military Intelligence Directorate which was under the control of the Army. He was not even trusted with War Office files. For instance, 7 October 1909 had been Cumming's first day in his new office at 64 Victoria Street, just next to the Army and Navy Stores. The entry in his personal diary that day told what was to be the story of his first few months: 'Went to the office and remained there all day, but saw no one, nor was there anything to do there.' By November he was still writing the same thing: 'Office all day. Nothing doing.' and in that month he told his superior officer, Admiral Bethell, the head of the NID, that he: '. . . had done literally nothing up to the present date except sit in the Office and I have only received one letter (containing my pay).' It was all Cumming could do to get permission from the War Office to purchase a typewriter – and then only if it was a cheap one. On the other hand, Kell, as a fellow army officer, was showered with agents and resources by the War Office. His organisation, which in 1916 was redesignated as MI5, prospered.

Over the next few years Cumming gradually acquired one or two agents from the War Office and an assistant from the Naval Intelligence Department, but he was still considered an irrelevance by most in the intelligence world. He did not open his first overseas station (Brussels) until 1913. The Foreign Office refused to have anything to do with him. They would not allow him either to contact or to use information from consular officers and insisted that he must not gather any intelligence about political developments abroad – that was their job. His role was largely reduced to gathering naval intelligence on the Continent – something the NID was already doing with far greater success.

Cumming was not helped by the fact that he proved to be a singularly inept spy – far from the mastermind he is often portrayed as. For instance, on 26 November 1909 he finally had his first meeting with a foreign agent, a War Office contact code-named 'B' who was actually a German named Byzewski who was producing very useful intelligence on German shipbuilding. Byzewski came to London for a debriefing at great personal risk. Since this was principally a matter of naval intelligence Cumming was entrusted with the task, but he made rather a hash of it. Cumming spoke almost no German and he and Byzewski spent the entire meeting with Cumming frantically flicking backwards and forwards in a phrase book. Only at the end of the meeting did he find out that Byzewski also spoke French, a language in which they were both reasonably fluent. Another meeting had to be hastily arranged.

On another occasion Cumming and his assistant, a Royal Marines officer, Major Cyrus Regnart, travelled to Brussels to meet an agent. Looking for somewhere quiet to debrief him they tried to book a room in a local brothel. The madam – faced with two men wanting a private room who said they were not interested in having a woman sent to them because they were waiting for another man – assumed that they were dangerous homosexuals about to take part in a highly illegal act. She threw them out into the street and they had to leave hurriedly before the police arrived.

Cumming even walked straight into the arms of his enemies at one stage. In 1911 an agent code-named 'TG', who was unhappy with the way he had been treated by the British government, was blackmailing Cumming. He said that he had compromising letters from the Bureau which he would release to the press or some other foreign government unless he was paid £2,500. The letters cannot have been *that* incriminating because he eventually agreed to hand them over for just £22, but the story then becomes even more bizarre. 'TG' said that he was storing the incriminating letters at his consulate. Astonishingly, Cumming actually went to the consulate to fetch the letters. But when he got there 'TG' had already left and the staff of the consulate became suspicious. When Cumming tried to leave they blocked his exit and locked all the doors. He was questioned by the Consul General for fifteen minutes – a considerable period, so they were clearly concerned about his reasons for being there. Cumming seemed surprised by this: '... I had taken off my hat as a mark of respect, but his attitude was not very pleasant ...' If they had realised who Cumming was, he would have been in a lot of trouble – the consulate was technically foreign territory. It would have been a disaster for the head of a British intelligence department to have been captured so easily. But Cumming was lucky. He later claimed that he escaped by spinning a story and pretending to not even notice that he was being detained. It is more likely that the consulate's staff released him because they could not believe that this tubby blunderer really was a British intelligence agent.

Although Cumming later described espionage as 'capital sport', he did not even like the people he was forced to work with. He confided to his diary in 1911: 'All my staff are blackguards – but they are incapable ones, and a man with a little ingenuity and brains would be a change, even if not an agreeable one.'

So why has this picture of Cumming as a master spy become so prevalent? The main reason is that MI6's records are jealously guarded – more so than the records of any other intelligence service in the world. Most people imagine that this is because the service is so effective. In fact, it is because the opposite is true: even today it is believed that it is better to preserve the myth of British intelligence rather than to allow the public (and the organisation's opponents) to know just how bad things are. Against this background of secrecy, only a few books were written by those who knew Cumming and these were heavily censored. It is hardly surprising that they paint a rosy picture of him. Much of the impression of

Cumming as a master spy was created by the former agent Sidney Reilly whose 'experiences' are almost complete fiction.

It is rare that anyone in a senior enough position to resist the censors was able to tell the true story. Someone who could was Sir Samuel Hoare, an MP who was the head of station in Petrograd from May 1916 until May 1917 and later rose to be Foreign Secretary. He described Mansfield Cumming in the following terms: '... jovial and very human, bluff and plain speaking, outwardly at least, a very simple man ... In all respects, physical and mental, he was the very antithesis of the spy king of popular fiction.' The mistaken assumption that those engaged at the very highest levels of espionage must be masterminds is an error which has continued to this day – despite all the evidence.

So, by the end of its first five years of existence, the Secret Service Bureau was in danger of being viewed as something of an irrelevance. Other departments had better organisations and produced better intelligence. The majority of historians who have studied the period have concluded that Cumming was pretty ineffective and when Winston Churchill arrived as First Lord of the Admiralty he came to the same conclusion, as one of his biographers notes: 'But what light could British spies throw on German intentions, and specifically on plans to invade or carry out raids? What was the naval, or foreign, section of the new Secret Service Bureau under Mansfield Cumming doing in the interests of national security? Churchill had to admit that the answer was "not much".'

Fortunately the First World War brought a change in Cumming's fortunes – as it did for all the intelligence organisations. At the start of the war, MI6 had a headquarters staff of just eleven people (a figure which included four clerks, two typists and two doormen) and one foreign station operating out of a furniture shop in Brussels. Four years later, the newly promoted Captain Cumming could boast an organisation of over 1,000 staff and agents with stations throughout the world including posts as far away as Tokyo and Buenos Aries. He had also established liaisons with the intelligence departments of every Allied country. At one point he was even offered an unlimited budget. He turned it down on the grounds that '... the supply of such a sum would probably lead us into great mistakes ...'

But now the war was over. Faced with massive debt and the need to provide employment for hundreds of thousands of returning troops, Prime Minister Lloyd George was looking to make savings wherever possible in order to create the 'land fit for heroes' which his election slogan had promised. That meant cuts throughout Whitehall, including the world of intelligence.

As every intelligence department fought to justify its continued existence, the future of MI6 seemed highly doubtful because Cumming had not had a good war. Both the Naval Intelligence Department (NID) and the War Office Secret Service (WOSS) had outperformed him. The NID had provided a superb decryption service working out of Room 40 in the Admiralty: it had cracked vital German codes and provided excellent intelligence. That organisation later provided the basis for GCHQ. The War Office had run over 6,000 agents, many of them in train-watching networks which gave an extremely accurate picture of the movement of German forces behind the Front. MI6 also ran a well-known train-watching network under the code name *La Dame Blanche*, but although *La Dame Blanche* was probably the largest and most successful of these networks it had actually been formed by Belgian patriots without any lead or assistance from MI6. In the one train-watching network that MI6 did initiate – in August 1917 – everyone had been arrested by March 1918.

Another problem was that Cumming's organisation was an orphan – both the NID and the War Office Secret Service had powerful government departments backing them. Additionally, although Cumming had finally achieved the rank of Captain, he was still far outranked by the head of the NID (a Rear Admiral) and the head of the War Office Secret Service (a Major General). The difference in ranks accurately reflects the relative worth of each organisation.

No one wanted MI6, except possibly as part of their own empire. Even the Foreign Office, which was nominally in charge of funding for Cumming's department, would have been quite happy to see it disappear – as long as no one else controlled it. In their opinion, secret agents were far too likely to cause some sort of diplomatic embarrassment and the Foreign Office believed that intelligence about foreign matters was far better collected by professional diplomats working quietly behind the scenes than by some sort of John Buchan-style adventurer.

In October 1918 Major General Sir William Thwaites, the

Director of Military Intelligence, proposed that all the various intelligence departments – MI5, MI6, MI8, MI9, the various cryptographic departments of the Admiralty and Cumming's organisation – should all be amalgamated into one body, which would be placed under War Office control. He pointed out that this arrangement would be more cost-effective, more efficient and far more suited to a peacetime organisation. Since the NID would be left intact the Admiralty had no objection. Winston Churchill was among a number of influential figures who supported the idea of an amalgamated intelligence service. At the end of the First World War it seemed that MI6 was doomed and that the only post left for Cumming was a quiet retirement.

However, although no government department wanted owner-ship of MI6 none of them wanted to see it controlled by any of the others, either. The Foreign Office suggested that the precise allo-cation of intelligence resources and funding should be left until after the Paris Peace Conference in June 1919 when government intelligence requirements would be known more clearly. Thwaites's plans were shelved and MI6 survived for just a little longer. Cumming had just a few short months to secure a spectacular intelligence coup which would convince Whitehall that MI6 was an organisation worth saving. From somewhere in the world he had to produce intelligence which no one else could get – not even the War Office Secret Service and the NID with their extensive network of military facilities. By the autumn of 1918, there was only one place where Cumming could find such intelligence – Bolshevik Russia. No other British organisation was there. In fact, no intelligence service from any Allied nation was there.

Gathering intelligence from Bolshevik Russia had been Cumming's best chance of saving the organisation he had created. But now his only agent, ST-25, was trapped. Unless Agar could rescue ST-25 and recover the intelligence, MI6 itself was probably finished.

But it would be two weeks before Agar could even reach Russia to launch his rescue attempt.

And in the meantime Cumming did not even know if ST-25 was still alive.

3

Froggy chooses Sinbad

As soon as his meeting at Whitehall Place was over, Gus Agar took a cab and then raced back to HMS Osea on the first available train from Liverpool Street. He had phoned ahead for a car to meet him at Maldon station. Soon he was being driven across the low causeway which connected the 600-acre island with the mainland twice a day at low tide. In the distance to the east he could see oyster boats amongst the shoals dredging for the day's catch, and further away on the island the slipway along which the CMBs had to be hauled before being stored in rows on either side of a long ditch known as the traverser pit. The car left the causeway and was soon driving swiftly along a deeply rutted track through the lines of temporary huts and tents that comprised the base. Flocks of ducks and chickens scattered ahead of the car. Osea Island had been commandeered by the Navy as a CMB base in 1917, but it was still a working farm and the sailors supplemented their rations by raising animals of their own, including pigs. In fact, the entire base was quite a menagerie. Agar's driver made straight for the old manor house, which was the only substantial building on the island. It was also where HMS Osea's commanding officer, Captain Wilfred French, had his office.

Captain French, known throughout the Royal Navy as 'Froggy', was the only other officer at Osea who would know about the operation. He and Agar were good friends and in many ways French had become like a father to Gus. It had been French who had originally recruited Agar to the CMB Service. The base at Osea had desperately needed an expert in mines and torpedoes but, with the prospects for promotion being better in the regular offices of the Navy, no one seemed to want the job. French had promised Gus that if he joined the CMB Service he would be given command of the first of a new type of CMB, a seventy-foot beauty that would carry four torpedoes. But before the boat could be built the war had ended and the order was delayed. Even so, French had kept Gus at the base. CMBs were sent on duty around the world – to Archangel in December 1918, to Riga in spring 1919, to the Rhine – but each time Agar had been passed over because he was required for training duties at Osea. As a result he became known throughout the Flotilla as 'the torpedo conscript'. Captain French had always promised that one day he would make things right with Gus and now that chance had come with his recommendation of Gus to Cumming for this secret mission. Gus was keen to get his commander's advice about how to tackle this seemingly intractable problem. As soon as Gus arrived, French dismissed his secretary and Gus told him the whole story.

Together the two men pored over maps of the area, trying to work out a plan of operations. The Gulf of Finland is almost 250 miles long but only thirty miles wide, narrowing gradually as it approaches the mouth of the River Neva where St Petersburg (Petrograd) is situated. Right in the middle of the last few miles of the approach to the city is the Russian island of Kotlin. It is five miles long and about a mile wide. Every inch of the surrounding water was swept by the powerful guns of the eight fortresses which lined its shore, the largest of all being the one at the south-eastern end and one of the most formidable in the world – Kronstadt. The defences of Kronstadt were supplemented by a chain of sea fortresses, nine to the north, six to the south, which formed a seemingly impenetrable barrier for any who might be tempted to slip past. Then there was the question of the minefields and the breakwater. In theory, a CMB could skim over a minefield – if the mines were set at the usual depth of six feet. But the breakwater was another matter. According to Cumming, the breakwater was three feet below the waterline. At full speed a CMB drew two feet, nine inches, leaving a clearance of just three inches. If Cumming was just slightly wrong the first that Gus would know about it would be when the bottom was ripped out of his boat. Of course, there was a route through the breakwaters to the south of Kotlin Island by going through the main shipping channel. But that would be so closely guarded that there was no chance of slipping through undetected. It would be little better than suicide. To the two British officers evaluating the task before them it must have seemed that the jagged coasts of Finland to the north and Estonia to the south were like the jaws of some gigantic monster waiting to slam shut on anyone who approached Petrograd by sea. The problem was not just how to get in and find the mysterious ST-25, it was also how to get out alive.

Gus and French both agreed that the first thing the team would need would be a secure base from which to operate. Cumming was sending Gus to Helsinki (which at the time was known as Helsingfors) where he had several secret agents who would do their best to assist Agar. But the distance between Helsinki and Petrograd was beyond the operational range of a CMB. If they were to drop the agents behind the Russian border they would need to be much closer. That meant some isolated inlet where they could hide the CMBs by day, but neither coast looked promising. To the north the coast of Finland was dotted with innumerable small coves which might be suitable. But Finland was strictly neutral. Finnish forces under General Mannerheim had only recently succeeded in expelling Bolshevik forces and achieving an uneasy truce. The Finns would be unlikely to support a secret mission which might undermine that hard-won peace. To the south was the coast of Estonia, but fighting between White and Bolshevik forces was raging back and forth across that country and it was impossible to know if a particular area would be safe by the time the CMBs reached the Gulf. Even if the team found a suitable base there would be problems of accommodation and supply. They would need hundreds of gallons of fuel and ammunition, together with workshop facilities to repair the temperamental engines. The problems just seemed to keep mounting up the more they considered the project. The worst thing was that there just wasn't enough detailed intelligence on what was happening there.

In the end Gus and Captain French decided on a two-stage plan: Gus would examine the Bolshevik defences upon arrival in Finland and see if he could get any accurate information about the depth of the breakwaters. In the meantime, the most Gus could offer Cumming would be to run agents from Finland across the Gulf to the coast of Estonia and drop them as near as possible to the front lines.

With a plan of campaign agreed the next problem was to select the members of the team. French advised Agar to take two 40-foot boats. Each 40-foot CMB required three crew members: a commander, a mechanic and a junior officer to act as a second in command and man the Lewis guns. This meant that they would need five more men. Since this was his first command, Captain French advised that Gus should only pick younger men. This was in line with what Cumming had requested and in any case older, more experienced hands might be more difficult for a young man like Agar to command.

Agar's first choice was his second in command of the boat. Sub Lieutenant John White Hampsheir was normally assigned to CMB 75. He and Gus were firm friends. This last fact was important: far from home and with a small team Gus would need someone he could trust. At five foot nine inches tall, Hampsheir was slight of build, blond and blue-eyed. He was a painfully shy man, but he was good at his job and Gus hoped that he would flourish in a small team.

The position of mechanic was in many ways even more important. The high-performance engines of the CMBs were notoriously temperamental. They were basically aeroplane engines, but conditions in a CMB were far worse than those in any aircraft. These delicate mechanisms were frequently doused with gallons of sea water and then pounded repeatedly by forces of several tons as the CMBs bounced across the waves. The engines and therefore the boats' very survival depended on the skill of the mechanics. They had to remain below decks in the forward engine compartments in cramped conditions, never seeing what was happening outside, drenched in sea water from the bilges, thrown around as the boats smashed their way across the waves and working in almost complete darkness because they were allowed only the light of one tiny electric bulb per boat. CMB motor mechanics were considered the very best in the Royal Navy. Now Gus had the pick of those on the base. He had no doubt. There was one engineer at Osea who was better than any other: Chief Motor Mechanic Hugh Beeley. Although only twenty-four, he seemed much older. Trained at the elite Rolls-Royce engineering works he was known on the Flotilla as 'faithful Beeley' because of his unflappable calm and his ability to get the best out of any machine. Be it Fiat, Sunbeam or Thornycroft, there wasn't a CMB engine that he couldn't fix.

Captain French had a very clear idea who should command the second CMB. Gus later recalled French's suggestion word for word: 'Young Sindall should do you well for the other one: nice chap; no brains; but very willing and adaptable.' Twenty-year-old Sub Lieutenant Edgar Sindall was a member of the Royal Naval Reserve. His nickname in the CMB Flotilla was 'Sinbad' because of his buccaneering attitude. He didn't much care what made a boat go, he just wanted it to go fast. But if his attitude was light-hearted, the one thing he didn't lack was nerve. As French had implied and Gus well knew, Sindall was as keen as mustard to get into the action. French suggested that they leave the choice of 'snotty' (midshipman) and mechanic to Sindall, provided he followed the rule that they should be young and without any close family ties.

For his second in command, Sindall chose nineteen-year-old Midshipman Richard Marshall. He was a close friend and the best shot with a Lewis gun on the Flotilla. He was usually assigned to CMB5, another of the 40-foot boats, so he would be familiar with their operation.

For a mechanic Sindall chose his friend Albert Piper. Barely nineteen his character was very much like that of his new captain. Gus described him as '. . . rather a happy-go-lucky sort and much younger than Beeley, but first-class at his job. Keen and eager to go anywhere and do anything.' He normally worked on one of the 55-foot craft, CMB46, but despite his youth he had already proved himself to be a first-class mechanic and like Beeley had qualified for his Chief Motor Mechanic rating.

Knowing the importance of keeping the engines in top condition, Gus begged for one other mechanic. He would not travel on any of the missions but would remain in Helsinki with the spare stores and could be called on as a reserve if necessary. Despite the acute shortage of trained mechanics at Osea, Captain French agreed and they selected 20-year-old Richard Pegler.

With selection of the team complete, it was now well into the evening and Gus and French left selection of the boats to the following day. When Gus went to bed that night his mind was still reeling at the pace of the day's events and he lay awake for hours wondering what would happen on the mission ahead. Above all he thought about the mysterious ST-25:

'Speculation about this man became an obsession. Who was he? What was he like? Was he still alive? Would I be in time to get to him? I must hurry – hurry the devil!'

*

The next day Gus and Captain French had to decide which of the 40-foot CMBs to take. The 55-foot boats would have been sturdier and carried more armament, but they were less manoeuvrable and their greater size would make them easier for Russian sentries to spot. On the way to the boats they collected Hugh Beeley to ask for his opinions on which engines had been recently overhauled and would be most reliable. He still had not been told that he was part of the team.

It was early morning and the mist still clung to the fringes of the island. The base was comparatively quiet at this hour apart from some hammering in one of the workshops and the distant lowing of the cows in the surrounding fields. There was space for 52 CMBs in the storage area, 26 on either side of the concrete traverser pit which contained the equipment for transporting them from the end of the slipway.

Much had been expected of these unusual weapons of war when they had first been designed, but in many ways their full potential had never been explored. Perhaps now they would justify the cost and effort of their creation. It was almost a miracle that they had ever been designed at all.

In the summer of 1915 three young naval lieutenants named Hampden, Bremner and Anson approached the boatbuilder Sir John Thornycroft with an idea. They were all serving with the Harwich naval force on convoy-protection duties. The conflict in the Channel had become a stalemate. The German navy lurked in their well-defended harbours and only occasionally made forays into the North Sea. On the rare occasions when the *Kaiserliche Marine* did appear the warships of the Royal Navy were usually too slow to reach the area before the German ships had returned to harbour. What was needed was a new kind of vessel, fast enough to reach the Germans when the alarm was sounded and somehow capable of evading their harbour defences to strike at them across the vast minefields which defended their coasts. The three young officers, desperate to see action, thought they had come up with a design which would do the job.

Fortunately Sir John Thornycroft was a brilliant engineer and inventor in the manner of Barnes Wallis (the man who was to design the Dambusters' bouncing bomb in the Second World War). Sir John had been designing motor boats for various navies around the world as well as for the private market since 1864 when he'd been just nineteen. By coincidence, he was already thinking on very similar lines to his visitors. Motor torpedo boats had been in existence for many years, but as time had passed and the operational demands on them had grown they had become larger and heavier until many of them were more like small destroyers. Like the visiting lieutenants, Sir John thought that torpedo boats should return to being smaller and faster. In fact, he had only recently submitted designs for a new kind of boat to the Admiralty.

This design was the result of over ten years of development work. Two things had revolutionised high-speed motor boats during that time. The first was the development of the internal combustion engine. This device, which in 1890 had only been able to push motor cars along at a few miles an hour, had now become powerful enough to launch aircraft and boatbuilders had quickly used them in speedboats where high revolutions by the propeller were needed for high speed. The other breakthrough was in the design of the hull. Sir John had pioneered the design of a hydroplane hull where, as the speed of the boat increased, the boat actually began to fly above the surface of the water rather than forcing its way through the waves like a conventional vessel. The loss in drag meant a tremendous boost in speed. It was a similar basis to the design which allowed Donald Campbell to break the world water-speed record in 1964. When conditions were suitable it also led to a smoother ride without a great deal of the bouncing around which was encountered in other vessels.

Thinking that the Admiralty had ignored his papers, Sir John was now keen to interview his unexpected visitors as men on the front line who would tell him exactly what the Navy needed. He was right. As young men eager to see action they wanted a boat which was fast – breathtakingly fast. The seagoing equivalent of a fighter aircraft. In order to make it difficult to hit it should also be small, no more than thirty feet from bow to stern. Next, the boat would have to pack a really big punch, at least one and preferably two eighteen-inch torpedoes. Finally, the boat must somehow have fuel tanks large enough to allow it to cruise, find its target, attack and return to base.

Sir John must almost have wished that he hadn't asked. To a boat designer the competing requirements of these young naval officers seemed irreconcilable. Speed was not the problem: Sir John had been working on a series of boats known as skimmers for the past ten years and his son Tom had raced them successfully on the international circuit. In 1910, one of the Thornycroft *Miranda* boats achieved a speed of 35 knots. Her hydroplane hull and specialised engine made her by far the fastest thing on the water. But carrying torpedoes, even one eighteen-inch torpedo, would soon put a stop to that. Each one weighed over three-quarters of a ton. It would be like attaching a caravan to a Formula One racing car.

And then there was the problem of launching the torpedo. In conventional motor torpedo boats the torpedo was lowered over the side of the ship on davits and launched while the boat was travelling at very low speed. But that system would be no use in this new kind of vessel because she would be a sitting duck as soon as she slowed down to fire. Torpedo tubes using compressed-air rams were used to launch torpedoes from warships, but these would be far too cumbersome for a high-speed motor boat.

Sir John and his design team wrestled with the problem all through the winter of 1915. They had produced an earlier design where the torpedo was launched over the front of the boat by an explosive ramming system using a cordite charge, but that had proved too dangerous as the boat tended to catch up with the torpedo and hit it in the rear as it entered the water – and then they both blew up. Another option was to fire the torpedo by means of a ram over the stern of the boat. But this meant that the boat would have to be sailing away from her target as she fired. Early torpedoes were tricky things to aim at the best of times and it would be damn near impossible to hit anything while heading the wrong way. This method would also entail getting far too close to the target before turning to aim as the attacking craft was sailing away. The CMB would probably be blown out of the water before it had a chance to fire.

Finally, Sir John hit upon the solution. It wasn't pretty, but *theoretically* it should work: the torpedo would be launched over the stern of the boat by a ram, *but with the torpedo facing forwards* so that it was travelling in the same direction as the skimmer. On the face of it, this seemed like a crazy idea. There were certainly three big problems. The first was that the hydraulic ram had to hit the nose of the torpedo (which contained the explosives) hard enough to shove it off the CMB but without causing it to blow up. The second was that the skimmer would have to be travelling very fast for the torpedo to launch, otherwise the streamlining of the torpedo would mean that it would go into a 'death dive' straight to the bottom of the ocean. In shallow waters this meant that it would blow up, probably taking the CMB with it. The exact speed would have to be determined through experiment. The final and for any skimmer crew the most pressing problem was that once the torpedo was launched the skipper would have a split second to swerve out of the way before the torpedo's motors engaged and sent it racing forwards much faster than the CMB could travel. Hesitate for a second and the skimmer would simply blow itself up.

There was also the question of range. As every car driver knows, high-performance engines guzzle fuel and a skimmer would require a very great deal of fuel indeed – and yet the skimmer had to be small and light. In order to get tanks big enough to give the skimmer a decent range, say 150 miles, everything else would have to be stripped out of the boat. And to keep weight down to the absolute minimum, the construction would have to be of plywood. There could be no weight allowance for armour so the fuel tanks would have no defence against bullets or shrapnel – even a near miss by a high-explosive shell might well cause the whole machine to split at the seams. It is hardly surprising that the boats came to be referred to as 'eggshells' by their crews.

Sir John summoned Hampden, Bremner and Anson to a meeting to announce the results of his research. But as he explained the design it was their turn to wish they had never asked. They had the fast boat they wanted, but only a fool would take to the water in it and only a maniac would try to launch a torpedo from one. Sir John was not even certain that his calculations were correct. The only way to be sure was to actually build the design and test it. For that he needed approval from the Admiralty. Nervously – knowing that *they* were likely to be the guinea pigs who were going to test this monstrosity – the three lieutenants agreed that they would support the project.

The Admiralty accepted the design and in January 1916 placed an initial order for twelve boats – provided that the first three prototypes passed trials successfully. The boats were built at the Thornycroft yard at Platt's Eyot (pronounced 'eight') on the River Thames, whilst the special V-12 engines were developed by Sir John's son Tom at their works in Basingstoke. Three months later, in April 1916, the first boats were complete and a unit from the

Royal Navy established itself in great secrecy in some disused sheds belonging to the South-Eastern Railway at Queensborough in the Thames estuary near Sheerness. The crews slept in the sheds with the boats which were launched from a slipway outside. Their job would be to show that the principles Sir John had worked out on the drawing board would work in reality. But there was more than one problem: not only was the team testing a completely new warship, firing a torpedo backwards at their own sterns, but now, because of the sensitivity of this new design, the Admiralty insisted that they were only allowed to take the skimmers out to sea at night!

Maintaining secrecy soon became a bit of a problem. When the throttles were full out and the hulls lifted clear of the water, the engine roar was tremendous. The early CMBs must have been quite a sight for anyone catching a glimpse of them as well: if the petrol mixture was wrong the engine would belch great jets of smoke and flame from its exhaust, which must have looked spectacular at night as they shot past. But, despite all the problems for the young crews, as the stern of the CMB settled down, the nose rose and two great wings of water were thrown up on either side of the cockpit, there was no more exhilarating feeling than the sheer sense of speed they achieved. They were travelling in the fastest boats on the water and they had a licence to test them to the limit.

It was dangerous work. Travelling at high speed at night was always tricky and visibility over the long bows of the CMBs soon turned out to be a problem. Although they were working with torpedoes without warheads, it was still scary launching a three-quarter-ton torpedo over the stern of the boat and risking it hitting you in the backside if you didn't get out of the way fast enough. The mechanics had their work cut out as well. Despite the careful work of the boatbuilders, under the strains of very high speeds and the battering as the boat bounced from wave to wave the seams tended to leak and the water and the vibration played merry hell with the high-performance engines. Half the work was just in keeping the engines dry. The mechanics soon found that the bilges could be drained when travelling at high speed by simply removing a bung from the hull. When the CMB was 'flying' this drain hole was clear of the waves and the excess water was forced out. But this method did have its drawbacks – as one captain found out when his CMB mysteriously sank after he returned from one trial run. After that mechanics had the importance of replacing the bung drilled into them . . .

Eventually, after nights of trial and (t)error, the determined crews finally got Sir John Thornycroft's crazy system to work. They found that the CMB had to be travelling at 30 knots or better for the torpedo to be launched successfully. This was fast enough so that the torpedo did not go into a death dive and fast enough so that the CMB could get out of the way, but not so fast that the crew were unable to aim.

The Admiralty were impressed with the results of the trials and confirmed the order. The skimmer was officially designated as the Coastal Motor Boat, abbreviated as CMB. As soon as the results of the tests were known, Sir John began work on a fifty-five-foot version which would have two engines and carry two torpedoes. It was ready for service by April 1917. A seventy-foot mine-laying version eventually appeared in 1919. In total, the Admiralty was to order more than one hundred CMBs.

This was more work than Thornycroft's boatyard could cope with. Other British boatbuilders had to be drafted in to help and soon the list of yards working on CMBs read like a *Who's Who* of the classic age of British boatbuilding: Hampton Launch Works, Salter Brothers, Tom Bunn & Co., Frank Maynard, J. W. Brook and Co., Will and Packham, Camper and Nicholsons and many others. Most are long gone now, but in 1917 they were the finest yards in Britain. Each CMB was built by hand and because they came from different yards they each had slightly different handling qualities. A new commander would have to get to know the characteristics of his particular boat just as a rider has to learn the temperament of a new horse.

But although the hulls could be provided there was a further problem. The CMBs required high-performance petrol engines of around 250 horsepower. The war was still raging in Europe and capacity in British engineering works was stretched to the limit producing engines for aircraft. There was no chance of switching production for a small run of marine engines. The Admiralty had no choice but to order that aircraft engines be installed and soon the skimmer flotilla was sporting a variety of Thornycroft, Green, Sunbeam and even Italian Fiat engines. This meant that the performance of each boat varied even more. Every individual coastal motor boat truly was unique.

Gus asked Hugh Beeley which two of the remaining CMBs he would recommend. The first choice was easy. CMB4 was one of the oldest and most reliable of the skimmers in the Flotilla. Beeley had spent days of work getting the engine just right and as Gus later wrote: 'he was as proud of it as a favourite hunter and gave it as much care.' She already had a considerable war record and had taken part in one of the CMB's first successful actions against enemy warships. On 8 April 1917, CMB4 under the command of Lieutenant W. N. T. Beckett was leading a hunting pack comprising CMBs 5, 6 and 9. They skimmed over the minefield just north of Zeebrugge harbour and were stalking the entrance at low speed to reduce the engine noise which might give them away. In the distance Beckett spotted four German destroyers off the Weilingen Channel. The CMBs increased speed and quickly moved in to attack. Beckett missed with CMB4's torpedo, but the rest of the pack were more accurate and two torpedoes struck the German destroyer *G88* below the waterline. She sank within minutes. The CMBs raced away into the safety of the darkness, using their ability to skim over the Germans' own minefield to escape pursuit. Beeley promised Gus that CMB4 would not let him down.

As for the other vessel, after pacing up and down the line several times they finally decided on CMB7, known in the Flotilla as 'the boat they couldn't sink'. Seamen, even those of the Royal Navy, are by tradition a superstitious bunch and if there was ever a boat which was lucky it was CMB7. She was almost as old as CMB4, but had seen far more combat. The events which earned her reputation had occurred over four days just a year earlier: On the evening of 30 April 1918, CMB7 and CMB13, based in Dunkirk, had been lying in ambush outside Ostend harbour. German destroyers were a menace to British shipping in the Channel, but as long as these raiders were in Ostend they were safe. The plan that night was to flush them out into the open waters of the English Channel. First, the RAF would bomb the harbour. The German destroyers would almost certainly seek the safety of the open sea. There the CMBs would be waiting to finish them off.

CMB7 was then under the command of Lieutenant Commander Eric Welman. It was often hard for the CMBs to pick out their targets because they were so low to the waterline. They had already been waiting for an hour and a half when Welman caught sight of a ship heading for the open sea, silhouetted for just a moment against the explosions in the harbour. He signalled to CMB13 and the two boats moved slowly across the choppy waters, running parallel to the course of the German ship, one on either side, hidden in the darkness as they moved out into the Channel. The problem for the CMBs was that the German guns had greater range and they had to get close enough to launch their attack without being seen. It was not the first time that they had tried this tactic and they edged closer, knowing that the destroyer's crew would be watching for them. But if the plan worked they would have the destroyer in a crossfire.

Suddenly they were seen. The destroyer opened fire and increased speed to try and get away from them. Both CMBs held their positions about half a mile out, too far away for them to launch their torpedoes but far enough to make them a difficult target. Welman could see that the destroyer was heading for the shallow waters of the coast. Sooner or later she would have to turn or risk grounding. The two CMB crews just had to stay alive long enough to take the shot.

Sure enough, the destroyer eventually put her helm hard over and the range between Welman and the destroyer closed rapidly. Welman opened up CMB7's throttle and raced towards his quarry with shellfire bursting all around him. As soon as the range closed to 400 yards Welman gave the signal and his midshipman fired the torpedo. Welman immediately swerved to one side and, glancing over the side, he saw the bubbling stream as the missile coursed past them. They raced away into the enveloping darkness and as the crew watched over their shoulders there was a flash and roar which announced that their torpedo had found its mark.

However, on 2 May, two days after the successful attack, the CMB base at Dunkirk was alerted that another German destroyer had nosed out into the Channel. Four CMBs – CMBs 2, 10, 13 and 7 – raced as a pack to intercept the destroyer's last known course. But on arriving at the position they found that there was not one, but a formation of *four* German destroyers. Because of their limited forward vision the CMBs had wandered right into the middle of them. Whether or not this was a deliberate trap laid by the Germans was never known, but the CMB pack was in any case in deep trouble. As the German ships opened fire the CMBs scattered in different directions. The German vessels, signals flashing between them, quickly decided to concentrate their fire on one – as luck would have it, it was CMB7.

Welman twisted and drove CMB7 through the waves, coaxing every knot of speed out of her as the shellfire came closer. The destroyers were fast, in the choppy sea almost as fast as a CMB, and they were soon close enough to open up with machine guns. With the high vulnerability of the CMBs because of their thin plywood skin and massive fuel tanks, it seemed impossible that CMB7 should survive such concentrated fire. Yet still she flew on, bouncing and zigzagging frantically, threatening at any moment to throw her crew overboard.

The other CMBs did not abandon her; seeing her plight their helmsmen returned to the attack. CMB10's engines began to fail and she was forced to abandon the run, but the other two pressed on and very nearly paid dearly for their bravery. The skipper of CMB2 was wounded as she was strafed and the crew were forced to flee to safety. CMB13 was hit and her steering gear was damaged, which meant that she began steering in ever-increasing circles – circles which would take her right through the centre of the German formation. As CMB13's crew fought to repair the damage, they continued to fight back against the destroyers as they passed through the formation. They launched their torpedo even though there was almost no chance of aiming. The torpedo duly missed, but it did force two of the German vessels to take evasive action. Finally, after passing through the formation twice and yet miraculously surviving, CMB13 was far enough out to sea to cut her engines, lie low and escape further attention from the destroyers which were still in hot pursuit of CMB7.

But CMB13 had done enough. As the sea calmed, CMB7 gradually outpaced the destroyers and one by one they gave up the chase. When they were finally able to stop, Welman and his crew had a chance to examine their boat. CMB7 had taken hits to her carburettor, her induction pipe (three times) the water-jacket of her engine and even her steering compass. Yet despite all this damage, when the loss of even a few knots might have proved fatal, CMB7's engine had not missed a stroke.

So, twelve months later, Hugh Beeley recommended CMB7 as the reserve boat for the mission – whatever it was. It was then that Gus told Beeley not to worry because he would be going on the mission as well. Gus explained that he could not tell him where they were going or why, but he wanted both boats overhauled and ready to sail within two days. Mindful of Cumming's cover story for getting them to Finland, he also ordered Beeley to paint the boats in brilliant white rather than their usual camouflage grey. As Gus and Captain French strode back to the manor house, Hugh Beeley stared after them as though they were barking mad.

Meanwhile Agar had two more meetings with Mansfield Cumming. At the first, on Friday, 9 May, he presented the plan that he and Captain French had developed in the past forty-eight hours. It did not amount to much. There were simply too many unknowns. Until Agar arrived and saw the area and in particular what kind of threat the forts presented he could not say exactly what the route he would take would be. However, if all else failed they would at least run a courier service over to the coast of Estonia and the couriers would have to take their chances from there.

Gus gave Cumming a list of the crews and details of the boats he was taking. Cumming checked once more that the crew members were young and unmarried – men who were expendable. Gus also outlined the fuel, food and ammunition requirements. Cumming promised that they would be met by his agents in Helsinki. He provided Gus with their names. There seemed to be little more to be said. Cumming told Gus to liaise with Commander Goff and Dorothy Henslowe over the transport arrangements. But there was one point that they had both overlooked. It was only as they were leaving the meeting that Cumming remembered that Gus would surely need money. Since the Navy had provided everything for him during his career, Gus had not thought of this either. Cumming asked how much would be needed. Gus was completely taken aback. He had no idea. After some thought he said:

'Um, about a thousand guineas, I think.'

Cumming immediately called his secretary on the intercom and told her to have the MI6 paymaster Percy Sykes bring in a cheque for 1,000 guineas made out to 'bearer'. Gus didn't know what to say. He had never had more than a few pounds in his pocket. As someone who had been a penniless junior naval officer himself, Cumming apparently sensed Agar's discomfort and said:

'I don't want you to keep detailed accounts – you will have other things to think about – but we shall require, later on, a rough statement showing how you have spent it. You will all, of course, receive your service pay, but not from the Admiralty.'

And with that he left the preparation in Gus's hands. There was a great deal to do. Although it had broken Beeley's heart the CMBs' normal camouflage grey had been covered with a coat of shining white paint. Now he and the other mechanics at Osea had to construct canvas covers to protect the CMBs from the elements as they were shipped to Finland. The machine guns and torpedo-firing gear had to be stripped out of both boats and then repacked in crates labelled as engine spares. Passage had to be booked on steamers leaving for Finland as soon as possible. MI6 found ships that they thought were suitable. Agents working at the MI6 station at Helsinki tried to source petrol and oil but, because of the turbulent situation in the Baltic, this proved to be extremely difficult.

Despite the urgency of the situation there was a host of bureaucratic delays and it seemed as if the team would never be able to leave. For instance, none of the team had a passport. These were issued by the Foreign Office on Thursday, 15 May. With a lack of attention to operational security the passports were numbered sequentially – Hampsheir's was 283727, Sindall's 283728, Agar's 283729 and so forth. A detail that might raise awkward questions with a sharp-eyed immigration official. There was also a great deal of discussion between government ministries about how the men should be described under the heading 'Profession'. There was a lot of unhappiness about the idea of them being shown as commercial travellers. In the end the Admiralty won out and they were recorded as officers of the Royal Navy. Next there was the question of visas. Finland was a newly independent state and the Foreign Office was keen to observe all the proprieties. So despite the need for secrecy applications were made at the Finnish embassy for visas. Naturally it could not be explained to the Finns why there was a need for these to be issued as quickly as possible. Still, the Foreign Office did their best and the visas were issued the following Monday, 19 May.

Even clothing was a problem. Despite what their papers said, the team had to look like civilians. But having spent almost all his life in the Navy, Gus did not even own a suit. He was sent to Covent Garden where he bought a rather cheap brown two-piece suit from Moss Bros. He was afraid to spend his operational money on anything more expensive.

Finally, on the evening of Wednesday, 21 May, the team were

ready to move. They would travel in two groups: Sindall, Piper and Pegler would be on the slow cargo ship with the boats. Gus, John Hampsheir, Richard Marshall and Hugh Beeley would travel on a slightly faster ship which MI6 had found for them. That night the Royal Navy tug HMS *Security* arrived secretly at Osea and cables were attached to CMBs 4 and 7 which were as ready as Beeley and his team could make them. The journey took all night because the boats could not be towed too fast in case they were swamped, but as dawn broke the next morning *Security* arrived at West India Commercial Docks in the heart of London and the CMBs were secured alongside the Swedish cargo ship SS *Pallux*. That evening Gus took the crews to dinner and then to the theatre where they watched the now forgotten comedy *'Yes, Uncle!'* It was to be their last night in England for quite a while. Possibly for ever.

The following day the boats and the stores were finally hoisted aboard the *Pallux*. Sindall together with the mechanics Piper and Pegler were left with their charges. While the other members of the team did some last-minute shopping, Gus went to a final meeting with Cumming at Whitehall Place. To celebrate their departure, Cumming took Gus on a hair-raising drive through London in his Rolls-Royce to dine at one of his clubs. During the meal Cumming did not talk about the operation at all and when the meal was over he simply patted Gus on the back, said: 'Well, my boy, good luck to you' and left. Gus walked to the Army and Navy Club, collected his few civilian belongings and then took a taxi to Euston station. There he met Hampsheir, Marshall and Beeley. They were due to take the 5 p.m. service to Hull – and were a little put out that MI6 had only booked them third-class tickets! But there was also a surprise visitor waiting for them: Dorothy Henslowe. She had brought some magazines 'for the journey', but it is clear that this was something more than attention to detail. These were young men who probably would not be coming back and she clearly felt a sense of responsibility towards them which Cumming did not. She stood on the platform as the train pulled out of the station. Gus hung out of the window and watched her until she was out of sight.

The train arrived at Hull at 10.30 p.m. It had been an awkward journey. No sooner had they boarded the train than Gus had been spotted by an old naval friend named Hunt who was also travelling to Hull to take command of a new ship. Gus was forced to engage him in conversation while spinning some story about where he was going. The others lay low and pretended not to know him. When the train arrived in Hull the local Senior Naval Transport Officer (SNTO) had sent a rating and a car. He conducted them to the nearby Railway Hotel where the SNTO had booked rooms for them.

At 9.30 a.m. the next morning Gus and his colleagues changed into their ill-fitting civilian clothes, had a meeting with the SNTO at which they handed over the cases containing their naval uniforms and from there were directed to the offices of Ambrose Good, shipping agent. It was here that their cover story began to unravel.

Good was puzzled by the exorbitant rate which his guests had agreed to pay. £15 would have been a high price for passage to Finland, but because of the need to get the team out there as quickly as possible, MI6 had agreed a fee of £45 per man. In Good's opinion this was ridiculous and quite frankly suspicious. He was convinced he could get a lower price and Gus agreed to let him try. Good telephoned the *Fennia*'s agent and soon had the price reduced to a more reasonable £20. But then there was another problem: the *Fennia* was not rated to carry passengers. To get around naval regulations the four men would have to be signed on as deckhands. They were taken to the shipping office to sign on and then went to the Aliens Office where their passports were stamped for exit. It was at this point that the naval men heard to their horror that the *Fennia* was a dry ship (she was Finnish-registered and Finland had introduced prohibition at the same time she became independent). Hampsheir was sent hastily into town to secure as much alcohol as he could find. He returned with a rather odd collection: four dozen bottles of stout and a dozen bottles of port. It would have to do.

Finally they arrived in their ill-fitting Covent Garden suits at the *Fennia*. Her captain ('a good sort, fat,' noted Gus) and some of the crew welcomed them aboard. The four Englishmen were clearly a matter of some curiosity. When Gus asked the captain about this, he admitted that this was the first time he had ever carried passengers as seamen. In his diary that evening Gus wrote despairingly that the captain gave him 'many eyewinks' at this point. Being a spy was going to be more trouble than he had thought: their cover story was already under suspicion and they had not even left England yet.

By 1.30 p.m. the *Fennia* was underway. Mealtimes on the ship were: breakfast at 9 a.m., dinner at 1 p.m. and supper at 6 p.m. Gus was horrified to find that there was no afternoon tea. As the *Fennia* moved slowly out of port, he noted in his diary that he was going to ask for afternoon tea to be served promptly at 4 p.m. each day and a late supper before bed as well. 'Expect to have a row about it,' he wrote cautiously. But in 1919 there were some standards which an Englishman simply could not let slip.

Gus wondered how ST-25 was faring.

4

Very special measures

ST-25 had missed afternoon tea. He had also missed dinner and breakfast. In fact, he hadn't eaten for more than two days.

He lay hidden in a clump of bushes in the marshes on a low hillock which was all that separated him from the stinking mud and slime of the lower reaches of the River Neva, which ran through the centre of Petrograd. Great clouds of persistent mosquitoes swarmed overhead in the pale half-light of the Baltic night, their high-pitched buzzing and continuous irritating bites hardly noticed now amid the pain of hunger, the itching of the lice which infested his tattered clothes and the racking cough which he knew must surely be the first sign of pneumonia. Or perhaps it was cholera? There was already an epidemic in the city. It had claimed over ten thousand people. As ST-25 lay there looking up at the stars, he tried to remember what the first symptoms of cholera were, but he was so tired that the details would not come to mind. Or perhaps it was typhoid. The water that now came out of the few working taps in Petrograd was brown and infected. Perhaps that was how it would end? Not with a shout, a dash from cover and the sudden searing pain of a bullet, but with a gentle drift into coma, death and just another withered corpse laid amongst the thousands of others which littered the countryside around the city – victims of famine, disease or simply the Cheka's deadly justice.

ST-25 slipped in and out of a restless sleep, occasionally waking with a start to listen for Cheka patrols. In his mildly delirious state it was hard to tell the difference between what might be the sound of approaching Cheka greatcoats and the swishing of the reeds in the inshore breeze from the Baltic. He knew they were searching for him. The cordon which had been tightening around him for weeks was probably about to close shut. There was a new officer in charge.

The Cheka knew that there was a British agent somewhere in the city and this new man had been summoned from Moscow specifically to hunt down ST-25. Apparently he had lived in England, spoke English fluently and even had an English wife. He was certainly good at his job. There was a new intensity to the manhunt. ST-25 had been chased from every safe house. The searches had gradually driven him further and further out into the suburbs until he wasn't safe anywhere in the city. They even knew his name and details this time:

Paul Henry Dukes. Age: 29. Nationality: British. Profession: concert pianist.

Someone had talked. Possibly one of his couriers they had picked up on the border. Possibly one of his friends from when he had studied for four years at the St Petersburg Conservatoire. Or perhaps one of his new networks had been penetrated by an informer as his first one had been shortly after his arrival in the country. It did not really matter. It was too late now. He had run out of everything: out of friends, out of money, out of time. Too weak to make the journey across the border, he knew that even if he had been well the patrols had been tightened to such an extent that he would never make it alive. He could not sleep because of the pain in his feet from the effects of frost-bitten toes which he had acquired in an accident during one of his trips into the country.

He only had one small hope. One razor blade's edge of a chance that kept him going: MI6. He had to believe that they would keep the promise they had made to him when they had convinced him to return for this, his third trip into Bolshevik Russia in less than a year.

Paul Dukes remembered that day clearly. Major John Scale, the new head of all MI6 operations in north-western Russia, had assured him that 'very special measures' were being prepared in London to ensure that he had an escape route. But that promise had been in February, four long months ago and still there was no sign of anyone.

Special measures! Paul laughed bitterly, a laugh which turned into a dry, racking cough. He buried his face deeper in the folds of his greatcoat to stifle the noise. He knew that the shore was heavily patrolled, even here in the marshes, and if he was found he had no excuse for being out after the 10 p.m. curfew. He would immediately be arrested or shot as a smuggler . . . or worse.

He had no doubt about the tortures that awaited him if he was caught. The Terror in place since September 1918 had changed everything. It seemed that the torturers of the Cheka competed to surpass each other: in Kharkov they went in for scalping alive and hand-flaying; in Voronezh prisoners were thrust naked into a barrel studded with razor-sharp nails and rolled around the interrogation room; in Poltava they used impalement; in Kremenchug they buried prisoners alive; at Ekaterinoslav it was crucifixion or stoning – very biblical; in Odessa they tied the prisoners to planks and slowly pushed them, alive and feet first, into the prison furnaces; in Aramvir they slowly crushed the prisoner's head with a vice until the eyes popped out and the skull cracked; in Orel they poured water onto chained prisoners and left them outside overnight so that they became ice sculptures and a warning to others. But the torture which Paul feared most came from Kiev where rats were tied in cages across the stomachs of prisoners before a blowtorch was applied to the bars of the cage. The rat could only tunnel out one way . . .

Paul's hand closed on the revolver in his pocket. He had no doubt what he would do with the last bullet if he had to. It was all so different from the future which he had planned when he had first arrived in Russia almost ten years ago.

Paul was born in the town of Bridgwater, Somerset on 10 February 1889. He was the third of five children – four boys and a girl. His father, the Reverend Edwin Joshua Dukes, was the minister of the local Congregationalist church. Surviving photographs show an austere man who always wore a high starched collar, pince-nez spectacles and a carefully trimmed goatee beard. He had returned from missionary work in China and married a local girl, Edith Mary Pope. The running of the church soon became a family affair with his brother-in-law as the church organist and other family members as officials.

Edwin was not a cruel man, but religion dominated his life and Paul remembered him as puritanical and cold. Cuthbert, Paul's youngest brother, later charitably described him as '. . . always a trifle haughty, serene and detached' and 'inclined to be unapproachable'. All the affection in Paul's early life came from his mother, Edith. She was an outstanding woman of her time. She had been born in 1862 in Sandford, a village not far from Bridgwater and was soon identified as a gifted child. Her father, the village schoolmaster, was keen that she should make the best of her abilities, so she was sent away to a boarding school in Gravesend. From there she went to the University of London where she matriculated 'taking first place among all the women graduates in England'. She then returned to Sandford to help her father at the school and to work in the local chapel, but she still found time to gain her Bachelor of Arts degree by correspondence course. Edith was then barely twenty years old. She might have gone on to a glittering academic career, but the other dominant force in her life was Congregationalism and two years later, in 1884, she married Edwin. The rest of her life was dedicated to her family and helping her husband run his church. But Paul never forgot the educational achievements of his mother and he always proudly referred to her as 'Edith Pope BA'.

The first nine years of Paul's life were idyllic or at least that was how he remembered them. Edith, whom he described as 'infinitely kind', provided all the love he required and he had the wonderful countryside of Somerset to explore. Much of this was done in the company of an elderly member of the congregation, Moses Turner, a delivery man:

> 'Moses would stop at our door and my mother would hoist me to his side dressed in a blue smock and clutching a precious package of sandwiches. Moses would click his tongue and jerk the reins, his hefty dray horse tugged obediently and off we jogged on pilgrimages that were to me an adventurous escape from the restricted atmosphere of a somewhat strait-laced home.'

That idyllic childhood was cut cruelly short by the death of Paul's beloved mother from a disease of the thyroid gland in 1898. She was just 35. Edwin, already in his fifties and as remote from the children as any patriarch could be, immediately ruined everything. One Sunday evening at the end of his sermon, he suddenly announced to the congregation that his family would be leaving Bridgwater. He was going to take charge of the Congregationalist chapel at Harrogate in Yorkshire. Even though he was only eight at the time, Cuthbert Dukes always remembered 'the long, long silence' which greeted this announcement. Sitting in the front pew, this was the first his children had heard of the idea. But they were not going to Harrogate. Edwin felt that caring for them would detract from his religious duties and soon they were packed off to various boarding schools.

It was Paul's great misfortune to be sent to the Congregationalist Boys' School at Caterham in Surrey. The school had been established in 1811 for members of the Church who wished to ensure that their sons were brought up correctly in the family religion. But for Paul, aged only ten, it proved a nightmare which was to undermine his belief in God for ever. As can often happen under the protective shroud of organised religious belief, a predatory paedophile was at work in Caterham School. He was Paul's housemaster and Paul soon became one of his victims. For a small boy who had lived such a happy childhood, to suddenly lose his beloved mother, to be taken from everything he had known and then to be exposed to this monster must have been terrifying almost beyond endurance. Separated from those he could confide in, he was also trapped by the code of the times which was that one did not 'peach' on others, no matter what their crime.

Eventually Paul could take it no longer and when he was home on holiday he summoned up the courage to tell his father what was happening. But Edwin either could not or would not believe that a man working at a school run by his beloved Church could possibly do such things. To his mind it was clear who must be in the wrong: he accused Paul of making the whole thing up and to teach Paul the error of his ways he then invited the housemaster to stay with them for the holidays, making sure that the two of them spent plenty of time alone together.

An experience as traumatic as this might have destroyed a lesser person. It might have produced a monster even more evil than this unnamed housemaster. But Paul survived and always said that he learned two lessons from this passage of his life. The first was that there was no God – for who could believe in a deity who had created such a world? The other lesson was subterfuge. In order to avoid the attentions of this paedophile, he learned to lie, cheat and evade. He dreamed up dozens of different ways of making sure that their paths crossed as rarely as possible and that when they did he appeared too sick or otherwise occupied for the housemaster to dally with him. Eventually a new crop of younger boys arrived at the school and the housemaster moved on to other victims. But Paul never forgot those lessons and he never forgave the father who had handed him over to such a creature.

Academically Paul was competent but not outstanding. He was a timid and rather reserved boy, but he did have a talent for music. He had been taught how to play the church organ by his uncle and at Caterham he became a fine pianist. He decided that he wanted a career in music and dreamed of studying in one of the great European academies. But when he left school his father was determined that he should follow a clerical career. A life of office drudgery seemed to be Paul's future.

The event which was to change the course of Paul's life occurred in September 1907. After being forced out of Harrogate in 1901 by a congregation who could not tolerate his dictatorial ways, Edwin had found it very difficult to get another ministry. He was interviewed by several churches, but discreet enquiries soon uncovered his reputation as 'an awkward man to get on with' and no post was ever offered. Eventually, in 1904, things took a turn for the better and he was appointed to a small church in Kentish Town. One day in August 1907, Edwin suddenly announced that in a few days time he was going to remarry to a forty-year-old widow named Harriet Rouse. As usual he gave his children little or no warning about this. Paul in particular resented the marriage, which he felt was a betrayal of his mother's memory. Perhaps because of his horrific adolescent experiences, he also seemed to associate his father's marriage to a woman twenty years his junior with some failure to control his sexual urges. In any case, the marriage provoked the final split between Paul and his father. Paul decided that he would now take any opportunity to escape. He was eighteen years old.

Edwin and Harriet were married on 2 September 1907. Their departure for a honeymoon in France gave Paul his chance. He packed all his belongings into a Gladstone bag, spent most of his meagre savings on a one-way ferry ticket to Rotterdam and set off from London. He had a vague plan to make his way to the Conservatoire at St Petersburg, which at that time was the most prestigious and exclusive music school in the world.

Paul's prospects were not good. He had almost no money and he spent practically his last sixpence on a German phrase book in the mistaken belief that it was the national language of Holland. The one hope he had was an advertisement from a language school in

Rotterdam asking for English teachers. When Paul arrived there, he found that the 'school' was run out of a small flat by a Mr William E. Birkett, a young Englishman in his twenties. He seemed completely perplexed when Paul arrived unannounced on his doorstep saying that he had come about the teaching job. At first he turned Paul away, but seeing the young man's desperation he eventually agreed to take him for a month's trial giving lessons in the town of Enschede, on the border with Germany. And so Paul began a slow journey across the Continent which was to last for the next two years.

After almost a year teaching for Birkett, Paul, now fluent in both Dutch and German, decided to move on. He began work for a German, Dr E. Kummer. At first this was in Germany, but within a few months he moved with Kummer to open a school in Warsaw, then part of the Russian empire, arriving there in January 1909. A few months later he was off again, this time opening a *Sprachsinstituten* for Kummer in Riga, the capital of Latvia. But the business was not a success and folded after a few months when it was discovered that Kummer was a deserter from the German Army and had a string of debts. Paul was suddenly left stranded a long way from home, without money or prospects. He scraped a living giving private lessons in English and German and was supported by the vicar of the local English church. By April 1910 he had finally saved enough money to make the last stage of his journey. He bought a rail ticket to St Petersburg.

The next four years of Paul's life were happy again. He was accepted by the Conservatoire and studied under the renowned teacher Anna Essipova, the school's principal professor of piano who also trained Sergei Prokofiev and Alexander Borovsky. Paul supported himself by continuing to give language lessons. He shared rooms with Sydney Gibbes, tutor to the Tsar's only son, Alexis. As a result of this friendship he had access to all the inside gossip about the Imperial family, including the activities of the monk Rasputin. But although Paul was a highly talented musician he soon realised that he had left it too late to play at the very highest levels. Instead he continued to play at occasional concerts but decided to direct the bulk of his energies towards a career in composing and conducting. He soon began work as assistant to Albert Coates, the principal conductor at the world-famous Imperial Mariinsky Opera. The pair first met in 1911 and it was a friendship which was to last for the rest of their lives. They were known locally as 'Big Boy Albert' and 'Dukelet'.

In August 1913 Paul graduated from the Conservatoire and began work at the Mariinsky full-time. But then, on 1 August 1914, Germany declared war on Russia. When Britain was dragged into the war a few days later (4 August) Paul went to the British Consulate to volunteer for the armed forces. But the medical examination revealed a defect in his heart and he was deemed 'unfit for service'. It was a shaming blow. Paul decided that he would do better to continue working in Russia than returning to live uselessly in Britain. However, in 1915 the chance to serve arose again. As Russia's failures on the battlefield multiplied, doubts arose about the nation's determination to stay in the war. The British government decided to open an 'Anglo-Russian Bureau' that would monitor conditions inside Russia and at the same time engage in propaganda activities designed to keep Russia loyal to the Allied cause. This included writing press articles and organising touring cinema shows. The Bureau was led by Hugh Walpole, the novelist, who was already in Russia on Red Cross duties. Paul was the first member of staff to be signed up. In 1916 he resigned from the Mariinsky to work for the Commission full-time.

Paul travelled all over the country, reporting on living conditions and writing summaries of reports and articles in the Russian press for transmission to the Foreign Office in Whitehall. There was some crossover between the work of the Bureau and the work of the various military intelligence agencies working out of the British embassy and it is possible that this was when Paul first came to their attention. However, during his travels Paul developed a great deal of sympathy for the plight of Russia's serfs and for the ordinary soldiers at the Front who were used as so much cannon fodder. He came to believe that revolution was probable, if not inevitable.

During this period Paul became close friends with the novelist Arthur Ransome who was then the Russian correspondent for the *Daily Chronicle*. Ransome suffered constantly from ill health and on some occasions Paul even wrote Ransome's column for the newspaper. The two men were in a prime position to witness the coming revolution at first hand. St Petersburg (renamed Petrograd in 1914 as a patriotic gesture by the Tsar) was the capital of the Russian empire and it was here that the drama was played out. When the first Russian Revolution broke out in March 1917 Paul supported it. Many of his friends from his student days at the Conservatoire were among the protesters who stormed the government buildings. Paul helped to turn the Tauride Palace into an arsenal, working through the night to help peasants and soldiers shift sandbags and weapons. He witnessed the street fighting at close hand and saw the rampaging mobs throw police agents from the roofs of buildings where they had been hiding.

But then the Revolution stuttered. Bowing to Allied wishes and unable to agree to German terms for a truce, the leader of the Provisional government, Kerensky, was forced to continue the hugely unpopular war. Paul, who desperately wanted democratic reform in Russia, could see the situation sliding out of control and, although leaders of the various factions talked and talked, there seemed to be nothing anyone could do to prevent it. In April 1917 Paul was at the Finland Station to witness Lenin's arrival from Switzerland. The Germans knew the trouble he would cause and had allowed him to pass through their territory in a sealed train. Paul witnessed the rapturous reception this man was given by his supporters and also saw the determined look of the men who arrived with him. Paul later claimed that he quickly realised that here was the most serious threat to the future stability of the country.

But Paul was to miss the Bolshevik seizure of power in November 1917. In July he was sent back to London as special liaison officer between the Anglo-Russian Bureau and the Foreign Office. The Anglo-Russian Bureau was primarily responsible to the Ministry of Information. The Ministry was led by John Buchan, the novelist and creator of the first great spy-hero, Richard Hannay. *The Thirty-Nine Steps* had recently been published, in 1915. Paul briefed Buchan and senior officials at the Foreign Office about the situation in Russia. Paul was shocked at their level of ignorance. Whitehall seemed almost completely unaware of the most basic facts about Russian life and of the very real threat from Lenin, Trotsky and the Bolsheviks. But then in July, shortly after Paul arrived, the Bolsheviks attempted a coup against Kerensky's Provisional government which failed miserably. Lenin fled to Finland, Trotsky and Zinoviev were captured. It seemed that Paul had been wrong after all.

Paul was reduced to writing digests of items in the Russian press and preparing propaganda pieces. But, sitting in his room on the top floor of the northern wing of the Foreign Office building, Paul listened to the Zeppelin and Gotha bombing attacks across the city as he worked through the evenings. He was stuck there, thousands of miles from the world which he really knew. Millions of men had died, many of them his friends, and he was working in an office. Being in London brought home to him how many young men had made the ultimate sacrifice. What did that make him, sitting here in safety and comfort? Was he a coward?

In September 1917 Paul went to see Buchan and asked for more active duty. He was sent to the Front in Flanders where he produced intelligence reports about the state of the armed forces. But it wasn't enough. If anything the sight of conditions at the Front and the sacrifices made there heightened his sense that he must do *something*.

In November 1917 Paul returned to London to astonishing reports. There had been a second coup and this time the Bolsheviks had been successful. Kerensky had leniently but stupidly released Zinoviev and Trotsky and then resentment at the war had finally brought them to power. The Bolsheviks did not control the entire country. They held Petrograd and Moscow, but the rest was in doubt. In the reports that he was reading Paul could see that the future of Russia, perhaps of the whole European war, was in the balance – for if the Russian Front collapsed Germany could turn her full strength against the struggling Allied armies. And here he was thousands of miles away. The sense of frustration was agonising:

'If only I, too, could have been a fighter! If only I, too, could have gone "over the top"! But my sorry lot was to be in mufti. As a needed "specialist", I had even been torn away from my base of operations – and was expected to comment upon reports that were now days old – months old if calculated in revolutionary time.

I *must* go back . . .'

But how? Paul agonised over the issue for several days and finally went to Buchan personally and begged for his help. In many ways John Buchan was a frustrated spy himself. He suffered from a digestive problem that had completely undermined his health so he sympathised with Paul's plight. Here was a chance to create a real-life version of Richard Hannay, the man he had already imagined.

He told Paul to work out a way to return to Russia, using official cover. He, Buchan, would smooth things with the Foreign Office. Once Paul was in Russia Buchan thought that it would only be a matter of time before the intelligence services decided to make use of him.

So, in December 1917, Paul headed back to Russia as a King's Messenger with dispatches for the British embassy in Petrograd. He then intended to travel the country as a sort of roving official observer for Buchan's department, commenting on a number of institutions including the Red Cross, the American YMCA and even the Boy Scout movement. John Buchan's plan worked perfectly and in June 1918 Paul received a message from the British Consul-General, John Wardrop, that he was required urgently in London.

But, by then, leaving revolutionary Russia was not a simple matter. It took Paul more than a month to get to the northern port of Archangel and then to get passage on various British warships along the northern coast of Norway. Eventually he was able to get a place on the troopship *Prince Arthur* bound for Scotland. As the ship chugged slowly across the North Sea, her crew keeping a careful lookout for mines or enemy raiders, Paul was very worried. The message from the Foreign Office that Wardrop had relayed to him had given no indication of the reason for his recall nor why it was so urgent, but Paul had a suspicion that he knew the answer. Paul believed vehemently that there needed to be reform in Russia rather than a return to Tsarist rule and some of his reports had been distinctly pro-Bolshevik. Certainly too much so for Foreign Office tastes. He suspected that he was being recalled in disgrace.

So he was surprised, when the *Prince Arthur* finally docked in Aberdeen on the evening of 26 July 1918, to be told by the Control Officer who checked his passport that he was to travel to London immediately. Paul boarded the sleeper to London, arrived at Kings Cross station early the following morning and found a chauffeur-driven car waiting for him. He was driven swiftly through the streets of London, around Trafalgar Square and into Whitehall before turning left into one of the side streets. The car drew to a halt outside one of the grey stone buildings.

All these elaborate arrangements and now the arrival at this anonymous headquarters led Paul to suspect that he had not been recalled in disgrace after all. Whatever this place was, it was not the Foreign Office, nor was it the War Office. The driver led him through the front entrance to the elevator and at the top floor Paul was shown into an office that was occupied by a young army officer.

This man was Lieutenant Colonel 'Freddie' Browning, second in command of MI6. In many ways he was the archetype of a MI6 officer – wealthy background, public school (Wellington), an Oxford blue (tennis), and a member of the MCC. He was a director of the prestigious Savoy Hotel and had previously worked as head of intelligence at the Trade Office. Sir Samuel Hoare MP wrote that he was 'famous upon every cricket ground and in every racquets court, the friend of more people in the world than almost anyone I knew'.

However, Browning also had a reputation as a playboy and in descriptions by some authors he comes across as something like a public-school bully. Upon his arrival at MI6 in 1916 he promptly installed a French chef in the staff canteen and set about organising regular parties. His popularity with the frequently lascivious Cumming was due, at least in part, to his ability to supply a bevy of pretty society girls for these events. Browning's rather vulgar sense of humour had also provided Cumming with one of his favourite descriptions of MI6: 'We have no use for the "usual channels" – except in the early morning!' In any event, this upper-class dandy certainly did not take to Paul Dukes.

Browning rather abruptly informed Paul that he had been recalled for work of national importance with the Secret Service. Paul was initially a little puzzled that he had been ordered to return all the way from Russia simply to be sent back to that country to do what sounded like exactly the same thing he had been doing before. When Paul protested that he was already doing precisely this sort of work for the Foreign Office, Browning appears to have misjudged his man. Rather than explaining what MI6 was thinking, he stated in a rather objectionable manner that Paul's work for the Foreign Office was neither here nor there and that in any case MI6 had the right to commandeer the services of anyone they chose. Furthermore, taking Paul's apparent confusion for weakness, he then sneered that if the danger was too much for him then of course MI6 would select someone else. Never one to duck a fight, Paul's reply was forthright – but unprintable.

Paul's return had caught MI6 slightly unprepared – Cumming was not available. Browning told Paul to go away and return at

4.30 p.m. the following day for a further briefing. Paul's meeting with Browning was quite possibly the most unpromising recruitment interview in the history of the British secret service.

The following day, Browning did not even bother to ask Paul if he was going to accept the job offer: he had clearly decided to pass Paul on to someone else. He took Paul to a book-lined office on a lower floor of the building where another senior officer was waiting. Paul always protected the identity of this person although he admitted, 'I had more to do with him than with any other person in the roof-labyrinth.' However, Paul did want tribute to be paid to this man one day in the future because he left clues in his writings which can now be deciphered. The mysterious person who had so much to do with Paul's recruitment was Robert Nathan, the head of MI6's political intelligence department, Section V. Nathan had entered the intelligence world from the Indian Civil Service. Ill health had forced him to retire from that role in 1914, but upon the outbreak of war he had joined the Indian Political Intelligence department, tracking Indian nationalists who were working with the Germans. He had then joined MI6 and served on the New York station before taking up this new post.

Although Paul found Nathan much more to his liking, he still found what MI6 wanted to be rather vague: '. . . someone to remain there and keep us informed of the march of events.' Not only that, but having dragged Paul out of Russia MI6 did not appear to have given much thought to how he should get back or how he would survive once he got there: 'As to the means whereby you gain access to the country, under what cover you will live there, and how you will send out reports, we shall leave it to you, being best informed as to conditions, to make suggestions.'

This approach was typical of the early years of MI6: a rather dilettante group of officers sat in London enjoying life away from the front line, sending out personnel willy-nilly into the world with no proper training or briefing, interfering when they felt like it and generally cocking things up. The novelist Compton Mackenzie was an officer in MI6's Athens station between 1915–1917 and his memoirs are stuffed full of the frustrations of dealing with 'fools in London', culminating in his satirical novel *Water on the Brain* where the character Colonel Nutting represents all the pompous inadequacies of the typical MI6 staff officer. Henry Landau, who was head of the military section on the Rotterdam station

1916–1918 and later set up MI6's first Berlin station, suffered similarly from the poor state of MI6 recruitment: after being interviewed by Cumming he was sent abroad the very next day without any training whatsoever.

The meeting culminated with Nathan offering to take Paul to see 'the Chief'. Paul consistently told a rather odd story about this moment. Nathan left the room to see if Cumming was available. While he was gone, Paul took down a book at random and was startled to discover that it was a dummy stuffed full of top-secret papers headed *Kriegministerium Berlin*. Paul hastily replaced the volume, whereupon Nathan returned and said that Cumming was not available and that Paul should come back the next day. When they arrived in the office the following day Nathan pointed to the very same book amongst all the dozens of others on the shelves and invited Paul to take a look at it, praising it as a particularly fine volume. Nervously Paul did so, only to find that the dummy had gone and the book he held in his hands was perfectly normal.

What did it mean? It might seem that Paul had made the incident up if he had not told the story so consistently. However, there is a history of MI6 using a similar exercise to test potential agents: in December 1910, in the very early days of the organisation, Cumming had a meeting with the wife of a German officer who was offering information. To test her trustworthiness Cumming left her in the room alone with his notecase. He either marked the notecase or observed her secretly because when he returned he knew that she had not touched it. This may all seem rather Boy Scoutish, but it was just the sort of trick which appealed to the swordstick-carrying Cumming. It was quite possible that something like this trick had been passed on as good tradecraft – and may even still be in use today.

But whether this was a test or not, Nathan took Paul straight up to see Cumming whom he introduced as 'Captain Spencer'. In fact, MI6 were still so uncertain of Paul's trustworthiness that he did not learn Cumming's real name for another eighteen months. Even so, the old man's genuine warmth and enthusiasm (and slight battiness) soon won Paul over. Ever since working for Buchan, he had longed to be part of the world of intelligence and this old man with his gadgets and maps, his swordstick and his talk of messages written in secret inks, sounded very much like the real thing. Although Paul never mentioned it in any of his accounts of the meeting we know from Cumming's own diary that another man, named Samson, was present. This was almost certainly Colonel Rhys Samson, a rather shy and bookish officer. He had been Compton Mackenzie's head of station in Athens and had got on well with him. With this background, Cumming probably included Samson at the meeting as a good judge of what sort of spy this concert pianist would make. Samson must have approved because the meeting was short and by its end Paul was officially a British agent. Cumming told Nathan to instruct him in codes and ciphers and to send him back to Russia as soon as possible. He had just one piece of parting advice for Paul:

'Don't go and get killed,' he said, smiling.

The conman and sometime MI6 officer Sidney Reilly later claimed to have been present during this interview and said that Paul had almost been rejected. He claimed that only a last-minute interest in Cumming's collection of guns had saved Paul – together with Reilly's personal endorsement, of course. Like many of Reilly's stories, this was so much nonsense: Cumming did not have a collection of guns in his office and Reilly did not meet Paul until after Paul's return from Russia. But like the tall tale of any good conman, it did convey a grain of truth: MI6 were indeed rather reluctant to recruit Paul. He did not fit the usual mould of an MI6 officer. Like the staff officers in London, almost all MI6 operatives in the field were from a military or naval background – even Reilly had served a brief stint in the Royal Flying Corps in Canada before he was recruited. On paper, Paul appeared to be simply a musician with a dodgy heart who just happened to have an intimate knowledge of a target country. The Great War had raged for four years and yet Paul had done nothing to prove himself. It is clear from the records of Browning's first interview with him that he was afraid that Paul might be a bit of a shirker. Paul had no military experience, let alone any experience of intelligence work and yet they were going to send him back into one of the toughest espionage environments in the world. It would hardly be surprising that both Browning and Cumming were doubtful.

Two weeks later Paul was told that it was time for him to set out again. Nathan asked how he thought he would return to Russia and Paul decided that the best way was the way he had come – via the northern port of Archangel. On Sunday, 15 September 1918 he set off by train for the port of Newcastle from where he left for

Archangel on a troopship. His cover was as a diplomatic courier under the alias 'Captain McNeil'.

But everything had changed in the ten weeks since Paul had left the country. Archangel was now occupied by an Allied force consisting of British, French and American troops under the command of General Poole. They were there to prevent war matériel which had been provided to Russia from falling into German hands and also to provide a secure haven from which White Russian armies might overthrow Bolshevik rule.

There was no MI6 station in Archangel, so Paul's principal contact was to be Colonel C. J. M. Thornhill, the chief of military intelligence who was attached to General Poole's staff. Thornhill had been head of the MI6 station in Petrograd between May 1915 and May 1916 and had then transferred back to War Office service as Second Assistant Military Attaché gathering battlefield intelligence on the Eastern Front. Paul was told that he could also call on Commander Andrew Maclaren of the NID who had served on the naval staff of the embassy in Petrograd and much later was to be MI6 station chief in Warsaw.

Paul's plans changed immediately. With the arrival of troops in Archangel and the expulsion of the diplomatic missions there was no way that he would be able to move freely around the country. But his Russian was good enough for him to pose as a native so he would travel as a Bolshevik. The question remained of what his cover would be and by what route he would travel. It was 600 miles to Petrograd and 200 miles of that distance would have to be covered on foot before he could reach a railway line. But there seemed to be no alternative. Paul worked at his fitness in preparation for the trek and grew a beard in the hope of disguising himself from those who knew him in Petrograd. Thornhill was horrified at the prospect of Paul trying to make it to Petrograd by the northern route through enemy territory and on foot at the height of winter ('You're a ruddy idiot!' were his exact words). Now that the Allies were at Archangel this was exactly the direction the Bolsheviks would be watching for any suspicious activity.

Paul was stubborn, but the combination of Thornhill's entreaties and the early arrival of the Russian winter eventually convinced Paul that he would not make it. Thornhill advised him to head for the MI6 station at Stockholm and try the western route into Russia through Finland or Estonia. But Paul was reluctant to remove his carefully cultivated beard and straggly long hair which he might need in a few days, so he could hardly travel as a King's Messenger again. He and Thornhill agreed that he might as well start disguising his origins as soon as possible. Thornhill provided him with papers of a Norwegian commercial traveller and the newly hirsute Paul took the passenger ferry to Stockholm.

In 1918 the MI6 station in Stockholm consisted principally of two officers: Major John Scale and Clifford Sharp who, in England, was editor of the socialist magazine *New Statesman*. He was on special war-service leave and had been in Stockholm working for MI6 since 1917.

While Paul was in the city Scale permitted what could have been a major operational blunder: the novelist Arthur Ransome had arrived in Stockholm on 5 August with his twenty-four-year-old mistress Evgenia Petrovna Shelepina. She had been one of Trotsky's secretaries in Petrograd and was now personal assistant to V. V. Vorovsky, the Bolshevik ambassador to Sweden. Intelligence reports stated that Ransome was a Bolshevik agent and he was widely regarded as a traitor. (In January 1918, Colonel Knox, the military attaché in Petrograd, had made no bones about his feelings for Ransome: 'You ought to be shot!'). By October 1918, when Paul arrived in Stockholm, the Foreign Office was considering whether to prosecute Ransome under the terms of the Defence of the Realm Act, possibly even for high treason.

Arthur and Evgenia had set themselves up in a cabin at Igelboda on the sea approach to Stockholm where Arthur could write and indulge his passion for pike fishing. Arthur was shunned by most members of local English society who, living in a city crammed with terrified refugees fleeing from Bolshevik atrocities, felt that he was, at the very least, a good deal too sympathetic to the enemy's cause. Those who did visit him included members of the MI6 station in Stockholm who: '. . . turned out years afterwards to have been less friendly than they pretended.' Pointing out that Arthur was in danger of prosecution back in England and that he needed to prove his loyalty, MI6 persuaded him to write some papers on the situation in Russia using his unique perspective obtained through his friendship with leading Bolshevik figures.

Paul visited Ransome at the cabin and he clearly told his old friend everything as Ransome later noted:

'Paul planned to visit Russia in secret and I told him that it would be easy but unwise, as, travelling clandestinely and in disguise, he would get much the same sort of view of Russia as a hunted fox gets of a fox-hunt ... it was impossible to take Paul seriously enough to dislike him, and I liked him as a link with the old days in Petrograd.'

Paul's recollection matched that of Ransome:

'I did not hesitate to reveal to him my design. He roared with laughter when he saw the beard that decorated my face, and entering into the spirit of the thing offered me every assistance, knowing that I would never give a verdict at variance with weighed convictions.'

To allow Paul to visit a man who lived with the secretary to the Bolshevik ambassador and who was under such suspicion of working for the enemy that even on his return to England six months later he was arrested as a Bolshevik spy was an appalling lapse of operational security. It showed that either MI6 did not have Paul under proper control or they did not have a clue what they were doing. Fortunately, Ransome was merely a naive idealist rather than a Bolshevik agent – but what about Evgenia? She had clearly been trusted to work at the highest levels of the Bolshevik administration; she and Ransome had met following a 'chance' encounter in one of the offices of the Commissariat for Foreign Affairs; she had arrived in Stockholm, the heart of Allied espionage attempts against Russia and a key target for the Cheka's counter-espionage effort, having travelled with an official Bolshevik group via Berlin; in short, her relationship with Ransome had all the hallmarks of a classic 'honey trap'. Even if Ransome was not a traitor, Paul's entire mission could have been given away if Evgenia had wanted to ask the right questions. Yet to all of these warning signs Stockholm station remained blind.

Fortunately, neither Arthur nor Evgenia were Bolshevik agents, but it soon became clear that if Paul was to find a way into Petrograd he would have to move closer to the frontier and that meant travelling into Finland. So at the beginning of November Paul boarded a steamer for Helsinki. Finland was the place from where most of the smuggling operations across the border were controlled.

One way or the other Paul should find what he wanted there. In the meantime Scale had provided Paul with a new set of false papers. He was now Sergei Ilitch, a Serbian commercial traveller.

Upon his arrival, Paul quickly learned that there were dangers as well as advantages in being closer to Russia. Helsinki was packed with desperate émigrés – desperate for money and desperate for any way out of Scandinavia to Paris or Berlin or even to America. The city was also rife with Bolshevik spies and those working for them, watching for counter-revolutionaries who were seeking a way back into the country. As Paul later recalled: '[Helsinki] at that time was one of the unhealthiest spots in Europe. Whenever necessity brought me there I lay low, avoided society, and made it a rule to tell everybody the direct contrary of my real intentions even in trivial matters.'

After several weeks one of Paul's contacts in Helsinki came up with a name: Melnikov. He was a former Tsarist naval officer who was now living in Viborg, the largest Finnish town close to the border. How Paul came by Melnikov's name is unclear. One account is that the name was given to him by White Russians in Helsinki. Another is that he was introduced to an American secret service agent who had just escaped from Russia and who provided him with a letter of introduction to Melnikov. But Melnikov had been one of Cromie's agents and although either of the other two stories may be true, the most likely answer is that Paul was given a letter of introduction to Melnikov by the MI6 station which was based in the British Consulate at Helsinki.

In any case 'Sergei Ilitch' now boarded a train for Viborg, a town just thirty miles from the Russo-Finnish border. There he checked into a hotel which Melnikov used in between his trips into Russia. Melnikov was already there and Paul, using his letter of introduction, made contact. Paul and Melnikov warmed to each other immediately: '... I had the peculiar feeling that somewhere, long, long ago, we had met before, although I knew that this was not so.'

Like all good case officers, Paul first tried to find out Melnikov's reasons for working against the Bolsheviks and whether they were genuine. Melnikov's politics were deeply monarchist and he hoped to see the Romanovs returned to power by the Allies (something Paul did not agree with), but that was not why Melnikov was risking his life:

'The searchers came at night. I had some papers referring to the insurrection at Yaroslavl which my mother kept for me. They demanded access to my mother's room. My father barred the way, saying that she was dressing. A sailor tried to push past and my father angrily struck him aside. Suddenly a shot rang out and my father fell dead on the threshold of my mother's bedroom. I was in the kitchen when the Reds came and through the door I fired and killed two of them. A volley of shots was directed at me. I was wounded in the hand and only just escaped by the back stairway. Two weeks later my mother was executed on account of the discovery of my papers.'

Melnikov wanted at least one thing before he died: revenge.

But revenge lay in the future. For the moment, there was something else Melnikov wanted from Paul: whisky. Between the harsh rule of the Bolsheviks and Finnish prohibition, good-quality alcohol was better than hard cash and Paul had brought a considerable amount of it with him. As with so many agents, the strain of being a hunted man and the danger of his frequent border crossings had turned Melnikov into a chronic alcoholic. For three days they sat in the hotel in Viborg making plans while Melnikov worked his way through Paul's supplies of good Scotch whisky. Only when it was finished did Melnikov reluctantly announce that it was time to leave, not realising that Paul had managed to preserve one last store of the valuable liquid which he kept hidden in a medicine bottle.

It might have seemed poor tradecraft for Paul to place his life in the hands of this vengeful drunk, but Melnikov could offer three things. the first was a contact, a former member of Cromie's network whom Melinikov could only remember as 'John M'. Paul later refers to this person as John Marsh, but today we know that this was almost certainly an English businessman called John Merritt (sometimes spelled Merrett) who worked for BECOS Traders – the British Engineering Company of Siberia. He and his wife had lived in Petrograd for some years and he had most recently spent his time and energy helping members of the British community to escape to Finland. Since one of Paul's main tasks was to resurrect Cromie's organisation this contact could prove vital – if Melnikov could find him.

The second thing that Melnikov could offer was access to a number of safe houses in Petrograd. It would be vital to Paul's survival in the city to have somewhere to hide in between meetings with agents. Melnikov gave him the address of a hospital where he had formerly lived and also a café operating out of a private flat in the city. The intention was that Paul should be able to contact Melnikov at either of these places and Melnikov could take him to safety.

The final and most important thing which Melnikov could offer was contact with a group of Finnish border guards who would, for a price, supply Paul with false papers and a way across the border. This was what Paul had been seeking for the past three months. It was now November. He had already wasted too much time.

Finally, on the evening of Friday 22 November 1918, with the whisky exhausted, Melnikov announced that he would go ahead of Paul and clear the way with the border contacts:

> 'At six o'clock he went into his room, returning in a few minutes so transformed that I hardly recognised him. He wore a sort of seaman's cap that came right down over his eyes. He had dirtied his face, and this, added to the three-days-old stubble on his chin, gave him a truly demoniacal appearance. He wore a shabby coat and trousers of a dark colour, and a muffler was tied closely round his neck. He looked a perfect apache as he stowed away a big Colt revolver inside his trousers.
>
> "Good-bye," said Melnikov again. He turned, crossed himself, and passed out of the room. On the threshold he looked back. "Sunday evening," he added, "without fail." I had a curious feeling I ought to say something, I knew not what, but no words came. I followed him quickly down the stairs. He did not look round again. At the street door he glanced rapidly in every direction, pulled his cap still farther over his eyes, and passed away into the darkness – to an adventure that was to cost him his life.'

On Sunday, 24 November, Paul followed. An associate of Melnikov's arrived to take him to the station. This contact, a former Russian officer whom Paul only ever refers to as 'Ivan Sergeivitch', also gave Paul one other piece of information which, as is often the way with secret-service operations, turned out to be more valuable than almost anything else. He gave Paul the address of his former flat in Petrograd. Although Ivan himself could no longer live there it should still be occupied by his housekeeper and, if Paul identified himself as a friend who had recently seen Ivan, she should admit him.

That evening Paul proceeded on the train from Viborg to Raiaoki, the last stop before the frontier. From there he followed the railway line for half a mile to the bridge over the River Sestro which marked the border. It was almost nine p.m. and fully dark, but he was close enough to see the Bolshevik sentry pacing back and forth in the glare of the floodlights on the far side of the bridge. Nearby in the little border village was the hut that housed the Finnish border-guard detachment. Paul knocked at the door and handed over a piece of paper with the password which Melnikov had written for him.

He was expected. The guards confirmed that Melnikov had gone ahead two nights before, although they had no idea what had happened to him. Bolshevik border security was getting tighter all the time. With a cheerful grin one of the guards told him: 'A week ago one of our fellows was shot as we put him over the river. His body fell into the water and we have not yet fished it out.'

There were four guards based in the house and Paul was uneasy. Although these men could speak perfectly good Russian, they spoke Finnish among themselves, a language which Paul did not understand. He had no idea if he was being double-crossed. He wondered what sort of bounty these men would get if they simply arranged for him to be captured when he crossed the border? It must have been tempting for them. His unease increased when the senior officer regarded him curiously and Paul found that thanks to Melnikov his identity was already blown and that his Russian accent had not fooled them: 'Melnikov says that you are somebody important – but that's none of our business. But the Redskins don't like the English. If I were you I wouldn't go for anything.'

Still, Paul had no choice but to trust them. There was no other way across the border. Over glasses of boiling-hot tea the guards told him the latest news from Petrograd: the cost of bread, they said, had risen to a thousand times its former price. People were hacking dead horses to pieces for food in the streets. All the warm clothing had been taken and given to the Red Army. The Chekists were arresting and shooting without question or trial anyone whom they thought suspicious. The guards seemed to take pleasure in telling Paul how bad things were in the city and how likely it was that he would be stopped, questioned and caught. Paul said nothing.

With the tea finished, conversation turned to his cover story. Melnikov had said that the guards would supply Paul with false papers and to his astonishment they now typed up papers which identified him as Joseph Ilitch Afirenko, a member of the Cheka, the very organisation that would be hunting him in Petrograd. Not surprisingly Paul was a little worried by this, but the guards simply laughed and said they thought it was the best possible cover – after all, who would question it? The guards also thought the name 'Afirenko' sounded Ukrainian, which would help to explain his rather strange accent.

Paul relaxed slightly when the guards produced a collection of the authentic paper and inks to use for the forgeries. They even had the correct official stamps which they had either copied from other documents or obtained from the Bolshevik sentries on the other side of the bridge in exchange for bottles of good vodka. Bolshevik identity papers were changed all the time to prevent forgery, but the guards claimed to be aware of all the recent changes – Paul hoped they were telling the truth.

With his papers safe in a waterproof wrapping in his pocket, there remained the question of how to get Paul across the border. The usual method would be to send him in a small rowing boat which was attached to a rope. Paul would row himself across and then the guards would haul the boat back. It was too dangerous for any of them to go with him. The risk of being shot was too great. The guards explained that they would put him ashore at a large meadow. Previously they had used some woods further along the bank as this appeared to offer better cover, but the Bolshevik border guards had become wise to this and often hid there. Paul cannot have been very reassured as the Finnish guards told him that the meadow seemed such a stupid choice that it was unlikely to be watched. His unease probably increased when they warned him that there was also a cottage in which the Russian border guards slept that overlooked the meadow. But Paul was facing the classic dilemma of the undercover officer: he could either put his life in the hands of these suspicious characters or he could walk away. But if he walked away he would never get into Bolshevik Russia. He decided to press on.

The guards waited until three a.m. by which time they hoped the Bolsheviks would all be asleep rather than staking out the banks of the river in the freezing cold. Paul and three of the guards trudged through the snow to the area where the rowing boat was stashed and then they dragged it down the bank to the ice at the edge of the river. In the silence of the freezing night air it seemed to Paul that the sound of every scrape of the boat must carry for miles. He watched the opposite bank nervously. At the far end of the snow-covered meadow he could clearly see the cottage containing the Bolshevik guards. The windows were dark, but Paul found that all he could think was that there must be soldiers hiding there. He shook his head and forced himself to concentrate.

Paul did not have to go far. The river was only about fifteen metres wide. But there were no oars so he would have to push himself across by using a long pole which lay in the bottom of the boat. With a rope attached to the stern and while wearing a bulky overcoat which was packed with all his food, money and other equipment, this was not easy. As he struggled and sweated, fighting against the river current to keep the boat steered in the right direction, the Finnish guards laughed at Paul's clumsiness and hissed mocking encouragements. It was certainly not the most elegant secret crossing of a border ever attempted.

When Paul reached the far side there was no way of holding the boat still as he disembarked. There was nothing for it but to drop the pole in the bottom of the boat and then make a clumsy leap for the bank. Naturally, the boat slipped from under him and he fell forwards, crashing heavily through the ice. The sound shattered the stillness. As he struggled up the low bank on the far side he looked up at the cottage which was now only about two hundred metres away. To his horror a light was suddenly switched on.

'Run hard!' called the guards from the opposite bank, but in his cumbersome overcoat, now heavy with freezing water, this was no easy task. Cursing and scrambling, Paul staggered forwards across the meadow, running as fast as he could. He had lost all sense of direction, forgotten all the instructions which the Finnish guards had given him and, looking up at the distant trees, he could see that he would never make it. He threw himself full length in the snow and waited for the tramp of Russian boots and the final shot. It never came.

Glancing back over his shoulder, Paul could see lanterns moving down by the water's edge and a few moments later shooting broke out. It seemed to Paul that the Bolsheviks were shooting across the river. But there was no return fire. The Finns must have left. After several volleys, the shooting stopped. Paul felt certain that the Bolsheviks would now follow his very obvious tracks through the snow from where the ice was broken, right to where he was hiding. He looked up and tried to gauge the distance to the trees. He was about halfway across the meadow. Could he make it?

But the Bolsheviks did not follow the tracks. Paul watched as the lanterns moved along the bank and then returned slowly to the cottage. After a few minutes the light in the cottage went out. Paul was alone in the darkness once more.

He was freezing, but he waited until he was absolutely certain that the Russian guards were asleep again before crawling forwards through the snow, stopping whenever he heard a suspicious noise. He found that in his panic he had run the wrong way across the meadow and that he now had to cross another small stream which the Finnish guards had warned him about. But since his coat and trousers were already wet, there was nothing to be lost by wading carefully across it. His boots were now thoroughly soaked and he wondered how well the secret writing material that he had hidden between the layers of his leather soles had fared. Well, there was no point in worrying about it now. Soon he was in the comparative safety of the woods.

Eventually Paul found a half-built house and he sheltered there until dawn, shivering and pulling on the medicine bottle of whisky in order to keep warm. After an hour it began to snow and he knew that he was in danger of hypothermia if he stayed huddled where he was. He had to keep moving. He moved cautiously along the side of the road that he knew must lead to the nearby railway station. However, it was not long before he came to a crossroads where he could see soldiers gathered around a bivouac fire. It was too dangerous to keep moving about. He retreated back to the half-built house and waited for dawn. Then, still shivering, he mingled with early-morning foragers shuffling in the direction of the station. No one gave him a second glance. At the gate he could see a soldier checking identity papers. The Cheka identity card prepared by the

Finns had survived his dunking, protected in its waterproof wrapping. Paul handed it over nervously, keeping his head down and his cap brim lowered. To his relief the soldier waved it away, having barely looked at it. Paul moved onwards with the crowd towards the station platform. Now all he had to do was wait for the train to Petrograd to arrive and endure the two-hour journey into the city.

As Paul stood on the crowded platform a feeling of elation swept over him. After four months of struggle he had finally made it. He was now the only British spy in Soviet Russia.

With a start, Paul awoke to find himself still lying amongst the clump of reeds. It took him a moment to realise where he was. He rolled over onto his hands and knees and looked around carefully, trying to suppress the hacking cough that had started up once again. He was frozen to the bone from sleeping on the damp ground and every joint ached as he tentatively stretched himself out and flexed his stiff fingers.

It had all seemed so difficult, getting into the country. But now, seven months later, he knew that it was nothing compared with trying to get out again. Everything now depended on Major Scale and his 'very special measures'. Where the hell were they? And who the hell was Scale sending? Paul could not imagine how anyone could get him out.

As he staggered to his feet and tried to stamp some life back into his limbs, Paul rubbed at the mosquito bites which covered his face and knew that one thing was certain: if he spent another night out in the open in these marshes he was going to die. He did not know if rescue really was coming, but he had to believe that it was. He had to find some way to survive for just a few more days.

Although he was starving and seriously ill, Paul still had the instincts of a spy. The first rule: maintain your cover. He stumbled around, gathering whatever pieces of dry kindling he could find. He would have to return to the city and there was a good chance that he would be intercepted by a patrol on the way. They would want to know what he had been doing out here in the early morning. The answer: gathering firewood. Petrograd was so short of every necessity that even a small bundle of firewood was worth selling. The patrol might fall for that.

Racked with coughing, clutching his meagre bundle of twigs

wrapped in a scrap of rag, Paul staggered through the reeds until he reached the deeply rutted cart track that he knew would lead him back towards Petrograd – and back towards the waiting patrols of the Cheka.

5

Peter Sokolov

The rescue team was making its way towards Russia, but progress was painfully slow. By five a.m. on Sunday, 25 May 1919, the *Fennia* was still just dropping her pilot near the mouth of the Tyne and preparing for her crossing of the North Sea. The weather was atrocious, the winds were against her and the old Swedish cargo ship pitched and rolled like a fairground ride. Gus had secured his precious afternoon tea from the Swedish captain (in return for a few of Cumming's one thousand guineas), but that home comfort hardly mattered to some of the crew. The captain and chief engineer of the *Fennia* had been paid to give up their cabin to their suspicious new 'deckhands' but, as that was the only available cabin on the ship Beeley, the only NCO, and Marshall, the junior 'snottie', were forced to sleep on benches in the ship's saloon where they were thrown about with every drunken lurch of the old tub. Beeley was battered and dreadfully seasick and with every retch must have wished that he was back in the warmth of the sheds at Osea among his beloved engines. Separated from the boats there was nothing for him to do and as the only NCO billeted with three senior officers there was no one for him to talk to, either. To make matters worse, halfway through that first day untethered mines were spotted floating in the water and the *Fennia*'s captain reduced their speed still further. Gus could barely contain his frustration and that night wrote irritably in his diary about how the captain had '... got the wind up'.

The weather on Monday was just as bad and the four Englishmen stayed in the saloon, trying to keep their playing cards on the table for games of piquet, interrupted only by Beeley's occasional dashes outside to throw up over the handrail. But at six p.m. a cry from the watch announced the coast of Sweden in sight through the murk and by the end of the evening the captain was able to inform them that the barometer was rising and there would be better sailing ahead.

He was right. The following morning the sea was calm and the sun broke through the clouds. Beeley turned a paler shade of green and the *Fennia* began her steady passage through the spectacular mountains and forests of the Scandinavian islands. For the next four days the journey felt more like a pleasure cruise than a desperate rescue mission, but even though the crews knew that time was ticking away for ST-25 there was nothing they could do to make the ship go any faster (although Beeley did spend a lot of time investigating the engine room) and the weather was so glorious that there was nothing to do but make the best of it. The crew played deck quoits (Gus and Beeley thrashing the snotties Hampsheir and Marshall) and more games of piquet. They read books. They snoozed in the sunshine. Gus spent a lot of time in the chart room on the bridge with the captain, learning as much as he could about sailing conditions in the Gulf – although the captain mainly wanted to tell him about his female conquests in Hull. Gus noted in his diary that the captain was: '. . . a bit of a gay dog when away from home'. Gus gave up the precious bunk in the cabin to Beeley on the slightly less than noble grounds that he was too tall to sleep comfortably on it anyway. For the first time on the trip the team's chief motor mechanic actually got some rest.

The *Fennia* plodded slowly on. Finally, at two a.m., on Friday, 30 May, the lights of the Finnish port of Abo appeared on the horizon. As experienced seamen Gus and his crew simply went back to sleep – they suspected that it would take quite a while for this civilian ship to negotiate its way slowly through the shoals and into the safety of the harbour. They were right. The *Fennia* crept forwards, had a long wait for a pilot to become available and were then held in a long queue of other vessels seeking docking permission. Despite Gus's polite suggestions that they should get a move on the captain seemed unruffled, more interested in sharing a carefully hoarded bottle of Scotch whisky with his highly profitable new deckhands than hurrying his own crew.

It was 7.30 p.m. before the *Fennia* finally docked. It had taken them seventeen agonisingly long hours to cover the last mile of the voyage. As soon as the gangplank was lowered the team grabbed their bags and, pausing only to show their Finnish visas at the

Immigration Office, they dashed for the railway station. They had to reach Helsinki as quickly as possible to make contact with the MI6 station there. But more bad news awaited them: they had missed the last train of the day by just a few minutes. The old stationmaster took some small pleasure in informing them that there would not be another train until 7.10 the following morning.

There was nothing for it but to head for the misleadingly named Hotel Grand and book rooms for the night. Gus arranged at the desk for an early wake-up call and they headed for dinner. This was Gus's first introduction to the economic realities of newly independent Finland where all commodities were in short supply. Having just emerged from a civil war in which the Bolshevik sympathisers had only been narrowly defeated much of the country was still in chaos and prices were astronomic. One thousand guineas had seemed like a lot of money when they left England, but having already spent over a hundred pounds on the journey Gus began to worry about how long the money would last. 'Everything ruinously expensive,' he noted gloomily in his diary that night.

Experienced officers know that on an espionage mission anything that *can* go wrong *will* go wrong. It was a lesson Gus began to learn the next morning. The hotel desk had forgotten the alarm call and the crew had to frantically grab their belongings and race on foot across town to the station. Unwashed, dishevelled and with their new suits stained with sweat, Gus and his crew arrived just in time to catch the 7.10 to Helsinki. Except that there wasn't a 7.10 to Helsinki. There *was* a 6.45 to Helsinki, but it had already gone. The stationmaster who had given them the wrong information yesterday was nowhere to be seen and Gus angrily demanded to know when the next train was: not until 4.30 p.m. and it wouldn't reach Helsinki until at least midnight. Dispirited, Gus sent the crew to the hotel while he took a cab to the harbour master's office to get news of the *Pallux* which was due to arrive with the CMBs the following morning. There he discovered that bad weather in the North Sea had delayed the ship's already slow crossing and the *Pallux* was not expected now until Wednesday.

Gus stepped outside the office feeling about as low as it was possible to feel. To make his day complete, it began to rain.

He hailed a cab back to the hotel, but even then his troubles were not over. On arrival at the hotel the cabbie demanded an outrageous price for the trip. After the numerous disappointments of the morning Gus was in no mood to be taken for just another gullible foreigner and he stood his ground. As the argument with the cabbie developed into a full-blown row, first the other cab drivers joined in and then a local police officer arrived. To Gus's astonishment he backed the Finnish cab driver against the foreigner and demanded that Gus pay up or be placed under arrest. Gus refused to back down and demanded that the British Consul be sent for. There was a long delay while telephone calls were made. Eventually the news arrived that the consul was out of town and couldn't be contacted. Gus had no choice but to pay up.

He trudged into the Hotel Grand where he and the crew spent the rest of the day having breakfast and lunch ('at ruinous prices') and playing cards. Tomorrow would be 1 June – just two weeks until the 'White Nights'. Then there would be no proper night-time, just a sort of hazy twilight, and it would be impossible to penetrate the line of Russian forts without being seen and shot at. Even if they made contact with ST-25 before that date, every day wasted meant fewer minutes of darkness each night and their chances of survival would be a little less.

However, the next day things did improve. The team had caught their train from Abo in the evening and arrived in Helsinki in the early hours of Sunday morning. They checked into the Grand Hotel Fennia in the city centre which had been booked for them by the local MI6 station They had several rooms together with a private sitting room, although Gus noted that all meals were served '. . . in the café downstairs at ruinous prices'. The next day Gus left his men to go for a walk around the city whilst he went to the British Consulate. There he met the British Consul Henry Bell and the Vice-Consul Raleigh Le May who was also, apparently, head of the MI6 station. Major John Scale, the head of the MI6 station at Stockholm and also in overall charge of all MI6 operations in northern Russia, had also travelled to Helsinki for the meeting. The poor weather in the North Sea had meant that the *Fennia* had cancelled her call at Stockholm during the trip over and Scale wanted to see what sort of man London had sent him.

This first meeting was essentially a briefing on the political situation in the area and Gus immediately learned that Cumming's idea of this being a top-secret mission had gone out of the window. The hotel had been insistently asking for their British passports, but Gus had been holding out because he had been told in London that they would be issued with passports in false names. Gus found that this plan had been dropped. The Foreign Office was insistent that the Finnish authorities must be apprised of the fact that the CMBs were operating in the area even if they were not told the exact details of the mission. The situation in Finland was extremely delicate. Officially Finland was neither pro-British nor pro-Bolshevik, and during the war had even been pro-German at one point. The British Consul, Henry Bell, was working hard to cultivate good relations with the new Finnish administration, but Finland could not afford any action which might antagonise her powerful neighbour and jeopardise their hard-won independence, least of all British sailors dashing around on secret missions sinking Russian ships. Democratic elections were due in a few weeks' time.

Le May was equally adamant that there was no way he could get the necessary stores of petrol and oil without official Finnish assistance. It was essential that Admiral Walter Cowan, commanding British naval forces in the Baltic, should be briefed on the mission. The Admiral was currently in Reval, the capital of Estonia, but he was sending a destroyer and Gus would be taken to meet him on the following day. Two Finnish ministers would also be travelling on the destroyer, heading for talks in Estonia. Gus's presence would be explained by saying that he was a diplomatic courier working for the Foreign Office.

Also at the meeting was an enormous Russian who was introduced to Gus as Pyotr Sokolov, although he very quickly became known to everyone simply as Peter. Gus was told that Peter was ST-25's chief courier, but that he was currently being held back in Helsinki by MI6 because the border crossing had become too dangerous. Gus formed the distinct impression that this was MI6's view, not Peter's.

Peter was twenty-eight years old. He had been a law student in St Petersburg when war had broken out in 1914 and had then served as an NCO in the Russian army. Like Melnikov, he was working against the Bolsheviks because of the way his family had suffered at their hands. He was blond, tall, powerfully built and Gus later learned that he was something of an athlete: both a boxer and footballer. Football in Russia was a fairly new sport, introduced by the English community, but it had caught on tremendously just before the war. Peter had played for St Petersburg Unitas, the national champions, and he had won four caps playing for Russia at the 1912 Olympics. Gus was not surprised that this huge Russian, who was about six foot four inches tall, played as a central defender. Le May told Gus that his first task would be to get Peter into Petrograd.

Although Peter spoke very little English, Gus could speak some Russian and soon warmed to him. Unlike Scale and Le May who seemed more worried about political complications, Peter was desperate to get back to ST-25. Gus told the others that he had to have a base nearer to Petrograd. Peter suggested the tiny harbour of Terrioki. It had previously been the home of the St Petersburg Yacht Club, but was now deserted except for a Finnish border garrison in a fort about a mile away. Terrioki was 30 miles from the British fleet's forward base at Biorko and just 25 miles from Petrograd, well within the CMBs' range of operations. It sounded ideal.

Peter had more good news when Gus asked him about the breakwater. Like Melnikov, Peter worked as a smuggler to raise money for his anti-Bolshevik activities and he knew from local sailors that there were several passages through the breakwater. This was fantastic news. It meant that the seemingly impregnable defences could be breached. It would still mean running in under the Russian guns, but with the combination of surprise and the speed of the CMBs, it just might work. Gus asked Peter if he could find a smuggler who would act as pilot for the team. Peter agreed to travel to Terrioki and hire one while Gus and the others had their meeting with Admiral Cowan.

Although it might have been politically necessary, it was a foolish move to take a long-serving naval officer such as Gus aboard a Royal Navy vessel and the next day his cover was completely blown. The destroyer HMS *Vanessa* docked in Reval at 11.30 a.m. and the party crossed to Cowan's flagship, the cruiser HMS *Cleopatra*, only to find that the Admiral had left for an official lunch. Diplomacy with the newly independent states was as important as military matters in this command. But as Gus was going aboard the *Cleopatra* he was recognised by a junior officer, Lieutenant James Rivett-Carnac:

'But surely you are Agar, are you not?' he challenged.

Gus knew James Rivett-Carnac so well that for a moment he was lost for an answer. Then he proved once and for all that he was not a natural spy by eventually blustering that he was actually a cousin of Lieutenant Agar, working for the Foreign Office, and that the two of them were often mistaken for one another. Rivett-Carnac didn't fall for this story for a second and continued to watch Gus curiously as he hung around the ship waiting for the return of the Admiral.

It was 7.30 p.m. before the Admiral finally returned. Admiral Cowan saw Gus and his colleagues in private with only his Flag Captain, Charles Little, present. Cowan was one of the most decorated sailors in the British Navy and Gus described his jacket as '. . . a blaze of colour from the many decorations he had received for war services . . .' (Indeed, Cowan was known to arrange his numerous campaign medals in an order which showed off their colours most pleasingly rather than in the official order.) Standing only five foot six inches tall, he was known throughout the Royal Navy as 'The Little Man' or simply 'Titch'. At 48 years of age, he had a record as a brilliant seaman, but also a reputation as a martinet, a trait which would eventually cost him promotion to the very highest offices within the Admiralty. By 1919 he had already suffered one mutiny under his command and was soon to suffer another in the Baltic. He was known both for his demand for the very highest levels of performance and for a tendency to inflict severe punishments for the slightest of offences. It was a tendency he was aware of himself and when he was in his seventies he wrote: 'When I commanded a squadron [*i.e. in the Baltic*] I made the mistake of expecting too high a standard of discipline.'

And yet this little man with the violent temper inspired tremendous loyalty and admiration amongst those officers who knew him well. Admiral Keyes described him as 'The gallantest little sportsman I ever met.' Charles Little was in many ways the perfect flag captain for him. When Cowan lost his temper over a misdemeanour and demanded a draconian punishment for the sailor responsible, Little would simply say, 'Aye, sir' and then do nothing, knowing that by the following day Cowan would have forgotten or thought better of it.

Cowan opened the meeting by explaining the difficulty of his position. Officially Britain and the new Soviet government were not at war. When challenged about what the Royal Navy were doing there, the British government had simply said that British forces were on 'a summer cruise'. And yet Cowan's light-cruiser squadron had been sent to the area to safeguard the independence of the Baltic States and Finland. His only guidance from the British government was to treat any Bolshevik warship found outside Russian territorial waters as hostile. The problem with this was that he did not have sufficient naval power to protect the Baltic States. It was all a gigantic bluff! Cowan explained that the Bolshevik Baltic fleet included three great warships: the battle cruisers *Petropavlovsk* and *Andrei Pevozvanni* and the armoured cruiser *Oleg*. At present they were lurking in their well-defended harbour at Kronstadt, but if they ever ventured forth and were well handled they could blow his force out of the water.

Knowing of Cowan's reputation, Gus, still dressed in his ill-fitting brown Moss Bros suit, had approached the meeting with some nervousness. But he also knew that he would need Cowan's help and wanted to prove to the Admiral that he could be an asset to the British naval force. He explained his purpose for being in the area and how he planned to penetrate the line of forts from a base at Terrioki. He joked that once his secret duties were complete it might be possible to reconnoitre and possibly raid Kronstadt harbour. Cowan laughed and said that if Gus managed to attack Kronstadt then he would recommend him for the Victoria Cross – a remark which turned out to be prophetic.

Captain Little was against the whole enterprise, feeling that if this sort of work needed to be done then it should be done by naval personnel in uniform, not by young officers masquerading as civilians. Together the naval officers studied confidential Admiralty charts which showed the disposition of the Russian defences and the lines of the breakwaters. Little listed all the hazards which Gus faced and then said that in his opinion the plan was outlandish if not impossible. But Cowan was of a different mind. He admired daring above all other qualities in a junior officer. He listened to Gus's account of how Sokolov had told him about the gaps in the breakwaters and the idea of using smugglers to find them. He was particularly interested to hear how CMBs could skim over the broad Russian minefields. Mines represented the greatest daily threat to Cowan's squadron throughout the mission and were to account for the loss of several British ships. It does not appear to have occurred to him before this meeting to use CMBs to counter that threat.

Cowan had a liking for unusual ideas (he had once captured an enemy submarine during a naval exercise by having his men lasso its periscope from the deck of his destroyer – and was reprimanded for the damage he caused!) and by the end of the meeting he had decided to overrule Little's concerns. To the end of his life Gus remained grateful to Admiral Cowan for his backing at this vital moment and he always remembered Cowan's words of support: 'Nothing is worthwhile doing unless there's a risk in it. Always choose the boldest course if you have any choice at all; it is always the boldest course that stands the best chance of success.'

Gus boldly asked for a destroyer to tow the CMBs as near to Terrioki as possible. Cowan agreed, announcing that only the day before the Finnish government had agreed that Cowan should be allowed to base his cruiser force at an advanced base at Biorko Sound. Gus also asked for a couple of ratings to be attached to his command to deal with routine matters such as cooking and guard duty. He would need his crews to be as fresh as possible for their courier work. Cowan agreed readily.

Then, as the meeting was breaking up, Gus raised a rather more tricky subject. Because the CMBs were being transported to Finland on a civilian freighter they had been unable to bring with them anything more powerful than small arms. They might be able to put up a fight against Russian patrol boats, but against larger craft they would be effectively defenceless. Gus wondered if Cowan would issue them with torpedoes?

Admiral Cowan was highly doubtful. This was a secret-service mission and he did not like the idea of people dressed as civilians racing around firing Royal Navy torpedoes: '. . . that would never do.' But then Gus told him how Cumming had given the team permission to keep uniforms and a small white ensign hidden aboard each of the boats. If Cowan issued the torpedoes, Gus promised that they would only attack the Russians under a British flag and wearing British uniforms. Cowan pondered this and then asked who would be responsible for the maintenance and priming of the torpedoes? Even in 1919 torpedo design was still at an early stage and they could be unstable and dangerous. Gus explained that he was a fully trained mines and torpedoes officer. Still not entirely convinced, Cowan said that he would give the matter further thought.

After three hours the meeting broke up at 11 p.m. HMS *Vanessa* took Gus and Scale back to Helsinki. It was three o'clock on Tuesday morning before Gus fell into his bed back at the Hotel Fennia, but he was up early the next morning to take the train to

Abo and make preparations for the arrival of the CMBs on Thursday. Gus was determined to move things along as quickly as possible. First he saw the harbour master and arranged that the *Pallux* should be able to dock right under the big crane that served the harbour. The CMBs might have been the last thing onto the *Pallux*, but they were damn well going to be the first thing off. Next he visited the Customs office. He had asked Le May to get hold of a letter from the Finnish Ministry of the Interior exempting the boats from Customs searches – since the mission was no longer secret from the Finns he might as well make use of any official help he could get. He had also hired a tug and a barge to transport the 2,000 gallons of high-octane petrol and other equipment off the *Pallux* and then take it to sheds where it could be stored before being sent on to Terrioki. Meanwhile Consul Bell and Vice-Consul Le May were negotiating with the Finns for permission to use the boats in Finnish waters.

The SS *Pallux* duly arrived shortly after midnight early on the morning of Thursday, 5 June, bearing CMBs 4 and 7 together with Sindall and the two mechanics, Piper and Pegler. True to Cowan's word, HMS *Voyager* had arrived promptly at 9 a.m. ready to tow them on the next stage of their journey. By 10.30 a.m. the two 40-foot CMBs, still in their fresh coats of gleaming white paint, were winched off the deck and lowered gently into the water. They were easily the most striking objects in the busy commercial harbour, their sleek lines attracting many admiring glances – and some suspicious ones: MI6 was not the only intelligence service operating in the country. Clearly Cumming's plan to pretend that these vessels were for commercial sale in a country as poor as Finland was never going to wash – there was already gossip all over the port. Gus ordered the mechanics to repaint the boats in their light grey camouflage colour immediately. Meanwhile he was forced to continue the round of unofficial diplomacy, this time leaving for a meeting with General Hubert Gough, head of the British Military Mission to Finland (as distinct from Cowan's naval mission), who was naturally curious to find that there was going to be a secret-service team operating in his area. The secret mission was definitely a secret no longer.

Their planned departure after dark that evening was delayed. Peter Sokolov had missed his train on the way back from Terrioki. There was no way the team could go without him. And then matters became worse. The Chief of the Finnish Naval Staff, whose name was Schultz, asked to be transported on the *Voyager* as he was travelling down the coast. Gus and the captain of the *Voyager* spent an agonising few hours working out where they would stash Peter so that he and Schultz did not meet. But eventually Schultz decided he would rather go by train so the problem was solved by the time Sokolov finally rolled up, profusely apologetic, late on Friday afternoon.

At 10 p.m., when it was finally dark enough, HMS *Voyager* set off with the two CMBs in tow. Hugh Beeley paced the aft rail ceaselessly during the night, nervously watching his beloved boats. Exposure to sea water was the greatest problem with running the CMBs' high-performance engines and he did not like the way the tow had been set up. He understood the fragile nature of the CMBs' hulls. They were loaded with stores and could easily split a seam under the pressure of a fast tow. Commander C. G. Stuart, captain of the *Voyager,* was doing his best, but the problem was that the streamlining of the CMBs had been designed for when they were driven by their powerful engines from the rear. Towed from the front, the balance was all wrong and as the speed rose above twenty knots they kept bucking and dipping their prows like nervous horses lowering their heads as they were dragged forward. Several times the tarpaulin covers that Beeley and his team had hastily made up at Osea were completely awash. He was convinced that the engine compartments must be getting drenched. The problem was that the *Voyager* had to travel quickly if she was to reach Biorko before dawn so Captain Stuart kept straining for more speed. Two hours or so into the journey Beeley thought that the CMBs looked heavier in the water, a sure sign that either a seam or the canvas cover was leaking. Gus agreed and just at that moment the hawser towing CMB7 snapped under the strain.

There was no time to check the seals on the tarpaulin or the engines. The destroyer halted briefly and a boat was sent out with a new line. For the rest of the journey, HMS *Voyager* reduced speed to try and protect the little boats, but nothing seemed to make any difference and at 5 a.m., with the race to beat the dawn already lost, CMB4 sank lower and lower in the water and finally her hawser parted as well. Beeley went out with the *Voyager*'s boats to attach a new line and announced through a loud hailer that she would have to be pumped out before she could be towed any further. He dreaded to think about the damage that must have been done to the delicate engines. More time was lost as they had to use the hand-operated pumps and it was noon on Saturday, 7 June, before *Voyager* crawled into Biorko Sound where Cowan and the rest of the light-cruiser squadron was already waiting.

For the next 24 hours Beeley and Piper worked hard. (As planned, Pegler had remained in Helsinki with the reserve stores.) They stripped the engines as far as possible and tried to repair the damage that the sea water had caused. On Sunday afternoon Gus ran the first trials of the boats across Biorko Sound. Sailors of the squadron with nothing better to do lined up on the decks to cheer on the little boats as the roar of their powerful engines resounded across the bay. CMB7, the 'lucky boat', had been lucky again and passed her test with flying colours. But, just as Beeley had feared, for CMB4 it was a different story. On her first run across the bay the engine would not make more than about 20 knots. She simply bounced across the choppy water like a car with a faulty clutch, never quite making the speed necessary for her aerodynamics to lift her out of the water. Beeley disappeared below to make some adjustments and then Gus took CMB4 on a second run. As she sped across the bay, the engine roared and speed increased until she was racing flat out. She rose out of the water and two great wings of spray, the trade mark of a fast-moving CMB at full power, flew high to either side in her wake. A great cheer rose up from the watching sailors. Drenched in the spray, Hampsheir, Beeley and Gus looked at each other across the cramped open cabin. The roar of the engines made speech impossible, but the grins and raised thumbs made their exhilaration clear as CMB4 pulled away from CMB7.

Then, just as they came to the end of their run and were about to throttle down, there was an explosion from the front of the boat and the scream of grinding metal. Beeley frantically made the sign to cut power as smoke began to billow around them. Gus slammed the throttle shut and CMB4 dropped back into the water, quickly gliding to a dead stop. Beeley disappeared into the engine compartment, holding an oily rag over his face against the fumes. He was gone for some time. Sindall and Marshall in CMB7 pulled alongside, looking concerned. Gus and John Hampsheir spent the time while Beeley made his checks finding a rope and organising a tow from CMB7, but they knew they were in trouble.

When Beeley clambered back into the cabin, his face and overalls were coated with oil and with smoke residue and he looked despondent. It was all bad news. CMB4 had run the big ends clean off two connecting rods and completely seized her engine. It was about as bad an accident as could have happened and with the tools that Beeley had available there was nothing he could do. The engine was a complete write-off.

As the two boats limped back towards HMS *Voyager* Gus was at his lowest point yet. With less than ten days to go before the onset of the White Nights one of his boats was already out of action. There was a spare engine with the stores at Helsinki, but he knew from experience that to install a complete new engine would usually take a team of mechanics several days even with the first-class workshop facilities at Osea Island. Out here, miles from anywhere and with only limited equipment, it would be impossible to get CMB4 ready in time. Gus looked towards the distant Russian coast. Either he would have to risk a run through the forts with just one boat or Beeley was going to have to produce a minor miracle.

6

The Zorinsky Enigma

Back in Petrograd, Paul Dukes knew nothing about the problems his rescuers were facing. In fact, he thought that his luck might actually be changing for the better.

That morning as he shuffled down the road towards Petrograd he had seen a broken-down fence surrounding what appeared to be a copse of stunted trees. Paul had never paid attention to this area before but now, with the instincts of a true scrounger, he forced his way between the broken palings in the hope of finding more firewood or perhaps something more valuable. To his surprise he found that he was on the edge of the enormous Volkovo Cemetery. He had not realised that it extended this far. He looked around and saw that he was in an enclosed area set aside for an obscure religious sect known in Russia as 'the Old Believers'. Judging by the overgrown and dilapidated state of the graves, no one came here very often.

Paul forced his way through the bushes and long grass, looking for anything that might be useful among the array of wooden crosses many of which were leaning at irregular angles, the names long ago weather-worn and rendered indecipherable. Here and there were one or two stone tombs, mostly collapsed, but at length he came to one which was in a slightly better condition. One corner of the tomb had fallen away and it was possible, with a bit of a squeeze, to climb inside it.

The air was foul, but the earth was dry and the stone walls provided shelter from the elements. Paul decided to rest there for a while before heading into the city. It would be good to stay somewhere fairly warm and safe for a few hours. As he lay there he reflected that he had been hunted by one means or another since the day he had arrived in the city . . .

*

When Paul had arrived in Petrograd on that first Monday, 25 November 1918, his first thought had been to find the apartment belonging to John Merritt. As a former member of Cromie's intelligence network he should have quickly been able to lead Paul to other former agents who had survived the Red Terror.

Paul left the Finland Station, took a few moments to orientate himself and then set off in the direction of the address that Melnikov had given him. He had not travelled very far when he came across an old man who was standing against a wall, sobbing. Forgetting where he was for a moment Paul stopped and asked the old man what was wrong:

'I'm cold and hungry,' whimpered the old man. 'For three days I have eaten nothing.'

Glancing around in case anyone was watching him, Paul reached into his pocket and quickly pushed a twenty-rouble note into the old man's hand, but the old man simply looked confused:

'Thank you,' he mumbled. 'But what is the good of money? Where shall I get bread?'

The full tragedy of life in the city came home to Paul at that moment. He pulled from his coat a small loaf of black bread which he had been saving for an emergency. At first he tore the loaf in half and offered a portion to the old man but, seeing his emaciated state, Paul then shoved all the bread into the man's outstretched hands. That was the last of Paul's food. Although he still had plenty of money, he had no idea where he could purchase more provisions. After a long cold night in the open he was already very hungry, but he had a suspicion that things would get a lot worse.

Less than an hour later Paul arrived at the address that Melnikov had given him. It was Paul's first test as an undercover agent and he immediately made his first mistake. He tried to slip into the apartment building unnoticed and was challenged by the caretaker who closed the door firmly behind him and then barred the way. When Paul asked for Merritt, the caretaker said that he had been arrested by the Cheka and, clearly suspicious, he asked what Paul's business with Merritt was. Building caretakers had become the stool-pigeons of the Cheka. They were mostly poor and uneducated, but many had been placed in charge of new house-committees, free to search flats and denounce residents at their will. Many were revelling in their new power. One word from them to the authorities and an occupant would be snatched away by a Cheka squad before they could even protest – leaving the caretaker and his cronies free to pillage the flat of the 'traitor'.

Paul knew all this from his time in Russia six months earlier and he knew that unless he could talk fast he was in trouble. His first instinct was to wave his Cheka identity card and try to cow the man into letting him out. But this man did not look as if he would be easily fooled and Paul was sharp enough to know that if he pretended to be Cheka the man would wonder why he had not known about Merritt's arrest. The caretaker was still watching him suspiciously and in desperation Paul said the first thing which came into his mind. He offered up the small parcel he was carrying which actually contained his spare clothing and some money. He said that he had no idea who Merritt was, but that he had been asked to deliver the package to him.

The caretaker looked far from convinced, but there was little he could do to challenge the story. However, when Paul said that he would take the parcel back to the person who had asked him to deliver it, the suspicious caretaker insisted that he leave it behind. Paul did so and hurried gratefully from the building.

This was a terrible blow so early in his mission. The one man he had hoped would be his chief contact was already in the hands of the Cheka. Worse, because of his poor tradecraft Paul had lost most of his belongings in a city which was desperately short of everything – especially food.

Paul did not know it but Merritt had been targeted by the Cheka because of a lead from an informant. In August 1918 they had arrested a black marketeer named Boris Borisovich Gol'dinger. Gol'dinger had done a lot of business with the British community in Petrograd who were desperate to get their hands on supplies and who, unlike most of the area's citizens, had the funds to pay black-market prices. Under interrogation by the Cheka, Gol'dinger quickly decided that his only hope was to turn informant and among the morsels he offered up was the name of John Merritt. Whether this was a lucky guess or whether Gol'dinger had been approached by Cromie or Merritt at some stage to work for their network is not known, but in any case the Cheka added Merritt to their list. In the wake of the Cromie murder they had to be careful before arresting such a prominent British citizen, but they soon discovered that Merritt was helping people escape across the border. They decided to bring him in, hoping that he would betray the rest of his network.

Meanwhile Paul had to move to his back-up plan – find Melnikov. Not feeling confident enough to fight his way onto one of the overcrowded city trams, he walked four miles across the city to the hospital in a street called Kamenostrovsky Prospekt where Melnikov had said he sometimes stayed with one of the doctors who was a relation of his. When Paul asked for Melnikov at the porter's lodge, he was told that he had not been seen for some time. Another dead end. That only left the café which was on the other side of the city from the hospital. Paul thought of the long weary trudge back across Petrograd. The adrenalin surge of sneaking across the border and arriving in the city had worn off by now and he felt hungry and weary. But then he had an idea: Melnikov had said that the café did not open until late in the afternoon so he had plenty of time. Paul decided to spend a little of his money. He bought some newspapers, some rather ropy-looking apples and some very stale biscuits. Then he hired one of the few remaining horse-drawn cabs and headed back to the Finland station where he had arrived that morning. He knew there was a waiting room there where he could sit in the warm and read until the café opened. He was also less likely to be stopped and questioned by a patrol there.

The journey in the cab depressed Paul utterly. Although he had only been away for six months the rapid decay of the city was frightening. The streets were strewn with rubbish and the faded red bunting which still hung across the streets from the celebration of the anniversary of the Revolution a few weeks earlier only emphasised the desolation. The Finnish guards who had told him about starving Petrograd citizens carving the flesh from the corpses of dead horses abandoned in the street had not exaggerated the situation. Everywhere Paul looked there was hunger, desperation and decay.

Late in the afternoon of that first day he finally made his way to the café. It was run by a mother and daughter in a top-floor apartment situated in a fashionable part of the city not far from the Nevsky Prospekt, the main street running through Petrograd, comparable with the Champs Elysées in Paris. Melnikov's name was enough to gain Paul admittance to the flat and he was relieved to hear that Melnikov had been there on Saturday, the day after he had set off from Viborg. At least Melnikov had made it this far. Paul decided to wait at the flat to see if Melnikov returned. He was about to make his second big mistake of the day and although it would take several weeks for the threat to materialise it was an error which was to almost cost him his life.

The café was empty when Paul arrived but soon about a dozen people came in, including four young men who, from their overbearing manner, Paul guessed to be former army officers. Paul soon learned that Melnikov had continued to be indiscreet as the younger of the two owners, named Vera, came to his table and told him that Melnikov had warned her that Paul might be coming:

'I shall ask no questions. You may feel quite safe here and nobody will notice you.'

But as Paul glanced around at his fellow diners, he knew that he was in an awkward spot. His ruffian-like appearance might pass out on the street where there were so many beggars and travellers from the countryside, but the patrons of the café were far better turned-out and he knew that they must be wondering who this unkempt-looking character was who they had never seen before. The four army officers seemed particularly wary of him. They were drinking and making a lot of noise, but casting occasional suspicious glances at him. As Paul wondered if he should pay the bill and leave without waiting for Melnikov, one of the officers suddenly stood up and walked over to Paul's table.

The officer was tall and thin, with sunken eyes, hair brushed straight back and a narrow black moustache. Paul was particularly struck by his slightly crooked mouth, perhaps the legacy of some injury. But he was not unfriendly. He sat at the table and introduced himself as 'Captain Zorinsky'. He said that he knew that Paul was waiting for Melnikov. Paul admitted nothing. Zorinsky continued nevertheless: he did not know when Melnikov would return but if, in the meantime, he could be of any assistance, Paul had only to ask. Paul thanked him for the offer, but showed no inclination to talk so Zorinsky simply smiled, bowed and returned to his noisy friends. Paul did not like the look of Zorinsky at all, but he knew that this was no gauge of the man's reliability. Even so, he decided that there were other leads he could try before he called on Captain Zorinsky.

However, one thing was clear: he could not remain here. He wondered who else Melnikov had told about him apart from the hostess of this café and Zorinsky? The Finnish border guards had jokingly referred to Melnikov as a 'chuckleheaded scatterbrain', but Paul was beginning to suspect that they were right. There was certainly no safety to be found here: if they would admit someone looking as disreputable as he did then it was simply a matter of time before a Cheka informant managed to infiltrate the place. He glanced at the other diners again. Perhaps one was already here?

In fact, the café was a well-known haunt of White sympathisers and the Cheka were already aware of it. It was just about the most dangerous place that Melnikov could have sent Paul to. Even though Paul did not know this he could sense that something was very wrong with the place: despite the delicious food and the attractive young owner who urged him to call again soon, after he had paid the bill he decided that he would never go back there again.

Out in the street it was already dark even though it was only six o'clock in the evening. Paul was almost exhausted. He had not slept at all the night before and then had spent much of the day walking. Although he had spent the afternoon at the railway station he had not dared to doze off in case a Cheka patrol arrived. If he was to find somewhere warm and safe for the night he had just one option left – the flat belonging to Melnikov's smuggler friend Ivan Sergeivitch. Paul had never intended to use this address as, apart from his brief meeting with the man, he didn't know Ivan at all, but now he had no choice. He turned up the collar of his coat against the cold and set off.

There were forty flats in Ivan Sergeivitch's apartment building near the Kazanskaya (the street leading to Kazan Cathedral). Ivan's apartment turned out to be on the very top floor. Once again Paul had to trudge up many rubbish-strewn flights of stairs, but at least this time there appeared to be no caretaker to ask difficult questions. And he was in luck. Just as Ivan had promised, the housekeeper was still living there. Although she was suspicious she finally allowed Paul to enter the flat. Her name was Stepanova and she was staying there with two other people, her nephew Dmitri and Varia, the family nanny. They were surviving on the meagre Red Army rations that Dmitri earned. But with typical old Russian hospitality they shared their cabbage soup and black bread with Paul and also offered him a place to rest for the night. As he fell asleep on the couch in the study with the snow falling again outside he could at least console himself with the knowledge that he had made it across the border and survived his very first day in the city. He might not have made contact with Melnikov yet, but there had been far worse starts to secret operations. He slept soundly.

The next day Paul paid Stepanova for the food he had eaten and then went back across the city to the hospital in Kamenostrovsky Prospekt. There was still no sign of Melnikov. The snow was now falling steadily and there was a biting wind. The previous evening's meal had not been very filling and Paul was already hungry again. But food was rationed and to get it one had to have a ration card. The Finnish guards had not been able to provide him with one so Paul wondered where he was going to get his next meal. He was also out of leads. If he was to rebuild Cromie's networks he was going to have to think of something.

He wandered the streets for the rest of the morning, hoping that an idea would occur to him while he kept an eye out for Cheka patrols. Not surprisingly, he drifted towards the area of the city where he had once lived and it was here that he found a small restaurant in a private flat run on the same basis as Vera's café where he had been the day before. It was risky, but he was so hungry that he took a chance. Inside the flat the food was only gruel (Paul now had a pretty good idea what happened to the horses), but there were mouldy carrots and fresh bread as extras and the woman in charge told him that he could eat there every day as long as he had money and as long as they didn't get raided.

It was still freezing cold and Paul didn't relish the prospect of a long night out on the streets, but the bread at the restaurant also gave him an idea. Purchasing three loaves of white bread, he returned to Ivan's flat that afternoon. He had only been supposed to stay there for one night, but Stepanova was so overjoyed by the gift of white bread rather than the gritty black bread which usually appeared in the rations that she invited Paul to stay another night. And Dmitri's army rations for that day included meat so the meal that evening almost counted as a feast. While the meal was being prepared, Paul made use of the telephone from the hall at the block of flats. He phoned the café which he had visited the day before. Unfortunately there was still no news of Melnikov.

That evening as Paul dozed off, he realised something: he had only been in the city for two days but he was beginning to relax. At first he had been panicked, living, as he said later: 'from minute to minute and hour to hour.' But now he no longer saw eyes on every street corner. Although he did not know it he was going through a process which all intelligence officers experience on a new mission and that sense of fitting in, of knowing that you have not been discovered and are truly 'undercover', is one of the best feelings in the world. He drifted slowly off to sleep . . .

The doorbell in the flat rang loudly and Paul awoke with a start.

He had slept late. Stepanova had kindly allowed him sleep in one of the spare beds and she had even found him an old pair of Ivan's pyjamas. There were no sheets, but there were plenty of blankets and Paul had been cosy and warm. Now it was 7.45 a.m. and here he was half-asleep and without his clothes. Suppose it was the Cheka at the door? In a panic he realised that he had no idea what to do. The windows of the apartment were too high for him to jump from and like a fool he had chosen a hiding place with no other exits. There was nothing he could do but produce his Cheka papers and demand to know what they were doing here. But as soon as he thought this, he knew that it wouldn't work – the Cheka would know if they were raiding the flat of one of their own. He was reduced to waiting nervously as he stood in Ivan's pyjamas whilst Stepanova shuffled to the door to find out who it was. As he stood there with his stomach in knots, Paul swore that he would never again sleep in a place from which there was only one exit.

It was as he was standing there in the middle of the room feeling like a fool that the door of the room burst open and in strode Melnikov. He was wearing new clothes and a pair of glasses, but it was definitely him. Paul was overjoyed. He had been increasingly convinced that the Cheka must have picked him up. And there was other good news as well because behind Melnikov stood a giant of a man with ginger hair and dressed in a tatty brown suit whom Melnikov introduced as John Merritt. The caretaker had been wrong: he had not been arrested. The Cheka had come for him, but he had escaped through a back window as they were smashing their way in through the front door. He had been on the run ever since. Merritt explained that he had managed to evade capture by shaving off his beard; few people seemed to recognise him without it (although now it was growing back and Merritt joked that he had better find a barber). However, he had nearly been caught in random searches several times. Once he had been stopped in the street by a Chekist and had been about to be arrested because his papers were not in order. But then he had asked for a cigarette and as the Chekist reached into his pocket Merritt had knocked him out with one punch and had run for it. Paul asked him why he had not just cleared out of the country? Merritt replied that although *he* had escaped the Cheka had managed to grab his wife. He had been hiding out in the city, trying to think of a way to free her. Then Melnikov had spotted him in the street the previous evening and they had been searching for Paul ever since.

Having brought the two British agents together as he had promised, Melnikov was keen to move on. He told Paul to meet him that afternoon at the 15th Communal Eating House just off the Nevsky Prospekt (a sort of soup kitchen for those who did not have ration cards). He also warned Paul that he should never sleep more than two nights in the same place – and then he was gone.

Over a cup of tea as Paul dressed, Merritt gave Paul the names and details of the members of Cromie's network who were still at large and were not so terrified that they might agree to work for Britain once again. Promisingly, one or two of them still occupied positions at the Russian Admiralty and Ministry of War. He would also take Paul to one or two safe houses he could use. The best ones were those belonging to people who were working (reluctantly) for the new Bolshevik administration. As government employees they were less likely to be visited by the Cheka. In the meantime Merritt had an appointment to see a member of the Cheka who he thought might be able to give him information about his, Merritt's, wife. The man was a former member of the *Okhrana*, the Tsarist secret police, but many of them were being re-employed because of their knowledge and experience. This man had no love for the Bolsheviks and – if the price was right – was prepared to help those in need. Paul agreed to go with Merritt. After all, this Cheka informant might turn out to be useful.

They left the flat and Merritt made his way through the streets to the south of the city. The risk of being picked up by a Cheka patrol was so great that the two men travelled separately. Merritt led the way and Paul followed about fifty metres behind so that if one of them was stopped the other had a chance to walk away unnoticed (but to walk, *never* to run). First, Merritt took Paul to a dilapidated flat where his former housekeeper was living. The flat had belonged to another British citizen whom Merritt had helped to cross the frontier and who had left him the keys in gratitude. Merritt introduced Paul (simply as 'Mihail Mihailovich') to the housekeeper, Maria, and said that Paul could use it as a safe house, describing it as '. . . one of the safest places in town'. The place was dirty and had very little furniture left, but it would do in an emergency.

Then they moved on to one of Merritt's contacts, a 35-year-old former journalist who was working as a clerk for the Soviets in the Department of Public Works. Like Dmitri (Stepanova's nephew who was in the Red Army) he was doing this simply to get an official ration so that he could live. At first, he seemed a little reluctant to go on assisting Merritt and he kept whining about his problems, but the gift of half a pound of gritty black bread was enough to transform his attitude and suddenly he was all smiles and cooperation.

Merritt was using the ex-journalist's flat in the Liteiny Prospekt (just off the Nevsky) to meet the Cheka informant whom Paul only ever referred to as 'the Policeman'. When he arrived a short while later, the Policeman turned out to be a short, red-faced, self-important little man. He told Merritt that his wife was being held in a communal cell with thirty or forty other women and that she was taken out and interrogated several times a day because the Cheka believed that she must know where her husband was hiding. There were no washing facilities, few bunks and very little food or water. The women were only taken from the cells at Gorohovaya for two reasons: to be interrogated or to be shot. The executions took place at exactly the same time each day: those who were dragged out at seven o'clock each evening knew what their fate would be.

John Merritt was distraught. He demanded to know how much it would cost to smuggle his wife out of Gorohovaya – he would pay anything. The Policeman smiled quietly and said that it could possibly be done – for thirty thousand roubles. Paul was shocked, but Merritt agreed to pay it without argument and handed over ten thousand roubles on account. Apparently he had already given the informant ten thousand roubles and Merritt promised the final ten on the day his wife was released. The Policeman said it would take a day or so to arrange and invited Merritt to come to his house the day after next and then offered him a bed for the night. The informant said it would be quite safe. Merritt agreed. If Paul was horrified at the risk Merritt was taking he never said so, but he must have known that the reward for handing over Merritt would be considerable.

After the Policeman had left, Paul asked Merritt about the risk. Merritt explained that everyone in the city was convinced that the British would invade any day now. The Policeman would do nothing that might compromise his future success. He also suggested that the ex-journalist should be told that Paul was a British agent. He was a coward, but a venal one. As long as Paul kept him well paid he would do as he was told and the flat would provide another safe house for Paul to use. After some thought Paul agreed and immediately won the ex-journalist over by giving him money to keep the flat well-heated, saying that he would return later that night.

Paul then left for his meeting with Melnikov at the 15th Communal Eating House. Things were going well and he was looking forward to seeing his friend who had been such an important part of his success so far. But when he arrived at the Eating House he was shocked to find that the building was encircled by the militia and by Soviet sailors who often provided the muscle for Cheka raids. The occupants of the restaurant were being led out in single file and others in the street were being searched. He hung around hoping to see if Melnikov was one of those who had been caught and while doing so he bumped into Zorinsky, the army captain from the café. Zorinsky told him that Melnikov had been one of the first to be arrested and taken away. Apparently the Cheka had been tracking him for several days. Zorinsky offered to take Paul back to his flat to talk about what might be done to get Melnikov released. Still not sure whether to trust Zorinsky, but reluctant to turn down any possible lead, Paul agreed.

Zorinsky and his wife Elena turned out to be doing suspiciously well, living in a well-furnished flat with plenty of food and a supply of good vodka. They could even afford to employ a maid. After dinner, Zorinsky explained that his wife was a successful actress in the theatre, which entitled her to extra provisions, and that he was signed on there as a manager. He did no work but drew pay and rations. That left him free to indulge in his 'hobby'. Zorinsky then boldly announced that his hobby was intelligence and produced a document which Paul was astonished to see was a copy of recent top-level negotiations between the Bolshevik government and their political opponents. If the document was genuine, it was just the sort of political intelligence that Cumming was looking for.

Zorinsky asked if the document interested Paul at all? Fearing a trap, Paul tried to act nonchalant and handed the document back, but Zorinsky waved him away and told him to keep it. He said there would be other reports available shortly if Paul would like to see them. Zorinsky then topped everything off by claiming that he had been one of Cromie's agents!

Paul tried to gather his wits. This was all just too good to be true. Merritt had not mentioned Zorinsky when talking about Cromie's network – but would Merritt have known all of Cromie's contacts? Every instinct was telling Paul to get out of the flat, but he was transfixed. If this man was genuine, he might be able to provide all the intelligence Cumming could ever want. Paul just did not know what to say. He was facing a common dilemma for any undercover officer: it is often the most dangerous and least trustworthy contacts who have the best information. Deciding on the right ones to trust is what separates good spies from dead spies. It was as Paul was wrestling with all these thoughts that Zorinsky landed his final punch:

'John Merritt has had hard luck, hasn't he?'

Still reeling, Paul made his most stupid mistake of the mission so far:

'John? So you know him too?'

Zorinsky instantly became very interested and leaned forward in his chair:

'I know *of* him. Tell me, you don't happen to know where he is, do you?'

Paul hesitated. For a moment he was on the brink of telling Zorinsky the whole story. It would make everything so simple. But then his instincts saved him. Paul said firmly that he had no idea of Merritt's whereabouts – it was just that he had heard about Merritt's arrest before he left Finland.

Zorinsky looked disappointed and sat back. He was probably not convinced by Paul's answer, but he clearly decided not to push this promising new contact too hard at this early stage. He had almost certainly concluded by now that Paul was a beginner at this game. He could wait.

Zorinsky offered to let Paul sleep in a spare room in the apartment that night. Paul accepted. Considering Zorinsky's odd behaviour this might seem like a terrible mistake, but Paul had been learning from John Merritt: if Zorinsky was some sort of Cheka agent then troops would have arrived and arrested him by now.

Zorinsky could have easily put in a call. Besides, like the ex-journalist, he would have known that the British were expected in Petrograd soon and that, together with the fact that there was probably more profit in keeping Paul 'in play', should have meant that Paul was safe for that night. And then there was the possibility that Zorinsky was genuine, that he really had been one of Cromie's contacts. If that was true then Paul might well make him the head agent, in charge of the whole network.

The next morning Paul left and headed for Maria's flat where he had agreed to meet Merritt. He did not arrive there until 11 a.m. but Paul deliberately took a circuitous route to throw off any followers that Zorinsky might have arranged the night before. John Merritt arrived shortly afterwards, his head covered by a large black shawl. He looked very shaky, far from his defiance of the evening before. Even Maria was frightened by his haggard appearance.

It soon became clear that it was the latest report about his wife that had caused the change. The Cheka had tried a new tactic in their questioning of her. She had been forced to stand in place for seven hours, without being allowed to move an inch, without food or water, whilst she was continuously interrogated. If she moved she was beaten. Eventually she had fainted. The Cheka had forced her to tell and retell her story over the past few days and now they had highlighted various inconsistencies as she had become more and more confused and disorientated. They were forcing her to explain the inconsistencies and she was getting herself more and more tied up in knots and giving away more and more information. Things looked very bleak for her unless she could be rescued from prison somehow.

The information she had given them so far was allowing the Cheka to close in on Merritt. They now knew that he had shaved his beard, which was the reason for the shawl, but with his height and build simply covering his face was no disguise at all. A special detachment of the Cheka had been formed to hunt for him and there was a large reward for information leading to his capture. It was only a matter of hours before a Cheka street patrol would pick him up. This flat was one of the last places which would be safe for him.

And so John Merritt had taken the terrible decision to leave the country. If he remained, all that would happen would be that the Cheka would get both him and Paul. Merritt begged Paul to take over the rescue plans that he had started to arrange with the

Policeman. He knew it was a risk on top of Paul's other espionage duties, but there was no one else he could turn to. Naturally Paul agreed. He promised that he would personally take Merritt's wife over the border to make sure that no harm came to her. This seemed to ease Merritt's anguish a little.

Merritt decided that he would leave the next day. First he agreed to visit a business friend of his in the local Jewish community who would provide the money that would be needed to bribe the guards to release Mrs Merritt. Before he set off, Paul asked him about Zorinsky. Merritt said he had never heard of him.

And with that Merritt was gone. Paul spent much of the rest of the day writing his first CX report for MI6, using invisible ink on a tiny scroll of tracing paper. Merritt would carry it out in the sole of his boot.

Paul saw John Merritt again briefly the next morning, Friday, 29 November. Merritt had covered his face in dirt and wore a driver's cap. He was carrying the identity papers of his former coachman. He hoped that these would be good enough for him to be able to travel north from the city by rail from the Okhta station. This was in the east of the city from where most of the rail lines headed deeper into Bolshevik Russia so it was less likely that the Cheka would be watching it. But one line branched and ran north towards the Finnish border. Merritt planned to leave the train at some point and then to cross the border on foot.

It was late in the day when Merritt turned and said his final goodbyes to his faithful housekeeper. They were never to meet again. Paul then escorted Merritt to the station, using the trams with Paul watching Merritt's back in case he was being followed. But Paul saw nothing. By the time they reached the station it was dark. The tiny wooden station was packed with refugees. When the train arrived they all surged forward and climbed into and onto the carriages any way they could, even sitting on the roof. Paul's last sight of John Merritt was of the giant British agent fighting his way through the window of an already overcrowded railway carriage and then burrowing deeply into the heaving mass of desperate passengers inside in the hope of avoiding discovery. In his pocket Merritt carried a loaded revolver and in his boot Paul's secret report. He had promised Paul that he would sell his life dearly if the Cheka cornered him.

And then the train was gone.

As he trudged back into the centre of Petrograd in the cold and the dark, a wave of depression swept over Paul. With the departure of John Merritt and the arrest of Melnikov, the last reliable links with Cromie's old network were gone. Meanwhile the mystery of Captain Zorinsky remained. Merritt had not heard of him, but that was not proof of anything. Paul decided that the best step was to have Zorinsky's document checked out. If that was genuine then there was still a chance that Zorinsky might be genuine as well. The only problem was how to do it?

Paul set to work. Over the next few weeks, he followed Melnikov's advice and never spent a night in the same house twice in a row. He was also careful not to let the occupants of any of them know about the other places. He began contacting the people on the list of former agents given to him by Merritt. Many of them believed that Paul's appearance meant that Britain would be liberating Petrograd any day now and his first job was to dampen these expectations and prepare them for a much longer haul. He was not entirely successful in this, but some of them listened and slowly he began to reconstruct the intelligence networks. He also arranged a back-up plan in case the Cheka finally got him. He had to pick one trustworthy agent and in the end decided that Merritt's former housekeeper Maria was the best. She was nervous, but she was reliable. Paul told her that if he disappeared she should wait several days and then send someone to the British Consul at Helsinki giving his name and as many details as were known about his fate. Soon Paul began entrusting her with all the details of his movements and told her at which safe house he would be sleeping so that if he did disappear MI6 would have a better idea of who had betrayed him. He even used her as part of his courier service and she hid all his reports in the flat while he was waiting for someone who could take them out of the country.

In between agent meetings Paul spent time attending public meetings where he collected general intelligence on opinions and conditions within Russia which the British government (and therefore Cumming) so desperately needed. Paul found the long public speeches unbelievably tedious, but he also had the opportunity to see Bolshevik leaders such as Trotsky, Zinoviev and Lunarcharsky at close quarters.

His other task was to free his friends. This meant dealing with the two agents he found most odious: the Policeman and Captain

Zorinsky. Obviously, he did not trust either of them but they seemed to have the best contacts. They also both seemed to have just one aim in mind – to bleed as much money from Paul as possible. For instance, the Policeman claimed to be part of a group who could seize control of the entire city – if Paul would only hand over 100,000 roubles 'for expenses'. Meanwhile, Zorinsky wanted 60,000 roubles to bribe the investigator handling Melnikov's case – although it would still take more than a month to release him and there might be a need for further payments to bribe other officials concerned with the case. Zorinsky recommended paying 30,000 roubles up front and the rest when Melnikov was released.

Paul went to see the Jewish banker whom John Merritt had spoken to before leaving the country. Although the banker was sympathetic there was no way he could raise the whole sum, but he did provide enough so that, adding in the remains of his operational budget, Paul could pay the first instalment for Melnikov's release. It was at about this time, in mid-December, that Paul decided that he must return to Finland. He had proved that it was possible to live in Petrograd undercover, but he needed to contact MI6 to get more money and to set up a reliable courier system. His intelligence reports were stacking up at Maria's flat and there were fewer and fewer people who might be able to take them. He also wanted to find out if John Merritt had got back safely and to check out Zorinsky.

But he did not want Zorinsky to find him gone and abandon the attempt to free Melnikov. So he told Zorinsky about his plan to return to Finland. Zorinsky immediately became very interested. He wanted to know how Paul was getting out of the country and when Paul pretended to be undecided, Zorinsky strongly recommended attempting to cross at Bielo'ostrov Bridge. This was the official frontier station leading into Finland and as such could be expected to be the most heavily guarded point on the border. Zorinsky replied that he had contacts there and for around 7,000 roubles he could bribe the commissar and the guards at the station so that Paul would be able to sneak across.

Once again Paul did not know whether to trust Zorinsky. If he really did have those contacts then crossing at Bielo'ostrov would be far safer than the dash through the open countryside. But there was something suspicious about the predatory way in which Zorinsky had reacted to the news and it was not the first time Paul had seen him react strangely. Risky or not, he decided to stick with his original plan. A few days later he told Zorinsky that he had abandoned his plans to travel to Finland but would be going to Moscow for a few weeks instead to make contact with agents there. If Zorinsky was some kind of double agent then Paul hoped that the prospect of being able to obtain information about a British spy network in Moscow would buy enough time for him, Paul, to escape over the border.

Meanwhile the Policeman's plan to release Mrs Merritt from prison was finally in place. He had hoped that she would have been moved from the Cheka headquarters at No. 2 Gorohovaya to one of the state prisons at Shpalernaya or Deriabinskaya where security was less stringent, but the Cheka had refused to let her go and it seemed that they were serious about their threat to execute her. If she had been English there would have been some hope, but she had been born in Russia and therefore the Cheka felt they could do as they wished because no one in England would care – what was one more dead Russian?

The only positive news was that since their spies had learned that John Merritt had escaped to Finland the Cheka had stopped their daily interrogations. There was no point now. That meant that if the Policeman could get Mrs Merritt out of whichever communal cell she was being held in then her absence might not be noticed for several hours, perhaps even days. But now was the time to act, before they started taking an interest in her once again.

And so at three o'clock on the afternoon of 18 December 1918, Paul set out for St Isaac's Cathedral. On the way he passed No. 2 Gorohovaya, looking for any suspicious activity. There had been blizzard conditions in the city that morning, and although these had eased at around midday it was still bitterly cold on the streets. People hurried along with their heads down. The Petrograd Cheka headquarters at No. 2 Gorohovaya was laid out like its sister building, the infamous Lubianka in Moscow. It was a grim stone building several storeys high and built around a central courtyard. There was one main entrance to this courtyard through an archway which connected with the main street. This made it easy to monitor those who went in and out of the building. As Paul walked past, hunched against the freezing cold and trying not to be noticed by the occasional Cheka patrols that left the building, he found it hard to believe that the odious little Policeman could secure Mrs Merritt's escape from such a place.

Inside No. 2 Gorohovaya, Mrs Merritt waited in her crowded cell on one of the lice-ridden pallets at the back of the room. Shortly before four o'clock the cell door opened unexpectedly and her name was called. Many of the other women looked up curiously: it was not the execution hour, but it was unusually late in the day to be called for questioning. What could it mean? Mrs Merritt sighed and stood up. She knew that whatever this was there was no point in struggling or protesting and besides she was too weak. She shuffled towards the door.

She did not recognise the face of the solitary guard beneath his peaked cap. He locked the door behind her and then signalled with his rifle that she should walk ahead of him. They passed along the stone-flagged corridors past the rows of other cell doors, but instead of going up one of the staircases to the offices of the Cheka above, the guard forced her further along to one of the numerous side passages in the cellar. He made her stop at a door and motioned her inside with his bayonet. Mrs Merritt could see that this was a women's toilet, but female prisoners in the cell were usually expected to use a bucket which was emptied once a day. These toilets were never used by them. She was immediately suspicious, but the guard refused to answer her questions and simply pushed her through the doorway.

Lying on the floor in one of the cubicles was an old green shawl, a shabby hat and two slips of paper. Nervously, Mrs Merritt picked them up and read them. One was a day pass to Gorohovaya issued to some relation of a prisoner in a name she had never heard of. The pass stated that the visitor had entered the building at four and must leave by seven o'clock. The other piece of paper simply said: 'Walk straight into St Isaac's Cathedral.'

It could have been a trap – she was smart enough to know that. But she was too worn out to care. What was the difference between a bullet in the back as she was walking out through the front gates or a bullet in the head as she knelt in the courtyard one evening just a few days from now? She destroyed the instructions, wrapped the dirty shawl around herself and stepped outside.

The guard had gone. Mrs Merritt walked back along the passage to the main staircase. There was a desk here where all visitors were checked in and out. She presented the pass. The guard barely glanced at it and waved her past. Hardly daring to believe her luck, she walked slowly up the stairs, trying to look ahead at each turn in the staircase to see if anyone was waiting to ambush her. But the staircase was empty.

She arrived in a corridor and at the far end could see the main doors through which she had been dragged in the middle of the night almost one month before. Tears were streaming slowly down her cheeks. Still clutching the shawl around her, she stumbled forwards. She passed office doorways where the clacking of type-writers and murmured conversations showed that the Cheka was still hard at work, but no one looked up. At the doors, a guard held one of them open so that she could pass through and she stepped into the twilight of the late afternoon.

The courtyard was busy with Cheka troops passing back and forth on various errands. The familiar canvas-covered trucks of the Cheka were parked here and there. The transport by which their victims arrived and in which the bodies were taken away. To Mrs Merritt's left was the archway and main gate of the building.

She stepped carefully down the steps into the courtyard. Still no one challenged her. She walked slowly towards the gates, not daring to hurry but at any moment expecting to hear her name called or a shot ring out.

Mrs Merritt was at the gates.

The sentry with a rifle slung over his shoulder took her pass and read it. He glanced briefly at her, added the pass to a pile of others on the desk behind him and then waved her through.

Fifteen minutes later Paul was still at St Isaac's and almost out of his mind with worry. He had been there for over an hour and had burned two whole candles as he knelt before one of the icons from where he could watch the entrance to the cathedral. He had never met Mrs Merritt and the Policeman had only told him to watch for a woman in a green shawl at around four o'clock. It was now a quarter to five but Paul could not afford to let his concentration on the door lapse for even a moment. He smiled wryly as he thought how impressed any watcher must be by his devotion to the blessed icon.

And then he saw the green shawl. It looked almost black in the candlelight in the cathedral, but it must be her, he thought. Mrs Merritt hesitated at the door. She appeared to be on the point of collapse. Slowly she advanced towards the altar and then Paul was by her side. Taking her gently by the wrist he told her that he was an Englishman who had been sent by her husband and that he would be taking her across the border to Finland that night. She almost collapsed in his arms. He led her to a pew to rest for a few moments, but he knew they could not wait for long. As soon as she felt strong enough to stand he led her out into the street.

It was a long way to Maria's flat and Paul wasn't sure that Mrs Merritt would make it. It meant taking a risk, but he hailed one of the horse-drawn sleighs from across the square. Even though the woman was weak, Paul could not afford to head there directly in case they were being watched. At an intersection known as Five Corners they left the sleigh and hurried through the deep snow down one of the side streets. With Mrs Merritt leaning heavily on his arm Paul led her through twisting alleyways, hoping to throw off any followers but taking care that they didn't turn a corner and bump into a Cheka patrol at the same time. Finally he felt that he had done enough and that John Merritt's wife could not take any more. He hailed another sleigh and they made their way as quickly as possible to Maria's flat.

Even here there was no time to rest. Maria was overjoyed to see her former employer but in less than an hour it was time to move on. Paul planned to use the same route as John Merritt to get out of the country and the last train from Okhta Station left at seven o'clock. Paul helped Mrs Merritt out of the hat and green shawl and wrapped her in a dark cloak which he had purchased at one of the unlicensed street markets that morning. She was very weak and Paul dreaded to think what conditions would be like at the station, but there was nothing he could do. After a last farewell to Maria he took Mrs Merritt downstairs and hailed another sleigh. He had to conserve whatever strength she had for the long walk across the border – if they made it that far.

At Okhta the scrum to board the train was every bit as bad as it had been on the day when Paul had seen John Merritt. Paul dragged Mrs Merritt through the crush, barking at her in Russian, hoping to look as little like an English couple as possible. But the press of people trying to get out of the city was so great and Mrs Merritt was so weak that it did not look as though they were going to make it before the train departed. Then, almost at the point of giving up, Paul saw that an extra boxcar was being fitted to the front of the train. The crowd surged forwards and Paul ran with them, half-dragging Mrs Merritt as she stumbled in the snow behind him. People were piling in through the open doors of the boxcar. In a moment the opportunity would be gone. Paul hauled Mrs Merritt to her feet and lifted her bodily above the heads of the others who were struggling to scramble aboard. She cried out in pain, but there was nothing for it. With a final effort, Paul forced his way in among the mass of passengers and their bags of belongings and then the door of the boxcar was slammed shut behind them.

Paul later said that the thing which struck him most about the journey was the almost complete silence in that boxcar. The people were all crammed in to the point of suffocation, but after the screams and oaths and struggles on the platform no one spoke – or if they did it was only in brief murmurs. Only one thing disturbed the quiet: a young boy who was jammed in next to Mrs Merritt coughed and coughed and coughed until Paul thought he might brain him. For five hours the train chugged steadily north, stopping occasionally at small stations for passengers to try and fight their way off the train before the boxcar door was slammed shut and they headed off through the snow again.

It was midnight by the time they reached the end of the line at Grusino. People streamed off the train and headed into the pine forests on their own private quests for food and firewood. It was bitterly cold and the snow here was deep. Paul helped Mrs Merritt to climb down. Paul had been told by John Merritt where to find a contact here but first he led Merritt's wife in the opposite direction to the border, in case anyone was watching them. When he was certain that they were safe he took her to the hut on the edge of the forest which Merritt had given him directions for.

The hut turned out to be occupied by several people. One was a sixteen-year-old boy named Fita. His father had been shot by the Cheka for 'speculation'. He now took revenge on the Bolsheviks and earned a meagre living by leading refugees across the border. There were four other people waiting for the journey to begin. Fita told Paul that one was an army officer who had been asking for a guide in the village for the past few days and had finally wound up here. He had brought three women with him. Two of the women, aged just fifteen and seventeen, were 'princesses', distant relations of the Tsar. The other woman was their governess. All four were dressed in rough peasant clothes in the hope of avoiding discovery. Paul dreaded to think what would happen if he and Mrs Merritt were caught by the Cheka along with these 'enemies of the proletariat'. But then, as a British spy he was in so much trouble by now that it probably wouldn't make much difference.

The party set off in two sleighs. Paul paid Fita a little extra for the fastest sleigh just in case they had to make a run for it. They travelled north because the direct route west to the Finnish border would be too dangerous. Even so, they had to make several wide detours to avoid border outposts. Normally the area was a combination of forest and impassable bogs and the outposts were designed to cover the few safe forest tracks. But with everything now frozen the sleighs could safely glide over the bogland and give the outposts a wide berth.

About fifteen miles from Grusino they reached a tiny village, barely more than four or five huts, deep in the forest. Here the party left the sleighs and Fita handed them over to the next contact. From here they would walk. This was the part of the journey which Paul feared Mrs Merritt would never manage.

The party said goodbye to Fita. They did not know it, but within a few weeks he would be dead, tracked down and shot by the Cheka for 'conspiring with counter-revolutionaries'.

The new guide was a highly disreputable-looking individual, little more than a vagrant. Both Paul and the officer protecting the princesses tried to persuade him to allow them to take the sleighs for the rest of the journey. The peasant replied that it was only about a mile to the border and in any case the snow was too deep for the sleighs to force their way through. The princesses seemed to have brought quite a lot of bags with them. Even though he had to support Mrs Merritt Paul helped the officer and the guide to carry as many of them as possible.

They set off through the trees. The peasant led them at a determined pace. Although the nights were long, it was important to cross the border before the morning when the patrols would become more active. Things were not helped by the fact that the officer insisted on stopping every fifteen minutes so that the princesses could rest. Far from the mile which the guide had predicted it soon became clear that the distance to the border was more like ten or twelve. Mrs Merritt's resilience astonished Paul. She seemed to have got her second wind: despite a month in the hands of the Cheka with almost no food and constant interrogation she trudged onwards through the snow and made her way with almost no assistance. She certainly handled the journey with greater fortitude than any of the other women.

Finally they arrived at a clearing beyond which was a broad ditch. The guide told them that this marked the border. They could see a black and white post sticking out of the snow on the far side. That meant Finnish territory and safety. He warned them that the Russian border posts were only a mile away on either side of them and patrols were frequent so they had to cross quickly. But there seemed no way to cross. There should have been a bridge, but as they walked up and down the bank there was no sign of it.

Then, as they were standing around wondering what to do, a figure carrying a rifle emerged from the trees behind them. For a moment there was panic, but no other patrolling figures appeared and, looking more closely, the guide recognised the man who was walking towards them. He was a hunter from a nearby village. After greeting the guide, the hunter told them that they had missed their mark and that the bridge was in another clearing a few hundred yards away. Ten minutes later the party was making its way gingerly across a thin, heavily iced plank of slippery wood which was apparently the 'bridge' into Finland. Once on the other side, the members of the party hugged each other in celebration.

'It's all right for you, you're out of it, but I've got to go back,' grumbled their guide.

As Paul looked back across the ditch he knew that he would have to go back as well. His work for MI6 had only just begun. With some more money he could really get Cromie's networks back on their feet.

And besides, he had a friend to rescue.

The Commandant of Terrioki

With CMB4 out of action, Gus asked for a conference with Harold Hall and Peter Sokolov, who had both travelled with him from Helsinki. He needed to know if they were prepared to risk a run through the forts with just one boat. They both agreed that they could wait a few more days. If ST-25 was still alive, then a few days were unlikely to make a lot of difference. Gus would take Peter in, Peter would collect ST-25 and Gus would take them both out. As long as there would be enough time to do that, then Gus could repair the boat. Gus told Beeley that he could have four days to repair CMB4.

Beeley looked horrified.

To remove the engine of a CMB meant taking out most of the deck first and then disconnecting and lifting out a solid block of metal weighing over half a ton. It was no small job and was never attempted at Osea unless the boat was in dry dock. To do it without proper tools while the boat was still in the water was insanity. But, true to his reputation, 'faithful' Beeley did not complain. He simply left in a hurry to see what equipment he could scrounge from the other ships in the squadron. In the meantime there was at least some good news. The captain of the squadron oil-storage vessel *Francol* asked to see Gus. On the deck under some tarpaulins he had two torpedoes which Cowan had ordered him to collect from Reval. Gus only hoped that would get a chance to use them.

HMS *Voyager* would be sailing in and out of the Sound on various missions so the first thing Beeley needed was a secure berth. Gus was given permission to moor CMB4 alongside the *Francol*. The captain offered to give any help he could, but this was specialised work and in the cramped conditions of CMB4's tiny hull it was really a one-man job. At the same time the engine of CMB7 was also giving trouble and since it was the only boat currently running it was vital that Piper sorted out the problem. Beeley would be on his own, although John Hampsheir would stand by and give whatever assistance he could. Beeley and Hampsheir spent the next few hours arranging shear legs on the deck of the *Francol* to help with the heavy lifting and then they set to work stripping the deck.

Meanwhile, Gus tried to make the best possible use of the time. He told Admiral Cowan of his plight and Cowan immediately dispatched the destroyer HMS *Versatile* to Helsinki to collect the spare engine and Pegler. As soon as CMB4's engine was removed Pegler would be sent with it to Reval where there was a submarine depot ship, HMS *Maidstone*, which had the facilities to completely strip and repair it. Gus telegraphed Le May in Helsinki and asked him to have everything ready – and to send a large supply of soda water with the engine. The squadron was running short of it and it would help to make valuable friends among the senior officers.

Gus dispatched Peter to Terrioki on horseback through the dense Finnish pine forests to try and make contact with the local smugglers and finalise the deal for a pilot. Gus also asked Admiral Cowan for a supply of rum from the squadron's stores with which to bribe the smugglers. Peter thought that the smugglers might want a lot of money, but to seal the deal it would help to have something extra: as in Bolshevik Russia, good-quality alcohol was prized in Finland at the moment and Royal Navy-issue rum would be like gold.

Beeley and Hampsheir worked straight on into the night. There was little that Gus could do but look on and offer encouragement as they toiled all the next day as well. It was not only the oncoming White Nights that gave them a sense of urgency. The weather was good at the moment, but if a storm hit Biorko Sound while CMB4's deck was removed and her structure weakened it could cause irreparable damage. Removing a CMB engine at Osea was a three-day job in a well-equipped workshop. Beeley and Hampsheir did it in two. And just as the old engine was being winched onto the deck of the *Francol* on the evening of Tuesday, 10 June, HMS *Versatile* was sighted entering the Sound. She signalled that she had the spare engine on board.

Beeley was already worried about this engine. It was the only complete spare engine he had been able to find at Osea and he had hoped that they would never have to use it. Usually, all new engines were run on a test bench before being fitted. This was to ensure that they were tuned and running properly as once they were in the boat it was the devil's own job to make adjustments without taking the whole engine out again. This engine had never been tested before, let alone tuned for best performance and Beeley would not vouch for it, especially when compared with the engine he was removing, the one which he had cherished so carefully until it had been soaked in several dozen gallons of sea water. Beeley and Hampsheir were doing their best and there was still a chance that CMB4 might be ready in time but, as Pegler set off for Reval with the old engine, Gus's worries were far from over.

That night Gus was woken aboard HMS *Voyager* by a message that Russian ships had been sighted venturing out of Kronstadt. The squadron had been expecting a raid now that they had moved up to their summer quarters at Biorko and Cowan had carefully placed three destroyers on watch. This looked like the first serious attack.

Quickly rousing the crew of CMB7, which was tied up alongside HMS *Voyager*, Gus obtained permission from the Admiral to intercept. Piper had been told to have CMB7 ready for immediate launch and soon they were racing away across the darkness of the Sound. The rest of Cowan's squadron would follow as soon as possible, but it took much more time for these larger vessels to get steam up and manoeuvre into position. In the distance, among the lights of the various naval vessels, they could see the superstructure of the *Francol* and beneath that the working lights Beeley had rigged up in CMB4. He was working through much of the night again.

As CMB7 skimmed across the Sound, it probably occurred to Gus that what he was doing was rather against the spirit of his orders. He was supposed to be on a secret-service mission for Cumming, but here he was risking himself and his one serviceable boat in an attack on an unknown number of more powerful Russian vessels. The chances were that he would be blown out of the water – and even if he wasn't there would probably be the devil to pay when Hall and Le May found out. Still, there was no time to worry about that now – this was too good a chance for his young crew to miss. With Gus at the helm, Sindall and Marshall clung to the fairing around the cockpit as the boat leapt forward, their eyes straining as they scanned the darkness for the first sign of the enemy. Piper nervously tended the engine in the lower compartment as Gus opened the throttle full out.

Unfortunately, the news from the outlying destroyers had been slow in reaching the squadron and although CMB7 was by far the fastest of Cowan's vessels to respond she only caught sight of the Russian ships in the far distance as they were returning to Kronstadt. The destroyers had been unable to engage as they could not risk entering the minefields. Only CMB7 could have reached the Russians. The move had probably been a feint, something which the Russians did periodically to test the British squadron's response times. The squadron intelligence officer believed that the Bolsheviks had already installed spies in the hills overlooking Biorko Sound to relay news of all the squadron's manoeuvres to Kronstadt. The Soviet vessels were now well behind the line of defensive forts and it would have been madness for Gus to pursue them. Disappointed, he eased down the engines and turned CMB7 for home.

But the evening had one benefit. Admiral Cowan had watched from the bridge of the flagship as CMB7 had set out across the Sound. He had been impressed by the speed with which the crew had responded and as soon as Gus returned he summoned him to the flagship to congratulate him. When Gus explained how the CMB could have skimmed across the Russian minefields if only the targets had not been on the wrong side of the forts, Cowan became even more interested. The arrival of a new weapon which could ignore the defensive minefields raised intriguing possibilities. If Gus did anything to prove the worth of the CMBs against the Soviet fleet then he could be sure of Cowan's support.

Meanwhile, as soon as the new engine had been unloaded from HMS *Versatile* Beeley set to work, with Piper stripping it down and preparing it for installation in CMB4. Mechanics from the *Francol* helped as much as they could. The overhaul was normally a two-day job in the relaxed atmosphere of the Osea workshops, but by noon the next day the engine was being lowered into the correct position in CMB4's hull. The mechanics had completed the task in just eighteen hours. Gus offered the captain and mechanics of the *Francol* some of Cumming's thousand guineas in recognition of their assistance, but they refused.

Now it was down to Beeley once more, crawling around in the tight confines of the little hull where every task seemed to be a three-handed job in a two-handed space. After three days' work with almost no sleep Beeley was practically spent. Hampsheir was hardly any better as he had matched Beeley every hour, on hand to pass tools and fetch missing parts. It was this extreme fatigue which almost certainly caused an incident that was to have terrible consequences later in the mission:

It was the afternoon of Wednesday, 11 June. There were just seven days to the onset of the White Nights and Beeley and Hampsheir were still working flat out. They were lucky that the weather had remained fine all week as there was no way they could have even attempted the job if it had been otherwise. Beeley was hammering away at a recalcitrant pipe somewhere in the depths of the engine and he called for Hampsheir's help.

There was no answer.

Gus always said that Beeley was never one to curse but he was so tired now that even his seemingly limitless patience was strained. Eventually he simply sighed and clambered out into the sunshine. He looked around. There was no sign of Hampsheir anywhere. Beeley clambered up onto the side of the boat and glanced at the scramble net running up the sheer metal sides of the *Francol*, wondering if Hampsheir had gone to fetch something. It was as he was standing there, with the hull of CMB4 gently rising and falling in the swell, that he noticed the bubbles coming to the surface of the water and in one terrible moment he realised what must have happened.

Shouting for help he threw himself into the water between the two vessels, aiming for the place where the bubbles were breaking the surface. In the dark and icy waters of the Sound he could see and feel nothing and he was soon forced to come back up for air, only to find that the swell had pushed CMB4 tight up against the *Francol* and that he too was now trapped. At that moment, something struck his foot and he reached down instinctively. His hand closed on the collar of Hampsheir's boiler suit. Beeley tried to kick for the far end of the boat, but with the dead weight of Hampsheir in his hands he was hardly moving through the water at all. Then, just as suddenly as the gap above him had closed, there was a sudden shaft of sunlight as it opened again and Beeley burst into the open air to find dozens of hands of the *Francol*'s crew pushing CMB4 away from the oiler. Several men, including Sindall and Piper, leapt into the water to help Beeley support Hampsheir, while others reached down to haul them both out. Hampsheir was gently lowered into the bottom of CMB4 and one of the crewmen from the *Francol* began applying life-saving techniques to try and empty his lungs.

After coughing up several mouthfuls of sea water Hampsheir revived, but was very weak.

Beeley and Hampsheir were immediately sent aboard HMS *Voyager* for dry clothes and a medical check. But, despite doctor's orders, Beeley was back at work within half an hour, determined not to throw away all the time that he had saved the team so far.

John Hampsheir was a different story. He had only been in the water for a few minutes and the effects of the 'bad dunking' (as Gus described it) were soon over. But HMS *Voyager*'s medical officer was worried. Hampsheir was still shivering and appeared to be disorientated. There was no sign that he had struck his head when he had fallen into the water. It seemed more like shell-shock or a nervous attack.

What no one knew was that Hampsheir, always highly strung, had suffered a terrible shock just six months earlier. William, his beloved older brother and a Company Quartermaster Sergeant in the Royal Engineers, had worked for a specialist Engineers outfit, the Inland Water Transport Unit. They were responsible for the enormous network of canals that supplied the British front line. William had survived the entire war only to die on 24 November 1918, just thirteen days after the Armistice. He was only 28 years old. The two brothers had been very close and the news had come as a terrible shock to John. To have lost his brother just when it had seemed to be all over was agonising. And now it seemed that it would be the same with him. His war service was complete and he had expected to be demobbed within a few weeks, but then Gus had asked him to come along on this top-secret mission and he had felt that he could not refuse. Now he knew what was involved, it seemed like a suicide mission. He was convinced that neither he nor his brother were destined to make it home. All Gus knew was that John Hampsheir was too badly shaken to be of much use at present. Gus pulled him off the repair duties and insisted that he rest for a few days. Richard Marshall and Bert Piper took over.

Meanwhile, although Beeley was doing his best to meet Gus's deadline, matters were taken out of everyone's hands. Just before nine o'clock on the evening of Thursday, 12 June, Hall received an urgent telegram from someone called Broadbent, an MI6 officer who had been sent to Terrioki to prepare for the CMBs' arrival. The telegram didn't say what the problem was, only that there was an emergency and that one of the CMBs must be sent 'at all costs'.

There was nothing for it. Gus told Beeley to leave the remaining repair work to Piper and then, having gathered Sindall, Marshall, Peter Sokolov and Hall, he set off immediately in CMB7. It was a sign of how far operational secrecy had broken down that word quickly spread around the squadron that one of the CMBs was leaving to 'give it to the Bolshies'. For the men of the squadron these little boats were important. Like Hampsheir many of them were 'hostilities-only' conscripts and they had expected to go home long before this point. Now they were facing an enemy who rarely ventured out beyond his defensive screen of minefields and they faced the prospect of being stuck there for months. The only vessel which could penetrate those minefields was a CMB. They knew nothing of ST-25 and naturally thought that the CMBs had come to the Baltic to attack the Russians. The sooner the CMBs did their job, the sooner everyone could all go home. The crews of the entire squadron gathered on deck to give three cheers as the little boat raced away across the Sound.

It was only about thirty miles to Terrioki and CMB7 could have covered the distance in less than an hour at full speed. But Gus did not want to risk CMB7's engine figuring that it was better to arrive at a steady pace than not at all. He also stayed well out to sea as he did not wish to be fired on from the shore by Finnish troops who might mistake his CMB for a smuggler's craft. He calculated that this added another twenty miles to the journey. It was difficult to navigate along the strange coastline in the dark. There were no villages, lights or other features along the thickly forested shore which might provide a landmark. Since Terrioki was a tiny unmarked inlet only three miles from the Russian border there was a serious danger of overrunning their destination and ending up in enemy waters. But Hall had wired a message to Broadbent to let him know that they were on their way and asking him to go down to the water's edge and signal with a torch every five minutes between midnight and 3 a.m.

They arrived off the mouth of tiny Terrioki harbour not long after 2 a.m. Gus eased the engines back. They coasted slowly towards Broadbent's flashing signal. Marshall was manning the twin Lewis guns. He flicked off the safety catch as they drew closer and nervously scanned the stone breakwater ahead. They had no idea what sort of emergency they were facing, but he was well aware that the Russian border was not far away.

Negotiating the mouth of a new harbour in shallow waters is always a tricky proposition, particularly in a forty-foot CMB where the helmsman has no view of the waterline at the bows (rather like trying to see over the bonnet of a particularly long car). Normally Gus would have asked Sindall to stand at the bows and give directions to make sure they didn't ground on a shoal or bank, but for some reason Hall claimed that he knew these waters and ran forward. He gave directions which Gus carefully followed. It was just as well they were travelling dead slow because although they didn't ground on any obstruction Hall ran them straight into the harbour wall.

CMBs had no reverse gear. Swallowing his anger with Hall, Gus put the helm hard over as Sindall and Beeley pushed them away from the wall by using boat-hooks. There was a nasty grinding sound and CMB7 lost some of her grey paint, but fortunately there was no serious damage done. Even so, this was not the way that any ambitious young captain of the Royal Navy wants to arrive in a new harbour and relations between Gus and Hall, already tense, became a little bit worse.

Gus now cut the engine completely and, using their boat-hooks as punt poles, they eased their way silently into the harbour, watching the shore for the first sign of trouble. The harbour was barely fifty metres wide, just about enough room to moor a dozen yachts. The waterfront was dominated by a long white two-storey building which was the old yacht club. The ghostly outlines of numerous chalets could be seen stretching away over the rising ground into the Finnish pine forests and silhouetted against the starlit sky were the towers of a Russian Orthodox church, which stood on a hill overlooking the harbour. The only other vessel present was one old fishing boat still moored in the centre of the harbour. Gus directed CMB7 towards this and then tied up alongside it.

There was the sound of people moving about in the darkness near the yacht club and then CMB7 was hailed from the shore. For one moment the crew feared that it was the local Finnish sentries challenging them. Marshall cocked the Lewis guns in case someone opened fire on the boat – after all, they had been warned there was an emergency of some sort here – but then they were hailed again, this time in English. It was Broadbent. He had Finnish sentries with him and told the crew where they should moor the small rowing boat they had brought with them. Clearly the guards didn't speak any English because when Hall told Broadbent that they had 'a certain person' with them, Broadbent understood that this meant Peter and called that it was best to leave him on the boat as the sentries tended to treat any Russian who arrived as a possible Bolshevik spy. They would place him under arrest and take him to the commandant at the nearby fort.

The crew unlashed their small rowing skiff and, leaving Marshall to keep Peter company, they rowed to shore. The sentries were naturally very suspicious of this arrival in the middle of the night, but Broadbent assured them that, despite their civilian dress, these were naval officers who were assisting British and Finnish naval forces based at Biorko Sound. Hall produced an official document which the British Consul Bell had obtained from the Finnish government: it asked local forces to render them every assistance. The guards were still curious and wanted to search the strange-looking boat, but a gift of English cigarettes and a bottle of Royal Navy rum convinced them that there was no need to ask any more questions that night. However, they insisted that Gus and Hall had to appear before the commandant first thing in the morning.

Once the guards were out of the way, Beeley fetched Marshall and Peter from the boat and Broadbent then took the party deep into the woods to a villa where he was staying. As they walked through the trees Gus demanded to know what the mysterious emergency was. Whatever it was has not been recorded in any of the remaining documents, but it was so trivial that Gus was disgusted. He noted in his diary that night: 'Broadbent met us and we all went up to his house. There I was rather annoyed to find out that the matter was really not important and he need not have sent the wire . . . No good crying about it.' Gus wondered whether it had all been a ruse by MI6 to get one of the CMBs to Terrioki faster. If so, why hadn't they just asked? It certainly did not improve his faith in them. Still, Broadbent had asked the old woman who looked after the villa to have a hot meal ready and Gus decided that he might as well make the best of it: he would take Peter into Petrograd the next night. There were only one or two days until the White Nights would make the passage through the forts too dangerous in any case. The crew grabbed a few hours' sleep on the floor of the villa, knowing that tomorrow would be their first real test.

The next morning, Friday, 13 June, Gus and Broadbent were due to see the Finnish commandant. But before that meeting had even happened there was trouble. Marshall and Beeley had been sent down to the harbour to check on the boat and they had only been gone about twenty minutes when Beeley came running back to the villa. Whilst Beeley was on CMB7, Marshall had been on shore checking out the yacht club to see if they could store any of their gear there. As he was scouting around, he was challenged by some of the Finnish sentries. The guard had obviously changed since the previous night and the new shift was in no mood for argument. Marshall clearly wasn't Russian, but he *was* in civilian dress and didn't speak any Finnish either so, despite his loud protestations that he was a British naval officer, he was immediately placed under arrest and marched at bayonet point along the main street of the village to the fort. Beeley had hid out on the boat until the sentries and their prisoner were gone and had then run for help.

That was enough for Gus. Together with Sindall and Beeley he marched straight down to the boat and collected their uniforms and side arms. He also told Sindall to raise the white ensign at the rear of CMB7. The 'uniforms' they had brought with them didn't amount to much – sea jackets and a uniform cap – but they would have to do. Cumming might have insisted that they must only be used in an emergency, but as far as Gus was concerned that emergency was now.

He left Sindall and Beeley with the boat and then together with Broadbent marched off to the nearby fort. At the gate Gus identified himself as a British naval officer and demanded to see the commandant immediately.

Commandant Sarin was a former Russian army officer and as such he was in a difficult position by being in command of a Finnish frontier post. He had to show that he had no pro-Bolshevik sympathies and that this section of the border was safe in his hands. He had already received the report from his sentries about the arrival of this strange group of men in civilian clothes in the middle of the night and could see for himself from his view of the harbour that CMB7 was no ordinary patrol vessel. So when Gus and Broadbent told him that this was an operation sanctioned by the Finnish government and showed him their papers he was far from convinced. On the other hand, he knew that Finnish naval forces were now stationed with the Royal Navy at the new base just up the coast at Biorko so there might be some truth in it. But, he asked, why all this skulking around?

Gus knew that he did not have a chance with the cover story of their being motor-yacht salesmen which Cumming had dreamed up and which he later described as 'a cock and bull yarn'. He decided that the only hope was to tell the truth or at least a very substantial part of it. He told Sarin that he and his team were intelligence officers working for the British admiral at Biorko. Now that the British squadron was so close to Kronstadt it was obviously important for the exits through the minefields to be watched in case the Russians attacked. That was why they had come to Terrioki.

'You will appreciate, Commandant, that the essence of such work is secrecy and that therefore the fewer people who know about us the better chances we have of success.'

Gus sat back thinking that he had successfully dealt with two problems at once – explaining why they had arrived secretly and why the commandant should keep silent about their presence.

But Commandant Sarin was not stupid. He said that he would have to refer to his superior officers at Fort Ino and also to the Finnish naval ministry at Helsinki. In the meantime he had to insist that Gus and his crew should confine themselves to the harbour. If they tried to leave they would be arrested upon their return and their boat would be impounded.

Gus could not afford this. He had to leave with Peter that evening, but if he was seen it could cause a row that would stop him using the harbour ever again. However, he had one more card in his hand which he now played: Broadbent, who spoke fluent Finnish, was well aware of the local politics in the area and knew that although the local commandant was answerable to the commandant at Fort Ino further along the coast the two men were rivals. Gus pointed out that if Commandant Sarin allowed him to operate while he was making checks with Helsinki, then Sarin, as the nearest responsible military officer, would be the first person to receive all the intelligence which was gathered. This would make him look good with his superior officers and would certainly be better than any intelligence that Fort Ino could produce.

Sarin was tempted . . . but was still not convinced. He insisted that it was still his duty to consult with Helsinki. He would give his reply as soon as possible. In the meantime, he agreed to release Marshall and instruct his sentries that the crew were not to be molested. But he remained firm in his insistence that CMB7 must not leave the harbour.

This was agonising, but the British team clearly were not going to get anything more from him. As they left, Gus told Broadbent to get a message to Helsinki as quickly as possible to ensure that Bell and Le May secured the necessary permissions from the Finnish government *before* Sarin's enquiry arrived. As for the ban on CMB7 sailing, they would just have to ignore it and hope for the best.

But as events transpired they did not need to ignore Sarin's instructions. That afternoon the commandant sent for Gus again. Broadbent was away organising a telegram for Helsinki via the British consulate at Viborg. Since Hall didn't speak any Finnish there was no point in taking him so Gus went alone. Sarin seemed in a much more approachable mood. His wife was present because she spoke a little English and she acted as interpreter between the two men. In contrast to the frostiness of the morning's meeting Gus was even offered a cup of tea.

It seemed that Sarin had received new intelligence. The garrison of Krasnaya Gorka, the Russian fortress on the other side of the Gulf and a key part in the Kronstadt defensive system, had risen in revolt against the Bolshevik government and had raised the White flag. Apparently the garrison had expected the fortress of Kronstadt to join in the rebellion, but they had not and Krasnaya Gorka was now isolated and in a state of siege. The Bolsheviks had to take the fortress back as soon as possible because it controlled the southern approaches to Kronstadt. The fortress was almost impregnable by land, but there were rumours that the Russian navy was going to sail from Kronstadt and position its battlecruisers just to the east of the fortress. Since the main guns of the fortress were fixed and aimed north and west (the direction of any likely assault by a foreign attacker) the garrison would be unable to fire on them. The Bolshevik battlecruisers would be able to pound Krasnaya Gorka into rubble at will. However, it was possible that the garrison of Kronstadt might yet join the revolt. In that case the battlecruisers would move into position behind Kronstadt instead.

Sarin had been ordered to watch for any movement by the battlecruisers and note what it was. Could, he wondered, Gus and his boat undertake a small reconnaissance expedition to see if these vessels had sailed from Kronstadt harbour?

Gus must have almost choked on his tea at this point, but he managed to say he just might be able to take a small excursion that evening. Sarin was immensely grateful and his whole attitude to the presence of the British CMBs in his territory changed from that moment. Gus headed back to the harbour astonished at his good fortune.

That evening the team prepared to take Peter through the forts. Gus watched as Peter prepared for the mission. He was wearing his old army uniform, stripped of its former insignia. In his pockets he carried Red stars which he would affix to the cap and jacket once he landed ashore. He also carried a leather satchel. There was nothing unusual in this since at this time most people in Russia carried similar bags in case they found anything worth buying (or stealing). In the satchel Peter had various packets, including one containing sandwiches. Hidden in the sandwiches were slips of tissue paper with the latest messages for ST-25 on them. Peter also carried a revolver. He did not intend to be captured alive.

At the briefing before they set out Gus emphasised to Peter that he had to stress to ST-25 that this could be his last chance to get out. The White Nights would mean that Gus could make one more trip through the forts and after that he wouldn't be able to return until the end of July. With that message confirmed they headed for the boats. Gus gave one last letter for Dor to Sindall for safe keeping in case he didn't return.

It was still going to be necessary to keep his presence concealed from the Finnish sentries who would surely be watching – Sarin still hadn't been told about that part of the mission. So Peter was dressed up in Beeley's boiler suit in order to make the short journey through the woods from the villa to the boat. Peter had proved as good as his word and provided a local fisherman and smuggler called Veroline to guide Gus to the place where he believed there was a passage through the breakwater. Peter indicated that the two of them had done some smuggling together during the previous winter. Veroline looked a real ruffian with his dishevelled clothes and unkempt beard. He spoke only a few words of English and Gus didn't trust him one bit, but when Gus told Peter he merely laughed as if to say: 'Well, what did you expect?' Veroline himself was quite relaxed about the journey and said that the smugglers used the route all the time. But he did not work cheap. Gus had to pay 3,000 Finnish marks (about £75 in 1919) with 1,000 marks of the sum in advance. At that rate the remains of Cumming's thousand guineas would not last long. As Peter had predicted Gus also had to hand over two bottles from his dwindling supplies of Royal Navy rum.

At 10.30 p.m., just as the twilight was darkening, CMB7 chugged slowly out through the harbour mouth and into the open waters of the Gulf. The small boat contained just Gus, Beeley, Peter and Veroline. Sindall and Marshall were left behind on the jetty with Hall. Gus had no idea what their chances were of making it through the forts in one piece, but he did not want to risk more lives than he had to. He decided to dispense with someone to man the Lewis guns because if they were fired upon they would be either blown out of the water with the first shot or running for their lives – he did not plan to stand and fight. If they did not return it would be Sindall's job to fetch CMB4 together with Piper and Hampsheir from Biorko and make a second attempt. But Gus ordered him only to drop an agent on the Estonian coast – not to try and penetrate the line of forts again. In the torpedo trough of the boat, they carried a 'pram', a light rowing skiff which Peter would use to row to shore and then conceal in the reed banks until his return.

The line of forts was only about twelve miles from Terrioki, but Gus took a wide curving route which would bring him in towards the gap between two of them where the smuggler was sure the breakwater was not complete. If he was wrong this was going to be a really short trip. CMB7 travelled at a steady speed of about twenty knots, not her top speed but enough to lift most of her hull from the water. They skimmed over the defensive minefield without incident, although even in a CMB it was still a nerve-racking time and Gus was immensely grateful for the charts which had been provided by ST-25 so that he knew when they were clear. They settled down for the approach to the forts which in the half-dark at this distance appeared like a line of large fishing weights stretched along the horizon. The forts varied greatly in size. Some were considerable stone structures complete with a full garrison and eight-inch naval guns. Others were little more than platforms for a few searchlights and machine guns.

Gus had given a lot of thought to how to tackle this part of the journey. It seemed strange to think they had travelled over 2,000 miles to get here and that now the entire mission could be decided in just a few hundred yards. But should he burst through at high speed, trusting to the smuggler's judgement, or should he creep through, hoping to slip past unnoticed? High speed was the CMBs' usual method of dealing with a problem – they would be a harder target to hit and they would draw less water so they would be less likely to ground on the breakwater. On the other hand the tremendous noise of the engine would alert the forts from miles away. If they crept through there was only a small chance of alerting the forts as the CMB was very low to the waterline and very hard to see in the dark, But, and it was a big but, if the guards were alert and spotted them they would be blown out of the water with the first shot.

After a lot of thought Gus had decided to creep through. They would be in the killing zone for longer and it would be a real test of their nerves, but from his long naval experience Gus knew how dull sentry duty could be. The Bolsheviks weren't expecting them and he did not believe they would spot him.

So as the forts loomed out of the darkness, Gus throttled right back and called for complete silence in the boat. Peter grabbed the Lewis guns and released the safety catch – not that the machine guns would be much help, but anything was worth a try. Beeley stood ready in the engine compartment with a carpenter's mallet. At the first sign of trouble, Gus would let the throttle right out to full speed and the clutch plates had a habit of sticking under sudden strain. A quick smash with the mallet was the only way Beeley could force them into place – although that probably was not a technique Rolls-Royce had approved.

There were no searchlights active and the forts were in complete darkness which was a promising sign. Gus kept a close eye on Veroline who was crouched on the prow signalling whether to ease the boat left or right. As they came within the range of the fort's guns, Gus's last thoughts were of ST-25, the man they had come all this way to save. ' ... a man whom I did not know except by a cryptic cipher letter, yet I knew must be incredibly brave and courageous. Where was he at this moment? What was he doing? Who was he?'

The forts drew nearer and there was still no sign of movement. They were about five hundred metres apart and Gus aimed straight for the middle of the gap to give his boat the maximum chance. CMB7's engine was just ticking over, their speed little more than a steady drift. No one spoke. As they passed they were able to see the barrels of the forts' guns quite clearly. It felt as if the guns were being aimed right at them. Was the garrison alert? Were they watching right now and just waiting for CMB7 to drift into line before opening fire? The crew waited for the first explosion.

It never came.

Veroline stood up and raised his hand in a thumbs-up gesture to indicate that they were clear of the line of the breakwater, but still Gus kept their speed steady. The smuggler walked carefully across the deck and climbed back into the cockpit. Very, very slowly the forts slipped behind them and the few shimmering lights of Petrograd became visible in the far distance. To their right the immense silhouette of the Kronstadt fortress loomed.

Finally Gus decided that they were safe enough:

'Okay, Beeley, let her go!' he shouted.

The engine immediately roared, the bows rose and the stern sank as CMB7 rapidly increased speed. Soon the roar of the engine was deafening and the great wings of white water rose high on either side. They were flying again. Everyone in the boat, including the villainous-looking Veroline, grinned their relief to the others and they settled down to enjoy the ride.

It took less than half an hour to cover the remaining distance and they never saw another vessel. As the coast of Russia drew closer, Gus turned north and eased off the speed. Peter made the last-minute checks of his equipment and pinned the Red Army badges to his uniform jacket. Gus came to a dead stop about five hundred metres from the shore. He was close enough to see barges tied up at the northern mouth of the Neva river on which Petrograd was situated. Beeley clambered forward and unlashed the pram, lowering it gently over the side into the water. Peter and Gus clambered after him and Beeley held the pram steady while Gus helped Peter to climb down.

Peter sat in the boat and grasped the paddle.

'Until the night after tomorrow,' said Gus.

'*Dosvidanya*,' whispered Peter, smiling. He paddled away into the darkness.

Beeley and Gus watched him go. They found it hard to believe that they would see him again. After all, he was six feet four inches tall: he towered over the rest of the team and with his mop of blond hair they thought he must surely stand out just as much in Petrograd. He was certainly a brave man.

There was little to do now but wait for the signal by torch from the shore to show that he had arrived safely. As they waited Gus took compass bearings on a church steeple and a factory chimney as it would be vital that he should return to exactly this spot. Beeley busied himself by quietly attaching the compressor pump to the engine, which was the only way to restart it.

They did not have long to wait. Within a few minutes Peter's signal flashed from the shore. Gus replied and then gave the order for Beeley to start the engine. Soon they were racing away at full speed again. There was not much more of full darkness left and Gus still wanted to get a look at Krasnaya Gorka before dawn broke. But as they approached the forts for the second time Gus eased off the speed again. They had one trick up their sleeve for approaching the forts from this direction and he was determined to give it a try. Peter had presented them with an ensign which he claimed was flown by the boats of Bolshevik Commissars. The forts would be unlikely to fire on one of their own coming from the Russian side of the lines. Of course it would have been a different matter if they had tried the ruse on the way in.

But to be convincing, Gus would have to travel at the speed of a conventional motor boat so he reduced speed to about ten knots and watched the forts grow larger in the darkness once more. The one thing that bothered him was that they did not know any of the Bolshevik recognition signals. Still, he thought it was worth the risk.

Once again there was no sign of life from either of the forts as they eased through the gap. Gus wondered if they were actually manned at all. Once more he opened the throttle wide and headed south for Tolboukin lighthouse which marked the western end of Kotlin island. From there they should have an excellent view of the waters at the rear of Krasnaya Gorka.

Sure enough, as dawn rose they could see the massive shapes of the two great Soviet battlecruisers, the *Petropavlovsk* and the *Andrei Pervozvanni*, situated just to the east of Krasnaya Gorka. Both warships were armed with massive 12-inch guns that had a range of over ten miles. There would be nothing the garrison could do except wait for the end. Gus could see the White banner still flying defiantly from the battlements and he said later that it seemed to him to be a call for help as much as a symbol of allegiance. He was galled to see the two battleships just sitting there waiting to begin their attack, knowing that no one could stop them. They were beyond the protection of the southern forts, but they were still behind the minefields and they had a defensive screen of destroyers and patrol boats. There was nothing that Admiral Cowan could do. Unless . . .

It was madness, but Gus was sitting there with a perfectly good torpedo behind him, the rising sun to screen his approach and one of the fastest boats in the world beneath his feet. Why not?

Remembering his promise to Admiral Cowan, he told Beeley to get his uniform jacket on and to prepare the torpedo for firing. Beeley looked shocked, but began work priming the charge for the ramming mechanism. Veroline didn't speak much English, but as Beeley passed out Gus's uniform jacket and cap, he quickly guessed what Gus was thinking and grabbed his arm in protest. This was absolutely not what he had been recruited for. Gus angrily shrugged him off and gestured for him to sit down. Then Gus opened the throttle and sent CMB7 into a large circle to pick up speed for his attack run.

Gus was about two miles away from the screen of destroyers. There was no point trying to sneak around behind them – it was too light and he would be seen before he was halfway there. The only hope was to go in at full speed, fire the torpedo and then run for home, trusting to speed to save them. Gus hoped that surprise would give them the edge.

Beeley emerged and gave the signal that the charge was primed. The torpedo was launched by a lever in the cockpit: this fired a charge that operated the ram which shoved the torpedo along the central trough and over the rear of the boat. As CMB7 straightened out and picked up speed, Gus aimed for the silhouette which he knew was the *Petropavlovsk*. She was the larger of the two battle-cruisers, a heavily armoured pre-dreadnought displacing 23,370 tons and mounting a dozen 12-inch guns. She was the greater threat. He might not be able to sink her with one shot, but if he could cripple her the Bolsheviks might be forced to withdraw the rest of the naval force.

CMB7 would be hard to spot in the early morning haze. Gus knew that the Soviets had a lookout at Tolboukin lighthouse and wondered whether they had seen him yet. It didn't matter. Any message they sent would arrive too late. Gus tried to estimate the range.

There was an explosion and the sound of grinding metal from the forward compartment. Cursing, Gus shut off the engines as Beeley dived below. Gradually CMB7 sank back into the water, trailing a faint plume of black smoke. Gus looked around. Veroline was cowering in the bottom of the boat, his eyes screwed shut, his right hand clutching a holy medal around his neck. Gus slumped back on his seat and waited for Beeley to tell him the worst. As he sat there completely dejected, he watched the Russian destroyers carefully. If any of them had seen CMB7's approach and turned to attack now, the British boat would be defenceless.

Several minutes later Hugh Beeley clambered back. The engine had stripped a gear, but he thought he could rig something. It would not be enough for them to make another attack run – the engine would only produce a few knots – but it would get them home. Veroline had recovered from his attack of nerves and was jabbering away in Finnish. Gus did not understand it, but he imagined it was something along the lines of 'You're a dangerous idiot and I'm never sailing with you again.' Gus didn't blame him.

Half an hour later Beeley started up the engine once more. It backfired repeatedly, but CMB7 moved. Slowly she limped the twenty or so miles back to Terrioki, breaking down twice more on the way. It was 3.30 a.m. by the time they stuttered through the mouth of the harbour, two and a half hours overdue. Hall and Sindall were more than a little relieved to see them, but at least Gus was able to report that Peter had been landed safely – the first part of the mission was complete.

Gus stumbled off to bed. Before he fell asleep he had time to scribble in his diary: 'Came home, crawling in like a lame dog. Hall very pleased to see me back . . . I myself did not think the chances of return very rosy.'

The next morning, at 11 o'clock, Gus walked up the hill behind the village to the fort to brief Sarin. The commandant was pleased to have the movements of the ships confirmed and said that he hoped the British navy would now attack the Russian vessels before they had a chance to begin their bombardment of the fortress. Kronstadt was the key to Petrograd and if Kronstadt was to rise in revolt then it was vital that Krasnaya Gorka hang on. Gus had to explain to Sarin very carefully that there was no way Admiral Cowan could attack across the minefields and that in any case, with his force of light unarmoured cruisers, victory would be far from certain against heavily armoured battlecruisers such as the *Petropavlovsk* and the *Andrei Pervozvanni*.

In return for the information and as a sign of their new working relationship, Sarin took Gus to the Russian Orthodox church and together they climbed the tower there. There was a marvellous view that commanded the sea approaches in all directions. On a clear day it was possible, with a powerful telescope, to see clear across the Gulf. In the haze that morning Gus could not make out the Russian battleships, but he could easily make out the nearest sea forts. Sarin introduced Gus to the old priest who tended the church and said that he should be allowed to use the tower for observations whenever he wished.

Meanwhile, Gus had to fetch CMB4. Beeley was working hard on the engine of CMB7 – Commandant Sarin had given permission for him to open a workshop in the yacht club building, but there were still various specialised parts and tools he required. There was no way the boat would be ready by Sunday night to collect Peter. So with CMB7 out of action, the problem was how to get back to Biorko and collect CMB4. They had no immediate way of contacting Admiral Cowan and the roads were little better than dirt tracks. Peter had made the journey from Biorko overland on horseback, but there were no horses for hire in the village – and in any case Gus was not sure that he could ride one.

Fortunately Broadbent came to the rescue. He had a friend, Mr Fountovsky, who lived not far from Terrioki and owned a very old, rather beaten-up Benz saloon, a reminder of when the Germans had controlled the country. If Gus would supply cans of petrol, Mr Fountovsky would offer his son as a driver. Gus accepted gratefully.

This may not have been a wise move.

He had enjoyed many hair-raising journeys during his time with the Royal Navy – after all, he had trained as a naval fighter pilot at a time when the aircraft were little more than assemblages of canvas, wire and string. But that breakneck journey through the pine forests of Finland would live in Gus's memory for evermore. The first thing which should have warned him that something was wrong was the big axe on the back seat. Fountovsky junior merrily explained that trees sometimes fell and blocked the forest tracks and they would often have to be hacked out of the way before the car could proceed – sometimes they would have to leave the track altogether and drive through the forest until they found it again. Gus might also have been interested to know that there was no form of driving test in Finland at this time and that Mr Fountovsky's son was none too clear on the position of any controls other than the accelerator. This hardly mattered, though, because, as he explained to Gus as they kangarooed out of the village at high speed, most of the controls didn't work anyway ...

They left Terrioki at 5 p.m., paused briefly for dinner at the Fountovskys' villa at Oasikivoka (although Gus seemed to have lost his appetite) and then shot through the darkening forests and twisting mountain paths arriving at Biorko around 11 p.m. Thanking the son for his help and wishing him, not with much optimism, a safe journey home Gus tried to find a boat to take him to the *Francol*. The squadron was at sea and only the oiler and a cruiser, HMS *Dragon*, remained in the Sound. At the pier he found a midshipman in charge of one of the *Dragon*'s boats. Gus identified himself as a naval lieutenant and asked to be taken to the *Francol* where CMB4 was moored. Gus's papers were in order but seeing this dishevelled individual in a cheap brown suit with several days' growth of beard the young midshipman was naturally sceptical. He agreed to take Gus out, but said that he would have to inform his captain.

Gus was greeted warmly by the captain of the *Francol* and had just started to have a wash and a shave when a message arrived that the captain of HMS *Dragon* demanded to see him immediately. So off Gus went again and spent the next two hours explaining exactly who he was and what he was doing. Captain F. A. 'Figgy' Marten took some convincing. Gus looked highly disreputable with his five-day growth of beard and dirty civilian clothing, certainly nothing like a naval officer. But finally, at one o'clock on the morning of Sunday, 15 June, he returned to the *Francol* and was greeted by her friendly old captain once more. It might have been the nervous strain of the journey or it might have been the result of several nights with very little sleep, but after he'd reported to the captain Gus collapsed in his cabin. ('Made rather an ass of myself,' he wrote later). The *Francol*'s captain made him eat a meal and then cleared his own cabin for Gus while he spent the night in the charthouse. There was just time for Gus to be given an update by John Hampsheir on CMB4's condition. The final repairs had taken longer than expected because of problems with the new engine, but she would be ready by 9 o'clock the next morning. Gus's dash from Terrioki had not been in vain. He scribbled a note in his diary – 'Have promised to meet Sokolov at the mouth of the Neva 2330

Sunday night and must not fail' – and then he was fast asleep. It was the first time he had slept in a bed for at least four nights.

The next morning the squadron had returned to the Sound. Gus went to collect the two ratings who had been promised to him by Admiral Cowan as additional staff to help with routine duties around the villa and to guard the boats. Their names were Turner and Young but the team soon nicknamed them Lenin and Trotsky. Since they were now part of the secret mission, Gus had told them to dress in civilian clothes rather than in uniform. He noted later: '... ship's company delighted by this', a further sign that operational security was not all it might have been.

Although CMB4 was fuelled up and ready to go in the morning, it took some time to locate the stores that Beeley had asked for. But by 3 o'clock in the afternoon Gus, Hampsheir, Piper and the two ratings were ready to depart. It was a dull, overcast afternoon with the promise of rain to come, but as CMB4 picked up speed across the harbour, Gus's mood was cheerful. With only thirty miles to cover in daylight he should be back at Terrioki in good time to collect Peter and, hopefully, the mysterious ST-25. He ran the engine at a steady rate so as not to put a strain on the newly installed Fiat engine. Because they were travelling in daylight he did not make a long detour away from the shore as he had done previously, but instead flew the white ensign from the rear of the boat as a clear sign that they were a Royal Navy vessel.

They were just passing Ino Point, not far from the Finnish fort, when a heavy machine gun opened fire on them from somewhere among the trees which lined the shore. Whoever was firing was far too accurate and at least one round ricocheted off something metallic in the boat. Within a few moments, rifle fire started flying around their ears as well. Turner and Young threw themselves flat in the cockpit and Gus crouched low over the wheel as he opened the engine full out and swerved away into deeper waters. It took only a few seconds until CMB4 had taken them safely out of range and the firing ceased as suddenly as it had started, but everyone in the boat was pretty shaken. This far from the border it could only have been Finnish troops who had opened fire on them. Clearly no one had told them that they were supposed to be on the same side. For Turner and Young it was quite a welcome to secret-service work. For Gus it was a useful reminder that he could take nothing for granted out here.

As they drew closer to Terrioki a rolling boom sounded across the Gulf, shortly followed by another. One of the ratings joked about thunder, but Gus and John Hampsheir had both been in action and knew what it was: naval gunfire. The Russian dreadnoughts had opened their attack on Krasnaya Gorka.

They arrived at Terrioki at six o'clock that evening. Hall and Broadbent were very relieved to see them. There were only a few hours until Peter and ST-25 had to be picked up and the success of the entire operation – and possibly the future of MI6 – hung on the information that ST-25 would be bringing with him. If he was still alive.

Gus just had time for a quick bite to eat while Beeley and Hampsheir refuelled CMB4. Sindall told him that the bombardment of the fortress had begun early that morning. According to Commandant Sarin, although the battlecruisers had been in position for some time there had been a delay while the Bolsheviks carried out an infantry attack on a smaller nearby fort known as 'the Grey Horse'. Once the smaller fort had been taken and Krasnaya Gorka had refused to surrender, the naval shelling had begun. Ominously, the defenders had been told there would be no prisoners. Sindall said that the Russians had been at it all day, but the latest news was that the fortress was holding out and the White flag was still flying defiantly. Gus thought bitterly about his failed attack on the *Petropavlovsk* two nights before and wondered if he could have forced the Bolshevik fleet to retreat. But it was too late to worry about that now.

At ten o'clock, pausing only to gather Veroline – who seemed to have forgotten his vow never to sail with Gus again – they set off into the gathering darkness. It was a heavily overcast evening and visibility was very poor, but that suited their plan perfectly. Once more they chugged carefully and slowly through the gap between the forts as if sneaking past sleeping ogres. John Hampsheir scanned the forts carefully through binoculars but was unable to see anything in the darkness, not even a chink of light. Then Gus opened the throttle and CMB4 accelerated away to the location where they had dropped Peter just 48 hours ago. They were at the rendezvous ahead of time. There was nothing to do but sit in silence in the darkness and watch the few working lights of Petrograd. Once the city would have been a blaze of light at night but now there was only electric power for a few hours each evening.

The time passed very slowly. Hampsheir never moved far from the Lewis guns and Beeley had the compressed-air tank connected to the engine ready for a rapid departure: they had no idea if Peter had been captured, but if he had he might have given away the rendezvous. The Bolsheviks would have been very happy to nab a Royal Navy vessel in their waters on a mission to collect spies. The crew watched the shore carefully: they were close enough to make out the reed beds where the pram was hidden. The first sign that Peter was ready to row out to them would be his signal of three short flashes of a torch. Then they would give him a signal in reply so that he would know in which direction to row. But as the minutes passed doubt began to enter their minds: did Peter still have the torch? Had he remembered that he was supposed to signal to them first? It was very tempting to flash the signal to shore now to see if there was any response, but they knew that there were bound to be Bolshevik shore patrols on the lookout. Even so Gus whispered to Hampsheir that if there was the sound of shots or any sign that Peter and ST-25 were in trouble he was going to take CMB4 in close to give them covering fire.

A light rain squall passed over. Not enough to soak them, but there was no shelter in the boat and in the night air it was just enough to make them really cold. The time for the rendezvous came and went. Still there was no signal from the shore. Beyond Petrograd the darkness began to lift as the brief Finnish summer night came to an end. Gus calculated that they had perhaps an hour left before dawn. Veroline was watching the sky too and made it clear, largely through sign language, that he thought they should go. Gus made it equally clear that he was well aware of the time and that Veroline should sit down and keep quiet.

Half an hour passed. The eastern sky was really quite pale now and the cloud cover was starting to clear. Even Beeley and Hampsheir were glancing at it nervously. Gus told everyone they would give it just twenty more minutes. It would be cutting the return journey dreadfully close, but he was determined to give Peter and ST-25 every possible chance. Gus checked his compass bearing on the church tower to make sure that CMB4 hadn't drifted out of place on the current.

Suddenly Gus caught sight of a flickering light. Had it been the signal? He thought he saw it again, but nowhere near the spot where Peter was supposed to be. He ordered Beeley to start the engine and they coasted slowly along the shore. This time they saw the signal clearly and came to a stop as Hampsheir flashed the return signal. In just a few minutes they could make out the pram struggling towards them. Soon it was alongside. Peter stood up and half climbed, half fell onto the side of the boat. He was clearly all in. Gus grabbed his arms and helped him aboard as Beeley reached over the side with a boat-hook to stop the pram from floating away.

Peter sat shivering in the bottom of the boat, gasping, but smiling weakly. At first Gus thought he might have been shot, but a quick glance did not show any obvious wounds, although he was soaked to the skin from the rain and from wading out into the water with the pram. Hampsheir produced a flask of rum and they forced a little between his lips.

'Found . . .' Peter gasped. 'Found ST-25.'

Gus leaned over the side of the CMB, but the pram was completely empty.

'Where is he?' he demanded and then, in one of the few Russian phrases he had picked up in Murmansk: '*Gdye on?*'

Peter looked puzzled for a moment and then murmured:

'Not coming.' And passed out.

8

Melnikov's Marvellous Uncle

Just 48 hours before an exhausted Peter Sokolov mumbled these words, Paul Dukes had been having problems of his own: should he suffocate or be bitten to death?

The small tomb in the forgotten corner of the Volkovo cemetery which had seemed such a good idea that morning seemed less good now. Although Paul was not exposed to the cold and damp as he had been out on the bogland, he soon found that the air in the tomb was rank and unbreathable. So he had tried sleeping with his head poking out of the gap where the walls had crumbled at the corner of the tomb. He then discovered that this seemed to be the favourite haunt of every mosquito in Petrograd and within minutes his face was covered in bites. So he retreated inside the tomb only to be forced out again a few minutes later because he couldn't breathe. There was no ventilation at all and if he fell asleep in there he might never wake again. He was too tired and hungry for the irony of this possibility to amuse him.

Eventually Paul compromised by wrapping his scarf tightly around his head and then lay with his head outside the tomb once again. The constant high-pitched whine of the mosquitoes in his ears was annoying, but at least he was not being bitten. He tried to nod off to sleep as a way of forgetting about the hunger cramps in his stomach. His mind drifted back to the sumptuous meal he had been given by the mysterious Zorinsky when he had arrived to begin his second stint in Petrograd in January 1919. It was hard to believe that it had all been just five months ago . . .

'So how are things over there?' Zorinsky had asked.
  'Over where?'
  'In Finland, of course.'

This was not the first time that Zorinsky had almost caused Paul to choke on his vodka, but he was determined not to let it show.

'It is a pity that you didn't let me put you across the bridge at Bielo'ostrov as I suggested,' continued Zorinsky.

'Oh, but I got away all right. It was a long tramp, but not unpleasant.'

'I could have put you across quite simply – both of you.' .

'Both of us?'

'Why, you and Mrs Merritt of course.'

Paul sat back in complete bewilderment. He had only returned to Petrograd the previous day and yet already Zorinsky seemed to know everything about him. How did he do it? More importantly, who else was he telling?

Paul knew that he was taking a risk by coming back to Russia. There were indications everywhere that the Cheka were becoming more effective. The Red Terror of the previous autumn might have been brutal and provoked revulsion throughout the world, but it had also yielded a wealth of intelligence leads which the organisation was now following up. Escape lines were being closed down and conspirators rounded up. Paul knew that he had only a limited time in which to operate.

But he had returned for two good operational reasons: the first was that MI6 desperately needed more intelligence reports. Paul had been welcomed in Helsinki by the British Consul, Henry Bell, but he had been quickly transferred by steamer to Stockholm where he could be safely debriefed – in Helsinki there were too many Bolshevik spies and others who were watching the British Consulate closely. In Stockholm he had spent Christmas week staying with the head of the MI6 station, Major John Scale, and his wife. While there, Paul had been busy writing up all the notes he had smuggled out of the country in code on tiny slips of thin paper. Much of it was little more than his impressions of conditions in the city, the price of food, how people were reacting to Bolshevik rule and so forth, but so little was known in Whitehall about what was happening in Russia that even this was like gold dust. The British government still could not make up its mind whether to attempt to befriend the Bolsheviks in order to try and bring Russia back into the ranks of Western nations or to oppose them utterly and support the White counter-revolutionaries. Despite all the horror stories coming out of the country, the Labour Party and the trade unions were running a very successful 'Hands Off Russia!' campaign.

During his stay in Stockholm it became clear to Paul that MI6 had no other sources in Bolshevik Russia. Some officers who had fled from Petrograd in the autumn had been reassigned to areas controlled by the White armies, but as for the Bolshevik territories, he was the only agent who had been able to penetrate the border security and set up a working operation. The message from Cumming in London was unequivocal: 'Supply ST-25 everything he wants and convey thanks.' Scale briefed him in more detail on Cromie's NID agents and also on other MI6 contacts in the hope that he could resurrect the old networks.

The second and for Paul the most important reason for going back was that he had to rescue Melnikov. Despite his desire for revenge on the Bolsheviks who had murdered his parents, the main reason why Melnikov had gone back into Russia was to help Paul find Cromie's old contacts. He had barely lasted two days before the Cheka had arrested him and now Paul knew that it was his duty to get Melnikov out. He also hoped that Melnikov would become his senior agent in the new network that he was establishing. He had already proved his worth many times over. Unfortunately that meant dealing with the mysterious Captain Zorinsky. Paul was concerned to find that Zorinsky was 'no trace' in the records of both MI6 and the NID, but that was a risk he was prepared to take.

And so less than two weeks after leaving Russia, in the first week of January 1919 Paul was back again. The return journey had been surprisingly simple. He had been unable to find Ivan Sergeivitch at Viborg and so had gone to see the Finnish border guards he had used before. They were quite happy to help him as long as he paid his way. In fact they had a new, more sophisticated method of smuggling Paul across the frontier – they wrapped him in a big white sheet. This seemed mad, but proved to be surprisingly effective. Paul was put across into exactly the same meadow as before, but this time he was in no fear of being spotted from the cottage because the sheet was almost invisible against the deep snow that covered the landscape. He even managed to avoid the ditch into which he had fallen last time. Once again he rested in the half-built house, sipping whisky until dawn, and then caught the first train of the day into Petrograd.

After checking that his safe houses with Merritt's housekeeper

Maria and the civil servant were still operational, his first call had
been to Zorinsky to find out how the plan to rescue Melnikov was
progressing. Zorinsky had invited him to dinner at his apartment
that evening as he had 'news'. Now it seemed that quite a lot of that
news concerned Paul himself.

Zorinsky pretended not to be angry that Paul had lied to him
about going to Moscow, but he did make strenuous efforts to find
out how Mrs Merritt had escaped from the prison. Apparently the
Cheka were baffled. Paul was wise to Zorinsky's tricks by now and
pretended that he had simply met Mrs Merritt at one of his safe
houses after her escape and had no idea how it had been done.
Zorinsky was mildly annoyed at this obvious lie, but countered with
a piece of news of his own. He asked, quite casually, if Paul had
heard of a certain Cheka officer. He then named the Policeman!

Trying not to let the shock show on his face, Paul claimed that he
had never heard of this man, but he felt sure that Zorinsky must
have been able to see right through him. However, Zorinsky's
information cannot have been as good as Paul feared because
Zorinsky did not follow this up. He simply warned Paul that he
should watch out for this old contact of Merritt's as he was thought
to be working for the Germans. Paul then chanced his luck by
asking if Zorinsky thought there was a link between this informant
and Mrs Merritt. Zorinsky said he did not think so and to Paul his
answer seemed honest.

Despite the fact that Paul had returned with the balance of the
outrageous sum Zorinsky was asking to free Melnikov, the former
army officer seemed reluctant to talk about the subject. Paul found
that he had been right not to return to the café which Melnikov had
sent him to. The Cheka had raided it while he had been in
Stockholm and had rounded up the proprietors – including Vera,
the pretty young owner – and about twenty other White conspirators. Zorinsky claimed not to know whether this was because
Melnikov had talked under torture or because the café had been
indiscreet. However, Paul noticed that Zorinsky seemed strangely
satisfied about the raid. When he challenged Zorinsky about this
the man was unrepentant: the people who went to the café were
fools, said Zorinsky, they were bound to have been picked up
sooner or later. Paul reflected on the fact that Zorinsky himself had
been one of these 'fools' for quite some time, although he'd been
conveniently absent on the day the raid had taken place . . .

But, as always with Zorinsky, just as Paul was about to conclude that the former soldier must be some sort of Cheka agent, Zorinsky completely turned the tables. He leaned over and handed Paul a pen sketch of the Gulf of Finland drawn on blue oil paper. He wondered if Paul was interested in it at all? For a moment Paul could not make out the jumble of symbols he was looking at and then he realised: it was a detailed plan of the complete minefield system around Kronstadt! And this was the original document, not a copy. Zorinsky coolly suggested that if Paul was interested he had better copy it right away as it had to be back in its locked drawer in the Russian Admiralty building first thing next morning. Paul did not know what to say. With Cowan's squadron now operating in the Gulf this was an invaluable piece of intelligence, yet Zorinsky was handing it over as if it was nothing. Paul wondered if it could possibly be genuine. Upon closer examination the plan showed how the minefields were set in two distinct zones. The map also showed the route which a vessel would have to take to pass safely through them. Paul knew that he could not afford to take a chance with something as crucial as this. Despite the risk of working in front of Zorinsky he set about copying it there and then. He could check whether it was genuine later.

While Paul was hard at work, Zorinsky produced another piece of paper and offered it for examination. It was a certificate of exemption from military service. This was a vital document which had only just been introduced by the Bolsheviks. Every male of military age had to have one – even Paul's certificate stating that he was a member of the Cheka would not be enough to excuse him. The Finnish border guards had not been able to forge one as they had not yet seen an example and Paul knew that if he was stopped on the street without one he could be in serious trouble.

The exemption certificate was signed by the relevant commissar, but the name of the bearer was blank. Once again Zorinsky appeared to have pulled off a miracle. He said that he already possessed one so Paul was welcome to this. He also said that he obtained them from a friend of his who was a doctor who had acquired them when two patients didn't arrive for their exemption examination. Zorinsky offered Paul a pen and suggested that he sign the form at once.

It was then that Paul realised he was trapped.

He had carefully concealed his operational name, the name that was on his passport and other forged papers, from Zorinsky. But now he was caught – he must either write his new operational name down so that it matched his other papers, right here on the desk where Zorinsky could see it, or he could refuse and Zorinsky would know that the game had come to an end. Zorinsky would probably pass his name and details to the Cheka within the hour. The bounty for an English spy would be very high.

Zorinsky lolled in his rocking chair, watching Paul's hesitation with interest. Paul later confessed that he suddenly felt 'an intense and overpowering repugnance' for this man who was controlling him so easily.

Paul decided he had no choice. He sat at the desk and carefully wrote his new operational name, 'Joseph Krylenko', trying to match the handwriting to that already on the form. For a moment he thought he was in the clear, but Zorinsky glanced at the form and pointed to the line below. There was a space next to the abbreviation *zan,* which stood for the Russian word *zaniatia* – occupation. Paul tried to pretend to Zorinsky that he had no occupation and should leave it blank. But Zorinsky was not falling for that story for a moment. He told Paul to put whatever it said on his passport. Once again, Paul knew that he had no choice. In every respect the exemption form must match the new 'Krylenko' passport that the Finnish guards had recently forged for him. He took the passport from his pocket and wrote on the form that he was an officer of the Extraordinary Commission, the Cheka. He also wrote down his age from his passport: 36, six years older than his real age. He noted the reason for the medical exemption with bitter amusement: 'incurable heart trouble' – exactly the diagnosis that had prevented him from serving in the British army in 1914.

Standing over him, Zorinsky picked up the Cheka passport and examined it. He admired the quality of the forgery and then turned over the single dog-eared sheet of paper, looking for the registration of the bearer's address which should have been on the back. But that requirement was a very recent regulation and Paul's passport did not have it. Disappointed, Zorinsky handed it back.

And then, finally, as if he had now disposed of all the other business he wished to deal with in this meeting, Zorinsky turned to the subject that Paul had been trying to raise all evening: the rescue of Melnikov. Zorinsky said that unfortunately the investigator was now asking for the whole sum of sixty thousand roubles in advance. When Paul asked what guarantee there would be that the investigator would carry out his side of the bargain Zorinsky barely bothered to look up from the copy of *Pravda* he was reading:

'Guarantee? None,' he replied.

Paul had little choice if he wanted to save his friend. He considered asking the Policeman to look into the case but, having risked his neck to save Mrs Merritt, Paul knew that he dared not start asking questions about another of Cromie's former contacts. Reluctantly, Paul agreed to bring the money the next day.

Paul spent the night at Zorinsky's flat so that he could finish copying the map of the minefields, confident that Zorinsky would not betray him as long as there was the prospect of another thirty thousand roubles to be delivered. Paul was angry. He knew that he was being played for a fool. Zorinsky was not only older than him but clearly much more experienced. But the intelligence that Zorinsky had provided so far had been top-notch according to Major Scale and if this map of the minefield also turned out to be genuine then the risk Paul was running was well worth it. Other than the money for Melnikov's release, Zorinsky did not even ask for much, just a few thousand roubles for expenses now and again. If he really was trying to squeeze Paul dry then he could easily have asked for ten times what he was actually getting for the intelligence he was providing.

As he lay in bed thinking, Paul turned the exemption paper over and over in his hands. This paper had increased Zorinsky's control over him, but what could he do about it? He had to have one if he was to move on the streets safely. Paul decided to fold the certificate a few times so that it would not look brand new. It was as he did this that the paper separated into two pieces. Paul realised that this was not one exemption form, but two! Whoever had torn this from the pad had accidentally taken two papers that were stuck together and not even Zorinsky had noticed. Naturally, the second printed form was blank and had not been signed by the commissar, but the signature would be the work of moments to copy. Paul now had the chance to create a totally new identity about which Zorinsky would know nothing. But where could he get such an identity?

Paul went to sleep turning the problem over in his mind, but by the morning he was no nearer a solution. The trouble was that whatever identity he created would need all the other supporting papers to go with it and he had no means of forging those, nor a contact who could supply them. It was an issue he would have to shelve for the moment. All that he had resolved was to try and track down Melnikov's uncle at the hospital on the other side of the city. Melnikov had trusted him enough to stay with him and had spoken of him in terms which led Paul to believe that he knew something of Melnikov's work. With Melnikov in prison Paul needed to follow up any lead which might guide him to his friend's underground contacts.

Three weeks later, at 10.30 a.m. on Sunday, 25 January 1919, Paul was sitting in the flat belonging to Melnikov's uncle at one end of Kamenostrovsky Prospekt, just a short walk along the road from the hospital. Over the course of the previous three weeks, this man had become a firm friend, but their first meeting had not been auspicious. When Paul had arrived at the hospital and found the uncle's office, the man had at first denied all knowledge of Melnikov's activities. He certainly denied that Melnikov had told him about any Englishman. Paul had expected this. The man's nephew had just been arrested by the Cheka. What would be more natural than to send round an agent provocateur to see if they could trick him into admitting that they knew of his counter-revolutionary activities? Paul continued to insist that he was a British agent and told the uncle all about Melnikov drinking every drop of whisky before they set out from Finland. That one small detail seemed to finally tip the scales and convinced Melnikov's uncle that this ruffian on the other side of the desk must be the real thing.

Over the next few weeks Paul had come to trust the old man more and more. Like Paul he had initially been a supporter of the Revolution and like Paul he was now convinced that it had lost its way. Paul told the uncle all about the meetings with Zorinsky and valued his opinion on whether Zorinsky was telling the truth. On this morning in January, Paul was complaining about how Zorinsky had accepted the balance of thirty thousand roubles but they were no nearer to Melnikov's release. Every time Paul raised the subject Zorinsky would claim that it would just be another few days or that his contact was away from the city for a while.

Melnikov's uncle asked a few simple questions about Zorinsky. For instance, was he demanding a lot of money? Paul replied that

Zorinsky rarely asked for anything except a few expenses and some money to support Melnikov's sister . . .

Melnikov's uncle pounced: Melnikov had no sister.

This was the first time that Paul had caught Zorinsky in an outright lie. No wonder he could work so cheaply – he was taking all the escape money for himself. Melnikov's uncle pointed out that Paul had better go on paying for this non-existent sister unless he wanted to alert Zorinsky. But Paul's greatest worry was what all this meant for the chances of Melnikov's rescue. Was he being lied to about that as well? He decided that he would have to use the Policeman to find out what was really happening to Melnikov. It would take several weeks for the informant to come up with an answer and in the meantime Melnikov's uncle promised to see what he could do about procuring a new passport for Paul. One of Melnikov's contacts, someone named 'Shura', might be able to help.

Just a few days later Paul called to see the uncle again and found a brand new passport waiting for him. It was in the name of Alexander Vasilievitch Markov, who was a 33-year-old clerical assistant at the main Post and Telegraph Office in Petrograd. The real Alexander Markov had been sent to Petrograd from Moscow on temporary duty, but because his wife had fallen sick he had returned to Moscow after just one week and the mysterious 'Shura' had purchased the Petrograd passport from him. Markov would simply tell the authorities in Moscow that he had lost it. Paul used the uncle's typewriter to change the name on the form to 'Markovitch' and then filled in the blank exemption form to tally with his new identity. The Markovitch passport would be valid until the end of May 1919. Paul hoped that his mission would be over by then and if it wasn't then at least he had plenty of time to deal with the problem.

In the meantime, Paul had committed another foolish mistake, one which could probably be attributed to his lack of training as an agent by MI6. It is strange how many espionage operations are brought down by the most mundane of details, but whilst Paul had brought a great deal of money with him into Russia he was desperately short of clothes, especially underwear (this was long before the days when 'going commando' was thought to be an option for a respectable gentleman – or even a secret agent). He was also constantly changing his appearance but the sort of articles he wore a lot of – such as hats and jackets – were in short supply in the

Petrograd second-hand markets. He borrowed as much as he could from contacts but all the time he kept thinking about his own clothes, which were still locked away at his flat.

Eventually Paul could resist the temptation no longer and broke every rule in the book by returning there. It was very likely that someone in the building would report the presence of a stranger to the Cheka. Fortunately, it seems that his current disguise of long hair and shaggy beard was so successful that even his own housekeeper did not recognise him and it was only with great reluctance that she accepted a letter from 'Mr Dukes' stating that this Alexander Markovitch was an old friend who should be given every assistance.

When he was finally admitted, Paul found that he had taken the risk almost in vain. The flat had already been ransacked both by the Cheka and a family of peasants who had used it as a squat for several weeks. All the good clothes had been taken and those that had been left behind had been ripped to shreds. Paul did find some of his underclothes, but it was a poor return for such a risk. It seems strange to think that the entire operation almost came to grief just so that Paul could have a pair of pants.

Another risk that Paul took was to contact one of his old friends who was still living in the city. In the middle of January he had lost Maria, Merritt's old housekeeper, when she had returned to the countryside. She told Paul that he could still use the flat, but a young stable boy from Merritt's former farm outside Petrograd came to live there in place of Maria and although the lad was honest he was not very bright. Paul could not be sure that the youngster would not make some stupid comment which would give him, Paul, away.

And then, at the beginning of February, Paul also lost the flat occupied by Stepanova, Ivan Sergeivitch's housekeeper. Her nephew Dmitri had already been transferred with his regiment to another city, which meant that she was always short of food. One day Paul made his usual telephone call to check that it was safe to visit the flat. He asked Stepanova if her father was well – this was done in case the line was being monitored by the Cheka. This time Stepanova said that her father was ill, in fact he was probably dying. This was the signal that something was badly wrong. A few hours later Paul met Stepanova in Kazan Cathedral, their emergency rendezvous.

It turned out that Varia, the nanny, had become involved with sending messages to Finland. Eventually a man arrived who said he had come from Ivan Sergeivitch and that she should return with him to Finland, bringing some things for Ivan's wife. Varia had left with the man and the next thing Stepanova had heard about her was that she was in the hands of the Cheka. Apparently Varia and her companion had gone to the Finland Station where they had been supposed to meet a man who would get them out of the country. But somewhere on the journey the Cheka were waiting for them: the three of them had been ambushed and arrested. Stepanova could not find out what was going to happen to Varia, but she had been told that the two men were going to be shot. It was only a matter of time before the Cheka raided the flat. It might already be under surveillance. Varia might even have been tortured and told the Cheka of the mysterious Englishman who often stayed there. Stepanova insisted that Paul must never risk returning to the flat again. He agreed. Paul did try to find out what had happened to Varia, but because of all the difficulties in getting information about the Cheka's activities he never managed it. He never saw Varia or Stepanova again.

With Zorinsky appearing to be less and less trustworthy and Paul's safe houses disappearing one by one, Paul desperately needed somewhere else to go. Unfortunately MI6's network in the city had been so poor that there were no new contacts who were suitable. Once again Paul was thrown back on his own untrained resources. He decided, against all the rules of espionage, that the time had come to contact an old friend. She was a pretty young English governess, Laura Ann Cade.

Paul had known Laura from his earliest days in the city when they had both been members of the St Petersburg Guild of English Teachers, a social club for tutors and governesses. The Guild organised parties and staged plays and reviews. Teaching work had dried up since the Bolsheviks had taken control of the city, but Laura Cade still occupied the same spacious flat where her English school was based, together with a rather fat female servant known to one and all as 'the Elephant'.

Paul telephoned to make sure that Laura was still at the flat, but replaced the receiver as soon as she answered in case the line was being monitored. Unfortunately this scared the life out of Laura because she thought it must be the Cheka who were calling. She very nearly refused to let Paul into the flat when he arrived in his ruffian-like disguise. However, once he had convinced her who he was he

was allowed in and, as he had suspected, she was happy to take part
in his cloak-and-dagger activities. She agreed to store his reports,
hidden between the pages of old textbooks, at the flat. There were
hundreds of these books in the disused classrooms and it was
unlikely that the Cheka would have the patience to go through
them. Paul also found in one of the classrooms a hole in the wall
that he thought would make a good hiding place for larger items
such as disguises. Because the apartment housing the school was
quite large and consisted of several rooms, Laura warned Paul that
she was sometimes forced to have Red Guards billeted there for
several days at a time. This was a danger, but Paul could also see it
as an advantage – the Cheka would be far less likely to search a
place that was used regularly by the Red Army. Even so, Laura and
Paul decided that it was best to arrange a recognition signal: she
would place a flowerpot in a certain window if it was safe to come
up to the flat. If it was not there, Paul would know that the Red
Guards were in residence.

With Laura Cade's combined apartment and school and one or
two other places found for him by Melnikov's uncle and the
Policeman (who, despite his rather repulsive character, Paul was
beginning to trust more and more) Paul soon had a new set of safe
houses that he could use. However, he still followed Melnikov's rule
of never spending more than two nights in the same place – in fact,
no more than one if at all possible.

Paul was managing to get a fairly steady stream of intelligence out
of the country. He sent the reports out in two batches, using two
different couriers. One of them did not return: he was a well-known
White sympathiser and the risk for him was too great. But the other
courier, a former army NCO and law student whom Paul contacted
through Melnikov's marvellous uncle, turned out to be the best of
the lot: Peter Sokolov. Peter went out to Finland and returned. But,
disappointingly for Paul, whoever had enciphered the message in
Helsinki had made a mistake and the message from MI6 was undecipherable. So Paul asked Peter to return again that very night. He
went, but never returned. Now Paul was without any means at all
of contacting MI6. He had no idea what he was expected to do next.
He was also running dangerously short of funds. Most of the money
he had brought with him had been spent either in paying the balance
for Melnikov's release or in supporting the owners of his various
safe houses.

But then, on 10 February, came the greatest blow of all. The Policeman finally returned with news about Melnikov. The information had been some time in coming because Paul had been careful not to express too much interest in the case lest the Policeman should string him along as Zorinsky had done. Now, when he called the Policeman, he was told that there was news about a 'family member'. This was the code phrase for news about Melnikov. Paul hurried to the Policeman's flat.

At first the Policeman was confused. He checked Melnikov's real name with Paul. Paul confirmed it.

'He was shot by the Cheka between 15 and 20 January,' said the Policeman, reading from a strip of paper.

Zorinsky had been lying all along.

Paul was still not sure what to do now. Although this news might have seemed damning there was still the fact that most of Zorinsky's intelligence had been genuine. Paul had even managed to verify the map of the Kronstadt minefields with one of Cromie's old agents at the Russian Admiralty. The map had been so well guarded that the agent had not been able to take it away, but he had seen it and from map references given to him by Paul he confirmed that Zorinsky's map was genuine. Paul thought long and hard. If Zorinsky was a Cheka agent why had he given Paul a genuine map? Why not a forged one which the British navy would use – and thus run their ships onto the mines? And just because Zorinsky had strung Paul along about Melnikov did not mean that the man was a Cheka agent. It was only natural that Zorinsky should try and get as much money from the relationship as possible.

And yet . . .

Paul decided to wait a little longer. He had enough money for perhaps two more weeks. He would get what intelligence he could from Zorinsky and his other contacts and then make a run for it. Peter Sokolov had told him of a new route across the border: by pony sleigh over the frozen waters of the Gulf. He had given Paul the name of a smuggler who would make the run – provided he was well paid.

But once again Paul was forced to change his plans. Before he even saw Zorinsky again, Melnikov's uncle asked to see him. Like Paul he had long been suspicious of Zorinsky and he had also been checking with Melnikov's old friends to see what they knew. It was the mysterious Shura who came up with the answer: he confirmed that Zorinsky was working for the Cheka.

On its own this was not enough – after all, the Policeman worked with the Cheka, but he was reliable. Paul was not so naive as to believe that someone who could provide intelligence as good as that provided by Zorinsky would have clean hands. But together with the other information – the way that people whom Zorinsky knew seemed to end up in the hands of the Cheka, the money for Melnikov's non-existent sister, the death of Melnikov – this news made Paul's mind up. It was time to leave. The only way he could continue to work in the city was if he got out of the country, threw Zorinsky off his trail and then returned with a new identity and new resources.

The next night Paul gathered the last of his reports from the hiding place at Laura Cade's academy and headed for the remote suburb where Peter's smuggler contact lived. The area was known as Staraya Derevnya – the Old Village. It was right at the mouth of the river Neva. In summer it was busy with holidaymakers and the exertions of lumber yards dealing with timber brought down the river. But in winter it was a desolate place. The heavy snow meant that it was impossible to tell where the shore ended and the frozen sea began and the flat featureless expanse was swept by bitterly cold northern winds. Peter's smuggler contact owned a tiny wooden hut on the very edge of the shore. With a small pony and sleigh he was able to travel out across the ice and make the journey of a few hours to the coast of Finland to collect black-market goods. Paul was lucky. The smuggler, who was actually Finnish, had just smuggled a load of butter into the city. Now he was about to make the return journey. Since he was going anyway it did not take much persuasion to allow Paul to ride with him on the sleigh.

They set off just after midnight. Overall, the distance was about 40 miles because they needed to give the shore a wide berth. The journey should take between four and five hours. Conditions were clear, no snow was falling. This would make their progress faster, but on the other hand they would be easier for the patrols to see. Paul snuggled down in the hay in the back of the sleigh and prepared himself for the long ride. The smuggler twitched the reins and the sleigh set off.

Once they were out on the sea ice the sleigh soon picked up speed. The ice was surprisingly flat and because the layer of snow on the surface was frozen solid there was good traction for the pony's hooves. Even so the ride was not without risk. The sea ice was not absolutely level and twice they hit ice ridges that capsized the sleigh completely. The Finnish smuggler was unperturbed and seemed to accept this as a normal hazard of the journey. It was simply a matter of righting the sleigh, loading everything back on and setting off again – as long as no one had broken their neck . . .

In the silence and darkness the whine of the sleigh blades cutting through the ice was surprisingly loud and Paul eyed the coastline nervously. It seemed to him that the smuggler was steering far too close to it, but, as if sensing Paul's concern, the man pointed to the massive silhouette of Kronstadt fortress where it sat in the middle of the Gulf. Powerful searchlights played out from the battlements of the fortress and the risk of being caught in the beam of one of those was far greater than the chance of being heard by a patrol on shore.

Even so, as they drew abreast of the fortress Paul peered intently at the coastline. The searchlight flicked past them once or twice and illuminated the shore for just a moment. This was Lissy Nos, the narrowest point of the strait. Paul estimated that they were now a mile away from the coast, maybe less, and he was amused by the way that at this distance the waving tops of the pine-forest trees looked like the sabres of charging cavalry.

Then it dawned on him that the 'trees' *were* charging cavalry!

Paul sat upright and thumped the smuggler hard on the back. The old man looked round and immediately saw the half-dozen horsemen who were riding down on them. He gave a moan and lashed the pony. The sleigh leapt forward.

'Ten thousand marks if we escape!' bellowed Paul into his ear, but the smuggler did not need any encouragement. They both knew that these were Russian Bolshevik troops and that the penalty for speculators was death.

Paul pulled a small revolver from his pocket. He looked back. The riders were gaining fast. He raised his pistol to take a shot, but it was impossible because the sleigh was bouncing around over the ice. It was all he could do to stop himself being thrown off, let alone aim.

There was a crack and a zing as a bullet narrowly missed Paul's head. Then another and another. Paul could clearly see the flashes coming from the rifles of the riders. They were good shots, possibly Cossacks. At the sound of the shots the smuggler's nerve seemed to fail him and the sleigh began to slow up. Paul immediately held the revolver to the man's head and shouted that he would blow his brains out if he did not keep going. With another heartfelt groan the smuggler lashed the poor pony harder and the sleigh leapt forward again. Another bullet fizzed past so close that Paul had to throw himself flat in the hay. The riders were almost upon them. And then disaster struck. The sleigh hit an ice ridge, slewed sideways, crashed into another ice ridge and came abruptly to a complete stop.

Paul did not hesitate for a second. He threw himself off the sleigh and pounded away across the ice. He had only one chance now. The horsemen would be more intent on looting the sleigh than chasing one lone fugitive – at least for a while. It was pitch black and he might get away in the darkness. As he ran he reached into the pockets of his overcoat and pulled out a package, ready to fling it across the ice. It contained all his secret dispatches for Cumming in London. He knew he was dead anyway if they caught him, but he was damned if they were going to get the reports as well. Glancing back, he saw that some of the riders had dismounted to search the sleigh and arrest the driver, but he knew that at any moment they would remount and be after him.

Paul ran on. Then, to his horror, he heard hoofbeats closing in again. He kept running and running, his lungs burning with the effort, knowing that at any moment there would be one last shot and the whole adventure would finally be over.

The hoofbeats grew louder. They must be right on top of him. He looked around wildly for cover, but the view was flat and barren in all directions, just mile upon mile of sea ice, great patches of dark grey and black.

Black!

Paul threw himself flat and at the same time sent the package skittering across the ice, trying to remember the direction it went in so that he could find it later. He lay there gasping as quietly as possible, dragging freezing air into his aching lungs. His gloved hands were over his head, his eyes shut tight like those of a child hiding under a blanket from imaginary monsters.

The hoofbeats clattered up alongside his head and horses skidded to a stop all around him. There were shouted orders. The horses trotted backwards and forwards, stamping and snorting heavily in the cold night air. Paul waited and waited, but still the final shot did not come. He risked a quick glance. Some of the hooves were almost close enough to touch, but the horses seemed keen to avoid the slippery black sea ice and kept shying away to the grey areas where a thin layer of snow gave them firm footing.

There were more barked orders. They were in Russian but the dialect was hard to understand. After a minute or so of peering into the darkness, the riders galloped on. Moment by moment the sound of their hooves drew further and further away. Beneath him, Paul could hear the sea rumbling and gurgling under the covering of thick ice like a distant underground train. He waited and waited until there was silence. Eventually the intense cold and sheer curiosity forced Paul to push himself up on his elbows and look cautiously around.

There was nothing to be seen in any direction: the horsemen, the sleigh, the driver – all had disappeared. Paul was alone on the ice with the distant searchlights of Kronstadt as the only sign of life. Brushing himself down, he walked over to where his document package lay. He picked it up and stuffed it back into his pocket. He then tried to judge his location from the position of the Kronstadt fortress on one side of him and the dark line of the coast on the other. Then he looked at his watch: it was half past one. He estimated that the sleigh had travelled less than halfway before they had been caught. He had a very long walk ahead of him, perhaps six hours or more in freezing conditions. But there was nothing for it. He pulled his overcoat tighter around himself and trudged on.

Paul later described the walk across the ice that night as the hardest journey he had ever had to make. The sea ice was slippery and he skidded or stumbled almost every step of the way. In addition he had not realised how tired he was from the nervous strain of living undercover – half-sleeping each night, waking at the slightest sound in case it was the Cheka. Soon he was at the point of exhaustion. He had to stop frequently to rest, peering ahead through the gloom, but the coast of Finland seemed no nearer.

At one point as he was resting he heard footsteps approaching across the ice. Repeating the trick he had learned when fleeing from the cavalry, Paul threw himself onto a patch of the black sea ice and lay completely still. The footsteps grew louder and shortly afterwards the silhouette of a figure passed just a few metres away. Someone was hurrying in the opposite direction, towards Petrograd. Paul never found out who this was or what they were doing. Once the footsteps had receded safely into the distance, he moved on.

It was dawn before Paul finished his journey. He wanted to make sure that he was in Finnish territory, but he did not have a map or compass so he decided to keep going until he was absolutely certain. It would not do to be picked up by a Russian patrol just when he was so close to getting away. At last he saw a signpost on the shore in Finnish and he knew that he had made it. This stretch of the journey had taken him almost eight hours instead of the three it would have taken by sleigh. He staggered forward into the trees that lined the shore and started to make his way through the pine forest which came right down to the shoreline. Even though he had no map, he reckoned that if he stayed within sight of the shore he should reach a town eventually and he could ask for directions from there. But he was so tired that he soon gave up. He collapsed out of the wind in the lee of a fisherman's hut and promptly fell asleep.

Paul dreamed that someone was barking harsh orders in a foreign language and opened his eyes to find two Finnish soldiers armed with rifles standing over him. They prodded him with their bayonets and demanded that he put his hands up. Paul protested that he was an English officer, not a Russian refugee, but with his long hair and ragged clothes they refused to believe him. He was marched at bayonet point to the nearest coastguard station where he was stripped of all his belongings and thrown into a cell. A few hours later he was marched several miles further inland to the border fortress at Terrioki. In February 1919 this was not under the command of the kindly Sarin but of an unnamed German officer. Many German officers working under General Mannerheim had assisted Finnish forces during the civil war against the Bolsheviks and had stayed on after the war was won. Following Germany's recent defeat by Britain and the Allied Powers this officer was not well disposed towards Paul. He took away all his money and papers, but finally allowed him to ring the British Consul-General in Helsinki. As soon as Henry Bell heard that Paul was being held at Terrioki, he arranged for him to be transferred to the British Consulate immediately. Paul was finally safe. He slept for a day and a half.

Bell sent a message to Stockholm and it was an indication of Paul's growing importance that this time Major Scale came to Helsinki to see him. Apparently Paul's other courier had never reached Finland so half his reports had been lost. Paul spent the next few days recreating these from memory and also decoding the other notes he had brought with him. They were everything that Cumming could have hoped for. Not only was Paul reporting on naval and military movements but he was able to produce complete sets of top-secret minutes from within the Petrograd Soviet. Even today, intelligence-service analysts acknowledge that these reports were better than any intelligence that MI6 had ever produced before. When reaction to them arrived from London, Scale impressed upon Paul just how valuable they were. Other than interviews with Russian refugees, the British government had no way of knowing what was happening inside the Bolshevik state. And then Scale asked the obvious question: would Paul go back again?

Paul later confessed that the excitement of working undercover had got to him. It had become a passion and he actually could not wait to go back. He was suffering from a problem common among operational officers: he was hooked on the adrenalin high of having his life in constant danger. The most important issue was: how was he to get out if he had to? He had barely made it this time and the land border was now almost impassable. The same problem would apply to his couriers. There was no point sending him back into Russia if he could not get the intelligence out.

Major Scale was honest: he had no answer to that question. All he could do was give Paul his absolute assurance that 'very special measures' would be taken to solve the problem and that MI6 would make his safe return their top priority. There was nothing that Paul could do. He would just have to take their word for it. He wondered what that might be worth?

Within a week he was on his way into Bolshevik Russia for the third and last time.

Paul lay in Michael Semashko's tomb, coughing and occasionally swatting at the endless, relentless mosquitoes. They had even managed to crawl inside the scarf wrapped around his head. In the distance he could hear naval gunfire. It seemed that the long-threatened revolt by Kronstadt and Krasnaya Gorka had happened at last. Very special measures indeed! Well, he had found out what the word of MI6 was worth. Peter Sokolov was the last of the couriers and he had worked wonders keeping Paul's dispatches moving across the border for the past four months. But each journey had been more dangerous than the last and he had failed to return from the last journey, so presumably the Bolsheviks had finally got him. He had been a brave man. But now Paul was trapped. The money had run out, the last safe house had gone. As he lay there in the dark he reckoned that he had only a few days left before his health gave in completely. Then he would face the choice: the revolver in his pocket or a last desperate attempt to get away – which would almost certainly mean arrest, torture and death. A peaceful end at his own hand seemed like the better option.

Dawn finally crept into the sky above the cemetery: the curfew was over. Paul clambered slowly and painfully out of the tomb. He staggered away down the road which led into Petrograd.

Just one last time . . .

9

Too late the hero

Peter Sokolov recovered quickly, but he was clearly so cold and exhausted that the crew had let him rest during the journey back from Petrograd. Because they had waited until the very last moment for him it was now 1.30 a.m. and almost daylight. Gus told John Hampsheir to fix the Commissar's flag to the staff at the rear of the boat. It then took a considerable test of nerve to reduce speed and cruise between the forts at about twelve knots as though they had every right to be there. Gus kept one hand on the throttle ready to make a run for it if they were challenged, but once again the forts were silent as they cruised though the gap selected by Veroline.

Gus had planned to sail out to Tolboukin lighthouse from where he could take another look at the battlecruisers shelling Krasnaya Gorka, but there was no time for that now. The most important thing was to get Peter and his precious messages back to Terrioki as quickly as possible.

Once Peter was safely back at Broadbent's villa in Terrioki, he was wrapped in blankets and given hot cocoa. Everyone gathered round to hear the story of how he had found ST-25 and, more importantly, why ST-25 was not coming out.

Peter had rowed the pram into the safety of the reeds which lined the shore of Krestovsky Island, made it secure and covered it over with vegetation. He picked out a particular tree as a landmark so that he would be able to find it 48 hours later. He was very careful – there were plenty of patrols in the area and he might need to find it in a hurry. Then, checking that his pistol was loaded and still dry, he had set off south towards the road which led into Petrograd. He had hardly travelled more than a mile when there was a shout in Russian, ordering him to stop. He never saw the patrol but had instantly plunged away into the undergrowth, keeping as low as possible. There had been a shot and he had thrown himself full length in the tall grass, but there were no sounds of pursuit. He lay still for some time, but heard nothing else and eventually stood up. At well over six feet tall, it was not easy for a man like Peter to remain inconspicuous, but all seemed quiet now so he pushed on towards the main road.

He headed for a set of rooms on Vasili Island, an apartment which had belonged to him when he'd been a law student before the Revolution and which he still rented. He had used it on his other runs into Petrograd to see Paul, but each time he'd had to check carefully before entering the building in case the Cheka were lying in wait for him. But everything seemed safe: his 'tells', objects left in certain positions around the room, had not been moved and there was a thick layer of dust over everything. Peter rested there for a few hours and then around noon he set off for the gardens of the Winter Palace. Paul had told him that this would be the fall-back contact point if they ever became separated for a long period. He would try and be there between midday and one o'clock each day. The gardens were an excellent choice: there were a large number of exits and entrances and the place was always full of people hanging around with nothing to do but listen to the dozens of public speakers who harangued the crowds from every possible vantage point. In such a busy and open area it would be hard for the Cheka to monitor any particular individual.

Peter wandered through the gardens for some time, looking for Paul but watching for any Cheka stooges as well. He knew that Paul would probably have changed his appearance, but although he saw several possible suspects none of them was him. The hour was nearly up and Peter was standing pretending to listen to a factory leader from one of the Soviets when he felt a tug at his sleeve.

He turned and looked down (everyone in Petrograd was shorter than Peter) at an old man in unkempt clothes and the dirtiest fur cap he had ever seen. The old man mumbled something and Peter thought he was begging for some money. He shrugged the old man off, only to feel a tug at his sleeve again. Once more he looked down and was shocked to realise that he was staring straight into the grimy but grinning face of Paul Dukes! Peter was horrified by the change in Paul's condition in just six weeks – his eyes were sunken, his cheekbones could be seen through his skin and he had a dreadful

pallor. But before Peter could say anything Paul had limped off
through the trees. Peter waited for a few seconds and then wandered
in the same direction, casually glancing around to see if anyone was
paying undue attention. He followed Paul to a secluded and
enclosed part of the gardens where he found him slumped on a stone
bench.

Peter sat down next to him, but instead of the warm greeting he
expected Paul immediately asked to see his papers. Peter handed
them over and Paul quickly sorted through them, checking the dates
and stamps. The untrained undercover officer of a year before was
now a consummate professional. He knew that the greatest danger
to them at that moment was that they would be approached by a
Chekist patrol and asked for their papers. The stamps were being
changed regularly these days, particularly for those who were pretending to be soldiers on leave as Peter was. If Peter's papers were
not up to scratch then they would both be arrested.

Next, Paul asked if he had brought money. Peter handed Paul a
thick package wrapped in brown paper. Paul held the package for a
moment and Peter was shocked to see that there were tears in his
eyes. Then Paul shoved the package inside his own grubby black
leather jacket. Money was the next most important thing in case
they were suddenly split up and had to make a run for it. Only then
did Paul embrace Peter and demand to know how on earth he had
got back into the city.

Peter's explanation was very confused. He told Paul that when
he had arrived in Helsinki on his last run across the border a man
called 'Lemay' had told him that he must wait before going back.
Paul had no idea who Lemay was, but it was clear that Peter did
not have a very high opinion of him. Weeks had passed, but every
time Peter asked about leaving he was told to wait a little longer.
And then a man had arrived in a wonderful craft which looked like
a boat, but which flew. Peter described it as being like 'a
monstrous bird'. The description was so confused that at first Paul
assumed it must be some sort of aircraft – such as a seaplane. Peter
described how this craft, driven by a man called 'Captain Eggar',
flew over the water at incredible speeds and had brought him all
the way to Petrograd without the need to cross the border. The
same craft would be ready tomorrow night to take both of them
out of the city again to safety. Peter then emphasised that this
would be the last chance to get away as after this the White Nights

would make it impossible for Eggar to return until late July or early August.

Paul was clearly sorely tempted by this offer, but he told Peter that there were people in prison whom he must rescue before he could leave. There were also some valuable contacts he had only just met and it would take time to prepare them to work for the British before he left. Things had been bad – he told Peter how he had been sleeping rough for several nights – but now, with the money that Peter had brought him, he thought he could survive for another four weeks.

Gus had prepared for this possibility. Peter gave the British agent a small slip of paper from 'Captain Eggar' which listed three dates in late July when the mystery machine would be able to pick him up. Paul promised to do his best to be there.

The two men spoke for several hours, with Peter relaying various messages from MI6 as well as the latest news from outside Russia. Then they left, Paul for the cemetery, Peter for his old student rooms, but travelling most of the way together. It might seem that Peter had the best of the deal, but he did not sleep much that night. He had used these rooms for a very long time and he did not know whether someone in the building might have given him away. He lay awake most of the night, clutching his revolver and listening for the slightest creak on the stairs which might give him some warning of the Cheka's arrival.

The next day the two men met in the gardens once again so that Peter could collect the various intelligence reports that had been stacking up since his last visit and which Paul had hidden away. Then Peter would make his own journey back to meet the CMB later that night.

The journey had been uneventful, though in order to avoid the curfew Peter had set out for Krestovsky Island in good time. But he had not realised how heavily the shore was patrolled. Time and again he had to turn back or skirt around a roadblock. At one stage he had to lie up in the reeds for half an hour as he edged past a Chekist outpost. Lying half in the water he had become soaked through and was soon very cold. His hands became so cramped that he could barely use the signal torch when he finally arrived at the rendezvous. If the situation did not improve, he doubted that Paul would be able to make the rendezvous in one month's time.

By now it was three in the morning and the party broke up to get some sleep. The only sound was the steady boom of the guns of the Soviet battlecruisers pounding the fortress of Krasnaya Gorka. The garrison there was apparently still holding out. Gus stood at his window and watched the flashes in the night sky. He had managed to get word to ST-25 and that work was finished for at least a month. But now, as he watched the horizon, he wondered if he could save the garrison of Krasnaya Gorka as well.

The next morning, Gus and the CMB crews moved to a new residence, the Villa Sakharov. Gus had rented it because Broadbent's villa was just too far away from the harbour and he wanted to be able to keep watch over the boats and any suspicious activity by the Finns at the yacht club. The cost was 3,600 marks a month (which, Gus noted in his diary, was 'pretty ruinous') but the villa had its own tennis court and came complete with a burly female housekeeper so it was a fairly comfortable choice. The housekeeper had a blonde-haired eight-year-old daughter who was always hanging around and the crew soon adopted her. A few days later Sindall produced a boxer dog called 'Dinah' from somewhere and then a variety of Russian refugee families who were billeted at neighbouring villas began to call. As a base of secret operations, the Villa Sakharov was quite lively.

To top it all, on that very first day the French military attaché from Helsinki called to see the operation. Clearly something was very wrong with MI6's operational security in the Finnish capital. Gus and his crews were as welcoming as possible, although they hid Peter away upstairs and stuck carefully to the story that this was simply an advance post for Admiral Cowan's forces. But with their lack of uniforms (still stored on the boats as per Cumming's instructions) and general lack of order, they certainly did not look like a crack unit of the Royal Navy.

During the morning Gus visited the local fort to see Commandant Sarin again. The local troops were still causing problems, hanging around, being nosy and now the villagers had refused to loan the British any boats to get stores to and from the CMBs. Sarin apologised profusely and promised that he would sort it out. Together the two men walked the mile or so to the tower of the little Russian Orthodox Church behind the village.

From there they could just make out the battlecruisers still pounding the Krasnaya Gorka fortress, Gus using his favourite telescope, Sarin a pair of binoculars. After a lull, the bombardment had recommenced at eleven o'clock that morning. The resounding boom of the guns echoed around the Gulf. Gus said that it was a shame to watch Russians killing each other. Sarin explained that the garrison of the fort were not Russians but Ingrians. Ingria was a region on the coast of northern Estonia. These people were not just fighting the Bolsheviks, they were fighting for their independence. Sarin lamented the fact that Cowan could not move in and destroy the battlecruisers or force them back into Kronstadt. He speculated that to prevent their families being taken as hostage many of the Ingrians would have moved their wives and children inside the fortress before the revolt began. In a strange echo of the last stand at the Alamo in Texas, the Ingrians had risen believing that they only had to hold the fortress for a few days before the White army under Yudenitch would arrive to save them. But, as with the Alamo, help was not coming. The leaders of the White armies, aristocrats and Tsarist snobs to a man, wanted the old Russia back and for them this meant the Russian empire complete with all its subject peoples. They had no interest in helping Ingrian nationalists.

Sarin pointed out that if the fortress fell, then all those women and children who had not already been killed in the bombardment would surely be executed. It was all so short-sighted of the British and the Whites. The intelligence that Sarin was receiving from interviews with refugees held in the quarantine camp was that the garrison of Kronstadt was considering whether to join with Krasnaya Gorka and if Kronstadt fell to the Whites the Bolsheviks could not hold Petrograd. And if they could not hold Petrograd, they could not hold Russia. In Sarin's opinion, he and Gus were watching not just the fate of one fortress as they stood on the church tower, they were watching the fate of the entire Bolshevik revolution. The Ingrians could hold out for one day under the ferocity of such a bombardment, maybe for two, but not more.

Gus tried to explain to Sarin yet again that it was not Admiral Cowan's fault. The minefields made it impossible for the British squadron to attack and, even if they did the guns of Kronstadt, the sea fortresses and the Russian armoured battlecruisers would destroy the lightly armed British cruisers before they could engage. It would be a massacre. But he did not tell Sarin something else: he still had one hope. He had sent a telegram to Cumming in London asking for permission to attack the Russian battleships. He had explained the vital balance of the current position and said that if his two CMBs could sink or even just damage one of the battlecruisers then he was sure that they would be forced to return to Kronstadt and the Krasnaya Gorka fortress would be saved.

But he was to be bitterly disappointed. Around midday, Hall appeared with Cumming's reply. It was curt and undeniably clear:

TAKE NO OFFENSIVE WITHOUT DIRECT INSTRUCTIONS FROM SNO BALTIC STOP

Cumming knew that Admiral Cowan would not order Gus to attack without secret-service support and in any case there was no time now to consult Admiral Cowan all the way over at Biorko Sound.

Gus listened to the guns on the far side of the Gulf. The White flag was still flying. He could not bear the thought of all those people trapped there, unable to fight back, just waiting for the end. And to know that the fate of Kronstadt hung on this revolt as well! What was the point of the CMBs being here if they couldn't be used for offensive action? Cumming was a fool.

All through lunch he turned the problem over in his mind. The repeated sound of the guns, easily audible wherever he walked in Terrioki, kept emphasising over and over again that something *had* to be done. These people could not just be left to their fate. Gus decided there was one last chance: it was possible that both CMBs might be destroyed in the attack and Cumming was obviously afraid that this would endanger the link with ST-25. Fine. But they could not make a run to Petrograd for another month because of the White Nights. Even if he and Sindall were killed that still left plenty of time to send two more boats from Osea. Now that he had shown there was a safe passage through the forts, the Admiralty could hardly object.

Gus knew that Hall and Broadbent had a radio at their dacha. From there they could contact Le May at Viborg and then a message could be relayed via Helsinki and Stockholm directly to Cumming in London. Gus ran all the way to the dacha and hastily dictated a second telegram. He emphasised the desperation of the situation. He explained that more boats could be sent. Finally he let Cumming know that if permission were given he could attack across the minefields that night.

Now all he could do was wait. He told Sindall to prepare both CMBs for launch that evening. Knowing that the courier runs were over, Sindall looked confused but he did not question his commander's orders.

The rest of the afternoon passed slowly. Gus confided in Sindall and asked what he thought of the problem. Young and impetuous as ever, 'Sinbad' was all for taking the boats out and damning Admiralty orders. Hall and Broadbent already knew what Gus wanted to do. Broadbent did not express an opinion, but Hall disapproved strongly. As far as he was concerned the CMBs had been sent to work for MI6 and that did not include waltzing off on glory trips. Gus ignored him. He had already formed a pretty damning opinion of Hall's worth. It did not matter anyway. Everything hung on Cumming's reply.

The telegram arrived late that evening:

ADMIRALTY DOES NOT APPROVE OF ANY FURTHER BOATS BEING SENT STOP YOU MUST DO THE BEST YOU CAN WITH THE MATERIAL AT YOUR DISPOSAL STOP BOATS SHOULD NOT BE USED FOR ANY OTHER BUT INTELLIGENCE WORK STOP

So that was it. His orders were clear.

And yet . . .

Gus felt sure that if he attacked the Soviet battlecruisers, he would have Cowan's support. The Admiral's parting words – 'Always choose the boldest course!' – kept coming back to him.

He reread Cumming's telegram. He handed it back to Hall.

'Get the crews together,' he told Sindall. 'We're going out.'

As soon as Gus said those words the pressure lifted. The decision was made – now all that remained was action. Damn Hall, damn Cumming and damn MI6! If they could not realise what was happening out here then he would disobey his orders and go it alone.

And it would be either death or the end of his career if he failed.

Down in the little harbour Piper and Beeley had already fired up the CMB engines using the compressed air pumps. The covers were off the Lewis guns, all crew members were wearing their uniform caps and the white ensign was flying from both boats. Shortly before 11 p.m., as soon as it was as dark as they could hope for, the two CMBs chugged slowly out of the harbour mouth and then picked up speed in line astern as Gus changed course to the south-west. His plan was to travel in a wide circle away from the battlecruisers and then sail along the southern coast of the Gulf right under the guns of Krasnaya Gorka. This would keep the CMBs away from the protecting screen of destroyers and make them less likely to be seen against the darkness of the coastline. Gus also calculated that the Russians would be less likely to expect an attack from the south and afterwards the CMBs would have a straight run at maximum speed back north to Terrioki. With only two torpedoes they did not have much of a chance, but Gus decided he could maximise that chance if they concentrated both torpedoes on the *Petropavlovsk*: she was the more heavily armed of the two. If he could cripple or sink her, then the Bolshevik fleet would be more likely to withdraw.

The guns were silent now. As on previous nights they might open up for a few rounds to continue the war of nerves on those trapped inside the fortress, but otherwise they would wait for full daylight before continuing the attack. This meant that there would be no cover for the tremendous noise of the CMB engines as they approached and Gus made sure that they gave the Russian ships a very wide berth as they swung across the Gulf.

They had been travelling at a steady speed for almost half an hour and the southern coast was clearly visible ahead when Gus felt John Hampsheir tap him on the shoulder. Gus looked back and saw that CMB7 had dropped far behind and was now almost invisible in the distance. He swung CMB4 about and headed straight for them. CMB7 was dead in the water. All three men looked pretty shaken.

They had struck some kind of obstruction, almost certainly a loose mine. By rights Sindall and his crew should have been dead. It was no wonder they looked shocked. This mine had not exploded but it had smashed something on the bottom of the boat, almost certainly the propeller shaft. The engine was still running, but they were getting no forward momentum at all.

It was dreadfully cruel luck. The odds against a small boat hitting a loose mine in the middle of the Gulf were astronomic. But there was nothing for it. Gus could not leave them stranded out at sea. The attack would have to be abandoned and CMB7 towed back to Terrioki. Gus reflected grimly that at least his career was safe for another day.

It was 3.30 a.m. but already daylight by the time they limped back into harbour. Piper immediately stripped off and dived overboard to inspect the damage. He confirmed that the propeller shaft was smashed clean through. There was also a gash in the hull and CMB7 was steadily shipping water. They had no spare propeller shaft, not even at Helsinki, although one was being shipped from England sometime in the next few weeks. There was nothing they could do. Gus sent the crews to get some sleep.

Later that morning Gus wrote in his diary that Ed Sindall was '. . . heartbroken as he is so keen to do a bit' and then added: 'If only he was more solid and paid more attention to details and spade work and treated his boat less like a motor car plus chauffeur complete. But then I suppose we all have our failings.'

Gus rolled over and tried to get some sleep but a few hours later he was back in the church tower, watching the battlecruisers through his telescope. It was now Tuesday, 17 June. Commandant Sarin was already there. They had both been disturbed by the same thing. The bombardment had not restarted at its usual time that morning and each of them was wondering what the Bolsheviks were up to. They could see that both the battlecruisers were under way and together with their escort of destroyers were making the short journey back into Kronstadt military harbour. But the White flag was still flying over Krasnaya Gorka, so what was going on? Had the sailors of Kronstadt finally risen in support? If this was a reprieve for the fortress it seemed too good to be true.

An hour later the answer became clear. The same force of four destroyers which had guarded the *Petropavlovsk* and the *Andrei Pervozvanni* during the bombardment escorted the powerful armoured cruiser *Oleg* out of port. She displaced 6,645 tons, had a crew of 565 and was armed with 12 six-inch guns – more than enough to finish the job. Other than the two battlecruisers she was the largest warship in the Russian fleet. The *Oleg* was soon taking up a position to recommence the bombardment and in the early afternoon the pounding of the fortress started once again.

Once more Gus spent an afternoon of anguish wondering where his duty lay. Yesterday he had been prepared to risk everything by attacking with two boats. If he attacked tonight he would only have one. There was almost no chance with just one torpedo. Even if he made it through the destroyer screen without being detected and launched his torpedo, half the time the underwater missiles did not strike what they were aimed at. Why should he risk the lives of his men and his entire career on such a dreadfully slim chance? His orders from London, both from the Admiralty and C, were clear: he *must not* attack. The Navy was all he had known since he had joined as a young cadet. Even if he returned from such a mission he would be dismissed from the service in disgrace, his whole career thrown away.

But having disobeyed his orders the day before, this time the choice was strangely easier. If there was only one chance that the lives of those in the fort could be saved then Gus felt that he was honour bound to take it. If he stood here and let those people die, then what kind of man was he?

That night CMB4 set off from the little harbour again. On board were Gus, Hugh Beeley and John Hampsheir. It was just before eleven p.m. and fully dark. There was no sound from the direction of the *Oleg*. She had shelled Krasnaya Gorka for about four hours and had then ceased fire some time before 7 p.m. But Gus had seen from the church tower that she was still there and he was still determined to do what he could, either to sink her or force her back into Kronstadt. Everything seemed to be urging him to return. Weather conditions were far worse than on the previous day. A southerly wind had sprung up at about 9 p.m. and, blowing across the current in the Gulf, it created a choppy sea. It was not enough to slow CMB4 down, but it made for a rough ride and the boat threw up so much spray that it was hard for Gus to see where they were going. Soon all three men were soaked to the skin.

Once more they circled around and attacked from the south to give themselves the clearest run, but they would still have to penetrate the destroyer screen. Gus eased the engines back to dead slow and they began to edge forward between two of the destroyers, keeping watch all the time for a small motor patrol boat which was cruising in the area. The destroyers drew closer until they were only two hundred metres away on either side. Ahead the distinctive three funnels of the *Oleg* could be seen against the pale night sky. Gus whispered to John Hampsheir to get ready for the attack run. This meant removing the safety pins from both the torpedo and the cartridge that fired the launching ram.

Keeping his eyes trained on the destroyers, ready to throw open the throttle at the slightest indication that they had been seen, Gus was vaguely aware of Hampsheir climbing onto the forward deck of the CMB. It had taken them fifteen minutes to creep this far through the destroyers. They were almost there. Out of the corner of his eye Gus saw Hampsheir come back to the cockpit.

Still there was no sign that they had been seen. Suddenly there was a muffled bang and CMB4 shook hard through her whole length. Gus looked around wildly, wondering what had happened – it did not feel like an explosion, more as though they had run aground. But CMB4 was still moving freely.

John Hampsheir grabbed Gus by the shoulder. There was panic on his face. He crouched down and hissed at Gus to turn back – the cordite charge for the launching ram had fired prematurely. It had almost taken his hand off and now there was no way of launching the torpedo. Gus looked behind. The torpedo was still there. The metal stops which held it securely in the trough had prevented the torpedo from launching when the ram had fired. But surely the hydraulic ram must have been damaged?

Beeley had rushed up from the engine compartment at the sound of the explosion. Their stares met. If the ram would still fire then there was a spare charge in the boat which was kept in case the original cartridge became soaked and refused to fire. But replacing it would be a tricky job and they could both see that Hampsheir was badly shaken. Also, the boat was still pitching heavily in the rough seas. Gus was grateful that the noise of the explosion had been muffled due to it having been enclosed in the cartridge chamber. Even so, every ship in the Russian fleet must now have lookouts on deck – how much longer did they have before they were spotted? If he had any sense they would make a run for it now while they still had a chance.

'Set a new charge,' ordered Gus, reducing the engine's revolutions until it was barely idling.

'You hold her steady sir. I'll help Mr Hampsheir,' said Beeley, clambering into the cockpit.

Keeping low in the darkness of the cockpit, Beeley could not see what had happened to make the charge fire, but he could guess. The safety pin in the cartridge was no more than a small T-shaped piece of metal. In order to help remove it the pin was usually attached to a length of brightly coloured lanyard. But if whoever was priming the charge yanked too hard on that lanyard it was apt to come away in their hand, leaving the pin still in the charge. Feeling around on the floor of the cockpit compartment Beeley found a pair of pliers. He guessed that Hampsheir must have accidentally pulled the lanyard off and had then tried to remove the tiny pin using the pliers. It must have been the devil's own job trying to get a purchase on that slippery piece of metal in these rough seas. When Hampsheir had succeeded he must have given a hard tug and somehow struck the lever which set the cartridge off. They were lucky that they had not all been killed. The stops were down, preventing the torpedo from launching. It could well have blown up under the pressure from the ram. It was the sort of accident that could have happened to anyone – but no wonder Hampsheir was shaken.

Using a screwdriver, Beeley prised the remains of the cartridge out of the chamber and then, using only his sense of touch, he cleared the chamber and checked for any damage to the mechanism. It still seemed strange to him that the stops had held against the power of the hydraulic ram. Reaching around, he found that the union nut connecting a copper tube to a piece of the mechanism known as the explosion bottle had worked loose. That was why the pressure had not been enough to launch the torpedo. Beeley shook his head in amazement at their luck. John Hampsheir had actually done them a favour: if they had committed to the attack run and tried to fire the torpedo, the ram would probably have failed. Now they had a chance to fix it. Using the pliers Beeley tightened the nut. The rest of the mechanism felt as if it was OK. The arm of the ram might have been warped by the pressure and if so it would jam next time. They would just have to take a chance.

Hampsheir had fetched the new cartridge and now he helped Beeley to lower it into position. The job only took a little over five minutes, but for Gus, standing in the cockpit with nothing to do but watch the silhouettes of Russian warships all around him, this brief delay seemed to last an eternity.

Finally Beeley tapped Gus on the shoulder.

'All clear, sir,' whispered Beeley. 'Let's go'.

Gus slowly eased the engine back into life and they crept forward once again. They could not afford to start the attack run too soon because the noise of the engine would wake every sailor in the entire Bolshevik fleet, but he had to judge the distance precisely so that there was enough distance for CMB4 to reach launch speed and release the torpedo at the right point. In the darkness and the heavy spray it was an almost impossible task. For another ten minutes they continued to creep forward until Gus decided this was about as close as they could expect to get.

'OK – this is it!' he shouted and threw the throttle wide open.

Immediately the stern of CMB4 was thrust down into the water and her nose rose. Gus fought to correct the CMB's natural desire to swing to the right and then corrected her course, aiming for the funnels of the *Oleg* which was about all he could see against the night sky. Next to him John Hampsheir crouched low over the fairing, holding a stop watch. As first officer it was his job to time the run of the torpedo.

The CMB's engine noise immediately alerted the Russians. The first Soviet destroyer opened fire with surprising speed. It was as though they had been waiting for CMB4 to make her run. The first shot went wild over their heads and landed about one hundred metres away. Gus stuck grimly to his course, watching the funnels of the *Oleg* grow steadily larger. Hampsheir bellowed the revolution count into his ear. There was no other accurate way of judging their speed and the right moment to launch.

Tracer fire lit the sky above their heads. Over the roar of the Thornycroft engine they could not hear it but they knew that they had been spotted now. Another fountain of spray directly ahead showed them where another shell had struck. Gus took CMB4 straight through the churned-up sea water.

'One thousand rpm!' bellowed Hampsheir.

At this point they were about nine hundred metres from the *Oleg* and now she too was opening fire. The first shell from her guns whistled over their heads. That was close enough. Gus pulled the toggle which fired the cartridge and there was a loud hiss behind them as three-quarters of a ton of eighteen-inch torpedo slid smoothly out of the trough. It was precisely three minutes past midnight.

Gus immediately put the helm hard over to the right and the *Oleg* disappeared behind a wall of spray as CMB4, freed of the weight of the torpedo, accelerated and fought to stay in the water. Leaping from wavetop to wavetop, Gus took the boat almost in a full circle. He headed west for home. Next to him John Hampsheir was shouting out the time every ten seconds. There was no point in manning the Lewis guns – they were being thrown about so violently that there was no way he could have hit anything.

'Thirty seconds . . . Forty seconds . . . Fifty seconds . . .'

They had missed! The torpedo should have struck by now. The sea was erupting all around them and it seemed to Gus that every vessel in the Soviet Baltic fleet was firing at them as they raced for a gap between two of the destroyers. He threw CMB4 violently from side to side as he tried to make them as difficult a target as possible. But some of the shells detonated as close as ten metres away, throwing great cascades of water across the boat.

Above the roar of the engine they felt rather than heard the tremendous explosion behind them. There was a brilliant flash which lit up the entire night sky and, glancing behind them, Gus had a brief vision of a column of thick smoke billowing into the air just behind the *Oleg*'s foremost funnel. Her sirens wailed as she immediately began to keel over.

CMB4 broke out of the Russians' defensive circle, but the warships were still firing and now the sea fortresses had joined in with their massive guns, even though there was no way they could have seen what they were shooting at from this distance. Gus felt himself being slapped on the back and looked round. Although he could not hear anything, both Beeley and Hampsheir were standing alongside him in the cockpit, laughing and cheering as they were thrown about. Hampsheir threw his cap into the air and it disappeared over the side in the slipstream. Even though they were still being shot at, Gus laughed with them.

CMB4 was in range for another five minutes, but the firing was very erratic and soon seemed to go in all directions as if the Russians were not sure what they were shooting at. Gradually the shellfire fell further and further behind. Gus was sure they could not be seen any more. He watched the compass and kept them on a bearing north for Biorko Sound. The brief night was over and it was almost full daylight now – he wanted anyone who saw them to think that the attack had been launched by Cowan's squadron rather than from a secret base. When they were within sight of the coast he turned east and they headed for Terrioki.

At the harbour mouth Piper and Sindall were standing on the wall, waving and cheering. Even from Terrioki they had heard the explosion and in the early light of dawn a column of thick acrid smoke on the horizon marked the spot where the *Oleg* had been struck. Hall and Broadbent were nowhere to be seen. But the victory had not been without cost. John Hampsheir had collapsed during the journey home and he had to be helped from CMB4 into the skiff. He had been vomiting and Gus had thought this was due to seasickness from the very rough ride in the choppy conditions. But now Hampsheir was shaking all over and it was clear that something very serious was wrong. Gus asked Sindall and Marshall to take Hampsheir to their dacha. He glanced at his watch. It was still only 12.50 a.m.

Leaving the others to look after the boat, Gus went straight to Broadbent's dacha. He sent two signals, one to Cumming in London via Stockholm, the other to Admiral Cowan at Biorko: 'Have attacked *Oleg* and have hit her.' He did not dare to hope that he had sunk an armoured cruiser with just one shot, but hitting her was good enough. He then wrote a quick report about the attack while the details were fresh in his mind. Then he returned to the 'Villa Sakharov' where the three men who had taken part in the attack posed for a photograph on a bench outside. Hampsheir looked as though he barely registered being there.

At 3.30 a.m. Gus finally clambered into bed but was too excited to sleep. He scribbled a long letter to his beloved 'Dor' about how his last thoughts before they had started the attack run had been of her. And then, eventually, there was just time to scribble one last note in his diary: 'Hope all the decent sailors were taken off by the destroyers.' He finished by writing: 'What a life!' Minutes later he was asleep.

By next morning it was clear that Hampsheir needed professional medical care, but he refused to be sent home. He insisted that he would be fine in a day or so. Gus knew how much it meant to him to be with his comrades and did not have the heart to send him away. They would not be making another courier run for at least a month. He hoped that with plenty of rest John Hampsheir would have recovered by then.

Gus had planned to tow CMB7 back to Biorko for repairs, but the weather had continued to deteriorate overnight and the journey would clearly have to wait at least until the next day. Gus was just wondering what to do about the problem of reporting to Admiral Cowan (chiefly to explain why he had disobeyed orders) when a summons arrived from Commandant Sarin. Together with Broadbent as an interpreter, Gus strode off from the dacha for what he guessed might be a difficult meeting.

He was right. Sarin was confused and extremely angry. Gus had never told him that the CMBs were armed with torpedoes and the Finnish guards had never seen them because the troughs at the rear of the boats had been covered with tarpaulins. The sound of the guns firing at CMB4 had been audible right across the Gulf, news of the disappearance of the *Oleg* had already spread and it was clear from reports by Sarin's shore patrols that Gus and his boats were somehow behind it. He demanded to know what was going on.

Gus explained about the torpedoes and gave a brief outline of the attack. Sarin was astonished that such a small boat could launch an assault but, like Admiral Cowan, he was absolutely appalled at the idea that Gus had carried out this attack while pretending to be a civilian. It was against every rule of war. Gus then had to explain about the uniforms and the white ensigns. When he'd attacked he had done so not as a civilian but as an officer of the Royal Navy (although even as he said it he had his fingers tightly crossed that Admiral Cowan would back him up on this ...) Sarin's next worry was that it would not take Bolshevik spies long to find out that Terrioki was the base for the CMBs. Didn't Gus know that Russia had seaplanes based at Orienbaum and could launch a bombing raid within minutes? Some of the closer sea forts could even bombard Terrioki directly. He was putting the lives of everyone in the area at risk.

Gus took some time to explain that the CMBs were the only weapon that could drive the Russian battleships back into their port. He had broken none of the rules of war and, whilst he apologised to Sarin for any deception, he had only misled the commandant because of the need for absolute secrecy. Hadn't Sarin himself asked why the British would not save Krasnaya Gorka? That was why they had attacked.

Gus's little speech must have worked because when he had finished Sarin came around the desk, embraced him and said something that Gus did not understand but which was obviously meant sincerely. Broadbent later told Gus that it was a saying in Russian about being in the presence of a very brave man and that if he could ever do anything to help Gus could rely on him. However, as the meeting broke up Sarin also suggested to Gus that it would be a good idea to take his boats out of Terrioki for a while in case the planes came looking for them. Since CMB7 needed to be towed to Biorko for repairs anyway, Gus was quite happy to agree.

All that afternoon Gus and members of the crew watched from the church tower, eager to see what the results of the night's work had been. Of the *Oleg* and her destroyers there was no sign. They could just make out Krasnaya Gorka. Worryingly, the White flag was no longer flying there but there was no sign of a Red flag either. Instead, there was just a haze of smoke as if many fires were burning. Gus didn't know whether his gamble had paid off or not.

The next day, Thursday, 19 June, dawned fine. Gus was none too sure what sort of welcome awaited them so they did not set off until three o'clock in the afternoon and arrived at Biorko Sound at about 7.45 p.m. To the astonishment of all of them, the entire squadron was waiting. As they eased past the outlying destroyers they could see that the rails along the decks of every vessel in the Sound were lined with sailors. Warships began to sound their klaxons and crews waved their caps in celebration. As they passed each ship in turn the little boats were given three resounding cheers. By the time they were tying up alongside HMS *Dragon* it was all Gus could do to keep the tears from his eyes. In all his time in the Royal Navy he had never seen such a reception.

That evening Gus was invited to dine with Admiral Cowan on the flagship HMS *Cleopatra*. Champagne was served and Cowan insisted on hearing every little detail of the attack. Slightly embarrassed, Gus stressed that he still did not know if they had actually sunk the *Oleg*, but Cowan told him not to worry and that he would wait for confirmation before claiming too much at the Admiralty. Gus had been dreading the meeting, knowing that everything hung on whether or not the Admiral backed his defiance of Cumming's order. He need not have worried. Cowan understood the courage this act had taken and when he heard how the first attack had failed his admiration grew. Cowan told Gus that he could forget whatever MI6, the Foreign Office or even the Admiralty said – he, Cowan, would tell them that the attack had had his full support right from the outset (even if he hadn't known about it, he added with a twinkle in his eye).

This was just as well because the reaction in Whitehall was highly negative. Labour Party politicians who were strongly pro-Soviet claimed that Gus's actions had destroyed any hope of ever reaching a peaceful accommodation with the Bolsheviks, MI6 was outraged that their explicit orders had been defied and the Foreign Office complained that months of patient diplomacy had been undermined. The Bolsheviks had turned the attack into a propaganda victory, claiming that they had been attacked by the entire British fleet which had been forced to retreat before the Bolshevik navy's heroic defence and the sacrifice of the valiant *Oleg*. Only the British press received the news of the attack with approval. If it had not been for Cowan's backing Gus would have been in a very tight spot indeed. He remained deeply grateful to Cowan for the rest of his life.

But something else happened at the dinner. Cowan told Gus that the principal value of the attack was in letting the Bolsheviks know that the British squadron now had a 'sting' and that they were not afraid to use it. Even so, the *Petropavovsk* and the *Andrei Pervozvanni* remained afloat and the newly independent Baltic states would never be sure of their freedom as long as the warships remained to threaten their coasts. Yes, the attack on the *Oleg* had been audacious, but Cowan wondered: if Gus were provided with a dozen or so more CMBs, could he repeat it? Could he do what he had offered to do at their very first meeting and hit the Bolshevik navy at its very heart in Kronstadt harbour?

At first Gus was stunned – it seemed impossible. Kronstadt was the most strongly defended harbour in the world and within its narrow confines the CMBs would lose their greatest advantage: speed. He knew that the harbour was enclosed on every side apart from a narrow entrance and that it was ringed with artillery and machine guns. The flimsy CMBs would truly be like fish in a barrel.

But the more the two men and Cowan's flag captain, Commander Clark, discussed the proposal, the more interesting it became. After all, the CMBs had originally been created for just this sort of raid. If the Great War had not ended in November 1918 they would have been used to attack the German High Seas Fleet at Wilhelmshaven, so why not Kronstadt? Still, there was the problem of the Russian guns. None of them could see the way around that particular problem, but they agreed to think about it and reconvene in a few days' time for a planning session.

The next day, Friday, 20 June, CMB4 returned to Terrioki with Hampsheir and Beeley, under the command of Ed Sindall. Gus remained in Biorko at Admiral Cowan's suggestion. As has been noted the attack on the *Oleg*, launched from Finnish territory, had caused quite a storm. Gus was expected to go to Helsinki to brief the Consul-General and representatives of the Finnish naval staff. Then Cowan recommended that he should travel to Reval where General Gough was currently staying. HMS *Vanity* would be leaving for Helsinki and Reval the following day.

Gus spent the rest of the day making arrangements with the Finnish naval liaison officer, Lieutenant Foch, to have CMB7's damaged propeller shaft repaired in the naval dockyard at Helsinki. He then travelled to the nearby Finnish seaplane base at Fort Ino. Arrangements had been made for him to take a flight to inspect the site of the attack on the *Oleg* and confirm her fate.

Gus's pilot was actually a Swede, Arthur Reichel. Gus mentioned that as well as looking at the *Oleg* he hoped to be able to get a look at the Kronstadt naval base. The Finnish commandant in charge of the squadron said that sadly they were forbidden to fly over Kronstadt because it was Russian territory and the Kronstadt anti-aircraft batteries were known to be disturbingly accurate. Then he smiled and said that, on the other hand, if Reichel's compass was out a few degrees and they accidentally flew over Kronstadt he could hardly be blamed for such a basic navigational error ...

Gus climbed into the front seat of the aircraft and, together with another seaplane flying as escort, they set off south for the *Oleg*'s last known position. At six o'clock that evening Reichel descended to 2,000 feet and there they could see the wreck of the great ship lying on its side in just six fathoms of water. Parts of her superstructure were breaking the surface. Gus later described it as looking like 'a great dead whale' and his first reaction was not one of triumph but of revulsion that he had caused the death of so many men. But then Reichel turned south for a look at Krasnaya Gorka and Gus's feelings changed. As he had seen from the church tower, the White flag was no longer flying. Now in its place flew not one but *three* Red flags. And so, even after all that he and his team had risked, the fortress had fallen. It had all been for nothing.

Gus learned later that he had sunk the *Oleg* only a few agonising hours too late. The garrison of Krasnaya Gorka had held out against the initial bombardment, but when the *Oleg* opened up on the afternoon of 17 June she very quickly smashed a final breach in the weakened defences. There was no way of holding the defence and the garrison had surrendered that evening hoping for mercy – once they had destroyed the locks of the fortress's great guns, thus rendering them useless. But they were not to receive any leniency. Gus was later told how the survivors, including the women and children, were lined up in pits and machine-gunned. Many of them were not killed by the Bolshevik bullets but were buried alive. It was every bit as horrific as he had imagined. The man who commanded the assault on Krasnaya Gorka was a then relatively unknown Bolshevik leader. His name was Josef Stalin.

Gus was still pondering matters when he realised that Reichel had taken them within sight of Kronstadt. For the first time Gus was able to get a complete view of the sea fortresses and understood how they linked to form a defensive line. He also saw the heavy defences of the port itself. The harbour guns commanded every vantage point. It did not seem possible that a CMB would survive longer than a few moments if it tried to attack that target.

Gus had much to think about as they turned for Finland once again. Then the engine of the aircraft suddenly cut out and despite his best efforts Reichel was unable to start it. Reichel put the plane into a shallow glide. He signalled to the second aircraft that they would not be able to make it back to Finland and that he was going to have to ditch in the sea. Since this was a seaplane it was not quite the problem it might have been. As a pilot himself, Gus was not unduly worried: aircraft engines were as unreliable as the engines of CMBs and during his training he had suffered several problems like this himself. On the other hand, he had never had to make a forced landing at sea before. It promised to be . . . interesting.

He need not have worried. Reichel was an excellent pilot and put the aircraft down smoothly in the water just a few hundred metres from the shore at Stirs Point. The second aircraft landed in the sea a short distance away and taxied over to them. Reichel invited Gus to hop across from the float of one aircraft to the other so that he could fly home. Reichel stayed with his aircraft and waited for a boat to come and tow him to shore where they would make repairs.

Gus made his way back to Biorko Sound, but it took a long time and it was well past midnight when he arrived at the flagship. Admiral Cowan was already in bed. Even so, he insisted on sitting up in his cabin to hear the news that the *Oleg* had definitely been sunk. As for Krasnaya Gorka, Cowan told Gus not to worry – he doubted that the Whites could have held the fortress for long even if the attack on the *Oleg* had been in time.

Gus also gave Admiral Cowan his opinion of the Kronstadt defences, particularly the number of guns. Cowan acknowledged that it sounded like a tough nut to crack, but he had already enquired about the availability of more CMBs and still thought it was worth considering further. As Gus was leaving, Admiral Cowan told him, informally, that he had recommended him for the Victoria Cross.

The next day Gus travelled with Marshall and Piper in the destroyer HMS *Vanity*, which was going to tow CMB7 to Helsinki for repairs. They set out at 9 a.m. but even before he left Gus received worrying news from Terrioki. Apparently Raleigh Le May had arrived from Helsinki with Harold Hall. They had told Sindall that they intended to send Peter Sokolov back into Petrograd that very evening. Gus sent a strongly worded telegram back to Terrioki telling them to wait as it was far too light now to attempt the run. He then sent another telegram to Mansfield Cumming in London summing up the current position:

1 BOAT OUT OF ACTION STOP 3 WEEKS TO REPAIR STOP REQUEST 2 MORE BOATS STOP 1 SPARE ENGINE, 1 MORE CREW STOP OLEG SUNK STOP OCCUPATION OF PETROGRAD BY ALLIES THOUGHT IMMINENT END.

Gus wanted to achieve several things with this telegram. In the first place, he thought that Cumming had overestimated the capabilities of the CMBs and that more resources were needed if the courier system was to be reopened in late July. He also wanted to let Cumming know that his disobedience to orders had been worthwhile and, in the last line, to give the very pressing reason for that disobedience: that the situation in the Baltic was now very delicately balanced. But if he had hoped for understanding from Cumming on any of these points he was to be sorely disappointed.

The tow to Helsinki took almost 24 hours because HMS *Vanity* had to crawl along to avoid swamping CMB7, which was still leaking badly. At eight o'clock on the Sunday morning they finally crawled into the harbour. Gus left Marshall and Piper to arrange the repairs and immediately went to the Consulate to see Henry Bell, the Consul-General. He also met Raleigh Le May's new and enthusiastic young assistant whose surname, he thought, was 'Card'. Gus contacted Le May at Terrioki for a second time and told him to wait to make any decision about a run through the forts until he returned on Monday. Le May said he would. Le May lied.

Later that day, HMS *Vanity* made the short run across the Gulf to Reval where Gus hoped to be able to brief General Hubert Gough. He was disappointed in this and for the first time encountered the professional jealousy which Victoria Cross winners sometimes have to endure.

Upon arriving in Reval, Gus asked for General Gough, but was instead directed to his naval intelligence officer, Captain C. W.

Bruton. Commander Goff at the Admiralty in London had privately warned Gus about Bruton before he had left. One of the reasons Bruton had been sent to the Baltic as an 'advisor' had been to get him out of the way. He had an exaggerated sense of his own importance and as the man responsible for naval intelligence in the Baltic he was likely to feel that MI6 had no business nosing around in his area without referring to him first. Goff warned Gus that, as a young naval officer under MI6 orders, he might find himself particularly unpopular. So Gus was prepared for a difficult meeting. What he did not know was that news of the sinking of the *Oleg* and Gus's recommendation for the Victoria Cross had already reached Bruton. Who was not pleased.

Despite Goff's warning, Gus at least expected the meeting to start with polite congratulations. Instead, Bruton immediately laid into Gus, saying that he had received numerous complaints from Raleigh Le May that Gus had been uncooperative, had caused friction and that he had kept a very important courier for Petrograd waiting for over a week and a half with no good excuse. What, demanded Bruton, did Gus have to say for himself?

Gus was caught completely off balance. He realised that Bruton must be referring to the delay while CMB4 was repaired. Gus protested, quite honestly, that Le May had never complained to him and that the delay for essential repairs had been agreed by MI6. But Bruton persisted with his accusations and the tone of the conversation very quickly turned nasty as Gus unwisely retorted that, in any case, he was very surprised that Le May would discuss secret intelligence matters with 'a third party'.

Bruton was livid. As a senior officer he took great exception to the term 'third party' and demanded that Gus withdraw the phrase. Gus would not. Then, in a scene straight out of a Patrick O'Brien novel, Bruton coldly reminded Gus that he was a mere lieutenant talking to a post captain and that he would soon learn damned well that it did not do for mere lieutenants to get on the wrong side of post captains!

Still Gus refused to back down. He countered that he might only be a 'mere lieutenant' but he was under orders of a 'very particular department' in London so he had nothing to fear from a post captain, one who, he noted, was only a post captain working in a staff position (a clear gibe that Bruton had not been entrusted with a ship).

And so it went on. At increasing volume, Bruton said that Gus's 'particular department' was only part of the NID and therefore Gus came under his orders. As the senior NID officer in the area he demanded that Gus tell him everything, including what his orders were. Gus refused. Bruton then changed tack and pretended that it did not matter anyway as he knew what Gus's orders were. Besides, he continued, he had been warned about Gus and given very particular instructions about him. Gus knew that this was a lie and a pretty poor one at that. He shot back that he too had been warned and had been given very particular instructions about Bruton.

Gus did not record how the meeting ended, but the upshot was that Gus did not get to see General Gough. It is hard to know who Gus was more angry with: Bruton for his attitude or himself for allowing the situation to escalate out of control. 'Pompous ass,' he wrote that night, 'I think he will work tooth and nail to get me placed under his orders, but sooner than do that I will take the boats home ... Wish I had never set eyes on this blooming evil genius. Why the devil can't he mind his own business and let people alone as I feel that if there is going to be any misunderstanding it is entirely due to him and no one else.'

Bruton had seemed disturbingly sure of himself when he claimed that MI6 was unhappy, and at Helsinki Gus had been unable to get any information at all out of young 'Card'. It seemed very suspicious and Gus now began to worry about what was happening at Terrioki during his absence. As soon as he arrived back at Biorko Sound, he borrowed a car from the commander of the Finnish squadron he had flown with a few days before and drove at breakneck speed to the base at Terrioki. He radioed ahead to say that he was coming and when he arrived at 2 a.m. on Monday, 23 June he found Ed Sindall and Peter Sokolov waiting for him. From the looks on their faces he could immediately tell that something was very wrong.

Apparently Raleigh Le May had arrived at Terrioki on Saturday, 21 June. He had been full of energy and had told Sindall to prepare to take Peter into Petrograd that night. Ed Sindall knew as well as anyone that it was now far too light to take a boat through the forts, but Le May, backed by Hall, seemed determined that they would go anyway. When Sindall asked what Gus had said about this Le May sidestepped the question and reminded Sindall that both he and Gus were under MI6 orders and MI6 would make the

Captain Augustus Agar: '…the last of the Edwardian gentlemen.
If he said a thing would be done, then it would be done.'

A typical street scene in Petrograd before the famine began to take hold showing the sort of horse-drawn sleigh in which Paul Dukes helped Mrs Merritt escape from No. 2 Gorohovaya.

A soldier working for the Cheka forces his way in through a window during a house search.

Recently arrested suspects are marched under guard through the streets of Petrograd.

A suspect is stopped and searched in a Petrograd street. It was just this sort of random detention that John Merritt had to fight his way out of.

The frozen bodies of victims of the Cheka. These people were from Omsk. In all 4,000 bodies were found. All had been tortured before they were executed. Every day of his mission, Paul Dukes knew that this was the fate awaiting him if he were caught.

Midshipman John Hampsheir, whose bravery was possibly all the greater because he was struggling against a nervous breakdown.

Sub-Lieutenant Edgar Sindall, Agar's buccaneering second-in-command who eventually joined MI6.

Midshipman Richard Marshall, the team's crack shot who refused to be left behind despite the prospect of overwhelming odds.

Chief Motor Mechanic 'Faithful' Hugh Beele the mechanical genius of the team in a self-portr using a mechanism that he had designed himse

CMBs on their storage racks at Osea Island. From front to rear the versions are: 55-ft, 40-ft, 70-ft, 40-ft, 55-ft and 55-ft. The 40-ft version used by Gus Agar seems tiny when compared with the 55-ft version used on the Kronstadt Raid.

The engine compartment of a CMB. This was the cramped space in which Beeley had to work on every mission, often in complete darkness.

The layout of a 40-ft CMB. Note the cables running to the rudder wheel at the left rear of the boat. It was one of these cables which was severed by shell splinters during Agar's last rescue attempt. There are petrol drums in the torpedo trough.

CMB4 and CMB7 on tow behind HMS *Voyager* en route to Biorko Sound. Eventually the cables snapped, both boats were swamped and the seawater ruined CMB4's delicate engine.

The view aft from a 40-ft CMB. The wheel at the top of the rudder post is on the right clearly showing the steering cables which were shot through on Agar's last mission.

Hugh Beeley (*left*), Chief Motor Mechanic
Albert Piper (*centre*) and Vic Jones (*right*)
relax after a swim at Terrioki.

Villa Sakharov, the team's
base at Terrioki.

Dinah, the team mascot.

The daughter of the housekeeper
at the Villa Sakharov who was
unofficially adopted by the team.

...d Sindall rendering assistance to a 'distressed'
...ussian refugee at Terrioki.

John Hampsheir (*left*) in the only known
photograph of MI6 officer Raleigh Le May
(*right*), the man who destroyed Hampsheir's
health and tried to have Agar dismissed.

The MI6 radio operators Vic Jones
(*left*) and John Busby (*right*).

The Russian Orthodox Church
at Terrioki showing the tower
from which Agar and Commandant
Sarin watched naval movements
around Kronstadt.

The courier and ex-prize fighter Gefter in a typically arrogant pose.

The gentle giant: Peter Sokolov. Agar's friend and Dukes's saviour.

Peter Sokolov (*second from left*) in the Russian football team at the 1912 Olympics.

A desperate race against time. The team play deck quoits aboard the *Fennia*.

The team victorious: Beeley (*left*), Agar (*centre*) and Hampsheir (*right*) photographed outside the Villa Sakharov just hours after their successful attack on the *Oleg*. Capless, Hampsheir already shows signs of the mental breakdown he was struggling against.

A shot of the armoured cruiser *Oleg* illustrating her formidable array of armament.

An aerial view of Kronstadt Harbour taken shortly before the Raid.

Y: 1. *Petropavlovsk* 2. *Andrei Pervozvanni* 3. *Pamiat Azova* 4. *Gavriil* (possibly)
Hospital ship 6. Military harbour 7. Dry dock

HMS *Vindictive* with her improvised flight deck and six of her complement of aircraft, their wings folded. Two 55-ft CMBs are tethered aft and the smaller CMB7 is tethered alongside.

Bill Bremner arrives at Biorko Sound with CMB79 in preparation for the Kronstadt Raid.

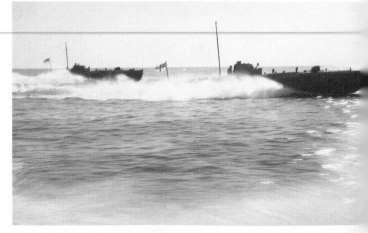

Two 55-ft CMBs reach attack speed.

Richard Marshall setting up CMB4's Lewis guns on the roof of the old Yacht Club the day after Russian planes bombed the secret base at Terrioki.

A close run thing: the almost completely submerged wreck of CMB7 at Terrioki after the team's miraculous final voyage.

1967. After almost fifty years at Platt's Eyot, a weather-beaten CMB4 is taken to her new berth in Southampton. It was arranged that the low loader would stop outside Agar's cottage in Hampshire. Here he salutes her one last time. He died the following year.

Paul Dukes in 1920 on the eve of receiving his unique knighthood.

decisions about when to go or not to go. He pointed out that there had never been any trouble from the forts before and there would be none now.

Ed Sindall had the distinct feeling that, following Gus's disobedience and the attack on the *Oleg*, Le May had either decided – or had been told by Cumming – to come to Terrioki and lay down the law. Sindall was still reluctant, but then Le May hinted that perhaps he had cold feet and lacked the nerve of his more successful senior officer. That did it. Sindall told Le May that he would take Peter in that night. Peter, who spoke very little English, could see that something was wrong, but he had long been resigned to simply going whenever and wherever MI6 told him.

Shortly before 11 p.m. CMB4 set out from the harbour with Sindall, Beeley, Peter Sokolov and the smuggler Veroline. Also in the boat was John Hampsheir. He was still very ill, but had left his sickbed because it was Sindall's first time through the forts. He thought Sindall might need his help. He was still shaky and it must have taken tremendous courage to go out again.

Hugh Beeley was also very unhappy about the trip. CMB4's engine was giving problems after the strain of the *Oleg* attack and badly needed an overhaul. The induct was shaking violently and the boat was making a lot of exhaust noise even at low revolutions. He warned Ed Sindall that he could not vouch for the engine if they suddenly needed full speed.

Because of the number of passengers, CMB4 was towing the pram as she moved steadily towards the forts at midnight. It was barely even twilight, but this was as good as it was going to get. The forts grew larger, looming black and silent as they always had. Just as Gus had done on the first trip, Sindall aimed for the middle of the gap that Veroline indicated. They crept forward until they were only four hundred metres away.

Suddenly the guns of the forts roared into life and two shells whistled low over the boat. Sindall uttered an oath and threw open the throttle, putting CMB4 into a rapid turn as he did so. But although the stern of the boat sank down for maximum power, the helm did not seem to respond – it was like trying to accelerate with the brakes on. Hampsheir opened fire with the Lewis guns, knowing that they were almost out of range but hoping it would do some good.

A third fort now opened fire. These were massive eight-inch naval guns (by comparison, the *Oleg*'s guns were six-inch). With that calibre of shell the forts did not need a direct hit: anything close was likely to reduce CMB4 to matchwood.

Sindall shouted at Beeley, asking what was wrong. Beeley leapt up from the engine compartment, knowing that the engine was working flat out and that the problem must be elsewhere. He pointed at the back of the boat, shouting, but no one could hear him over the roar of the struggling engine. Peter glanced back and understood immediately: the sharp turn had dragged the skiff under water and she was now acting like a sea anchor. As Sindall applied more power to get away it only dragged the skiff deeper.

Shouting in Russian for Sindall to stop, Peter began to fumble with the knot of the rope, but it was impossible to untie: the spray from the churning propeller had made his hands wet and the strain between the skiff and CMB4 pulled the rope bar-taut.

A second salvo of shells now bracketed CMB4 about twenty metres on either side and the entire boat rocked with the shock. The forts had found their range and they all knew that if they did not move now they were dead. Peter gave up the fight with the knot and fumbled for his pocket knife to cut the rope. But just then an axe wielded by John Hampsheir whistled past his head and sliced the rope in two.

That action probably saved their lives. CMB4 sprang forward, suddenly freed of her burden, but almost immediately stopped dead in the water again. Sindall hammered at the controls, but nothing happened. The clutch had sprung out under the sudden strain and now the engine was running full out but delivering no power. The detonation from the next shell was so close that it lifted them clean out of the water and drenched them with spray. Down in the engine room CMB4's watertight seams began to split.

Hugh Beeley had been thrown off his feet as he tried to get back into the engine compartment but now he scrambled across the floor of the cockpit, reaching for his carpenter's mallet. He dealt the engine one thunderous blow, the clutch re-engaged and CMB4 accelerated once more, almost throwing Peter and Veroline over the stern. As their speed increased and they roared away Sindall twisted and turned the little boat as the forts continued to fire, but after twelve minutes the gunfire finally ceased. CMB4 had disappeared into the night-time murk.

At first the crew thought they had escaped unscathed. They had lost the skiff, but that was a small matter. Then they saw John Hampsheir curled up on the floor at the rear of the cockpit with Peter Sokolov tending to him. He might have been suffering from shock before but he was in a very much more serious condition now.

Sindall told Gus that John Hampsheir was still in bed suffering from complete nervous shock and exhaustion. Even after two days he seemed no better. He would have to go home this time.

Once he had heard the whole story, Gus left the dacha and headed straight through the forest to Broadbent's residence where Le May and Hall were staying. He hammered on the door until he had roused them out of bed. These men had endangered his crew, ruined the health of one of his closest friends and blown any chance that a CMB could sneak through the sea fortresses safely in future. Gus never said what he did when the door of the dacha finally opened, but he would have been justified in punching Raleigh Le May clear across the room.

However, although Gus didn't record what he did, he did make a note of what he told them. In the first place, he reminded them that Cumming had chosen *him* to lead this mission and insisted that in future only *he* would decide when and where they went through the line of forts. In the second place, he forced Le May to agree that there would be no more attempts to get through the forts until at least the end of July. He then asked Le May if he had spoken to Bruton. Le May admitted that he had. Gus was disgusted and left Le May in no doubt that if he went behind his back again there would be very serious consequences. Finally, he told them that the Consul-General had found a sanatorium where Hampsheir could be cared for until he recovered. Since they were responsible for his medical condition one of them would be taking him there tomorrow. Harold Hall sheepishly agreed that he would go.

Gus then stormed out. He noted in his diary that night: 'I don't think they expected a full frontal attack – the air is much clearer now.'

Unfortunately he was soon to find out that the air was going to become very murky indeed.

Failure to communicate

Gus Agar was not the only person who had been badly let down by MI6. At the same time that he was having a row with them in the dacha at Terrioki, their incompetence had almost reduced Paul Dukes to tears.

Everything about his intelligence operation in Petrograd depended on money – money to bribe officials, money for agents, money to buy food in the famine-ridden city. He had not eaten for two days. When he had met Peter Sokolov in the gardens of the Winter Palace, it had not been safe to open the parcel there and then. He had just torn away a small corner of the wrapping to see what it contained and then stored it in a tomb in the Smolensk cemetery where he kept all his operational papers. But when he finally tore open the parcel he could not believe his eyes. The money consisted of forgeries – such poor forgeries that he would never be able to use them. There were twenty- and forty-rouble notes, but the dye was poor and the design on some of the notes was smudged. The paper was also too thin: anyone holding it would immediately look at it more closely. It simply *felt* wrong.

He had been holding out for this money. All his hopes rested on it. Paul later wrote of that moment:

'I sat down, staring at the parcel, futilely counting the sheets. I whistled softly. It was the best substitute for weeping, and I could almost have wept.'

He knew now that he should never have come back to Russia. From the moment he had set out from Finland, the third stage of his mission had been dogged by disaster . . .

Getting back into Russia the third time at the very end of February 1919 had been harder then ever. Paul had expected to return across the ice of the frozen Gulf as Peter Sokolov had done. But he made the mistake of telling the commandant at Terrioki about this. The German commandant who had been forced to release Paul just a few weeks earlier was determined to do all he could to stop him now. Even orders from the Finnish government that Paul should be given every assistance carried no weight with him. He ordered that anyone seen on the ice should be shot on sight. The smuggler who had agreed to take Paul immediately refused to have anything more to do with him. Paul knew that he was being watched in Terrioki by German agents working for the commandant and that if he made an attempt to get onto the ice even without a guide he would probably be seen.

Eventually Paul told the commandant that he was going back to Helsinki to complain to the Interior Ministry about the way he had been treated. The commandant looked rather smug, happy to have upset a British intelligence operation – but in fact Paul had lied. He had other ideas.

His first thought was to use the Finnish border guards who had helped him before, but he found that they had been moved on. So he headed next into the far north of Finland where there were fewer villages and border patrols would be less frequent. He hoped to find a peasant who would conduct him across for money, although he had no idea how he would find such a person. Fortunately, on the train to Rautta in northern Finland he met the newly appointed commander of the Finnish garrison there and, using his papers from the Finnish War Ministry, Paul asked for his help in finding a guide.

Two nights later, Paul set off in the middle of the night on a sleigh with a local guide from Rautta. At a forester's hut they left the sleigh and Paul's guide checked on the latest news about Bolshevik patrols in the area. Then at midnight they proceeded on skis for the twenty-mile journey to a village across the border. At first Paul managed to keep up with his twenty-year-old guide, despite the fact that the skis were the wrong size for him. Their progress was quite fast but, every so often, the two men would stop to listen. The temperature was twenty degrees below zero, the forest was in complete silence and every sound seemed to carry for miles in the freezing air. In these woods they would hear a Russian patrol long before they saw it.

After an hour they crossed the border. This was marked by a wide strip of snow which had been cleared of all vegetation. Crossing this no man's land was a great risk. The forest was so dense on either side of the strip that the first you would know if a patrol was hiding there would be as they opened fire. The only way to be sure was to sit and watch. But Paul found that every slight movement of bushes in the breeze seemed to be a sign that the Cheka were there. There was no way of knowing and they would just have to take their chances. Eventually his guide dashed across and Paul followed. They were safe, but their ski tracks in the snow remained for any passing patrol to find. Paul asked if they should attempt to cover them, but his guide simply shrugged and said that no one would be likely to follow them. Paul was not reassured, particularly since, as the man at the rear, he was the one most likely to get a bullet in the back if a patrol caught up with them.

The guide pushed on. Paul soon found himself in trouble. He had packed a large number of provisions about his person, especially chocolate and tins of condensed milk. In the famine conditions of Petrograd these commodities were worth almost as much as gold. He was also carrying large bundles of cash. These packages were all strapped to his body or carried in the voluminous pockets of a massive overcoat that he was wearing, but the sheer bulk and weight of all this meant that he found the journey much harder work than his guide who was in no mood to hang around waiting for this apparently fat and certainly very slow Englishman.

They pushed on for another three hours, frequently crossing frozen boggy areas where the additional weight meant that Paul had to struggle through muddy slush while his companion simply glided across and disappeared into the distance. But after a while it became clear to Paul that the young man was lost. Still the guide pushed on and Paul had no choice but to follow.

Finally, just as the morning began to get light, the guide came across a track and claimed to know where they were. He said it would only be another mile. Paul was almost at the end of his strength, but he promised himself that as soon as they reached the village he would sit down and rest as long as he wanted. He kept falling further and further behind and his guide became more and more agitated. As long as they stuck to the path there was a great risk that they would be spotted by a patrol, but they had to stay on the track or risk getting lost again.

The promised mile came and went and yet there was still no sign of the village. Paul's chest and throat ached from continuously gulping great lungfuls of frozen air and the muscles in his legs were so tired that he could barely lift the skis. His guide had disappeared. Working automatically, Paul kept going: right ski, left ski, right ski, left ski ...

The trees thinned out abruptly and Paul stopped in surprise. There was a hissing sound from the side of the track and Paul found his guide hiding in some bushes there. Paul collapsed onto the snow next to him and wondered if he would ever get up again. His legs and feet were so cold that he had lost all feeling in them.

The guide pointed across the clearing ahead to where a group of huts were situated at the base of a hill. He explained that Red Guards were based there. They would probably emerge some time in the next hour or so for the morning patrol. The guide said that they had come too far south, but that if they could cross the dyke ahead and make it past the huts without being seen they would only be about three miles from their destination.

Paul looked ahead and could see a small dyke in which a fast stream was running. He was about to ask his guide where the bridge was when the youth leapt up without a word, skied up to the dyke and simply used a thrust from his ski poles to leap right over it. Then he was gone, keeping low and gliding swiftly across the open snow past the huts.

Paul hauled himself upright by clinging to a nearby tree. He looked up and down the length of the dyke but there was no sign of any footbridge, not even a fallen log. If he waited much longer he would lose his guide completely and anyway the dyke was only about four feet wide. Under normal conditions he wouldn't have thought twice about it.

Paul slid forward and tried to leap the dyke, using his ski poles to thrust him forward just as his guide had done. Two things immediately struck him: one was that his legs were so numb that he had hardly left the ground at all; the second was that in clearing the dyke his companion had dislodged a lot of snow and frozen soil from the far side and that it was now about twice as wide as it had been before.

Paul disappeared into the dyke and there was a loud splash.

Thirty seconds later, two skis were thrown out of the dyke onto the snow on the far side. Two gloved hands appeared as Paul tried to haul himself after them. The dyke was only about five feet deep, but Paul's clothes and his huge overcoat were now drenched with freezing water after falling in the stream and he weighed almost twice as much as before. Also, he couldn't get a purchase on the snow-covered ground. He scrambled frantically with his feet to boost himself upwards, but the embankment of the dyke simply turned to mud beneath him and he kept sliding back down into the fast-flowing water. From one of the nearby huts, he could hear the sounds of people stirring.

A strange combination of exhaustion and fear caused Paul to giggle quietly to himself even as he became more desperate. This was it. Britain's top secret agent in Russia was going to die in a very small ditch! It seemed to him ridiculous at the time – he knew the ditch was not an enormous obstacle, but in the slippery mud and in his exhausted condition he just *could not* scramble out. Every time he tried he simply pulled yet another little avalanche of snow down on top of himself and made the slope even more slippery. All the time he was getting wetter, colder and heavier.

Finally, after thrashing around for ten minutes, he waddled further along the dyke and managed to grab the roots of a nearby bush. The first few times that he tried to pull himself up and out the damp roots slipped from his frozen fingers, but eventually he got a secure hold and inch by inch he hauled himself onto the snow.

Paul lay there, panting heavily. He did not care who could see him from the huts – he was simply too tired to move. Let them shoot him. He could not feel any part of his body and in the freezing conditions his soaked clothing was rapidly turning into a mass of ice. He laughed weakly at the thought that this was certainly no life for a concert pianist.

He was falling asleep from cold and exhaustion and wrote later that although he knew that this meant death he could not stop himself drifting away into pleasant unconsciousness. It was full daylight now. He lay there staring up into the clear blue sky and wondered if he should bother to move again.

But somehow it was the sight of that sky which helped Paul to gather his strength and force himself to his feet one last time.

He followed the ski tracks through the snow. He was by now in an almost trance-like state where he felt neither fatigue nor cold. He made no effort to remain concealed for there was no strength left for that. He only had energy for going forwards. He knew that if he stopped moving his skis that would be the end. He would just fall down, go to sleep and die.

He followed the guide's tracks for another three miles. He climbed up hills and slid, almost helplessly, down long tree-covered slopes. He was aware that now and again he was passing people, peasants out gathering wood for the early-morning fires, but he did not have the energy to look left or right, only to go on, to follow the tracks which continued endlessly in front of him.

And then they stopped. They simply faded into the snow and the snow had merged into a muddy track.

He looked up and saw a village at the top of the hill at whose foot he was standing. He unfastened his skis and trudged slowly up the hill. He did not care if it was the right village, he was going into it. When he reached the top of the hill he looked around. Every wretched hut looked the same and there was no sign of his guide or anyone else in the bitter wind which blew flurries of loose snow along the street. Paul staggered to the nearest hut. He propped his skis against the wall and knocked quietly on the door. No one answered. He didn't care. He opened the door and stepped inside.

The hut consisted of just one room. There was an old woman lying in a bed in one corner and five children of various ages and levels of grubbiness who had obviously just risen from a variety of straw pallets scattered around the floor. There was almost no furniture, but for some reason a small harmonium stood in one corner. The inhabitants of the hut stared at the apparition before them with a mixture of curiosity and fear. Paul crossed himself in front of the religious icons on the wall, staggered over to the stove in one corner of the room and slumped into a chair.

A few minutes later an old man in his mid-fifties entered. Paul mumbled an explanation about being on a foraging expedition. The man looked down at the growing pool of water around Paul's feet as the ice in his clothing gradually melted. Paul said that he had fallen in a stream. The old man seemed not to care.

The family went about their business, getting dressed and preparing breakfast. No one said a word to Paul although the children occasionally glanced curiously at him. They carefully set out their meagre breakfast, tea and tiny pieces of black bread. The old man laid one small piece in front of Paul and apologised that they did not have more. Paul marvelled at their unselfish hospitality, so typical of every Russian peasant he had known. They had almost nothing at all, but what they had they would share.

Paul stayed there for the rest of the day. The family were very wary of him as well they might have been: he could have been a Bolshevik official come to spy on them. But everything changed when Paul hauled himself over to the harmonium and began to play. It was a simple instrument and Paul was reduced to playing the hymns of his childhood which he had learned when he had first watched his uncle play the organ in the tiny Congregational church in Bridgwater. The family – particularly the old man, who also played – warmed to him immediately. A man who played such music could not be a Bolshevik.

The old man explained that he was the children's grandfather. The old woman was their grandmother. He never said what had happened to the children's parents. He had lived there all his life. He explained how the Bolsheviks had come to the village one day. They had told him that he was a 'capitalist' because he owned three ponies and five cows. They had taken two ponies, four cows and half his land for redistribution to the 'poor'. He looked around the broken-down one-room hut and wondered where these poor people lived. He had just been told that his remaining cow was to be confiscated so that the 'poor' could start a commune. All he hoped for now was that the Tsar would return and make everything better again.

The old man could see that Paul was in no state to walk any further. He said that Paul could stay as long as he needed to.

The old man planned to leave for Petrograd the following morning with his eldest granddaughter to smuggle into the city a small churn of milk which they hoped to sell. Paul set out with them. He was in a bad way. His feet were badly frost-bitten and he could barely walk. But he could not stay here. The family would not have made him leave, but they had so little that he could not find it in his heart to force himself on their hospitality any longer.

They set off well before dawn. Paul's young guide had reappeared and he took them in a sleigh as far as the railway station. It was four o'clock in the morning when they arrived to catch the only train of the day. It was not due to leave until six but already the station was packed with desperate passengers. Once more Paul found himself fighting his way across a platform to try and get a place in an over-crowded carriage. Men shoved and cursed, women and children screamed or cried and every boot which trod on his frost-bitten toes drew cries of anger and pain from Paul. But, clutching the hands of the old man and his granddaughter tightly, Paul eventually elbowed his way into a carriage. It was designed to seat six people, but there were fourteen crammed in when the train finally pulled away. Many more people were squeezed into the corridors, lying on the roof of the train or clinging to handles and buffers on the outside. One of the men jammed into the compartment knew the old man and recognised Paul as a stranger. He asked if Paul had come from 'over there' – meaning Finland. The old man gave him a tremendous kick on the shins and the questioner minded his own business for the rest of the trip.

The journey was long and slow. Despite the overcrowding it was also cold because there was no heating in any of the carriages and many of the windows were broken. Then, halfway into Petrograd, the train braked to a sudden halt. A disturbance began at one end of the train and the news quickly spread along the corridors that troops were boarding it. There were panicked cries everywhere as people fought to get away. Some people scrambled out through windows and fled across the snow, others tried hiding beneath the train. But Paul's feet were too badly damaged for him to run and he was too far from an exit of the carriage to get away. He sat there, resigned to his fate. But he need not have worried. The troops were not interested in checking papers only in looting the food which they knew these people would be bringing to sell in Petrograd. There were scuffles and shouts as they took whatever they could grab and as soon as they were gone the train moved on again.

Things were just as bad at Okhta station in the city. They arrived at nine o'clock and immediately there was a great scrum to leave the train. Troops had gathered at either end of the platform to stop people escaping. Once again they were going to search them, but, as before, the intention was to steal food rather than search for spies. Many people clambered out of windows or climbed under the train and ran away across the tracks. The granddaughter, who was the fastest of the three, told her grandfather that she would see him later at an address they knew and then disappeared under the train, clutching the precious churn of milk. On the platform the lines of soldiers quickly broke up as they dived into the crowd, seizing whatever took their fancy. People fought them or shoved past, hoping to get away with their precious goods in the confusion. Screams and cries of anger rent the air. Some soldiers fired their rifles over people's heads to try and restore order, but this only increased the panic. Women and children were pushed to the ground and trampled underfoot and Paul was swept away by the crowd before he could bend down to help them. He saw one woman clawing with her nails at the face of a soldier as she was held on the ground. It was a scene from hell.

The crowd surged apart as more soldiers advanced and Paul was separated from the old man as they were carried along towards different exits. In his exhausted state and with his frost-bitten feet there was nothing Paul could do to fight against the tide. The sheer weight of the crowd carried him out of the station, clear across the Okhta bridge and into the city before it slowed down. Once there people rapidly dispersed in all directions through the snow-covered streets and only then did Paul have a chance to stop and catch his breath.

He stumbled on into the city. The pain was almost unbearable now and he had only one aim in mind: to get to a safe house and rest. By chance, he saw the old man near the centre of the city as he was shuffling along. The old man caught his eye and crossed the street to say goodbye to him. Paul tried to offer him money in return for the food and hospitality. With a typical Russian peasant's stubborn pride, the old man would take nothing. All he would say was that if Paul ever needed help, then he should call on them. But Paul was never to see the old man or his family again.

And in the meantime things were about to go from bad to worse.

About an hour later Paul reached the safe flat that John Merritt had shown him three months ago. On the journey through the city it had seemed to him that security was tighter than ever. Squads of Mongolian and Lettish troops were hurrying here and there and many more people were being stopped in the streets. At the flat he banged on the door and was greeted sullenly by the stable boy from Merritt's country estate who now lived there instead of Maria the housekeeper. Paul was almost at the point of collapse, but he had only been inside the flat for a few moments when the stable boy told him that the Cheka had been there that very morning. This had been their second visit. They were looking for Paul under the name of Krylenko. The stable boy had not known the name because Paul had never trusted him with it, but the Cheka officers had given an exact description of Paul, including the fact that he had a front tooth missing. Fortunately, the stable boy had told them that Paul had gone away on a long journey and would probably not be coming back. This was good news, but Paul knew that he could never use this flat again. The burning question was: if they knew of his Krylenko identity, did they also know of 'Markovitch'?

Paul told the stable boy to stick to the story that he had gone away. Out in the street he wrapped his scarf around his head in the hope that no one would recognise him. This was not quite as silly as it sounds since many people were wrapped up against the cold in any old piece of clothing and with the lack of medical care in the city a lot of people were suffering from untreated ailments. With Paul's shabby clothing the scarf around his head did not look out of place, but it was a disguise which he could not rely on for long.

He headed for Laura Cade's language school. But even as he sloshed through the melting snow towards her building he could see that the flowerpot was missing from the chosen window. That was the warning signal: 'Stay away!' But was this because of the Cheka or just because Laura had troops billeted with her once again? Paul had no way of knowing. He turned down a side street and headed away from the area.

Paul was desperately tired, cold and hungry. Of his remaining safe houses he decided to head for the one belonging to the civil servant because it was the closest. He did not think he had the strength to go much further.

He stood in the street watching the entrance of the clerk's building for some time. If the Cheka knew of the other flat they might well have traced this one as well because both were linked to John Merritt. But after half an hour he decided that he could wait no longer and shuffled through the entrance.

He crept slowly up the stairs. The clerk lived in a flat on the first floor. But before Paul had gone more than a few steps he heard whispering coming from the floor above. He stood absolutely still. There seemed to be two or three different voices and they were right outside the clerk's front door. He heard the Russian word for 'lock pick' and a sound as though keys had been passed from one person to another.

That was enough for Paul. He turned and made a run for it. But in his haste he stumbled on some loose tiles and kicked them away across the hall, causing a clatter which was obviously heard on the floor above. There was the sound of boots running down the stairs. Paul kept running, thinking that he stood a better chance of getting away out in the open, but because of the agony of his frost-bitten feet his run was little more than a quick shuffle. He dived out through the door, but before he could even start down the steps a burly hand had grabbed him by the collar and the barrel of a revolver was jammed against the side of his head. The officer from the Cheka, wearing a leather jacket crossed with two belts of cartridges, threw him up against the wall and demanded to know who he was and what his business in the building was?

Paul acted on instinct. He pretended to be slightly retarded and a craven coward. It did not require a lot of pretence. He rolled his eyes and slobbered slightly. He stuttered that he had been looking for number 39 and had wandered into the hall of number 29 by mistake. As cover stories went it was pretty pathetic but, bowing and scraping, Paul eased past the officer and shuffled away down the steps.

At any moment he expected to be either shot or told to stop, but nothing happened. As he limped away and pretended to look for the right building number, out of the corner of his eye he saw the officer lower his revolver and stride back inside. As soon as he was gone Paul hurried into an alleyway and almost collapsed with relief.

So that was another safe house gone. Paul wondered if this was a routine search or if the Cheka had been tipped off? He also thought about the cowardly little clerk. If the Cheka had got him he would almost certainly talk. Paul tried to work out what was happening. There was a change in the mood of the city. He could sense it but he did not know what it meant. He bought one of the Bolshevik newspapers and looked for news about a security clampdown in the city. There was nothing, so perhaps the search was especially for him. The most likely possibility was that Zorinsky had at last cashed in all his chips by giving his information to the Cheka. But how did Zorinsky know so much about where Paul had been staying? He had always been so careful not to leave any clues and to make sure that Zorinsky didn't have people following him. It was a mystery – a mystery that would kill him if he did not solve it soon.

Paul had two more safe houses left. One was that of Melnikov's uncle. But that was clear across the other side of the city. Paul almost wept when he thought of the frostbite pain he would have to endure. But Melnikov's uncle had never failed Paul before and, even though he knew he might be causing irreparable damage to his feet, Paul set off. The journey took several long hours, but finally Paul was able to look for the warning signal. This time it was that a large box would be placed in a certain window where it was visible from the street. He almost dreaded to look up as he approached the hospital, but the box was not there. With great relief he turned up at the door of the surgery. He was barely able to stagger in. He need not have worried about a cover story for being there – he was so ill that Melnikov's uncle immediately booked him in as a patient.

He was amazed that Paul had made it into the city. His contact in the White underground, the mysterious 'Shura', had found out that Paul had become target number one for the Cheka. They seemed to know all about his movements and even had a photograph of him which showed his missing tooth. When the doctor saw Paul's condition he was even more astonished. He immediately prescribed several days' bed rest because of the frostbite injuries. Paul protested, but he did not have the strength to resist. His security was now in the doctor's hands.

For two days Paul remained at the hospital. His boots had to be cut off, taking a great deal of the skin from his feet with them. His toes looked black and rotten. The doctor shook his head and said that Paul would not be able to walk for weeks and might never recover completely. Paul replied that he must walk again soon, even with crutches, and begged the doctor to find him another pair of boots.

Paul's plan was to adopt a new identity and make the Cheka think that another British agent had arrived in Petrograd. The first step was to change his appearance. Paul needed to get rid of his shaggy beard and long hair. Melnikov's uncle only had an aged and very blunt razor and a tiny sliver of soap. Paul described that shave as one of the most painful experiences of his life as he scraped his face red-raw until he was completely clean-shaven. Melnikov's uncle then cut his hair and dyed it pitch black with some mysterious German hair lotion he found in the depths of the hospital. Finally, Paul replaced his missing tooth. It had fallen out while he was in Archangel in September 1918. He had saved it until he could see a doctor, by sewing it into the lapel of his trusty leather jacket. Now, using some tissue paper as wadding, he jammed it back into place. He looked in a mirror. He looked a bit bizarre, but at least it was nothing like his Cheka photograph. With his radically different appearance, almost all his former agents believed that he was a different man when they first saw him.

Melnikov's uncle also provided a complete new set of clothes. They were threadbare, but Paul knew how hard the doctor had tried to get hold of them. There was also a pair of wire-framed spectacles which made Paul look like 'a pale intellectual'. And from somewhere the doctor found him another pair of boots. These were very hard to find in Petrograd at that time and must have cost a great deal. They were several sizes too big, but with his feet bandaged it wasn't too bad. Paul would be able to travel around the city – albeit it at the pace of a crippled shuffle.

It was dangerous for him to stay longer. Although he was still not well, on the second day he limped out of the hospital leaning heavily on a walking stick. There was no hope of running away from a Cheka patrol, but in fact the lameness from the frostbite proved to be a blessing in disguise. Several times over the next few weeks he was caught in random searches in the street. At first he panicked, but he was always allowed to limp on through without even being challenged. Becoming a cripple seemed to have made him invisible.

A few days later Paul solved the mystery of the identity of the Cheka's informant. It was, as he had expected, Zorinsky. But the information came to light in an unusual way. Paul was limping alongside one of Petrograd's many canals when he caught sight of a figure he thought he recognised on the other side of the street. It was Melnikov's friend, the smuggler Ivan Sergeivitch. Paul had not seen him since that train journey to the border in Finland. Ivan was dressed as a soldier. Paul limped up behind him and tapped him on the shoulder, scaring him half to death.

Paul took Ivan to the gardens of the Winter Palace and finally convinced him that he really was Paul Dukes. It was then that Ivan told him to be on his guard: Zorinsky had spilled everything to the Cheka and there was now a substantial price on Paul's head. Ivan knew this because Zorinsky had actually crossed the border into Finland hoping to find him, planning either to trick him into returning to Petrograd or to kill him and claim the bounty anyway. Zorinsky had arrived in Terrioki only a day or so after Paul had left. Ivan confirmed that Zorinsky had betrayed both Melnikov and the café where White sympathisers had gathered. The Cheka had paid him a rate per head for that job.

Ivan Sergeivitch had a long history with Zorinsky who was indeed a former army officer. Zorinsky had denounced Ivan to the Bolsheviks and he had been arrested, but had escaped from the Cheka on the very night he was to be shot by breaking away from his guards and throwing himself over a parapet into the Neva river. That was why he had fled to Finland. If he had known that Paul had met Zorinsky he would have warned him to have nothing to do with him. The genuine intelligence that Zorinsky had provided must have been bait to lure Paul into providing as much information about British intelligence operations in the city as possible – and to line Zorinsky's pockets, of course.

Whilst Paul was not surprised, he still did not understand how Zorinsky had known so much about his other identities and safe houses. But after a short discussion with Ivan they thought they had a good idea. It could have been surveillance, but Paul had been very careful. It was more likely that Zorinsky had traced Paul's telephone calls. He had either told the Cheka to monitor the calls Paul made when he came to dinner or he simply used the operator to find out where Paul was ringing from. Paul had called Zorinsky's apartment from both the safe flats which had now been compromised. He could have kicked himself, but it was too late now: half of his network was blown.

Ivan then gave Paul the same advice that Melnikov's uncle had given him: get out of Russia fast. It was too dangerous now. A simple change of disguise would only buy him a little time – the Cheka would hunt him down and corner him just as they had destroyed Cromie's operations the year before.

Paul thought long and hard about it. He knew that both men were talking sense and he was highly tempted to make a break for it. And yet, when he considered the matter without panic, there were still possibilities. Zorinsky could not know of the Markovitch alias – Paul had guarded that so carefully that he had not even taken the papers back to Finland. So that, together with his new disguise, should give him a measure of protection. He could make new contacts. It would take time, but he knew that MI6 had no one else in Bolshevik Russia. If he did not do it, who would?

But in the end it was not bravado or a desire for glory which settled the issue, it was a purely practical matter. If Paul left Russia now he would have to walk across either the border or the sea ice and he was not in a condition to do either. He had to stay.

For the first few weeks of March 1919 he hardly moved about at all. As feeling returned to his feet almost any sort of movement was just too painful. He could do little to rebuild his network and relied almost completely on Melnikov's uncle. Paul needed new agents for his network and new safe houses if he was to repair the damage that Zorinsky had done. He relied increasingly on women. Men were being drafted into the army, but women could move about the country freely and were less likely to be suspected. They are known to us today only by their pseudonyms.

One was 'Aunt Natalia', the pseudonym for a Miss Marple-like character who turned out to be the mainstay of Paul's Petrograd network for the next four months. He had first met her in February 1919 through one of his other contacts who had suggested that her flat could be used for a meeting. Now that he had been deprived of so many other safe houses she came into her own. Aunt Natalia was an elderly spinster. Paul described her as 'looking like a typical German *hausfrau*, small, neat and tidy, plain ... she was always cheerful and composed and possessed amazing sang-froid'. She believed in non-violence but was passionately opposed to the Bolsheviks. Her brother had been one of the Tsar's librarians. He had paid dearly for that association when he became one of more than five hundred people selected for execution by the Cheka in revenge for the assassination of Uritsky.

At first Paul used Aunt Natalia's flat as a safe house. She would store his papers in a tightly bound little rubber bag which she hid in the bottom of a tub full of laundry. By coincidence, in April 1919, on the very first occasion when she used this hiding place, the Cheka arrived in the middle of the night. It was a routine search of the entire block but terrifying nevertheless. Paul's Markovitch alias and supporting papers stood up to examination by the senior Chekist officer, but they still searched the flat.

Once the Cheka had left, Aunt Natalia revealed that she had known all along that there would be a search by the Cheka that night. When Paul demanded to know why the hell she had not warned him, she replied that it might have been called off and in any case she had not wanted to worry him! It says something about Paul that he found this an endearing trait rather than a sign of advancing senility ... Fortunately, the hiding place had never even been suspected and Paul used it frequently over the next few months although he adapted the idea by placing the little bag in the toilet's cistern which was mounted near the ceiling and was therefore harder to search than a modern cistern would be. Later, when he was cut off from his couriers in May and June 1919, Paul stored the large quantity of intelligence which was building up in Aunt

Natalia's family tomb in Smolensk Cemetery on Vasili Island in the west of the city.

By the middle of March disturbances in Petrograd factories had become so severe that Lenin himself planned to visit the city. He and the other two leading members of the Bolshevik party, Trotsky and Zinoviev, were going to address a meeting at which they would announce new measures aimed at restoring control of the city. But the security situation was so uncertain that the Bolsheviks could not risk a public meeting. Instead, the trio would be addressing a meeting composed only of specially selected party members. It was vital that Paul should find out what these new security measures were. He also knew that a report about the views of the Bolshevik leadership during this crisis would be a high priority for MI6. Somehow he had to pass himself off as a loyal Bolshevik and get into that meeting.

He asked if the mysterious Shura could help. Melnikov's uncle passed a message and in a few days' time the reply came through that Shura had arranged everything. Shura had asked to attend the meeting with a staunch party member named Rykov. At the last moment he would drop out, but would ask if 'Markovitch' could go instead. Paul would have to be careful because Rykov did not know he was a British agent. Shura would tell Rykov that Markovitch was a Bolshevik sympathiser who was in the city recovering from a long illness. It was risky, but on the other hand Shura thought the fact that Rykov was so widely known as a loyal Bolshevik meant that Paul was less likely to be questioned.

Paul added to his disguise for the meeting, pretending to be a virtual invalid by using two sticks instead of one and playing up the extent of his illness (although this was not far from the truth). He need not have worried. Rykov was so busy helping Paul up and down stairs that he barely had time to ask difficult questions. As Paul and his new friend approached the People's Palace where the meeting was to be held, they could see that the building was heavily guarded by machine-gun emplacements and detachments of Lettish troops, the most loyal of the Bolsheviks' supporters in the army. Even so, Lenin had to be smuggled into the building through a side door because of the risk of another assassination attempt. Security was strict, but Shura had been right: Rykov was recognised by one of the guards and Paul was not even asked for his papers. In the massive vaulted hall which was the centrepiece of the Palace, Lenin announced that all rail travel into Petrograd would be stopped for four weeks to prevent 'speculators' bringing food into the city. Instead food would be 'requisitioned' from the peasants in the countryside, brought into the city and distributed by the Bolsheviks – but only to true supporters. That would be how they would beat the famine in the city. Paul noted wryly that Zinoviev, the leader of the Bolsheviks in Petrograd who only two years before had been a stick-thin agitator, now weighed almost twenty stone. While the people of Petrograd lived in famine conditions, he was housed in luxury at the former Astoria Hotel.

Lenin also announced that there would be a new wave of suppression aimed at weeding out 'counter-revolutionary elements'. More house searches would be conducted and, to cleanse the factories of 'conspirators', suspects would no longer be allowed to work in them. The Bolshevik leadership worked their audience into a frenzy of hatred. The Cheka would be given a completely free hand to pursue their objectives.

After the meeting Paul was able to produce a full report for London. It was one of the most timely and illuminating pieces of intelligence that MI6 had ever produced, right from the heart of the Bolshevik leadership. But the meeting also led Paul to change the nature of his operation. He now realised that it was no longer enough simply to report on conditions in the country. The Bolsheviks were potentially a threat to the whole of Europe. He needed to infiltrate the Bolshevik party if he was to be really effective.

To this end, Paul infiltrated the Comintern, the Bolshevik body dedicated to spreading world revolution. The chance came about almost by accident. Thanks to one of Cromie's former agents in the Russian Admiralty, Paul used to visit a building near the docks which mainly housed sailors from the Baltic Fleet – 'all rabid Communists', as Paul described them. This was an excellent source of intelligence about what was happening in Kronstadt and the level of support for the Bolshevik leadership in the Russian navy. No one suspected Markovitch, the lame old man who played the piano to entertain them. It was the second time that his musical skills had enabled him to win people's confidence. No one seemed to suspect a musician. The sailors were told by Cromie's agent that Markovitch's frail condition was due to months of torture in an English prison where he had been locked up for refusing to fight for the capitalists during the war. The sailors loved him all the more for that. From that house, Paul was able to meet those working for the Comintern and produced detailed intelligence about this secret organisation and those working for it. At one point there was even a proposal to send Paul to England as a Bolshevik spy. This would have been a useful way to escape from the country, but Paul decided reluctantly that he would be of more use in Russia and fortunately the idea was forgotten.

One of the greatest problems for Paul was raising money to support his ever-growing number of agents. By April 1919 he was short of funds once again. The Admiralty spy ring he was in touch with had their own ways of raising money, including bank robberies. Paul's contact with the Admiralty network was a young naval first lieutenant called Kolya Orlov and Paul became closely involved with one of his raids. This was to provide one of the most memorable episodes from his time in Russia.

Kolya's group was going to raid one of the 'People's Warehouses'. These were buildings where all the goods seized by the Cheka and Red Army troops were stored, supposedly for redistribution to the poor but actually to be sold to line the pockets of the Bolshevik hierarchy. The warehouses were stuffed full of cash, jewellery, works of art and furniture. Kolya and his friends hoped to 'liberate' some of this loot to raise money for the network.

They had already raided two of these places successfully. Paul said later that he did not ask them to carry out the raid for him, but there was much that he could not tell and we cannot be certain. He was certainly present at Kolya's house before they set out for the raid. He said that he was there because Kolya had invited him, claiming that it would inspire the group. Whatever the reason for Paul's involvement, there was little he could do. The affair was to end in disaster.

There were six men in the team, including Shura Marenko, the mysterious 'Shura' who had provided Paul with his Markovitch passport and some of his best intelligence leads. One of the team had carried out a reconnaissance of the warehouse and reported that it was guarded by only two officials and a couple of sentries. It looked easy. The group armed themselves from a stash of weapons at Kolya's house and then travelled to the warehouse by separate routes. When they arrived at the rendezvous one of their number, Shura Marenko's brother Serge, was missing. They were too young and inexperienced to realise that this meant trouble. The remaining five gang members went ahead with the robbery.

At first it all seemed to go according to plan. It was the end of the day and the warehouse would be closing at any minute so there should have been no members of the public left in there. Shura Marenko went into the building and made a last-minute check on the positions of the guards. He returned and said that all seemed to be as they had expected.

The five men then crossed the street to the warehouse. They overpowered the guard stationed just inside the main door. This guard, two terrified officials and two more sentries were taken into the ground-floor office where they were tied up and gagged. The gang began emptying the safe – and that was the moment when the net closed. There was a sound of trucks pulling up outside. Stupidly, the gang had not left a guard on the main door to watch the street and before they could move to cover it a gang of heavily armed Chekists burst through.

Gunfire erupted almost immediately, men throwing themselves across the warehouse in a desperate attempt to find cover wherever they could. The gang fought bravely, but they were heavily outnumbered. More and more Chekists poured through the entrance. One of the gang who tried to escape through the back door of the warehouse was cut to pieces in the alleyway. It had been a trap and they were now completely surrounded.

One by one the gang were killed, including Kolya Orlov, until only Shura Marenko was left. His revolver was empty and one arm hung limp at his side. Feebly dry-firing his now empty revolver at the advancing Chekists, he knew it was all over.

Suddenly there was a burst of gunfire from the doorway of the warehouse. A dark figure stood in the archway, silhouetted against the daylight and firing a revolver rapidly to cover Shura's escape. Caught by surprise, the Chekists were cut down or threw themselves into cover.

As he sprinted towards the doorway Shura knew that it had to be his brother Serge. He was late, but anyway Shura thanked God for his arrival. Shouting for Serge to follow him, Shura dashed through the doorway and into the street. To his amazement there seemed to be no Chekists outside so he dashed down a side street, expecting at any minute to hear the Chekists charging after him. Shura ran as fast as he could without looking back, twisting and turning along every alleyway he could find, hoping to throw off any pursuit. Finally he turned a corner and found himself on the edge of a railway station goods yard. Despite the fact that he had only one good arm, he sprinted alongside a departing goods train and hauled himself into a boxcar. As the train gathered pace he crawled to the doorway and looked back. There was no sign of the Cheka – but there was no sign of the mystery gunman either.

Shura stayed on the run. He made his way to Murmansk where he handed himself over to the Allies and from there he went to Finland. Two thousand roubles which he had stuffed into his pocket during the raid were enough to pay for everything for the next few months. It was while he was staying in Finland some months later that he found out what had gone wrong with the raid and the true identity of the person who had rescued him. The story was so astonishing that at first he could not believe it. His saviour had not been Serge. Serge, his own brother, had betrayed the gang to the Cheka. The person who had saved him from certain death had been Kolya Orlov's young sister, Sonia.

Paul Dukes had seen Sonia sitting quietly in the background during the meeting. He described her as 'about nineteen, dark, curly-haired, good-looking, very reserved'. She resented the fact that Kolya would not let her take part in his anti-Bolshevik activities just because she was a woman and she constantly begged him to change his mind. On this day he had finally agreed that she could keep watch from a coffee shop on the corner of the street and let them know if anything happened. After the gang had left the house, she had dressed up in men's clothing so as not to attract attention in the street. Then, with the assistance of the family retainer Akulina who had the key to the cellar where the weapons were kept, she had selected a revolver and left for the coffee shop. Kolya of course had never intended that she should be armed, but Akulina, who had once been Sonia's nanny, thought differently.

Sonia had seen the gang go into the warehouse, but the Chekists had arrived and charged into the building so suddenly that there was nothing she could have done to warn her colleagues. Then the shooting had broken out and without thinking she had run across the street to help her brother. When she burst in through the entrance she probably had no time to realise who it was that ran past her and called for her to follow. The bitter twist to the tale was that Shura was her fiancé.

But Sonia had survived. Having emptied her revolver, she had tried to run out of the door again but before she could get away she had been bundled to the ground by several burly Chekists. She had fought back so furiously with arms, legs and teeth, and it took so many of them to subdue her, that Shura got clean away.

Sonia was trussed up and taken in the back of a truck to the Chekist headquarters at No. 2 Gorohovaya. She was interrogated every single day for three weeks, but she was incredibly brave. Even her interrogators grudgingly admired her. It was a classic Cheka interrogation. First she was deprived of sleep, food and water. Then she was dragged down into the cold, damp basement where a glaring lamp was shone directly into her face. There were slaps, barked orders and repeated questions until she was completely disorientated and almost unconscious. She was threatened with various ingenious tortures, including red-hot needles stuck under her fingernails, flogging or being locked in an isolation cell where she would be force-fed salted food without being given any water – she was told that prisoners went insane before they died in agony. At one point they even pretended that they were going to execute her. A revolver was held to her head and fired several times. Only when she realised that she was still alive did she see that the barrel of the gun had been moved slightly at the very last moment. She still refused to talk. In a way she was lucky. Her interrogator, Yudin, was considered one of the gentler Chekists.

After three weeks Sonia was moved from No. 2 Gorohovaya to Deryabinsky prison. The conditions were a little better there, but only just, and every few days she would be forced to walk all the way back to Gorohovaya for yet another interrogation. During one of these journeys she saw Shura Marenko's brother Serge marching out of Gorohovaya in a Chekist uniform. She immediately denounced him to Yudin. Yudin questioned Serge and Sonia together, trying to use them to find the names of the conspirators. Serge had been working for the Cheka under an assumed name. He seemed to be horrified that there was a living witness to his terrible crime. That night he hanged himself in a cell with his belt, overcome with remorse at what he had done.

That night was also the worst so far for Sonia. Yudin tried a new tactic. He left her in the care of a female Chekist named Strunseva. Sonia later said that there was something very threatening about this woman. All her gestures were masculine and she smoked constantly. Sonia described her as having 'a square face, square body in a black leather jacket, with dark eyes set in square sockets'. Strunseva sat very close to Sonia and began caressing her hair. She said: '... the truth is you are a bitch of a counter-revolutionary and you shot some of our men ... how can you expect to be let off? But I can tell you, you needn't lose heart – if you are sensible ...'

Sonia, who had had a sheltered upbringing, had no idea what this meant, but as Strunseva sidled up closer to her Sonia was overcome with revulsion and suddenly pushed her away so hard that her tormentor flew backwards and fell over something on the floor. Strunseva stood up and grabbed Sonia by the hair so hard that she soon blacked out. Sonia remembered being dragged away but said that the rest of that night was just a blank in her memory. Perhaps it was. In any case, Sonia was to remain in prison for the next four months when she was to cross Paul Dukes's path again.

In the meantime, the strain of living constantly among his enemies was beginning to tell on Paul. One day in May 1919 he visited one of his agents, a former general in the Tsarist army. Paul was only there long enough to collect a small packet containing the latest intelligence (and presumably pay the agent). He hid the tiny packet inside his hat band, but the sun was shining so brightly and the day was so beautiful that he took his hat off as he walked along so that he could feel the sun on his face. Earlier that afternoon he had been to a performance of Tchaikovsky's Sixth Symphony in the Winter Palace gardens and he was lost in remembering it as he sauntered along. He felt so good that he even forgot the state of his feet.

Suddenly he felt a tug on his arm. A young man handed him the small packet which he said Paul had dropped. With sudden horror Paul realised that it must have fallen out of his hat. The packet later turned out to contain precise details of Trotsky's plans for an attack on the White forces under Admiral Kolchak. If some inquisitive person other than the polite young man had opened it, the agent who produced the intelligence and possibly the entire network would have been caught. This close shave was yet another reminder to Paul that he must never lower his guard even for an instant and increased the strain on his nerves still more.

That strain was increased by silence from MI6. Now that he was thoroughly familiar with working undercover in Bolshevik Russia,

Paul was producing more and more intelligence. He had even managed to recruit a source right inside Trotsky's 'Revolutionary Council of the North' and was able to copy the minutes of their meetings. He was amassing an ever greater store of excellent reports, but they were of no use unless he could get them to London. He had sent two couriers, but neither of them had returned. Major Scale had promised in February that 'very special measures' would be taken to ensure that he had couriers and an escape route. Where on earth were they?

By May 1919 the position had become critical. The future of Communist Russia was in the balance. The Red forces were under pressure from the White armies on all sides. In Estonia forces under Yudenich had advanced as far at Gatchina, only 20 miles from Petrograd. There was panic. Zinoviev, the Bolshevik leader in Petrograd, even packed up his things and prepared to flee to Moscow. On 1 May, Paul's contacts in the Russian admiralty told him that the garrisons at Kronstadt and Krasnaya Gorka were ready to revolt. If Kronstadt fell to the Whites then there was no way that the Bolsheviks could hold Petrograd. All that the conspirators were waiting for was a sign from the British that they would come to their aid.

Paul had to confess to his contacts that he had no idea what the British were doing. He could feel the opportunity to win the civil war slipping away. Shortly after he was told about the plans for a revolt, he also heard that Leon Trotsky, the Bolshevik Commissar for the Army and Navy, planned to appoint former Tsarist officers to their old positions in order to strengthen the armed forces. With these officers in place and discipline restored, the Bolsheviks might really be able to beat the Whites. Paul was running short of money and he needed to get his intelligence reports out of the country so that the British government could realise the importance of the situation. On 31 May Pravda printed a now infamous statement from Lenin and Felix Dzerzhinsky headed 'Death to Spies!' because the various White intelligence networks were providing so much help to their enemies.

Where was MI6?

Paul had to find a way to let them know that he was alive and still operating. In desperation he considered one last throw of the dice. He knew that the Red Army had powerful radio transmitters in the city. From his contacts in the army he knew of one radio operator who might accept a bribe. Paul devised a plan by which he would bribe this operator to broadcast a message which the British naval squadron cruising in the Gulf would have to pick up. He knew that the bribe would take all his remaining money. But the bribe had to be big because the man who sent the message would have to flee across the border immediately and would never be able to return. Paul had no idea how he would survive without more money, but the longer Cumming's silence continued the more he became convinced that it would have to be done.

But before Paul could put his plan into operation, disaster struck. Yudenich's thrust towards Petrograd had failed. The advance had been so successful because it had been led by six tanks driven by British soldiers who had volunteered for the mission. The Red forces had no answer to them and it seemed as though Petrograd must fall. But when they reached Gatchina, just 20 miles south-west of Petrograd, the British soldiers woke in the morning and found that the tanks had been sabotaged. Someone had poured sand into the gearboxes and without the proper spares the tanks had been reduced to so much scrap metal. The tanks had been sabotaged by officers of the White army. They were angry about British support for the independence of the Baltic states and Finland which they felt should remain part of the Russian empire. And they resented the idea that their former capital was about to be liberated by the British. The incident neatly summed up every reason why White resistance to the Bolsheviks failed.

With the White advance defeated the Bolsheviks took renewed heart. The Cheka began a new wave of crackdowns. And as part of this renewed offensive the Bolsheviks appointed one of their most brutal and feared officers as the new head of the Cheka in Petrograd: Iakov Kristoforovich Peters.

In many ways Peters was the perfect spycatcher because he knew what it was like to be on the run and how to organise espionage networks in a hostile foreign country. He was dedicated to his cause and had suffered heavily for it. More than any other Cheka officer he was responsible for destroying the Allied and White Russian agent networks which threatened to undermine Bolshevik Russia between 1918 and 1920.

He had been born in Latvia in 1886, the son of a farm labourer. As a youth he joined the Latvian Social Democratic Party and took part in the Russian Revolution of 1905. When the revolution failed, he was brutally tortured and then imprisoned for eighteen months. After his release in 1908, he travelled to London where he worked as a tailor's presser – although most of the time he was unemployed. But his experiences under Tsarist rule had led to his politics becoming ever more extreme and in December 1910 he was arrested on suspicion of involvement in the 'Houndsditch Murders'. This was an attempted burglary of a jeweller's shop by Latvian terrorists which had led to the murder of three London policemen. Most of those responsible were later killed in the infamous 'Siege of Sidney Street'. Peters survived and was tried with several co-defendants at the Old Bailey in May 1911. He was acquitted following the seemingly incredible defence that the murders had been committed by his Anarchist cousin who was so like him that they were often mistaken for twins. After his acquittal, Peters had gone back to work at the tailor's shop and he later married an Englishwoman, May Freeman.

In April 1917 he had returned to Russia, leaving May behind in England. He helped to establish the Cheka and soon rose rapidly through the ranks, becoming deputy to Dzerzhinsky himself. He had certainly earned a reputation for brutality: he was known as the 'Robespierre of the Russian Revolution' from the eagerness with which he signed the death warrants of those arrested by the Cheka and 'the Executioner' because of the number of prisoners he had shot personally. To the British press he was known as 'the Red Terrorist'.

He had already managed to break America's leading secret agent in Russia, in September 1918. Xenophon Kalamatiano had been captured trying to reach the safety of the American consulate in Moscow. He was using the alias 'Serpukhovsky' and his papers appeared to be genuine. At that time the Cheka had no idea exactly who they had captured, but his interrogators had the feeling that he was far more important than he seemed. However, a body search had revealed nothing and he was refusing to answer any questions. Peters was summoned and with his perfect knowledge of English and Western mannerisms he quickly and cleverly broke Kalamatiano. As the pressure of the interrogation intensified, Kalamatiano remained cool, but Peters noticed that the American agent's eyes occasionally flickered briefly towards the heavy walking stick he had been carrying when he was arrested. Peters ordered that it be examined more closely and it was soon found to be hollow. Inside were ciphered intelligence reports and receipts identifying more than thirty of America's top agents in the country. This had been a great counter-espionage coup for the Cheka and at a single stroke Peters had wiped out American intelligence operations in Russia.

On 8 May 1919 Peters was appointed 'Chief of the Petrograd Fortified Area' as part of the Bolsheviks' attempt to maintain control of the region in the face of Yudenich's advance. Upon his arrival he was fascinated to learn that there was a British 'super agent' operating in the city, just like Kalamatiano. If Peters could find him and interrogate him he could destroy MI6 just as he had destroyed the American espionage effort. Peters made it his personal mission to hound Paul Dukes out of every one of his hiding places, drive him into the open and then capture and break him.

In one of his CX reports, Dukes was soon describing the terror measures introduced by Peters as 'exceeding everything previously known'. A conspiracy was uncovered in the Red VIIth Army and anyone connected with it was ruthlessly dealt with. The Fleet based at Kronstadt was given a new set of political commissars and anyone whose loyalty was even the slightest bit suspect was taken away from the island. Everywhere people were stopped, searched, and questioned. Where there was any suspicion, people were shot. The Bolsheviks believed that they were engaged in a life-or-death struggle and they did not intend to lose.

As part of this renewed search for Paul, the Cheka raided Aunt Natalia's flat while Paul was staying there. Fortunately, he did not know about the arrival of Peters and was fairly relaxed about the search since the Markovitch papers and his military exemption form were still valid. But they were due to expire in a little over a week and Paul noticed that the Chekist who examined them made a careful note of the expiry date in his notebook. Paul decided he had to find another base of operations.

Melnikov's uncle had moved to a house in the suburbs, but the house where his medical practice was based was still in use. Paul stayed there together with a nurse who is today only known by her pseudonym 'Klachonka' (which means 'little cart horse'). Like Aunt Natalia, Klachonka soon became one of Paul's main agents. As a woman she could move around the city comparatively freely and as a nurse she was unlikely to be suspected if stopped. She also proved to be very quick-thinking . . .

It was 10 June and Paul was fast asleep on a sofa in the study of the flat. It was a very dangerous time for him. The Markovitch papers had now expired and Paul had been unable to renew them. He had almost no money and there was no news from MI6. The resistance movement was dispirited because of recent Bolshevik victories. Paul had decided that he would have to return to Finland, despite the fact that he had promised all his contacts that he would not leave them until the British arrived. To get across the border he had prepared some army identification papers. They would not pass inspection by the Cheka in Petrograd because they would immediately ask why he was not at the front, but they would probably be sufficient nearer the border where he could claim that he was reporting for duty or was on an errand. Paul planned to leave in two days' time. In the meantime, he had one other protection: Melnikov's uncle had suggested that Paul should pretend to be a patient being treated for epilepsy. He had taught Paul how to simulate a fit and it worked well – once they stopped laughing.

Knowing that he would be leaving in a day or so, Paul had let his guard drop and it almost cost him his life. In the middle of the night there was a loud banging at the door and shouting in Russian. It was the Cheka. Peters had increased the number and intensity of house searches, knowing that Paul must be hiding somewhere in the city. There was no time for Paul to react. He heard Klachonka hurrying along the passage and he thought she would delay them for a few minutes, but within moments the door of the room suddenly burst open and a Chekist officer strode in.

There was nothing Paul could do but pretend to be asleep. The forged army papers were in his pocket. As soon as they were found he was finished.

For a moment he thought he had got away with it. The officer glanced round and started to leave the room, but then a second officer standing in the hall pointed out that someone was sleeping on the sofa. The Chekist strode forward and wrenched the blankets back. Paul lay still, his eyes closed. There was nothing else he could do.

'This must be the invalid – he's asleep,' said the Chekist and they marched out of the room. Paul knew that Klachonka had told the porter that there was a patient staying at the flat who was being treated for a severe medical condition. The Cheka must have spoken to him before coming up to the flat.

Paul leapt up from the sofa. His first thought was to put a match to the forged army papers. He burned them as quickly as possible and then mixed the ashes with those in the fireplace. Now he had only the expired Markovitch papers. He could hear the Cheka searching the dining room next door, but then he heard booted feet advancing down the corridor and knew they were coming back to the study. There was nothing to do but climb back under the covers, but as soon as they asked to see his papers it would all be over. He did not even have a gun with which to shoot his way out. He only carried his revolver when absolutely necessary. Now he was caught in exactly the sort of trap he had always sworn to avoid.

The door opened. Klachonka bravely barred the Chekists' way, protesting all the time that the patient was in a very disturbed condition and that if he was woken suddenly it could '. . . provoke a fit at any moment!'

Those last desperate words were clearly directed at Paul. He took the hint. As the searchers approached the couch, he suddenly went into spasm. He began rolling around violently and howling incoherently. He was now able to fake a fit so well that he could even foam at the mouth. It must have been an Oscar-winning performance because the Chekists were completely baffled. They had never seen anything like it. Klachonka rushed to Paul's side and shouted at the Chekists to get out. She must have been even more convincing because, astonishingly, they obeyed her.

They left shortly afterwards, but it was clear that Peters had forced someone to talk. Klachonka told Paul that the Cheka had been looking for an English spy 'who limped because he had severe frostbite.' They also had a more recent photograph of him. Paul was lucky that he had changed his appearance so radically. There was no way Zorinsky could have known about the frostbite, so Paul realised that there must be a new informer somewhere in the organisation. The Cheka must have gone for now, but Klachonka had been told that she must report to the Cheka headquarters at No. 2 Gorohovaya the next morning for further questioning. They seemed to know that Paul was somehow linked with the hospital.

It was now more imperative than ever that Paul should get out of Russia. If there was an unknown informant then he had no idea where he would be safe. He left Klachonka's flat early the next morning. Without his army papers he needed to find somewhere to stay while he planned a new escape and it had to be somewhere that was not linked to his new organisation.

Paul tried everywhere he could think of. He hadn't seen the Policeman for some time, but when Paul called he said that his daughter had been arrested for carrying compromising papers and that he expected the Cheka to arrive at any moment. Paul then tried to contact the network at the Admiralty which was independent from his own organisation, but there was no message at the dead letter box site they used and he had no idea that his usual contact had been killed recently.

Paul now had no identification papers and as long as he stayed on the streets he risked being stopped and arrested at any moment. As he moved swiftly from alleyway to alleyway watching for the Cheka, he noticed posters announcing a new 10 p.m. curfew were pasted to every wall. Anyone out on the streets after that hour would be arrested on sight. Paul had to find somewhere to stay. The 'White Nights' had almost begun and there were now 20 hours of daylight in every 24-hour period. There would be nowhere to hide from the patrols.

But by the evening he still had not found anywhere he could stay. The Cheka appeared to be everywhere. Even Laura Cade who was currently storing many of his intelligence reports had placed the flowerpot in the window which meant that she was under suspicion.

Finally, in desperation, Paul set out for the house belonging to one of his contacts with General Yudenich's organisation. He did not like dealing with them because they were mainly former Tsarist military officers and aristocrats and therefore exactly the sort of people who might come under suspicion. But because he had little to do with them it also meant that it was unlikely that the informer was one of them. It was a gamble. There were only three hours until curfew and it would take Paul most of that time to get there, but he now had nowhere else to go.

Two hours later the officer who was his contact with the Yudenich group turned him away at the door. He protested that his family were in the house and that, because Paul was a British agent, it was just too big a risk to take him in. Paul begged him, saying that there was nowhere else to go and only a few minutes left before curfew, but the officer slammed the door.

Paul had trudged out of town towards the marshes. It was the only place he could think of. Even here there would be patrols looking for 'speculators' trying to enter or leave the city, but at least there might be reeds or bushes he could hide in.

Paul had not eaten for two days. Living on a poor diet and under constant nervous strain for the past nine months had seriously undermined his health. His frost-bitten feet made walking painful and still needed constant attention. He had no money, nowhere to hide and no news from MI6. It seemed that Peters's plan to drive him out of hiding was working. He could not survive much longer.

That night, as Paul lay shivering in a small clump of bushes in the middle of the Petrograd marshes, all he could think was that his mission had failed.

He did not know it, but just thirty miles away Gus Agar was already on his way in with Peter Sokolov.

11

Gefter

Paul lay in Michael Semashko's tomb and took stock of his situation. He could hear the deep boom of naval gunfire somewhere out in the Gulf. Sadly, Paul knew nothing of the Ingrians' life-or-death struggle at the Krasnaya Gorka fortress. In common with the rest of Petrograd he was convinced that this was British naval gunfire, not Russian, a sure sign that the British were actively supporting the drive of the White army along the Estonian coast towards Petrograd. That sound gave Paul hope. There was still a chance to win through if only he kept his nerve. The loss of all the counterfeit money from MI6 had been a blow, but the fact that he was in contact with the outside world again had changed everything. He could now let Cumming know how delicately events in Russia were balanced and how crucial British intervention could be at this time. Paul knew that his time as a spy in Russia must be limited, but he thought he could survive for one or possibly two more months. That should be enough for British and White Russian forces to arrive and remove the Bolsheviks.

His first task was to arrange a new identity. He could not go on creeping around the streets knowing that if he was stopped he would be arrested for lack of identity papers. Then he would have to get money. He could not count on MI6, so Paul decided that he would have to break a rule he had set for himself and contact the small British community still living in Petrograd. It was a considerable risk because the Cheka would be watching such people closely, but he had no other choice.

Then there was the question of how to hasten the end of the Bolsheviks. Paul was increasingly convinced that this could not be done from Petrograd. The centre of Bolshevik power was Moscow. After giving the matter considerable thought, he decided that he would continue to operate in Petrograd but would travel more frequently to Moscow. It might seem strange that until now Paul had chosen to remain in Petrograd rather than go to Moscow, but there were three reasons for his choice. First, Petrograd was the city most likely to fall to the White armies and, with the port of Kronstadt through which the Allies could pour men and supplies, it was probably the key to all of Russia. Second, it was the place where he had been able to infiltrate the Comintern, the Bolshevik organisation established to send secret emissaries abroad to spread world revolution. Naturally this was very high on the list of intelligence requirements for MI6. Finally, although the security situation in Petrograd was severe, it was the city Paul knew best having lived there for the past ten years. It was here that he had the most contacts and here that his chances of survival were greatest.

As well as a new identity, Paul needed a new safe house. Peter Sokolov had said that Paul could stay at his student flat. That would suffice for a few days, but it would not be enough. If Peter were picked up crossing the border, the Cheka would raid any address that he was connected with. For the long term, he had to find somewhere else to stay. Paul thought about his current list of agents: Klachonka, Aunt Natalia, Laura Cade. But every option seemed too dangerous. He needed somewhere new but at the moment he had no idea how to solve that problem,

Meanwhile the hunt for Paul continued. Following his earlier wave of searches, Peters struck again on 14 June. The targets this time were foreign mission premises, church property and 'bourgeois households'. The operation was led by the Cheka's 'Special Department', men hand-picked for their loyalty and ruthlessness. They were assisted by 20,000 Bolshevik supporters who were only too happy to ransack their way through the city. The search became an excuse for general looting, rape and murder. In a way, Paul was lucky that he was living rough in the disused cemetery, otherwise he might well have been caught.

Altogether Paul stayed in the tomb for four nights before moving to Peter Sokolov's flat. But during that time he did at least solve his first problem: he was able to adopt a new identity. He became Alexander Bankau, a draughtsman working at one of the factories in Petrograd. Paul was never very clear about how he came by this identity, but intelligence about levels of support for the Bolsheviks within these industrial centres was a key requirement for MI6. Paul was always on the lookout for informants and in one case a little kindness brought him a valuable agent. Although Paul does not link this incident to his Alexander Bankau identity it is possible that it concerns the same factory.

One of the things which most moved Paul amidst the terrible conditions in Petrograd was the plight of the children. More than any other section of society, they suffered under Bolshevik rule, principally from dirt, disease and famine. One evening Paul travelled to a church with Aunt Natalia. She was going to show him the family tomb where he could store his intelligence reports. There was a service being conducted at the church – in secret because the Bolsheviks had banned all religion. Paul had difficulty getting into the church because of the number of people carrying coffins. The priests, all hunted men like himself, moved hurriedly from coffin to coffin, sprinkling holy water and murmuring prayers. It was as Paul looked around the church that he realised that almost all these coffins were quite small: they were the coffins of children. Worse still, he soon realised something else: wood was expensive in Petrograd and even cheap timber was far too precious to be wasted on things like coffins. The coffins were rented for as long as it took for the priests to give a blessing and then the children were carried outside and buried in a communal grave. The coffins were then rented to the next group of mourners. There were dozens of families clustered outside waiting for their turn.

Few experiences affected Paul as much as that evening in the chapel. Whenever he could, he stopped to give any food he was carrying to children he found begging in the street. There was one small girl, aged about seven, who always used to beg in the same place. Paul would give her a piece of bread when he passed – if he was lucky enough to have found any that day. One morning he noticed that she looked quite ill. He asked where she lived and he took her back to her family. Over the next few days he gave the family money to find medical treatment and even sought the help of Melnikov's uncle at the hospital. But sadly nothing could be done and she died soon afterwards, possibly of typhoid. Despite the tragedy, her father, a factory foreman, was so grateful that he and Paul became friends and later he agreed to work for Paul as an agent. It is possible that it was through this friendship that Paul made the contacts who provided him with his Alexander Bankau identity.

A piece of paper from a factory was not much, but it was a start. Within the next few days Paul was also able to visit Klachonka who had finally been released by the Cheka. She had told them that she knew Lenin personally because she had sheltered him when he had been on the run in Russia many years before. At first they had refused to believe her, but eventually she was sent under guard to Moscow so that her story could be checked out by the local Cheka. Every word was found to be true. When he heard of her arrest, Lenin personally ordered her release and the officer who had arrested her was forced to make a grovelling apology.

Paul also found out that Klachonka had been very clever. She had been arrested because the Cheka had received information that she had recently treated an Englishman suffering from severe frostbite. She could have denied this, but instead she admitted that she did remember a man with frostbite calling at the clinic a month or so before. His Russian had been poor, but she had not known he was an Englishman, assuming him to be Lettish or Finnish. She told the Cheka investigators that the man had let slip that he needed his feet treated because he was leaving the country and planned to walk across the border.

Klachonka's acting ability had bought Paul valuable time. This information coming from a personal friend of Lenin himself would be believed and the Cheka would assume that Paul had returned to London. For the moment the hunt was off. Even so, there was still the question of the informer and Paul did not want to push Klachonka's luck any further. He stuck to his decision not to use the flat any more.

Meanwhile Paul strengthened his Alexander Bankau identity by enlisting in the Red Army. Through one of his military agents, he was put in touch with a senior officer in the 8th Army and given a position in the Automobile Section. This might have seemed an odd choice, but in fact it was exactly suited to Paul's needs. First, he was given all the supporting documentation he needed to pass an inspection by the Cheka. Second, membership of the Red Army brought additional rations and travel privileges. But the 8th Army automobile section had no vehicles so Paul did not have to worry about being sent to the front. Furthermore, his senior officer arranged for Paul to be sent around the country to find petrol, tyres or motor spares which gave him a perfect cover story for travelling to Moscow and elsewhere. When he was in Petrograd, the commandant's accommodation also provided Paul with a vital safe house.

Paul's new cover story was helped by the fact that his commander, who was aware that he was a British agent, had a reputation as a loyal Bolshevik. He had gained this reputation quite by accident a few months earlier: during an advance by the Whites towards Petrograd he had received an order to blow up a key bridge. Instead, the commander gave his men orders to destroy a different bridge, intending to cut off the Red Army's retreat and trap them in front of the White forces. Unfortunately his poorly trained troops blew up the right bridge by mistake and he was hailed as a hero.

It was shortly after joining the Red Army that Paul finally tried to deal with his financial problems. This was an issue for all the anti-Bolshevik forces working in Russia, but it was particularly acute for Paul. He was running a large network and every single agent required money – for food, for bribes and simply to survive. Paul was now about to make one of the biggest mistakes of his career as a spy, but it is hard to see what else he could have done. MI6 should have supplied him with money, but when they failed he had a stark choice between abandoning his hard-won agents or taking the only course open to him. And so Paul turned to the British community in Petrograd.

Despite all the hardship, there were still a few of these people living in Petrograd. Some were businessmen who were desperately trying to protect their investments. Others stayed because they did not have either the funds or the contacts to escape across the border. These were the sort of people that John Merritt had been helping.

The wealthier British citizens had set up a committee to aid the less fortunate. This was known as the 'Committee for the Relief of the British Colony in Petrograd'. Paul knew from the persecution of John Merritt that the Cheka took an especial interest in this body, certain that it was nothing more than a nest of spies. The chairman of the Committee, Mr Gerngross, had been arrested just a few days before on suspicion of espionage. Yet, despite the risk, Paul now turned to the secretary of the Committee, George E. Gibson, a British businessman who worked for the United Shipping Company in Petrograd. John Merritt had introduced Paul to Gibson just before he escaped from Russia. The problem was that in the six months since Paul had met Gibson his appearance had changed radically, so when a man dressed in Red Army uniform turned up at his door and claimed to be 'Paul Pavlovitch', a British spy whom he had met six months before, Gibson was more than a little sceptical. He had already been imprisoned once, in August 1918, when the Cheka had found a revolver hidden at his apartment during a routine search. Fortunately, Paul gave a password that had been agreed between the Foreign Office and the Committee in case a British spy needed to contact them. This password was a name, 'Henry Earles'. Once Paul had used this, he eventually managed to convince Gibson that he was the same person Merritt had introduced.

Paul told Gibson that he had run out of funds and badly needed a loan from the Committee to continue his intelligence work. Paul asked for approximately 100,000 roubles. This was not an easy sum to raise, but Gibson told Paul to come back the following day and he would have it for him. Gibson could only raise such a large sum by contacting several other people in Petrograd, which was in itself a dangerous enterprise, but the following day Paul collected the money and gave Gibson a receipt signed 'Captain McNeill', his MI6 cover name. He promised that MI6 would refund all the money and over the next two months Paul borrowed a total of 375,000 roubles. In reality, Gibson had a terrible time trying to get MI6 to refund the money.

Meanwhile the defeat of the Ingrians at Krasnaya Gorka strengthened the hand of the Bolsheviks even more. First the attack by Yudenich had failed, now the Bolsheviks were able to show that even if the Russian people rose up against them the British still would not come to their aid – even if they had a massive fleet just a few miles away. (The Bolsheviks did not mention the minefields, of course.) With the opposition cowed, the Bolsheviks now turned their attention to internal security and they instituted the first-ever purge of Communist Party membership. This was not a purge in the Stalinist sense, with show trials and opponents hauled off to gulags in Siberia. Instead this was a reduction of party membership to those who could truly be trusted. In Petrograd alone, party membership was reduced from more than one million people to little more than four thousand.

This should have made Paul's position much more difficult, but in fact it helped him tremendously. As part of his new identity, Paul was able to join this new 'elite' Communist Party. His contacts with the sailors at Vasili Island were a great help in this. He was after all a man who had supposedly been tortured by the English for his Marxist beliefs. He was a serving Red Army soldier. His sponsor was Rykov, the man who had taken him to hear Lenin speak at the People's Palace in March. Rykov was still unaware that Paul was a British agent (or so Paul claimed), but Paul had been able to strike up a friendship with him and once more it was music which came to his aid. Rykov was a keen balalaika player and with Paul accompanying him on the piano they used to entertain at Communist Party gatherings on behalf of the Commissariat of Cultural Enlightenment. To the Bolsheviks, such a person was first-class Communist party material.

There was only one danger. Since March, when he had first visited Vasili Island, Paul had changed his name from Markovitch to Bankau. Fortunately the first name 'Alexander' remained the same and since everyone referred to him by his diminutive 'Sasha' he was able to get away with it. But the danger that someone would realise that Bankau and Markovitch were the same person was always there. It was a tremendous risk. Every moment Paul spent among the Communists yielded more superb intelligence, but those same moments also stretched his already frayed nerves just a little further towards breaking point.

His membership of the 'elite' Communist Party was a great help to Paul. During house searches or checks at roadblocks, he would present his Communist Party card and would rarely even be asked for his other papers. Since his Red Army papers were genuine as well, he had developed almost the perfect cover story. Paul was even elected from his regiment to the Petrograd Soviet, the Bolsheviks' governing body in the city (in part because no one else wanted what – to them – was just a boring task). Paul soon found out that although the Soviet seemed to be powerful, the huge number of delegates (approximately 3,000) meant that it was little more than a raucous debating shop – all the real decisions were made by the Chairman, Zinoviev, and a small band of his cronies on the Central Committee. Even so, just being part of the deliberations yielded more vital intelligence on how the Soviet system worked and on its leading figures.

Despite the more rigorous security and the increasing effectiveness of the Cheka, thanks to his new cover story Paul later referred to July and early August as the quietest period of his mission. Even so, he knew he was near the end of his time in Russia. The strain of living constantly among his enemies was beginning to tell. He was always tired and woke shaking in fright at the slightest sound in the night. He knew that 'Captain Eggar' would be making his last trip in the middle of August. Paul also knew that he must make that rendezvous or he might never get out.

Security along the shore had been tightened up to such an extent that it would be impossible to steal a boat. Every vessel required a licence. Armed guards patrolled the shore and motor boats challenged all outgoing vessels. No one was allowed to sail at night for any reason at all, so any vessel spotted would be shot at and destroyed. Paul decided that his only chance would be to swim out to 'Eggar'. The distance was about two miles. Paul was a strong swimmer and he did not doubt that he could make it if the sea was calm, but it was the temperature of the water that worried him. Even in the warm summer months the icy waters of the Gulf of Finland could sap a swimmer's strength. Paul began to prepare himself for the journey by immersing himself in ice-cold baths to build up his tolerance to the cold. As he lay there he considered all the things that might go wrong, but his greatest fear was that 'Eggar' might not make it through the Russian defences alive. Then Paul would have to swim all the way back to shore. Strong swimmer though he was, he doubted that he would make it.

But then Paul had a stroke of luck. On or around 10 August he learned from one his contacts that a new courier was in the city trying to find him. Paul was suspicious, but went to the address where this new courier was hiding. He turned out to be a former Russian midshipman named Gefter. He was different to Peter Sokolov in almost every way. Whereas Peter was tall and thin, Gefter was short and stocky. He was also much older than Peter. In his time he claimed to have been a prizefighter, an artist and an actor. He was certainly full of a strong sense of his own importance. As Paul described him: '. . . a thick-set little man, indisputably brave, but inclined to exaggerated self-assurance'.

Gefter said that he had hidden the skiff in some reeds near the suburb of Lakhta and that his orders were to take Paul with him to meet Gus on the night of Friday, 14 August. Paul should make arrangements to be ready. However, when Gefter reappeared two or three days later he admitted that he could not remember where he had left the skiff and despite a thorough search of the dense reed beds along that stretch of the coast he had been unable to find it. Instead he bought an old fishing boat which they would use and then abandon. (He had paid for the boat in potatoes which at this time in Petrograd were worth more than hard currency.) The fact that Gefter had lost the skiff did not increase Paul's confidence in this cocky little courier and he particularly did not like the idea of involving a third party in their escape plan. It was quite likely that the fisherman would simply arrange for the Cheka to ambush them when they arrived to collect the boat and then pocket a fat reward. But the arrangements were already in place and he had no choice.

Before leaving, Paul had some loose ends to tie up. One of these was the rescue of Sonia Orlov. Despite the fact that Paul later claimed he had had nothing to do with the raid, he became deeply involved in attempts to rescue her. The fact that she was now held in the Deryabinsky prison rather than the Cheka headquarters at Gorohovaya meant that something might be done. Sonia's nanny Akulina had, by a combination of judicious bribery and a little flirtation, managed to get into prison to see Sonia. She had even been able to smuggle in a little food to strengthen her for the strain of the escape. Thanks to these visits Akulina knew the guards and every detail of Sonia's captivity. By August 1919 Sonia had been in prison for four months and, despite Akulina's ministrations, her health was beginning to suffer. If she was not rescued soon she would probably die in prison.

Paul took part in discussions about how she would be freed. Whether he remembered the ruse which had freed Mrs Merritt or whether it was Akulina's idea as he later claimed, the group decided on a very similar plan to the Merritt escape. First, Paul provided enough money to bribe one of the prison guards. Then Akulina travelled to the prison in the evening, accompanied by a Red Cross nurse who was a friend of the family. Paul and Shura Marenko were to follow at a discreet distance to act as bodyguards if there was trouble. Both men were armed with revolvers.

Paul claims that neither he nor Shura had any idea how the escape was to be effected – which is a little hard to believe – but apparently they were both disappointed when Akulina and the nurse emerged from the prison about thirty minutes later. The two men shadowed the women back to the Orlovs' house as arranged. They wondered what had gone wrong.

But when they arrived at the house they found Sonia sitting in the kitchen, waiting for them. The two men were stunned. It was like the finale of a magician's trick. She was dressed exactly as Akulina had been and the two men realised that it must have been Sonia they had seen walking with the nurse. Akulina arrived at one o'clock that morning. She told them how she had gone to Deryabinsky wearing two identical sets of clothes: black skirt, brown blouse, red scarf and a black shawl wrapped around her head. She had bribed one of the guards to allow her to take Sonia into a separate room where she had given Sonia one of the two sets of clothes and her pass. Then Sonia had walked downstairs from the cell, met the Red Cross nurse in the courtyard and had walked through the main gates with the other visitors. When the men on the main gate were replaced at midnight, the guard who had been bribed took Akulina there and explained that she had lost her day pass and was leaving very late because she had been attending a sick prisoner. It was a tremendous risk since the story was wafer thin, but the guards at the main gate fell for it and let her through. Paul does not say what happened to the guard who was bribed, but it is pretty clear that the escape would have been quickly traced to him if there was any sort of inquiry. Presumably the money which Paul put up for the bribe was enough for the guard to leave the country.

Shura and Sonia soon left Petrograd. But Sonia's health was too poor for her to risk crossing the border and so they headed to the countryside where it was planned that they would be sheltered by friends from Akulina's village.

With this last loose end tied up, Paul was finally free to leave. He made arrangements for his network to keep running. The new head of the network would be a woman later referred to by the Cheka as 'Petrovskaya'. Nothing more is known of her and it is possible that this was either Aunt Natalia or Klachonka. Whoever she was, Paul gave her Gibson's name and address together with the all-important MI6 password. Petrovskaya was told to go to Gibson if she needed more money to keep the networks running. Within a few weeks, Paul hoped that either he or his replacement would be back to take up the reins once more. On Friday, 14 August, he collected the last of his intelligence reports, said a tearful farewell to both Aunt Natalia and Klachonka and then set out for the Finland Station.

Paul travelled to Razdielnaya, about halfway to Finland, where he disembarked. Gefter was also on the train, but the two of them did not join up until they were well clear of the station and had checked that neither of them was being followed. Gefter led the way to the fisherman's hut. There they found the son of Gefter's contact. He told them that the boat would be delivered by his father to a point further along the shore in just a few hours. In the meantime they sat and drank tea, always keeping one ear open for the approach of a shore patrol. Paul's cover story was good, but he would have a hard time explaining what a soldier from the 8th Army transport division was doing at a fisherman's hut in the dead of night.

At about 10 o'clock it was fully dark and the young fisherman led them to the rendezvous. As promised, the fishing boat was there just offshore and the youth carried them out to it on his back so that they would not get soaked before their journey. In the distance the massive fortress of Kronstadt brooded in darkness. The searchlights were not yet active.

Then, just as they were getting ready to leave, a light which became increasingly brighter grew around the fortress. At first Paul assumed it must be some Allied attack or that the fortress was on fire, but it later turned out to have been a fire in the dockyards. The sight of Kronstadt burning added to the strange feeling of unreality as Paul left Petrograd for what he thought was the very last time.

The boat was heavy and difficult to handle. Gefter was an experienced seaman and, watching the sky overhead, he said that he did not like the look of the clouds. They could expect the weather to get worse very soon. The two men rowed as hard as they could, but progress just seemed to get slower and slower. They were now rowing into a strong headwind and the waters of the Gulf were becoming increasingly choppy. From his years in Petrograd, Paul knew that this was one of the sudden changes of weather for which the Gulf was notorious. Within half an hour of setting out they were rowing through a proper squall and water was pouring in over the gunwales with every stroke.

Even allowing for this, it seemed to Paul that the boat was lower in the water than it should have been. They were now hardly moving at all. Suddenly Gefter leapt up from his bench with an oath and opened a big locker in the centre of the boat. It was the fish locker, an enclosed area of the boat with a valve for filling it with sea water in order to keep the catch fresh. Either the valve had been left open or the bung had been shaken loose – either way the locker was awash. Gefter frantically tried to block the inlet valve, but it was no good. The water continued to pour in and they were sinking fast.

There was nothing in the boat to bail with. Paul tried frantically throwing water over the side with his leather cap but there was so much coming in that his efforts were useless. He peered out at the horizon and tried to get his bearings from the Elagin lightship which marked the Eastern end of Kotlin Island. He estimated that they were still more than a mile from the rendezvous, but they might still make it. Paul grabbed his oars and shouted to Gefter to keep going. There was nothing for it now but to row as hard as they could and get as close as possible before they sank.

Both men pulled at the oars with every ounce of strength that they had. The wind howled around them and rain poured down into the boat. They knew that this freak change in the weather would only last a matter of minutes, but that would not save them now. The current also seemed to be working against them and as Paul became more tired it seemed to him that the distance to the rendezvous was growing. As the boat sank lower, Gefter tried using one of the oars in a yawing motion in the stern to keep it afloat as Paul rowed and for a while it seemed like they were winning. They began to hope that they might outlast the squall and make it through to calmer waters. But they were out of luck. Eventually Gefter shouted that they would have to turn for shore. Peering ahead, Paul was forced to agree. He was a strong swimmer but even he did not stand a chance of making it to the rendezvous through these waves.

They fought their way back towards the shore. These had been hard-won yards and it was bitter defeat to have to give them up, but the squall showed no signs of abating. At least when they were heading in this direction they were taking less water on board. Somehow the little boat floated until they were about half a mile from the shore. Paul could just make out the trees in the moonlight. Behind him, Gefter tugged off his thigh-length seaboots and threw them into the water. Paul shouted at him to stop, but it was too late. Gefter protested that he would not be able to swim with them on. Paul asked him how he would walk across the sharp stones on shore. Gefter shrugged and kept rowing. A few strokes more and the boat gave up the unequal fight. The water swept over her sides and she slid quietly below the waves. The two exhausted men found themselves treading water.

Like many sailors, Gefter was not a good swimmer. He used one of the oars to help him float but in his exhausted state it was still a struggle for him to reach the shore. As Paul had feared, the bitter cold of the water was devastating and Gefter was not trained for it. With Paul's help he was just about able to stagger onto the beach.

The squall passed eventually and the Gulf was calm once again. As the two men lay there, gasping for breath, there was a faint roar like an aircraft engine in the distance and Paul could see what looked like a small white feather moving along the horizon. He knew from Peter's descriptions that this was the plume of water thrown up by the CMB. It was cruel luck. Paul could see from his watch that Gus was exactly on time. For a moment he was tempted to wade back into the water and to swim for it. He knew that Gus would wait as long as possible and he felt that he was strong enough to make it. But he knew that Gefter would not. Paul forced himself to turn his back to the sea and together the two men began their long walk home.

Gefter's lack of boots soon became critical. The boat had been swept several miles along the coast and they had a long walk ahead of them. They did not dare use the paths because of the risk of patrols so they had to force their way through the rocks and thick undergrowth. Soon Gefter's feet were bleeding heavily. Paul tried carrying Gefter on his back over the worst stretches, but they were both at the end of their strength and Gefter was heavy. They were both soaked to the skin and even though it was summer the cold night was beginning to chill them and they were both shivering.

They rested under a tree about halfway back to the city and then Paul stood up, nudged Gefter and told him that it was time to move on. Gefter slumped forward. He had stopped breathing and Paul could not find a pulse. Frantically, Paul rolled him over on the ground and began artificial respiration. For several minutes he thought Gefter was beyond hope, but then he coughed and began to revive a little.

Paul knew that there was no way they could push on in the darkness. Gefter was too weak and there were too many patrols. They rested until about seven in the morning when he knew the night patrols would return to barracks. The two men then managed to stumble to the fisherman's cottage from where they had set out the night before. Paul left Gefter there to be cared for by the fisherman's family.

But Paul could not stay. He would have no excuse if he was found there. The only place where he would be safe was back in the city. Within an hour he was on the train heading into Petrograd. But the event that would lead to the collapse of his entire network had already occurred. Although Paul did not know it, Peters and the Cheka were already starting to close in for the last time.

The Kronstadt Raid

Although the White Nights meant that the CMB courier service was out of operation for most of July, Gus Agar had not been idle. Like Paul Dukes, Gus could see that there was a very limited window of opportunity for the White forces to overthrow the Bolsheviks and he wished to do all that he could – within the constraints of his operational commitments – to help them. He had seen General Yudenich and his bunch of cronies at first hand, resting in luxury in their Helsinki hotels, and he was not impressed by them. But he thought the Ingrians were tough fighters who might be able to tip the scales if they were properly supported. Gus learned from Raleigh Le May that a force of Ingrian volunteers was going to mount an attack from Finland on Bolshevik forces. Gus offered to have his CMBs transported to one of Finland's larger lakes to support this attack. For once Gus's plans were in step with those of MI6 who hoped that the Russians would counter-attack and that this would bring Finland into the war on the Allied side. This matter was urgent as elections were due any day in Finland and it was expected that a strictly neutral Socialist government would replace the anti-Bolshevik administration of General Mannerheim. Unfortunately Scale tried to get clearance for this scheme from the difficult Captain Bruton so the plan came to nought.

However, on 26 July Agar did take CMB4 along the coast to support an attack by a small force of Ingrians. The trenches guarding the Russian border ran right down to the sea. Gus was able to get close enough to the shore to give covering fire into these trenches from a distance of five hundred metres. It was thought that this would draw Russian defenders towards the attack, thus weakening the area to the north where the Ingrians would attack. Certainly, shots were fired back at CMB4 but in the darkness they were well wide of the mark. Still, the effort was wasted: the attack by the Ingrians was successful, but the advance was not consolidated by Yudenich and the ground was recaptured some days later by the Bolsheviks. Even worse was the fact that the Russian pilot, who was supposed to know the area, ran CMB4 aground shortly after the attack. Her propeller shaft and engine mountings were badly damaged. Although Beeley did his best, the engine had been so badly affected that he would not vouch for the boat on long voyages or at high speed. The newly repaired CMB7 would have to be the mainstay of the courier service from now on.

Gus never publicly referred to this little adventure afterwards. The reason is clear: by using the Ingrians to provoke a Russian counter-attack, MI6, together with the outgoing government of General Mannerheim, hoped to create a situation where Finnish forces had to defend themselves. Finland would then be forced into the war on the Allied side. The fact that a Finnish officer accompanied Gus on this mission indicates that General Mannerheim may well have given his support. A declaration of war could have led to the cancellation of the forthcoming democratic election which Mannerheim was bound to lose. The fact that MI6 tried to trick the Finns into war was obviously a source of great embarrassment to the British government which is why the mission has been kept secret to this day. One question remains: did MI6 have government approval? Today it is (supposedly) unthinkable that MI6 would act without ministerial backing. However, in 1919 the situation was very different and the lines of command were not always clearly drawn. Certainly it seems odd that a British Cabinet which could not agree on intervention should suddenly authorise a move as provocative as this.

But despite the defeat of the Ingrians Gus was not too depressed. On the same day as the attack he received a telegram from Admiral Cowan informing him that he had been awarded the Victoria Cross for his sinking of the *Oleg*. There was no official citation and because the nature of his work was still a secret Gus was referred to in the press as 'the mystery VC'. John Hampsheir had been awarded the Distinguished Service Cross and Hugh Beeley the Conspicuous Gallantry Medal. It may seem unfair that Gus was awarded the Victoria Cross and that the other two received lesser medals even though they ran the same risks, but in this case the real burden had been his alone. It would have been his career that would have been destroyed if they had failed, it was his decision to ignore Cumming's order not to attack and it was his determination that drove the attack home despite the loss of CMB7 and the premature detonation of the torpedo charge. He alone had gambled everything on one shot – and he had won.

So the team was in high spirits when it reassembled at the beginning of August to resume the courier service. They were badly needed. Having fallen out with Gus, Le May and Hall had been trying to send new couriers by land. But it was now incredibly dangerous: the Finns had sent six couriers in two weeks and not one had returned. One of the new MI6 couriers was Vladimir Constantinov, a young officer from the Russian Guards Regiment. On 27 June he was sent with a guide to try to cross the border into Russia from Finland despite Peter Sokolov's warning that it was too dangerous. Constantinov returned the following morning with a Russian bullet in his shoulder. Either knowingly or not, his guide had led him straight into a trap and he had been lucky to escape with his life. Constantinov refused to attempt the crossing again. Instead he remained at Terrioki as an interpreter and camp helper. At the end of July, Le May finally convinced Peter Sokolov to try the route from Estonia. Peter disappeared and MI6 assumed that he had been either killed or captured. Gus had a different theory. He thought that Peter had run away to join the White forces in Estonia preferring to fight openly instead of having to deal with '. . . all the messing about he got from the people at Helsingfors . . .' (i.e. Hall and Le May).

MI6 tried to deal with the unreliability of the courier system by sending radio operators to Terrioki. These were Victor Jones (ST-35) and John Busby (ST-36). Not much is known of Busby, but Jones was a former RNVR Chief Petty Officer who had been demobbed and was working for the Post Office Wireless Department. When he and Busby arrived at the dacha they found that there was only one problem – MI6 had not provided them with any radios! So they spent several weeks doing very little except sunbathing and playing games of cards for haricot beans with the other residents of the dacha. Although radios arrived later, they were never successfully used for agent communication. Couriers carried by CMB were still the only reliable link with Paul Dukes.

But the resumption of the CMB courier service did not run smoothly. Hall and Le May were still determined that Gus would only do what they told him to do. On Monday, 4 August, Le May arrived from Helsinki. Major Scale had returned to England to report on the current situation, so Le May was now effectively in charge of the whole operation. He called a meeting with Gus, Hall and the latest of the couriers, Gefter, who had arrived at Terrioki two days before. Le May immediately annoyed Gus by laying out a series of plans for runs through the forts which the team had not been consulted about. Le May said that he wanted Gefter to be taken in that evening. It was highly dangerous, but Gus duly left to make preparations. A few hours later Hall arrived to say that Le May had abandoned the idea and that Gefter would go later in the week. Gus began to feel like a chauffeur.

The following day Le May called another meeting and once more began to lay out plans for courier runs, all without having consulted Gus at all. When Gus suggested that some of these ideas might prove difficult Le May insinuated that Gus was getting cold feet. He seemed to think that there was no risk at all in going through the forts. At one point Hall interjected:

'Now come on, Agar, which particular forts are you afraid of?'

Gus was stunned by Hall's ignorance. Very slowly and carefully he replied:

'All of them.'

Eventually Gus could stand it no more. He said that if ST-25 must come out now as Cumming was insisting, then he, as leader of the team, would decide how it was to be done. He insisted that an urgent telegram be sent to Cumming to have this confirmed and refused to discuss plans any further. He pointed out that once before Hall and Le May had interfered and that it had almost resulted in the death of his men. Hall breezily replied:

'Oh, that doesn't matter.'

Gus looked at him coldly and then left the dacha without saying another word. He refused to speak to either Hall or Le May again and instead made plans to see Admiral Cowan first thing the next morning. That night he wrote in his diary:

'This may be the end of our whole show, but things cannot proceed on with this sort of dual or triple control and again Le May said to me "We have spent a lot of money on the boats and they have done nothing." I didn't remark to him that while he and his people were sitting in nice comfortable places at Helsinki we had been doing the work … Anyway there's a bust-up and things have come to a head, either I have control and run the show as best I can without him or else they must get somebody else. In the meantime J is stuck in Petrograd and must come out.'

'J' meant Paul Dukes. Clearly Gus had only heard the name spoken as he consistently spells the name 'Jukes' from this point on in his diary, but it shows once again how operational security had broken down. This lack of security at Terrioki would shock a modern intelligence officer. Not only was the site visited by various Allied military attachés and dignitaries, but there was even a journalist staying at the base at one point. This was Hugh Muir, special correspondent of the *Daily Express*. It was Muir who first referred to Gus as 'the mystery VC'. Gus's papers include several photographs of him relaxing with the crews at the dacha. He appears to have stayed there between 2 and 10 August and seems to have known a great deal about the operation because Gus's diary entry for 10 August reads: 'I said I would send him a wire if anything happened' (!) This is particularly odd since most journalists were granted no access at all to military operations in the area. Even *The Times* correspondent was only granted one very brief interview with Admiral Cowan. One possible explanation is that Muir was actually working for MI6 – this combination of journalist and spy would not have been unusual in the early days of the Service, but no suggestion of this has ever appeared in papers which have been released to date.

Even Eric Brewerton, a very junior officer who had arrived from England on HMS *Vindictive* just two weeks before, knew by 10 August what Gus was really doing in the area. He wrote in his logbook that Gus was 'taking spies up the River (i.e. the Neva) and dropping them off.' If these men knew all about Gus, it is hardly surprising that, a few weeks later, Bolshevik agents knew exactly where to find him. This seems to be yet another lapse by Le May and Hall because they should have been responsible for the security of the mission.

Once Gus had spoken to Admiral Cowan, a telegram arrived from Cumming confirming that Gus was in complete control of the naval aspect of the operation and Gefter was finally landed by Sindall in CMB7 on 8 August with instructions to bring Paul Dukes out on 14 August. But relations between Gus, Hall and Le May had now broken down irreparably.

Meanwhile, the other project which had occupied Gus's time during the White Nights of July was coming to fruition: an attack on the Soviet Baltic fleet in Kronstadt harbour. To a certain extent, Admiral Cowan's hands had been untied on 4 July when the British Cabinet had finally decided that, whilst they would not formally declare war on Soviet Russia, it should now be considered that 'a state of war' existed between the two nations. Now Cowan could plan to attack the Soviet fleet in its lair without fear of recrimination. But as he and his staff spent many hours working on the plan, they always came up against the same problem – the noise of the powerful CMB engines would give the boats away as they passed through the forts (they dared not send such a large number of vessels through at low speed) and by the time they reached the harbour the defenders would be waiting for them. The harbour was only about 800 metres wide in any case. Without the element of surprise they would truly be like fish in a barrel.

But finally they came up with the answer. The aircraft carrier HMS *Vindictive* was due any day. She was only armed with a ragbag collection of old aircraft, but if they could time a bombing run to coincide exactly with the passage of the CMBs through the forts then the boats might not be detected. Furthermore, the harbour gun crews might still be in their shelters when the CMBs arrived. Such precision timing between aircraft and ships at night had never been attempted before, but it was their best chance. Cowan authorised the operation and gave it the code name 'R.K.' after the British Admiral Sir Roger Keyes who had commanded a famous blockship attack on the harbour at Zeebrugge in 1917.

HMS *Vindictive* arrived in Biorko Sound on 20 July. She was a 'composite aircraft carrier' – an old cruiser which had been retrofitted with a wooden deck from which aircraft could be launched. However, the launching of aircraft from ships was still in its infancy and was highly dangerous. If at all possible, pilots preferred to take off from dry land or even the sea (the *Vindictive* carried four seaplanes). HMS *Vindictive* was commanded by Captain Edgar 'Dasher' Grace, son of the famous English cricketer Dr W. G. Grace. On 6 July while en route to Biorko he had committed the ultimate naval sin of grounding his ship. She had been just outside Reval harbour. It took eight days to refloat her and at one stage it looked as though she would have to be abandoned entirely. Two thousand tons of stores had to be manhandled onto shore before she was finally towed clear thanks to a freak high tide, three tugs and the efforts of hundreds of sailors jumping up and down on her deck to shake her clear – a ludicrous sight. Cowan was furious at this delay to his plans and Edgar Grace was determined to make up for his error. The *Vindictive* was to be the base ship for all the CMBs as well as all the aircraft. It was a job which Gus and other officers quite frankly thought could not be done, but Edgar Grace and his men did it.

HMS *Vindictive*'s aircraft were a motley bunch. They were really fighter aircraft rather than dedicated bombers and although she carried twelve aeroplanes only eight of these were eventually to assist in the attack, due to maintenance and other problems. Four were Short seaplanes each with a crew of two (pilot and observer). Two were 'Ship Strutters', a variation of an old Sopwith aircraft, the Strutter, which first saw service in 1916 and by 1919 was practically obsolete. The Strutter had originally been designed as a two-seater, but the shipborne version was a single-seater in order to reduce take-off weight and therefore reduce the distance necessary to launch it. It was armed with a forward-firing machine gun and carried up to four small bombs. Then there was another obsolete Sopwith two-seater called a Griffin with a similar bomb load and, finally, the best fighter aircraft of all, a solitary Sopwith Camel. Although the Camel had been replaced in front-line RAF service by the Sopwith Snipe, it could still more than hold its own against anything that it was likely to encounter around Kronstadt. It was armed with two fixed forward firing Vickers .303 machine guns capable of unleashing over 600 rounds per minute and carried either four small fragmentation bombs or a single 50lb (23kg) high-explosive bomb.

But none of the *Vindictive*'s flimsy aircraft could carry bombs large enough to penetrate the Soviet battlecruisers' armoured decks and there was also the problem of accuracy. These aircraft carried no bombsights. Bomb release was simply a matter of leaning over the side of the aircraft to see if the target was below and then pulling the release toggle. Sometimes the bombs did not release at all because mechanics made very sure to fix them tightly as they had a tendency to fall off and explode during take-off. There was a verse from a song sung in Royal Naval Air Service messes which summed up their feelings about aerial bombing:

> *There's a game that some people play for the whole of the*
>   *day,*
> *Of dropping a bomb from the air,*
> *And men grin with delight if they drop it aright,*
> *A contingency only too rare!*

The aircrew were under the command of Major David Grahame Donald. A former Scottish rugby international, Donald's bluff no-nonsense approach was ideal for the dangerous world of naval aviation in 1919 and he was highly respected by his young pilots. Two bases were built to accommodate the aircraft. The seaplanes were moored on the shore at Sidinsari within sight of Cowan's squadron. (This proved very popular as they were alongside the local nudist beach.) The remaining aircraft were to be based at an airstrip on the coast near the village of Koivisto. The two-hundred-yard-long stretch of runway was still being hacked out of the virgin pine forest when the *Vindictive* arrived. Major Donald and his young pilots went to take a look. They picked their way across the shattered terrain, which was still littered with the remains of boulders and tree stumps. As they stood at the end of the airfield and peered over at the steep (and probably fatal) drop into the sea on the other side, the dour Scotsman neatly summed up the feelings of all his young pilots: '*Jesus Christ!*'

Meanwhile, at Osea Island in Essex, as many of the twin-engined 55-foot CMBs as could be found were made ready. Eventually eight were dispatched. They were to be towed in pairs across the North Sea by destroyers. It was a difficult journey. The tows parted no less than sixteen times, all the boats were swamped and one was lost entirely. The first thing the mechanics had to do upon arriving at Biorko was to completely overhaul the engines. This raised another problem: whilst the boats were readily available, mechanics were not. Maintaining high-performance CMB engines was skilled work and could not be done by just any mechanic in the Royal Navy. It was like the difference between the engine of a normal vehicle and a Formula One racing car. Most of the mechanics at Osea were 'hostilities only' personnel which meant that as soon as the war was over they were demobbed. Now a message went out for volunteers to return for a one-off mission, even though they could not be told where they would be going or what the mission involved. Eight mechanics bravely answered the call.

On Friday, 25 July, the first CMB arrived. It was number 79A, commanded by Lieutenant William 'Bill' Bremner, one of the three junior officers who had first suggested the creation of Coastal Motor Boats in 1915. Although he had already won the Distinguished Service Cross for one action involving CMBs, he was keen to see them used in the role he had always envisaged – skimming across minefields and attacking an enemy fleet in its home port. The other CMB which had been towed across the North Sea with 79A was undergoing a complete overhaul at Reval because of the damage caused by sea water during the journey.

In the early morning of 30 July, Major Donald took nine aircraft on the first bombing raid over Kronstadt harbour. Since the airfield was not ready, they took off from the deck of the *Vindictive*. The mission was very nearly a disaster. Shortly after the planes were airborne, coloured flares were seen arcing into the night sky from somewhere in the forests beyond Koivisto. This was a signal from Bolshevik spies warning Kronstadt that an attack had been launched. But the British aircraft were not equipped with radios and by the time it was realised that they had been spotted there was no way to recall them. All of the Kotlin Island forts were alerted and Donald's planes first encountered anti-aircraft fire when they were still four miles from their target. At 0300, just as it was becoming full daylight, the aircraft arrived over the harbour. Major Donald and his men found the Kronstadt air defences waiting for them. In order to have some chance of hitting their targets, they bravely flew no higher than 4,000 feet. The anti-aircraft guns soon locked on to this altitude and gave them a very warm reception indeed. Altogether the aircraft dropped sixteen bombs, claiming four hits, starting two large fires and killing one person. Donald described the anti-aircraft fire as 'very effective throughout' and they were lucky to escape without any losses. Although the damage caused by the attack was minimal, the mission did serve one additional purpose – the defenders of Kronstadt now thought that any British attack would come from the sky, not from the sea.

Meanwhile, out at sea, CMBs 4 and 7 sat just off Tolboukin lighthouse, watching the flashes in the early-morning sky as the attack progressed. Their job was to rescue any aircraft that might be forced to ditch in the sea as a result of enemy fire or engine failure. After an hour it became clear that all the British aircraft had returned. But in the meantime a Soviet patrol boat had begun nosing around outside the line of the forts, possibly as the result of the CMBs being spotted by sentries in the lighthouse.

Ed Sindall in command of CMB7 cruised slowly towards Gus Agar in the crippled CMB4 and asked for permission to have a pot at the Soviet boat. Gus knew how keen his junior officer was to see action. Gus gave him permission to make one pass, but not to follow if the Soviet boat retreated behind the protective line of the forts.

CMB7 immediately swung into the attack, making a line straight for the distant Soviet vessel. Although Sindall was still two miles away the sea forts had clearly been warned by the lookouts in the lighthouse because two of them opened fire with their massive naval guns. The shots were well wide but, even so, Sindall began steering a zigzag course to throw off their aim, all the while closing on his target.

Either the Soviet patrol boat could not see CMB7 or she was trying to lure CMB7 in because she did not turn and run. She held steady to her course in front of the line of the forts. Sindall closed to nine hundred yards, ignoring the shellfire directed at him, and then Gus saw the tell-tale swerve which showed that CMB7 had released its torpedo.

Almost immediately Ed Sindall realised that the torpedo was going to miss. The Soviet patrol boat accelerated and changed course towards him. But rather than run 'Sinbad' headed straight for them. The patrol boat opened fire with a small-bore deck gun and a shot landed just yards away from CMB7's port bow. Sindall came on, giving the wheel just a slight nudge to throw off the Soviet gunner's aim. The two boats were now so close that the sea forts ceased fire for fear of hitting their own men.

At 400 yards' range Sindall put the wheel hard over and as CMB7 disappeared behind a wall of spray Richard Marshall let fly with both Lewis guns. Osea's marksman had the satisfaction of seeing his tracer stream into the Soviet boat, killing or wounding the gun crew. Sindall brought CMB7 around in a full circle to give Marshall another shot, but the Bolshevik captain had seen enough. He turned and ran for the line of the forts. Sindall chased him for half a mile, but although Marshall kept firing he failed to hit anything vital and the speed of the Soviet boat did not decrease. Finally, the sea forts opened fire again and, mindful of Gus's orders, Ed Sindall broke off the attack. Together with CMB4 they turned for home.

On 9 August the remaining CMBs arrived. They were all in a very poor state after the crossing. But Admiral Cowan was concerned that the Russian spies in the hills overlooking the harbour, who had already sabotaged Major Donald's night attack on 30 July, would see the CMBs, guess his intent and alert the commandant at Kronstadt. He allowed just four days to overhaul the engines and one day for a rehearsal of the attack. By the night of 15 August the CMBs had to be ready to go, come what may.

Most of the hastily assembled crews of the CMBs were junior officers and ratings who had never been under fire before. There were only four officers with considerable experience. The commander of the attack was to be Commander Claude Dobson, a former submariner and leading CMB captain. The second was Lieutenant Archibald Dayrell-Reed, a highly decorated CMB captain who had already sunk one German destroyer. He was known throughout the flotilla as 'Mossy' because of his luxuriant black beard. The third most experienced officer was Lieutenant Russell McBean, the best helmsman in the Flotilla. Together with Bill Bremner these men would form the core of the attack. As for the others, the Navy would just have to hope that they proved their worth when the time came.

On 12 August, Bremner and Dobson were taken on a reconnaissance flight over Kronstadt and had a look at the defences. The naval facilities at Kronstadt actually consisted of three harbours side by side. To the west was the commercial harbour where the cargo ships docked. They could ignore that. To the east was a small military harbour that contained patrol boats and other minor vessels. Although lightly armed, some of these would be quite fast and might chase or even intercept the CMBs on their way back. At least one CMB would have to be detailed to deal with this threat. In the middle of these two facilities was the main military harbour where the Baltic fleet was moored. The entrance to this harbour was surprisingly narrow – no more than fifty metres across. Bremner and Dobson were unable to see if there was a boom across the entrance but they assumed that there was and that they would have to deal with it on the night. But the key factor in the defence of the harbour was a destroyer posted just outside the entrance. It would have a point-blank shot at any CMB entering or leaving the harbour. Worse still, that destroyer was the *Gavriil*, probably the most ably commanded ship in the Soviet Baltic fleet. Her captain, V. Sevastyanov, was a former Tsarist officer and he had already taken his ship into several encounters with Cowan's squadron. Dobson reckoned that at least one CMB would have to be assigned to deal with the *Gavriil* before the others could get through.

Both men were also shocked by how cramped the military harbour was. There would be almost no room to manoeuvre and certainly no room for more than two or three CMBs in the harbour at a time. Bremner and Dobson decided that the CMBs should attack in two waves of three. The first wave would have to be allowed to get clear of the harbour before the second wave attacked. But this raised a difficult question: the attack force was divided between four experienced crews and three inexperienced crews. Should the youngsters go first or second? The first wave would have the advantage of surprise and therefore the best chance of sinking their targets. The second wave would be sailing straight into the full force of the alerted enemy defences. They would be lucky to get through at all. It would certainly be no place for an inexperienced crew. In the end, Claude Dobson decided that the most important point was that they cripple the enemy fleet. He ordered that the three most experienced crews, led by himself, Bill Bremner and Mossy Reed, would attack first. The other experienced crew under Lieutenant Napier was detailed to sink the *Gavriil* at the harbour entrance. The youngsters would have to take their chances in the second wave. Gus Agar, who was too valuable to risk in the main attack because of his secret-service work, was detailed to deal with any patrol craft which emerged from the small military harbour to the east.

That afternoon, Cowan called the CMB officers together for a briefing. He listed the five principal targets: the most important were the two giant battlecruisers *Andrei Pervozvanni* and *Petropavlovsk*. If they could be destroyed the Soviet fleet would be effectively crippled and would be unlikely to emerge from Kronstadt harbour for the foreseeable future. The next target was the submarine depot ship *Pamiat Azova*. Soviet submarines were a constant threat to Cowan's squadron. Reconnaissance photographs showed that this depot ship currently had two submarines berthed alongside, preparing to go to sea. If a torpedo caused the *Pamiat*

Azova to explode or capsize she might take one or both of these submarines with her.

The fourth target was more of a problem. The large minefields in the Gulf constantly restricted Cowan's freedom of operation and had sunk several ships. Cowan asked the CMB commanders to attack the *Rurik*, an ageing Russian cruiser which had been fitted out as a minelayer. According to intelligence obtained by Paul Dukes, she had been loaded recently with 300 live mines and was about to lay a new minefield. Commander Dobson politely pointed out that putting a torpedo into a ship containing 300 live mines would probably destroy the *Rurik*, half the harbour and every single CMB in the surrounding area. Cowan simply shrugged at this: he just outlined the targets – how the attack was accomplished was down to Dobson and his crews. (After the briefing Dobson privately told his crews that they should forget the *Rurik* and go for the dry dock instead. They might live longer. Only if every other target had been destroyed should the very last torpedo be sent into the *Rurik*.)

The fifth target was the caisson of the dry dock where the Soviet warships were repaired. The waters in the harbour were very shallow and although the CMBs might sink the dreadnoughts they would eventually be raised and repaired. Anything the CMBs could do to delay that operation would be invaluable. Taking out the dry dock facilities would be an important stage in that plan.

Dobson then addressed the crews and pointed out that in the confusion of the harbour one of the greatest risks would be a collision between the CMBs. To avoid this, after firing their torpedoes each of the boats would go to a 'waiting berth' until the other boats in the group had completed their attacks. Then all three boats in the group would leave together before the second wave attacked. The waiting berth was to be next to a hospital ship which was moored against the southern wall of the harbour. The Russian guns would be unlikely to fire in that direction for fear of causing casualties among their own men. Hiding behind a Red Cross was taking a bit of a liberty, but the flimsy CMBs needed every chance they could get.

Major Donald then briefed the CMB crews about the air support. He told them that he could buy them no more than fifteen minutes. His aircraft carried only a few small bombs and although they would do their best to cause a distraction they did not fancy going up against the Kronstadt anti-aircraft defences at low level with just tracer bullets. The CMB crews did not think that this would be a problem: after fifteen minutes the only people still left in the harbour would be dead.

On Thursday, 14 August Gus made his one last attempt to collect Paul Dukes before the Kronstadt attack. This was the rendezvous which Dukes failed to make because his boat was swamped and he was forced to swim back to shore with Gefter. However, the trip was not a complete failure because Gus was able to drop another one of Paul Dukes's agents. This was a Bolshevik officer named Kroslov whom Gus describes as looking 'like an intellectual with a high forehead and wearing pince nez.' He clearly liked this man a lot more than Gefter whom he described as 'bombastic' and someone who 'might give the whole game away to save his skin.' Whether Kroslov's mission was a success is not known. He is never mentioned again in any published record.

This was also to be John Hampsheir's last trip. He had been staying at the dacha in Terrioki with the rest of the crew and he had begged Gus for the chance to prove himself once more. Gus did not think that he was ready, but he also thought that to show a lack of confidence in his friend might lead to a further deterioration in his condition. Gus had waited an hour at the rendezvous point, but when it was obvious that Paul Dukes was not coming he had had to turn for home. At first the engine nearly did not start because the compressed-air bottle which acted as a starter motor had been leaking and there was barely enough gas left for one attempt. Everything depended on Hugh Beeley and his tending of the engine, but once again he triumphed. Then, as they were returning through the forts at about one o'clock in the morning, they were caught in a squall similar to the one that had swamped Paul and Gefter earlier. Despite the best efforts of the crew, waves poured in over the side and soon there was one and a half feet of water in the hull. CMB7 was reduced to a crawl. The water was up to the level of the flywheel and if it rose any higher it threatened to stop the engine altogether. John Hampsheir bailed frantically as Beeley fought to keep the engine alive, whilst Gus tried to gain them every yard possible to get out of the sight of the forts. After half an hour the squall eased and they were able to turn for home, arriving at Terrioki just before two in the morning. But Gus's fears had been realised. Following this further brush with a watery grave John Hampsheir's nerves were finally gone. He was never to make another trip in a CMB.

The following day Gus left for Biorko Sound in CMB7 to join the rest of the flotilla. His task would be to lead the attacking craft through the line of forts and around the eastern end of Kotlin Island to the harbour. He took two Finnish smugglers with him to help guide the attack force through the sea forts. One was the constant if not necessarily trustworthy Veroline. The other was a Finn named 'Huva' who had served on a Russian yacht cruising around the Gulf of Finland before the war and knew the waters well. During the war he had worked on an English cargo ship and could speak fairly good English so Gus suggested that he should travel in Dobson's boat in case the flotilla ran into enemy fire and became separated. Gus did not tell either of the Finns that this time they would be sailing right into Kronstadt harbour rather than just through the forts. When they arrived at Biorko and did find out, they immediately wanted to leave. However, the promise of double pay and two quarts of British navy rum each finally convinced them.

That afternoon, Friday, 15 August the crews held their one and only rehearsal for the Kronstadt attack. They had set buoys in the water to mark the dimensions of the harbour, based on the photographs taken during the reconnaissance flights. Different-coloured buoys marked the positions of the primary targets: the battlecruisers, the submarine depot ship and the minelayer. It was the first chance the crews had to get a real impression of the task ahead of them. The greatest problem was that the two battlecruisers were moored on the far left-hand side of the harbour. The CMBs would have to enter, turn hard left, reach attack speed, launch their torpedoes and then swing out of the way before the torpedoes hit their target. Russell McBean was the most experienced helmsman in the Flotilla and he would be steering CMB31, commanded by Dobson. He started up the engines and roared into the Sound to make the first attack run. He was closely watched and also cheered on by the other CMB crews from the deck of the *Vindictive*. He passed at high speed through the buoys marking the harbour entrance, turned sharply through 120 degrees and then lined up on the row of buoys representing the *Andrei Pervozvanni*. But he had mistimed his turn and although he managed to reach the torpedo-launching speed of 30 knots, he had run out of room. CMB31 rocketed straight through the buoys representing the *Andrei Pervozvanni*, then through the *Petropavlovsk* and finally through the thirty-foot-thick harbour wall behind them. If this attack had been the real thing CMB31 would now have been no more than a pool of flaming oil and wreckage decorating the waters of Kronstadt harbour.

It was a sobering moment. McBean was the best helmsman in the flotilla and on the night of the attack they would have the added distraction of the guns of the harbour defences firing at them at point-blank range. The men could also see that the distances they were working with were so small that, even if they hit the target, the chances were that the explosion would destroy them as well. The reactions of the watching CMB crews were not recorded, but they are likely to have been unprintable anyway.

The crews practised all that afternoon, sometimes making it, sometimes not. But there was no time for them to get better. The weather was closing in rapidly and soon the waters became too choppy to practise any longer. The storm grew in force and the attack planned for that night had to be called off. The storm then continued for another day and a half and at one stage was so bad that the CMBs were forced away from the *Vindictive* to seek shelter in a small inlet off the main bay. But finally, on Sunday, 17 August, the weather broke and Admiral Cowan authorised the attack for that night. Zero hour, the moment when the CMBs would pass through the forts to begin their attack run, was set for 0045 on Monday, 18 August 1919. At Z minus 5, the aircraft would begin bombing Kronstadt harbour in the hope that this would distract the forts from the boats' run.

At approximately 10.45 p.m. on Sunday the first CMBs left the safety of Biorko Sound. Conditions were perfect for the attack. The sea was calm. A half-moon could occasionally be glimpsed through the scudding clouds, but otherwise the night was fully dark. Eight CMBs headed for the first rendezvous. This was Inonini Point the site of the Finnish fort where Agar had been fired on by Finnish troops just a few weeks before. Here the flotilla waited. The plan called for their attack to be timed to the minute and they were not scheduled to move on until Z minus 50 (11.55 p.m.) or they risked arriving in the harbour during the bombing and being hit by their own aircraft. The schedule had been designed so that they should begin their attack on the harbour at Z plus 20 (1.05 a.m.) – exactly as the bombing finished.

As the CMBs sat bobbing in the water with their engines ticking over, gunners checked ammunition drums and mechanics made last-minute adjustments to their notoriously temperamental charges. The starboard engine of CMB86 was giving particular cause for concern. It was only firing on six cylinders despite frantic last-minute work to repair it. The boat was very nearly pulled from the attack, but Francis Yates, a young – and newly married – lieutenant commander with engineering skills had volunteered to travel with the boat and keep the engine running if it was at all possible. He was still working on the engines as the flotilla was sitting there. Another officer who had not expected to be part of the attack was Lieutenant Commander Frank Brade commanding CMB62BD. At the last moment he had volunteered to take the place of Lieutenant Richard Chapman who had fallen ill.

As the CMBs rocked gently in the cold night air, each man must have been wondering about his chances of survival that night. Some would have been thinking back to a CMB raid almost exactly one year earlier. On 11 August 1918, a cruiser force from Harwich under Admiral Tyrwhitt had carried out a well-planned attack against German naval forces in the Heligoland Bight. The Harwich force had sailed across the North Sea transmitting a series of fake wireless signals which had been carefully designed to tempt German naval forces out of their well-defended harbour to attack what appeared to be easy prey. The plan was that the CMBs, assisted and protected by naval aircraft, would then attack the heavier capital ships with torpedoes. At first all went well. The British naval force arrived at their rendezvous off Terschelling Island on schedule and at 0530 the cruisers lowered six CMBs into the water. They roared off to carry out the attack. But the seaplanes that were supposed to provide top cover never made it. Laden down with too much fuel and ammunition they were unable to take off in the choppy conditions. Not one of the CMBs returned. Every single one of them was cut to pieces by a combination of shore defences and German naval aircraft. Some of the crews made it to the shores of Holland where they were interned for the remainder of the war. It must have occurred to the crews for the Kronstadt attack that this plan was disturbingly similar – except that in this case they were going right into the harbour, the very heart of the enemy defences.

Finally, at almost midnight, Dobson lifted his flashlight, which was covered with a green filter, and gave the signal for the attack to begin. All around Inonini Point CMB engines roared into life, shattering the stillness.

Agar opened the throttle of CMB7 and led the flotilla away into the darkness in a line-astern formation. Behind him followed Napier in CMB24A whose job would be to take out the *Gavriil* at the entrance to the harbour. He would be first to attack. Then came Group One consisting of Bremner, Dobson and 'Mossy' Reed in CMBs 79A, 31BD and 88BD respectively. They were followed by Group Two consisting of the volunteer Brade and two young officers, Howard and Bodley, in CMBs 62BD, 86 and 72.

Almost immediately things began to go wrong.

For some reason, Dobson's smuggler pilot, Huva, urged him to head further south than the line that Gus was taking because he was sure that Veroline was heading for a gap that was closed. Dobson chose to follow the smuggler's advice and veered away. The rest of the flotilla followed him.

Glancing behind as he gathered speed for their attack run on the forts, Gus Agar could only see two CMBs still with him. The one immediately behind was Napier's. As Napier was immediately behind Gus he had not seen Dobson leaving the formation. The identity of the other CMB is not certain, but Gus said later that she was making a 'fearful din' and throwing out flames from her exhaust – a sure sign of a malfunctioning engine. This was almost certainly Howard's boat, CMB86. In the darkness to starboard Gus thought he could see the spray thrown up by what might be the rest of the flotilla, but he could not be sure. He decided that he had no choice but to continue with the attack as planned. He was sure that the noise of their engines would have been heard by now and he increased speed to make CMB7 a more difficult target if the forts opened fire. Sure enough they did, letting go with machine-gun and light-artillery fire. But for some reason they did not use their searchlights and all the fire was well wide of the mark.

Once they were out of range, Gus eased back on the throttle to about 20 knots and steered a course for the eastern end of Kotlin Island, right below the fortress of Kronstadt. Glancing behind, he could still see Napier doggedly maintaining position. There was no sign of Howard at all but Gus could not afford to worry about that now. He pushed on. It would take about 30 minutes to reach the mouth of the harbour.

In fact Howard's boat, CMB86, was dead in the water several

miles behind. He had followed Gus and Napier through the forts, but he had fallen further and further back until finally there was 'a frightful jarring noise' and the boat shuddered to a complete stop. Howard immediately thought that the problem was the trouble-some starboard engine, but Lieutenant Commander Yates quickly put his head up from the engine compartment and said that the port engine had shattered its crankshaft. There was no hope of restarting it. Howard glanced back over his shoulder – he was trapped on the wrong side of the forts and was within range of the enemy guns. Fortunately, since his CMB's engines were dead the flames from the exhaust had stopped and they were effectively invisible in the darkness. But when morning came the Bolshevik forces in the forts would see them and they would not stand a chance. Yates told Howard that he would see what could be done and disappeared back into the engine compartment with the other mechanic.

Meanwhile Dobson had been incredibly lucky. His Finnish pilot seemed to become confused by the speed at which they were travelling and he had chosen completely the wrong gap. It was one of those where the Russians had recently repaired the breakwater specifically to stop a vessel such as a CMB. The bottom should have been ripped out of CMB31 and out of every boat following Dobson. But the heavy gales of the past two days had caused such an enormous build-up of waters in the Gulf that the tide that night was about two feet higher than normal. Instead of encountering disaster, Dobson and the following boats sailed over the newly repaired breakwater with plenty of room to spare. They were not even fired on by the forts. Taking this different route had also saved them considerable time compared to Agar and Napier who were now some way to the north. The carefully prepared timetable which called for the *Gavriil* to be destroyed first had already fallen apart.

CMB31 and the other boats rounded the eastern end of Kotlin Island and arrived at the rendezvous five minutes earlier than planned. Even so, the air attack by Donald and his men had not yet started. They had experienced considerable difficulty getting airborne and they were very late. The harbour was still shrouded in silence and darkness. There were no lights visible on the *Gavriil* guarding the harbour entrance. Not knowing where Napier was nor why the bombing raid had not started, Dobson decided to signal for the attack to go ahead.

Bill Bremner in CMB79 moved forward steadily, passing around behind the *Gavriil* and heading towards the narrow harbour entrance. It was his job to destroy the boom or chain guarding the harbour entrance and he carried gun-cotton charges in his boat for just this purpose. But as he drew closer the rating who was poised in the bows to watch for the boom reported that the entrance to the harbour was not guarded by a barrier of any kind. This was another tremendous stroke of good luck. Bremner put CMB79 into a wide circle to pick up speed and then accelerated towards the harbour entrance. The wings of water rose up on either side and he lined up with the *Pamiat Azova,* which was visible in her berth directly ahead. Even as he did so Major Donald and his aircraft appeared overhead and the first bombs whistled down to explode among the docks.

As the first bombs struck, Bremner was picking up speed. Because the waters in the harbour were so shallow it was vital that the torpedoes were launched at the highest speed possible to prevent a 'death dive'. Bremner's young second in command, Sub Lieutenant Tom Usborne, shouted the revolution count into Bremner's ear above the deafening roar of the engine. Bill Bremner had no time to look down at the controls: there was no aiming mechanism for the torpedoes – everything depended on the skill and judgement of the captain – and he had to estimate the line of attack by sight, just using slight nudges of the steering wheel to correct the CMB's course. He could not afford to make a mistake: unlike Dobson and Mossy Reed's boats, his 55-foot CMB was designed to carry only one torpedo.

They were running out of room. From somewhere to his right a bullet ricocheted off the metal frame of the windscreen. Tom Usborne shouted that they had reached 1100 rpm and Bremner pulled the release toggle. There was a loud hiss as the hydraulic ram shoved the torpedo along the trough and over the stern. Immediately Bremner threw CMB79 into a tight turn to port away from the line of the torpedo and the central harbour wall where machine-gun emplacements were positioned. Within seconds there was a crunching roar and a shudder that shook the entire boat. The crew of CMB79 let out a collective shout of joy as a cloud of smoke and flame began to rise above the *Pamiat Azova* and she immediately began to heel over to her starboard side.

Bremner had no time to look back. He brought CMB 79 to a halt near the dry dock which was his 'waiting berth' because crossing to the hospital ship would have risked a collision with Dobson and Reed. Above them the sky was lit up by streams of tracer and red-hot shrapnel like a 5 November fireworks display. But as soon as CMB79 drew to a halt bullets began to whine and ricochet all around them. It seemed that the cover they had hoped for did not exist and at least two emplacements could fire on them. Bremner kept his head down below the windscreen and his gunners did their best to lay down suppressing fire. But it soon became clear that if they stayed there, they were dead. Muttering an oath beneath his breath, Bremner opened up both throttles and steered straight across the harbour between the lines of tracer bullets and the plumes of water that were being thrown up by the shells, just getting across before 'Mossy' Reed came racing through. He headed straight on for the alternative 'waiting berth' at the hospital ship.

Meanwhile Agar and Napier had arrived just outside the entrance to the military harbour. There was no sign of the other CMBs but since zero hour had passed and the RAF's attack had clearly begun Napier opened out the engines of CMB24 and headed straight for the *Gavriil*. The destroyer was in darkness and seemed unaware of the cacophony from the nearby harbour. The second in command, Lieutenant Osman Giddy, primed the charge so that they would be ready to launch the moment Napier had the right line. They were already under heavy fire. Giddy later estimated that there were at least ten different shore batteries firing at CMB24 at this time.

Suddenly Napier spotted another CMB making for the harbour entrance. Afraid of hitting her, he broke off the attack and put CMB24 into a wide turn to buy some time. The other CMB passed and Napier came out of the turn so that he could attack the *Gavriil* broadside on. As soon as his boat had straightened out, he pulled the toggle and the torpedo slid out of the trough behind him.

Almost immediately the length of the *Gavriil* lit up against the darkness as her main guns suddenly opened up. Either Sevastyanov's men were incredibly accurate or they were unbelievably lucky. There was a tremendous flash and an explosion. Giddy was thrown across the cockpit. He felt a searing pain in the small of his back and knew that he had been hit by shell splinters. He lay on the floor of the cockpit for a moment, completely stunned. The CMB seemed to have stopped dead in the water and all he could see was the night sky above him. But why had the *Gavriil* ceased firing? For a moment Giddy wondered if he was dead.

Then the voice of CMB24's mechanic, Ben Reynish, brought him back to reality:

'Well, that's sugared it.'

Ignoring the pain, Giddy hauled himself upright and looked around, trying to assess the damage. There was no sign of Laurence Napier. He must have been blown into the water, but in the darkness Giddy could not see him. No one else in the crew seemed to be injured and the two sailors who had been manning the machine guns, Charles Harvey and Herbert Bowles, were clambering back to their positions to return fire. Giddy decided that the shell must have been a near miss. He was about to go below and see what could be done to get the engines going again when first one and then another shell landed on either side of the boat, knocking him off his feet again as Harvey fell back with his right arm shattered at the elbow. Giddy looked down, saw that there was water pouring into the boat and realised with horror that CMB24 had been split along her entire length by the force of the explosions. He shouted for Bowles and Reynish to help him unlash the fenders from the side of the boat because these would float, but before they could do this CMB24 simply fell apart and sank below the freezing waters. As he floated in the water, held up by his Gieves life jacket, Giddy began to lapse in and out of consciousness but he could see that the *Gavriil* was untouched – either Napier had missed or the torpedo had malfunctioned. Either way, the remaining boats were now at the mercy of the Soviet destroyer which would have a clear shot at any CMBs entering or leaving the harbour.

Meanwhile, Claude Dobson and the crew of CMB31 had begun their attack run. Unlike Bremner and Napier's CMBs, their boat carried two torpedoes and both were intended for the dreadnought *Andrei Pervozvanni*, the main target of the attack. For the moment the *Gavriil* was occupied with machine-gunning the survivors of CMB24 as they floated in the water, but the shore defences were fully operational and were pouring in both shell- and machine-gun fire against their attackers. At the helm, Russell McBean took CMB31 through the narrow harbour at full speed, knowing that it was their only hope of getting through the curtain of fire directed against them. Ahead of them the *Pamiat Azova* was now heeled well over and was a useful landmark in the churning waters of the harbour, which were being swept by searchlights as the Russians fought to protect their ships. CMB31 was travelling so fast that she almost ran into the rear of the *Pamiat Azova*, but the afternoon rehearsal had not been in vain. McBean slammed the throttle of the port engine to a full stop and threw the helm hard over. CMB31 spun in a tight circle, threatening to throw the crew overboard, and as soon as the *Andrei Pervozvanni* swung into view McBean opened up the port engine again and they raced across the harbour. The defenders could see who her target must be and Dobson later said that it felt as if every gun in the harbour had opened up against them. With McBean at the helm, Dobson could concentrate on launching the torpedoes, but although the line was right Dobson had to hold his nerve as he knew that launching before they had reached the right speed would be fatal in these shallow waters.

The engines hit one thousand revolutions. Dobson let fly with both torpedoes and McBean instantly threw the boat hard to port to get out of the way. The wake of the torpedoes hissed past, the noise unheard against the deafening roar of engines and gunfire, but Dobson could see from the wakes that his aim was true. Both torpedoes slammed into the *Andrei Pervozvanni* and twin columns of smoke and flame erupted from her side.

Close behind Dobson was the last CMB in the first wave, number 88, crewed by Lieutenant 'Mossy' Dayrell-Reed and his second-in-command Lieutenant Gordon Steele. She too carried two torpedoes and her target was the *Petropavlovsk*. Reed and Steele were firm friends, having served together on the HMS *Iron Duke* for several years. They were also both very experienced in CMB work and were reckoned to be the best crew in the flotilla. As McBean had done before them, they rocketed through the harbour entrance at top speed, straight into the maelstrom of fire. Steele and Sub Lieutenant Norman Morley were giving return fire from CMB88's twin machine guns and, since their target was moored alongside the *Andrei Pervozvanni*, CMB88 followed the same course as McBean had done before them. As they roared towards the rapidly listing *Pamiat Azova* Mossy Reed brought one engine to a stop and threw his weight against the steering wheel to yank CMB88 into as tight a turn as possible.

Almost immediately, they nearly collided with Bremner who shot across their bows heading for the cover of the hospital ship. Gordon Steele watched as the shore batteries passed across the sights of his Lewis guns. He pulled the stocks tight into his shoulder and emptied round after round at the harbour wall, hoping to put at least one of the guns out of action. Incoming bullets whistled and ricocheted around him as the Russian gunners returned fire. Above him the sky was lit up by the beams of searchlights and the twinkling streams of tracer fire from the British aircraft.

But then it suddenly dawned on Steele that the boat was turning too far. He glanced over his shoulder and saw Reed slumped over the wheel. Almost automatically, Steele abandoned his machine gun and leaned across to help his dying friend. Mossy Reed had been shot through the head. Steele shifted the apparently lifeless body out of the way and hauled the wheel in the opposite direction. Both throttles were wide open and the massive steel wall which was the hull of the *Petropavlovsk* was hurtling towards them, growing taller at every moment.

For a second Steele considered going around for a second attempt, but the fire was now so intense that he knew that they would not survive another attack run. There was nothing for it but to go straight on. If necessary he would ram the *Petropavlovsk* and try to take her with him.

Steele throttled back as far as he dared and as soon as CMB88's bow came back on line with his target he pulled the lanyard which launched both torpedoes. He stopped one engine and swung the wheel hard to port, but almost as soon as he did so there was a tremendous explosion virtually alongside the boat. They had hit the *Petropavlovsk*. In fact, they were so close that the picric powder from the explosives in the nose of the torpedoes was thrown over the stern of the boat, staining it yellow. But Steele had no time even to let out a cheer. As the *Petropavlovsk* disappeared in a curtain of smoke and flames to his right, a barge tied up to the hospital ship where Bremner was waiting swung into view. It seemed impossible that they would miss it as they were still travelling at high speed. Steele hauled on the wheel with all his might and Morley stopped firing as he saw the barge loom towards them. But somehow, just when it seemed that they were finished, they roared past the barge with inches to spare and were back out into the open harbour with all the enemy guns firing at them once more.

Looking ahead, Steele could see Dobson and McBean in CMB31 heading for the harbour mouth. He swung into line behind them and together the two boats, with their machine guns blasting away at the harbour walls, shot back out into the open sea once more. The *Gavriil* was waiting for them. Both boats had to run the gauntlet of fire that was coming both from the destroyer and from the harbour. Morley poured a stream of tracer fire in the direction of the *Gavriil* before the two boats swung away to the east and headed for home. Then Morley went to check on Mossy Reed. There were still faint signs of life. With no training in first aid, Morley did what he could, bandaging up the massive head wound and forcing a morphine pill between Reed's lips to dull the pain. Now his only hope was the surgeon on board the *Vindictive*. Steele opened out the throttles and stayed close behind Dobson's CMB as they raced for home.

Meanwhile, the crew of CMB7 were witnesses to the second stage of the attack. Gus had been hanging on to his one torpedo in the hope of doing the most damage. He could see that the *Gavriil* was still firing and he knew that Napier's attack must have failed. With the destroyer still in place the attacking CMBs in the second wave were in a bad way and Gus was considering having a crack at her himself. But then Ed Sindall spotted activity in the military harbour as some of the Bolshevik patrol boats tried to put to sea and so Gus had no choice but to stick to the plan. He put CMB7 into a wide circle which brought him into line with the mouth of the little harbour. He opened out to full speed and then launched his single torpedo just before CMB7 reached the harbour entrance, swinging away at the last moment with Richard Marshall giving the Bolsheviks a taste of both barrels of the twin Lewis guns for good measure. The wake of the torpedo streamed straight and true through the harbour mouth. In the darkness they could not see the result of their action, but Gus had aimed directly for the most densely packed area of the moored vessels. There was a tremendous explosion and several smaller secondary explosions so he was sure they must have done a good deal of damage. CMB7 returned to her station ready to intercept any vessels that emerged. But none did.

As Claude Dobson had feared, the second wave of the attack was in tatters. Howard with CMB86 and her two torpedoes was still stranded on the wrong side of the forts north of Kronstadt. Lieutenant Commander Frank Brade in CMB62 and Sub Lieutenant Edward Bodley commanding CMB72 now began their attack run, but almost immediately ran into trouble. The air attack was by now almost exhausted. Several of the aircraft had turned for home, although one or two pilots, including Flying Officer Eric Brewerton in one of the Strutters, were hanging on as long as possible, diving at the shore defences with their machine guns firing in the hope of winning the CMBs a few more precious seconds of time. Brewerton had been circling the area since the beginning of the CMBs' attack and had an outstanding aerial view of the entire action. He was amazed at how the little boats had been able to survive the storm of fire that had been directed at them, noting that even the anti-aircraft pom-pom guns were now depressed to their minimum elevation so that they could join in the defence.

He saw Brade and Bodley racing forward. He realised that the tracer fire from their machine guns, which had been intended to help them direct accurate fire in the darkness, was actually betraying their position to the Soviet defenders. The *Gavriil* opened fire and was deadly accurate. Brewerton swooped and raked the destroyer stern to bow in the hope of forcing her to cease firing, but his assault seemed to have little effect. He watched as the second CMB, number 72 commanded by Bodley, was forced to break off her attack run even before she reached the harbour mouth. One bullet or shell splinter had pierced the carburettor, reducing her speed, and then another struck the launching gear, jamming it completely. With no way to fire his single torpedo, Ed Bodley knew that he would only be needlessly endangering his men if he entered the harbour. He veered away to starboard and headed for home.

Now the success of the entire second wave rested on the replacement officer, Frank Brade. He opened out the throttles of CMB62 and raced past the *Gavriil* without sustaining a scratch, but the heavily defended harbour mouth waited ahead. The air attack was over and, ignoring the two or three remaining RAF aircraft, the searchlight crews all trained their beams on the harbour entrance. Caught in the light of several of these at close range, Brade was blinded just as he entered the harbour. In a desperate attempt to get out of the light he threw CMB62 hard to port. What he could not see was that this put him on a direct course for CMB79 under the command of Bill Bremner, which was trying to fight its way out of the harbour. Enemy fire had put one of Bremner's two engines out of action and he had fallen far behind Dobson and Steele. Brade's CMB hit Bremner's boat amidships at full speed, partially riding over it and locking the two craft together. Several members of both crews were knocked unconscious by the force of the impact. Both boats came to a complete stop and the Soviet gunners now poured their machine-gun and rifle fire into this tangled mess of wreckage.

Frank Brade was one of the first to recover. He immediately assessed what had happened. There was no way he could break free of CMB79 so he opened out CMB62's throttles and forced his bow around to face the harbour entrance. Bullets were now hammering into the little wooden boats from every direction. Brewerton, Donald and the remaining RAF aircraft could see what had happened and dived desperately time and again at the harbour guns in an attempt to force the defenders to keep their heads down, but there were just too many of them. CMB62 tried to return fire to knock out the searchlights which were now zeroed in on them, but first Leading Seaman Sid Holmes and then Brade's second in command, eighteen-year-old Sub Lieutenant Hector Maclean, were cut down in the withering fire.

Bill Bremner came to his senses to find that all hell had broken loose. He could see from the damage around him that CMB79 was finished so he quickly organised his three crew members to help him lever CMB62 free of the wreckage. Shouting above the gunfire for Brade to give the engines of CMB62 everything they had, Bremner and his crew tried to force her clear of CMB79. Tom Usborne was cut down at Bremner's side as they struggled with the wreckage, but with a final grind of splintering timber CMB62 slid clear. Rather than race to safety and abandon Bremner and his men, Brade immediately cut his engines to give them a chance to scramble aboard. Determined to leave nothing for the Russians, Bill Bremner's last act was to ignite the cordite charge which he had brought to deal with the harbour boom and as CMB62 began to pick up speed and head for open water there was a tremendous roar as CMB79's fuel tanks exploded and took the remains of the boat to the bottom of the harbour. The explosion was so fierce that Gus reported later that it must have been the *Gavriil* which had been hit and successfully sunk.

Outside the harbour the *Gavriil* was waiting and she immediately opened up with a hail of gunfire of her own. Brade still had two torpedoes left and was determined not to take them back, so he shouted to Bremner that he was going to sink the Soviet destroyer. But fire was still pouring into CMB62 from both the harbour defences and the *Gavriil* and moments later Brade fell dead at the wheel as bullets pierced the canopy of the little cockpit. Bremner, who had already been hit several times, immediately hauled himself forward and took the helm from Brade's dying hands. He straightened CMB62's course and headed straight for the *Gavriil* once more. As soon as he had gained enough speed he launched both torpedoes. The *Gavriil* was only two hundred yards away, the torpedoes ran true, but to Bremner's anger and frustration they passed *underneath* the *Gavriil* and headed out into the open sea beyond.

Now the *Gavriil* opened fire once more and her shooting was as deadly as it had been when Napier had attacked. One of the first salvoes bracketed CMB62 and a shell splinter pierced her engine compartment, bringing the boat to a complete stop. Fire rained in on the boat from all sides as the current drifted her ever closer to the *Gavriil* which was now at almost point-blank range. Bullets pierced the hull time and again, killing CMB62's Chief Motor Mechanic, 21-year-old Francis Thatcher. Still Bremner refused to surrender, calling for his own mechanic, Henry Dunkley, to get below and see what he could do for the engines. Bremner manned one of the remaining machine guns as Able Seaman William Smith fell dead or dying next to him. Bremner himself was hit several more times but kept firing as they drifted closer to the Bolshevik warship, determined to buy Dunkley time to get the engines going. But then it was all over. The *Gavriil*'s guns unleashed a final salvo, scoring a direct hit on what was left of CMB62 and sinking her. As the Russian guns fell silent all that remained was a large pool of burning fuel on the surface.

As far as Gus could see there was nothing left to do but head for home. He put CMB7 about and with a final burst of machine-gun fire into the crowded boats of the military harbour he left the flames and smoke behind.

But getting back to Biorko was not going to be so easy. There was still the line of forts to be crossed and this time their gun crews were waiting for the CMBs. The first boats to run this gauntlet were Dobson and Steele in CMBs 31 and 88. The forts opened fire at considerable range, but were very accurate. The searchlights were creeping gradually nearer and both captains wondered how to get through the forts at point-blank range. Steele and Dobson knew that they would have to chance it together. One of them was almost certain to be hit, but at least one of them stood a chance of getting home.

Several hundred feet above them in the darkness Captain Randall, one of Major Donald's pilots, was flying the only operational Sopwith Camel. Shortly after take-off his engine began to give trouble. But rather than 'wash-out' Randall had bravely refused to turn back and had carried on, knowing that every aircraft over Kronstadt would buy another few valuable minutes for Dobson's team. So he had slowly pushed on, falling way behind the other planes. He had travelled most of the way to Kronstadt when the engine that he had been carefully nursing finally cut out and died. This was frustrating, but Randall was not unduly worried. As had been demonstrated during Gus Agar's trip to see the wreck of the *Oleg*, engine problems were not uncommon and Randall simply turned the Camel around and put her into a long slow glide back towards Koivisto. He was about halfway back when he realised that he would not make it – he simply did not have enough height. The dark waters of the Gulf of Finland drew closer and closer until, when he was just a few feet above the waves, the plane's engine suddenly kicked back into life. A lesser man might have run straight for home but Randall was an experienced pilot and, as he blipped the engine, he felt sure that it would keep running this time. He immediately set course for Kronstadt once more.

However, as he was passing over the line of sea forts the activity of the searchlights attracted his attention. Scanning the water, he could just make out the wakes of what had to be the returning CMBs. He quickly assessed the situation as he watched Dobson and Steele make for one of the gaps. He decided that the sea forts needed something to take their attention off the retreating boats. He shoved the joystick forward and put his Camel into a steep dive.

Dobson and Steele had no idea that someone was coming to their rescue. They were under heavy fire as they raced towards the sea forts when the searchlights which had been hunting for them suddenly switched their attention to the sky and a twin trail of tracer fire marked where a lone aircraft repeatedly dived, zoomed up and dived again. Its machine-gun fire shattered one searchlight and sent the forts' gun crews scattering for cover. Even though they did not know who the pilot was, both boats gratefully shot through the unguarded gap, Dobson using the smoke apparatus fitted to the exhausts of his boat to create cover for Steele. Once they were through he hung back to see how many of the other CMBs would make it, while Steele turned north for Biorko Sound and raced away in the hope that he could still save Mossy Reed's life.

Sadly, Captain Randall would not be able to help any of the stragglers: not long after Dobson and Steele reached safety, the engine of his Camel cut out for the final time. Reluctantly, he turned north and was just able to make the coast of Finland where he landed on the beach about fifteen minutes later.

On the other side of the forts Lieutenant Edward Bodley was furious, due to the fact that he had travelled all the way to Kronstadt only to have his firing gear damaged at the last moment. By pure luck he was returning towards the forts when he came within sight of Howard's crippled CMB86. Yates had managed to get one bank of the starboard engines restarted and they were limping back towards the line of forts at a speed of about seven knots. They had already seen Dobson and Steele streak past on their way home.

Bodley was picked up by a searchlight from one of the forts. He managed to lose this by zigzagging and then turned back to Howard's struggling boat. He pulled alongside and told Howard to throw him a line so that he could take CMB86 in tow. With the two engines working together they should make a speed of about twenty knots. It was not much but it might be enough. But as Bodley arrived two searchlights locked onto their position. Everyone froze, but for some reason the forts did not open fire. Unable to believe their luck, the two crews worked frantically to secure the towline. Above them Lieutenants Fairbrother and Walne in one of the Sopwith Griffins did their best to help, as Fairbrother later recalled:

'[We] of course attacked the searchlights of the fort with machine-gun fire, but the ammunition carried in an aeroplane does not last for ever, and though we managed to put the light out several times, we never seemed to get it out for good and when our last rounds were spent we yelled curses down at the Bolsheviks as we saw the light flash out again.'

As that happened Fort Alexander, one of the Kotlin Island strongholds, opened fire with her 11-inch and 8-inch guns. High-explosive shells began to drop all around the little boats. As Howard remarked things were: '... pretty gummy as the shooting was rather good.' Howard's second in command, Sub Lieutenant

Wight, now distinguished himself by virtually single-handedly attaching the towline. Bodley set off, but almost immediately the towline parted. Howard did not want to endanger Bodley any further and waved him ahead. Howard then ploughed steadily on at seven knots, with shells continuing to fall all around them. It took incredible nerve as at any moment the final shot might have come, but eventually CMB86 was out of range and Fort Alexander gave up. Bodley reattached the tow and the two boats headed for Biorko Sound.

Now only CMB7 remained on the wrong side of the forts. Gus was in sight of Bodley and Howard as they passed through the forts. He could see that they were under heavy fire, but he also saw that Fairbrother was keeping the forts occupied. Gus hoped that the Griffin would do the same for him. But then he saw it turn north suddenly and leave – he did not know that the aircraft was out of ammunition. Daylight was coming on quickly and Gus could see that the searchlights of the sea forts were very active: they were hoping to pick off any more stragglers. Gus knew that his chances of getting through were very slim but there was no point in delaying, so he headed for the passage which Veroline indicated. He was still eight hundred metres from one of the northern forts when a searchlight latched onto him. He managed to twist CMB7 out of the path of that one but almost immediately ran into the beam of another. Tracer fire arced out from the fort as the Russians tried to fix his range and for a moment Gus thought he would have to turn away into the darkness for another run. But once again salvation came from Major Donald's squadron.

Although Randall and Fairbrother had gone, Flight Lieutenant Albert Fletcher, together with his observer Pilot Officer Frank Jenner, had hung back in one of the Short seaplanes in case they could be of help. Fletcher saw CMB7 making for one of the gaps and getting picked up by a searchlight. He immediately dived on the fort from which the searchlight was shining and roared low past it so that Jenner could strafe it with the gun in the rear cockpit. Twice more he dived to cover CMB7's retreat. The forts were forced to turn their guns and searchlights skyward and, while they were busy trying to shoot down Fletcher, Gus raced through the gap. Gus wrote later that he was in no doubt that Fletcher had saved their lives.

*

By the end of the mission 17 men, almost half of those who had set out from Biorko Sound just a few hours before, were missing, presumed dead. Three of the eight boats – CMBs 79A, 62BD and 24 – had been destroyed. But when Major Donald took off on a reconnaissance mission as soon as it was light he was able to confirm what the survivors had suspected: the attack had exceeded even their most optimistic expectations. They had not sunk the *Gavriil* as Gus Agar had believed, but the *Petropavlovsk*, *Andrei Pervozvanni* and *Pamiat Azova* were all either sunk or badly damaged.

More good news came from Petrograd a few weeks later. Although eight men had lost their lives on the mission, nine of those missing had survived and were being held prisoner. Among that number was a large British naval officer who refused to be cowed by his captors but instead ordered them around like servants. A diplomat reported that he kept accusing the Russians of being 'brigands' and 'stealing my bloody toothbrush!' As soon as they heard those words everyone knew that it could only be one man: Bill Bremner. Although wounded an astounding *eleven* times, including a severe wound in his left thigh, he had been pulled from the water alive. Along with the other eight prisoners he would survive to be repatriated in March 1920. He was awarded the DSO, the medal for gallantry just below the Victoria Cross, for his part in the raid, although when all the facts became known most agreed that he deserved the higher award. However, two Victoria Crosses *were* awarded for the night's work: one was to Commander Claude Dobson for commanding the mission, even though he had probably had an easier ride than almost anyone else. The other was to Lieutenant Gordon Steele who had saved CMB88 when 'Mossy' Dayrell-Reed was hit.

Sadly, Dayrell-Reed did not survive. All through the journey home he had lapsed in and out of consciousness as Morley tried to keep him alive. Although he could not speak the crew told him of the mission's great success and they thought that he understood them. He had hung on just long enough to be congratulated by Admiral Cowan when they arrived at the flagship but he died a few minutes later. He was buried on 19 August and his grave remains at the British war cemetery on a hill overlooking Koivisto to this day.

In his report to the Admiralty, Admiral Cowan succinctly summed up the heroism of that night. He knew best of all how vital this naval victory was for the independence of all the Baltic nations and just how slim the prospects for success had been:

> '[Their] ... cool, disciplined, dare-devil gallantry ... turned what the outside world would have called a forlorn hope into a legitimate and practical operation which met with far greater success than I had ever hoped.'

But for Gus Agar, there was still one more trip to make through the defences of Kronstadt. ST-25 was still not safe.

13

Lucky Number Thirteen

The day after the Kronstadt Raid, Gus and the crew of CMB7 returned to Terrioki. Gefter was waiting for them. He had managed to find a route overland through the fighting in Estonia. Gefter explained how he and Paul Dukes had been within sight of CMB7 on the night of 14 August and how close they had come to being drowned. But he was sure that Peter Sokolov would be able to find Dukes and to bring him out to the fall-back rendezvous that Gus had agreed for 25 August.

But now it was not so simple. Gefter was confident that Sokolov and Paul Dukes would evade the shore patrols, but then Gefter was always confident – too much so for Gus's liking. Meanwhile the Kronstadt Raid had changed everything. The element of surprise had been lost. The Soviets now knew exactly what they were dealing with and they would have redoubled the defences to ensure that there was no repetition of the attack on the Baltic Fleet. The days of slipping through the line of sea forts unchallenged were over.

The reality of this observation was emphasised on the morning of 20 August. Two Soviet aircraft flew over Terrioki and dropped seven bombs. Fortunately the Russians had as much trouble with aerial bombing as the RAF had. The bombs fell harmlessly in the woods. Some even failed to explode because they still had their safety pins attached. Richard Marshall immediately asked for permission to remove the Lewis guns from the crippled CMB4 and spent the rest of the morning fixing them on improvised mountings to the roof of the yacht club. But, to Gus, that was not the point. The bombs had not been intended to kill them. They were a message: 'We know where you are.'

Another warning was delivered the following night. Two hand

grenades were thrown into the garden of the dacha. No damage was done, but the crew stood watch for the rest of that night and every night thereafter in case the attacks were repeated. They never knew whether it was a Bolshevik agent or disgruntled Finnish troops who were upset with the British for making Terrioki a target, but someone clearly wanted them out of the area and would probably try again. From Hall, Gus learned that the Russians had now put a price on his head, equivalent to 5,000 English pounds – dead or alive. Someone was clearly giving the Cheka very good information indeed. Since Gefter and Peter were accounted for, Gus wondered if the courier Kroslov had been intercepted and had talked under torture. There was no way of knowing.

Climbing to the church tower to watch the sea forts during the day, Gus and his second in command Ed Sindall could see boats moving to and fro between the fortifications. They seemed to be carrying out some sort of work along the line of the breakwater. The question was: were they repairing it, creating a new boom or perhaps laying some more mines that were designed to float at a more shallow level and take out the CMBs? Every night the searchlights swept the waters in front of the forts, occasionally swinging into the air if there was even a suspicion of an approaching aircraft. As 25 August drew closer the stakes were being raised very high indeed.

As Gus stood in the church tower, one question turned over and over in his mind: was there now any point in going in to rescue ST-25? The prospects of success were almost zero – even if they made it through the forts the first time, they would almost certainly never make it back. There would be no friendly aircraft to cover their retreat. Gus and his crew had won the highest honours and had proved their bravery time and time again. He himself had won the two highest awards for valour, the Victoria Cross and the Distinguished Service Order which he had been awarded for the Kronstadt Raid. There were no more prizes left to win. Why risk the lives of his crew needlessly?

For three days the question tormented Gus. If he refused to go then was he being a coward or just a sensible commander? A vision of Paul Dukes and Peter Sokolov waiting on the beach kept coming back into his mind. Those two men might risk their lives to reach a team of rescuers who were never coming. After all, despite all his achievements, this was what he had been sent to Finland for – wasn't it?

Those who knew Gus Agar remember that one characteristic about him stood out: like Horatio Nelson, the hero of Trafalgar, he believed that the most important calling in life was to do his duty. In the end it was this point that decided the issue. As far as Gus was concerned he had given his word to Paul Dukes that he would be at the rendezvous and, no matter how many Russians might be waiting for him, he would lay down his life to carry out that promise.

But there was no sense risking the lives of others if he could possibly avoid it. He would have to take Hugh Beeley because anything might happen to the CMB's engines and it would be pointless to be left stranded in the middle of the Gulf waiting for dawn and the Russian guns. Even so, Gus laid out the facts carefully and gave Beeley the choice of refusing. 'Faithful' Hugh Beeley did not hesitate. Of course he would go. Gus also had to take Veroline, the Finnish smuggler. In the darkness of the cockpit on the Gulf at night there could be no charts. There was no telling which gap between the sea forts he might have to use and for that reason he needed Veroline's first-hand knowledge. Unlike his briefing of Hugh Beeley, Gus did not lay out all the dangers this time: Veroline might have refused to go. Instead, he would have a bonus – if they survived.

Gus called a meeting at the dacha on the afternoon of 25 August and announced that he and Beeley would be going in for ST-25 that evening. He joked that there were several points in their favour: for a start, this would be the thirteenth trip through the forts. As the thirteenth child of his family, he had always believed that thirteen was his lucky number. The crew laughed dutifully. Then Gus pointed out that they would be sailing in CMB7, the lucky boat. If the Germans could not sink her he was damned sure the Russians could not. Finally, having laid out his contingency plans for all the different possible outcomes, Gus left instructions with Sindall that, if he failed to return, the remaining team members should close down the base at Terrioki and report to Admiral Cowan at Biorko as soon as possible.

There was nothing more to say.

But as he left the dacha to walk down to the harbour, Gus heard footsteps as Richard Marshall came running after him. Marshall was on the point of tears and begged Gus to take him along. He protested that he had come out to Finland to get the job done and now, just when the success of the entire mission was in the balance, Gus planned to leave him behind. He had been on so many of the other missions – had he not earned a right to come on this trip? Once again, Gus stressed just how dangerous this mission was. He had not wanted to say anything at the meeting but he and Hugh Beeley were almost certainly not coming back. Marshall asked him to imagine how it would feel to be the one left behind – how he would feel for the rest of his life. It was pointless. Gus did not have the heart to refuse him. He shook Marshall by the hand and told him to go and help Beeley prepare CMB7 for sea.

Later that afternoon Gefter too came looking for Gus. Like Marshall, he wanted to be taken on the trip. From the notes in his diary it is clear that Gus did not much like Gefter. But he thought that he had the right to be there as much as anyone else and it was possible that they might make it through the forts but be too badly damaged to attempt the return journey, forcing them ashore in Russia. If that happened Gefter would be invaluable. Gus told him to join the party.

That evening, as soon as it was dark, CMB7 set out with her five passengers. They were not carrying a torpedo. On this trip, Gus knew that speed would be everything. Gefter and Veroline sat in the empty trough so that there would be as much space as possible in the cockpit. Gus headed south-east at a steady 20 knots. It would take about 30 minutes to reach the line of sea forts. Grimly, he noted the important difference between this mission and his other runs through the line: ahead he could see the beams of the search-lights sweeping the water. Now and again a fort would be plunged into darkness for a few minutes as a searchlight was switched off and then it would it would suddenly light up again as if the men in the fort had set a trap and hoped to catch a boat trying to sneak through the gap.

After about 20 minutes Veroline clambered forward into the cockpit. The Finnish smugglers were well aware that the Soviets had been repairing the breakwater, but from their contacts with fisher-men on the Petrograd side of the Gulf they knew that the contractors were cheating their bosses and that some of the repair work was incomplete: there were still gaps in the defences. Then again, it was only the gossip of fishermen and smugglers . . .

Veroline counted the forts carefully and then indicated the gap which he had been told was still safe. With a nod of his head to let Marshall know they were going in, Gus opened out the throttle and put the wheel hard to port.

From his position manning the Lewis guns, Richard Marshall probably had the best view of what happened next. He could see that Gus was aiming for a patch of sea where the searchlight activity seemed less intense. Once or twice a searchlight beam passed over them, but like many sailors Marshall knew that it was very difficult to pick out an object at sea at night and that unless the beam was focused exactly on the target, then it was likely to remain unseen. Even so, these were unnerving moments and Marshall crouched low behind the shoulder stocks of the Lewis guns.

They were about eight hundred metres from the gap when a searchlight passed over them and then returned to hold them in its beam. Gus jinked CMB7 left and right to try and lose it, but the beam stayed doggedly on them. Then a second light joined in and at the same time the guns of the fortresses opened up and the sea erupted around them. At once, Gus knew that these were not the sea forts of old – this firing was far more rapid and accurate.

Gus clung determinedly to his course. Speed now was everything. In a few seconds they would be through the gap and the closer they drew to the forts, the harder it would be for the guns to depress their muzzles and to track them. Marshall was blasting away with the Lewis guns and managed to knock out one of the lights. For a moment there was hope. But then a third searchlight and then another latched onto their position. The intense glare completely blinded Gus. Afraid that they would run directly into one of the forts, he spun the wheel hard to starboard to head them towards the open sea.

Once more the sea around them erupted as shells fell so close that CMB7 was momentarily lifted out of the water. She landed between a gap in the waves so heavily that for a moment Gus feared she had broken her back. But the boat roared onwards and as Gus glanced down into the engine compartment he could see Beeley hunched low over the engines, making sure that they didn't fail.

But something was wrong. CMB7 was no longer properly answering her helm. Gus fought with the wheel, but she was gradually turning in an arc that would bring her back towards the forts. Gus knew that the rudder was connected to the wheel by two long ropes which ran along the side of the boat and turned a wheel at the top of the rudder post. He felt sure that one of the steering ropes must have been shot through, but there was no time to check on that now. All his skill and strength were needed to keep the wheel as straight as possible, to keep CMB7 heading out to sea.

Again and again shells whistled over the boat as the Soviet gunners tried to find their range. Gus had lost count of the number of searchlights trained on them because he was still blinded by the intense light. Above the roar of the engine he felt rather than heard the clattering of Marshall's Lewis guns, which told him that despite his efforts they must still be within close range of the forts. He knew that if he could not correct their course it would be only a matter of time until they were hit.

Gus shouted for Beeley to check the rudder, but down in the engine room Beeley could not hear him. Neither Gefter nor Veroline would know what he was talking about. There was nothing that Gus could do.

And then it was suddenly all over. The Russians found their range. There was one final tremendous explosion, a splintering crash of shattering timber and metal and then nothing. The searchlights continued to sweep the waters, but the wreckage of CMB7 had disappeared.

Back at Terrioki, Sindall and Piper had gone to the church tower to watch for any signs of how Gus and the others had fared. Although there was no hope of seeing the tiny boat in the darkness, they could clearly see the sea forts lighting up the entire width of the Gulf. About 30 minutes after CMB7's departure there was the distant roar of naval gunfire and for about three minutes the horizon was lit up by orange and white flashes far to the south. Then the gunfire stopped and gradually the glow on the horizon dimmed as the searchlights were switched off one by one. There was little doubt that CMB7 had been seen – but what had become of her?

Sindall and Piper were worried, but there was still hope. If at all possible Gus would have turned round and made a second attempt by a different route. Or he would be returning to Terrioki so that he could try again on another day. The two men made their way down to the harbour wall and sat watching out to sea, signalling with an electric torch to give the returning boat a guide back to the harbour mouth.

They sat there signalling for the rest of the night, waiting for the familiar roar of the Thornycroft engine as Gus returned home. But the engine of CMB7 was never to be heard again. Slowly their hopes faded. Gradually the eastern sky grew lighter as dawn rose and within an hour it was full daylight. The short Baltic night was over. Both men knew that there was no chance of Gus evading the Soviet guns in daylight. CMB7 was not coming home and Lieutenant Gus Agar's mission to rescue ST-25 was finally over.

14

Run for home

In Petrograd the following day Paul Dukes learned of the death of Gus Agar when the Bolsheviks proudly announced that they had sunk a high-speed motor boat caught trying to penetrate the Kronstadt defences. Dukes knew that this must be Agar since he had promised he would come on the 25 August. He assumed that either Peter Sokolov or Gefter must have been in the boat and that they too had perished. Paul was sunk deep in depression. Even if Agar had made it through the line of forts, it would all have been in vain. The shore patrols were now so numerous that there had been no way he could have reached the coast, let alone stolen a boat. Paul had even considered reverting to his idea of swimming out to meet the CMB, but the waters at the edge of the Gulf were very shallow for some distance and now that there were more patrols he was sure that he would have been seen.

But a few days later Peter Sokolov reappeared. He had managed to cross the Estonian border and had then made the dangerous journey into the city. He repeated Cumming's demand that Paul should return to London as soon as possible.

Paul knew it was time to go. Not just because Cumming ordered him to. There was the fact that with the death of Gus Agar his lifeline had now gone. Besides that, his Russian army unit was moving up to the Latvian Front and that would end the most effective part of his cover story. But most pressing of all was the fact that Iakov Peters's work was having an effect. The Cheka were starting to enjoy success and one by one Paul's networks were collapsing. If the radio network had been working then it might have been different, but the equipment delays caused by MI6 had proved fatal. Peters had attacked the weakest link in the network structure: the couriers. Now it looked as if he had managed to break the National Centre.

The National Centre was one of the leading opposition groups resisting the Bolsheviks and the one for which Paul had the most hope. It was based primarily in Moscow and had strong backing in the military as well as from wealthy former industrialists and landowners. Its aims were generally right-wing and rather vague: it supported strong government, free elections to a new National Assembly and the removal of the Bolsheviks. Problems beyond those general aims would be resolved at a later date, but it was the commitment to democracy that most attracted Paul. Unfortunately the National Centre's level of funding, high-level contacts with the White armies and support inside the military made it a principal target for the Cheka.

The first breakthrough for Peters had come on 14 July. Two couriers had been intercepted as they tried to cross from Petrograd into Finland. Papers that they were carrying, together with the results of a typically brutal Cheka interrogation, led to other contacts. As a result of this information, on 23 July Peters was able to arrest one of the leading National Centre organisers in Petrograd, a man named Shteininger. His agents had been responsible for providing General Yudenich with much of his military intelligence from within Petrograd. Within a few days the Cheka had also picked up V. N. Rozanov, a leader of the Union for the Regeneration of Russia, an associated group with whom Paul had also been in contact.

These were the first cracks, yet Paul's organisation had continued to function throughout August. However, just as Peter Sokolov arrived in Petrograd to tell Paul it was time to leave, Peters made his final and decisive breakthrough. On the night of 28/29 August, the Cheka arrested N. N. Shchepkin, the leader of the National Centre. Yet another courier had been intercepted just a few days before and the Cheka had skilfully used him to trace the line of cut-outs that led to Shchepkin. In his hiding place Peters found detailed lists of all National Centre members and intelligence contacts. The arrests began. Paul Dukes's name was on that list.

For Paul the only question now was: how to escape? The Finnish border was closed, Agar was gone. For various reasons, which he never explained, Paul did not feel that it was safe to take Peter's planned route into Estonia. They would need to look further south. In order to have a chance, he decided that they should bypass Estonia and head to the border with Latvia. The Latvians were still at war with the Bolsheviks and the border would be crawling with troops from both sides, but it was the best of several bad options. They would just have to hope that they could slip through somewhere in all the confusion. In particular, Paul thought that Lake Luban, which formed the border between the two countries for some eighteen miles, might provide a chance for swimming or even floating across at night.

Before he left Petrograd, Paul adopted a final change of identity. Obviously, if he was captured crossing the border using his papers as Alexander Bankau his activities and associates would be very quickly traced and people would be arrested. So his contacts in the army provided him with the papers of a soldier recently killed at the Front. Paul became 'Private Vladimir Piotrovsky'. As for Alexander Bankau, the commander would simply record him as 'killed in action' once they arrived at the Front. Paul's commander also provided the newly resurrected Private Piotrovsky with an order to report to an artillery regiment on the Latvian front near Dvinsk. This would give Paul a good excuse for travelling south as he searched for a way across the border.

Finally, Paul decided to take with him a young man from his regiment, a short and skinny youth known only by the pseudonym 'Kostya'. Kostya had worked for Paul as a runner carrying messages around the city and doing small jobs for the network. Neither Paul nor Peter Sokolov knew the geography of the area they were heading for, but Kostya's family were hiding out in the forests there. Kostya thought that if they could find his parents, then they would know a safe way across the border. Since Kostya was happy to desert from the army Paul decided to take him along.

Paul also had to decide which of his many intelligence reports to take with him. It was not an easy choice. He wanted to take the most important pieces, but he could not take anything that might incriminate his agents if he was caught. There was also the fact that, due to MI6's inability to provide him with a reliable courier system, the amount of intelligence in various hiding places had built up. Paul selected the very best, memorised what he could of the rest and then destroyed it. He packed the tiny strips of tissue paper containing his encoded reports into his army pouches, which he packed with salt. This was not as strange as it might seem, since salt was highly valuable and was often carried by troops, as well as by other foragers, for bartering purposes.

Before leaving Petrograd for the last time, Paul had a lucky escape from an old enemy. He was just stepping down from a tram in Zagordny Prospekt when he looked up – straight into the eyes of Captain Zorinsky. The last that Paul had heard of him, Zorinsky had been in Finland trying to claim the bounty which the Cheka had placed on Paul's head. Clearly Zorinsky had returned. He was dressed in military uniform and was about to climb onto a motorcycle.

Paul rapidly stepped back on to the tram and forced his way deep among the crowd of passengers. He was wearing his military uniform and had changed his appearance greatly, but there had been a flicker of recognition in Zorinsky's eyes. Paul inched his way to the front of the tram and risked a look back. He could see Zorinsky peering over the heads of the crowd, searching for him. Paul jumped from the tram while it was still moving, jumped onto another tram and then ran in through the main doors of the crowded Tsarskoeselsky station. He found a seat from where he could watch all the main entrances and waited to see if Zorinsky had followed him. He had been so shaken by this chance encounter that he sat there until the evening, not daring to leave. But Zorinsky never appeared. Paul never saw Zorinsky again, but the incident served to remind him that he had only a finite amount of luck and it was running lower all the time. Eventually, there would be another odd coincidence and perhaps then he would not be able to get away. It all served to emphasise to him that it was time to leave.

Once more Paul briefed the mysterious Petrovskaya and told her that he hoped she would not have to remain in charge of the networks for long. Paul also said goodbye for the very last time to Aunt Natalia. She was probably the agent he was most attached to, but he had not been able to visit her for some time because she had been arrested in a routine sweep of suspects by the Cheka. Soon after she was released Paul was able to visit her to tell her that he was leaving.

As soon as he saw her at the door of her flat he knew that something terrible had happened. Silently, she allowed him to enter. Paul knew that the only thing which had kept Aunt Natalia going since the execution of her brother were her two pet canaries:

'Like a flash I looked up at the canary cage and saw it empty – no, not empty, by standing on tiptoe I could see two little corpses. Starvation ... and in Aunt Natalia's puffed cheeks I read the same dread sign. She had no work, no more trinkets to sell, no food ration, and the only people who could have come to her aid had been arrested. I found a lonely woman slowly dying of hunger as her little pet birds had died.'

This old lady had been so helpful to Paul and so resilient in the face of all the hardships she had faced and yet this one seemingly trivial incident had finally broken her spirit. There was very little that Paul could do for her. She was too frail for him to take her with him and she would not have gone even if he could have. He left her what money he could, but when they said goodbye, they both knew that they would never see each other again.

With all their goodbyes said and their arrangements made, Paul, Peter Sokolov and young Kostya set out for the last time on the evening of Saturday, 30 August 1919. As before, the scrum to board one of the few locomotives out of the city was so chaotic that there was little chance of their papers being closely examined. The weather was now too cold to risk clambering onto the roof or clinging to the rails outside, but there was nowhere else to go and they had no choice but to hang on to the steps. However, half an hour into the journey Peter used his almost Herculean strength to smash a window and force a way for the three of them into the packed corridor of one of the carriages, despite the protests of the occupants – which tended to die down as they realised just how big Peter was. There the three of them remained for the rest of the night, wedged cheek by jowl with their stinking, snuffling fellow travellers as the locomotive chugged its way slowly through the darkened countryside.

They travelled for eleven hours and in the early hours of Sunday morning arrived at an anonymous stop far out in the countryside where they would have to change trains. The connecting train was not due until that evening so they spent the day huddled together on a grass embankment near the tracks. They tried to sleep, but a militiaman challenged them as they lay there. He was clearly a member of the grandly named 'Committee for Combating Desertion'. He demanded to see their papers. These passed his examination but they could tell that he was still suspicious, watching them intently as they retreated to a nearby field out of sight of the station. Fortunately there was no sign of him when they returned to the station to catch the train that evening, so they assumed that they had got away with it.

This train was far less crowded. Foragers (known as 'two-pooders' because of the amount of goods they were allowed to bring back to the city) were unlikely to roam this far from the city, so the trio were able to sit in some comfort in a second-class compartment. There were two other passengers, but no one spoke and they sat silently in total darkness. The suspicion of one Russian for another which was to become a feature of life under Soviet rule for the next seventy years was already in place.

At three o'clock on the morning of Monday, 1 September, the train came to an unscheduled halt. Peering out through the condensation-covered window into the darkness, Kostya announced that they seemed to have been shunted into a siding and that there were armed guards everywhere. Moments later, an official passed through the train announcing that it was about to be searched and that everyone should stay where they were.

Immediately the three fugitives remembered the suspicious militiaman. He must have reported something and it had taken until now for the Committee for Combating Desertion to have the train halted. Peter quickly scouted the length of the carriage, looking out of all the windows, but the train seemed to be very effectively surrounded. There was no chance of slipping away under the carriages as they would usually have done. They were trapped. Worse still, Paul knew that his secret documents were likely to be found. The three packets of paper he had crammed into the pouch could clearly be seen by anybody who looked. And this search was going to be thorough: Peter said that one of the search teams was already in the next compartment and they were searching every-thing, even the seat cushions. It seemed to Paul that, like Gus Agar, he was about to fail at the very last hurdle. In desperation, he pulled out the packets and thrust them under his seat.

The door of the compartment slid open and in the semi-darkness they could see a military official of some kind holding the stub of a candle. By its weak light he peered into the compartment. He asked where they were going. They quickly replied 'Rezhitsa', which was the next stop. The man muttered something about putting prisoners in the compartment and slammed the door shut. They heard his boots as he stamped away down the corridor. From the other direction they could hear the search teams getting nearer. Peter

Sokolov saw that Paul was shaking. He put a reassuring hand on his arm and murmured to him to keep his chin up.

The three men could see the torch lights of the searchers next door through the chinks in the partition. Then it suddenly went silent. The three of them sat there, listening. It seemed to Paul that the searchers were listening too. No one moved. They barely dared to breathe.

The door of the compartment was slammed open.

But once again it was the official with the candle stub. He muttered 'Ach – yes!' as if he realised that it was a compartment he had already spoken to and then he slammed the door shut. They sat and waited in the dark once more. They were the last compartment in the carriage and they were sure that theirs was the only one which had not been searched. They had to be next.

But nothing happened.

Slowly a pale dawn began to appear in the sky outside and after the train had been halted for just over an hour it finally began to move again. The three companions glanced at each other in astonishment. It looked like they were going to get away with it. The train crept slowly forwards. Several times it threatened to stop but it kept moving slowly but steadily and an hour later it came to a halt at Rezhitsa, their final destination. Paul and his friends let the other two passengers leave the compartment first and then they retrieved the packets of intelligence from under the seat – still unable to believe their luck.

Peter Sokolov and Paul bought tea in the station waiting room while Kostya went out to get his bearings. They had only been there a few minutes when he came dashing back and pointed to a troop train which was leaving the station heading north-east. The doors of the boxcars at the rear were open and they appeared to be empty. It was a chance that they could not afford to miss. No one thought anything of three soldiers rushing to leap aboard a departing troop train heading in the direction of the Front and soon they were slumped in the corners, laughing and smiling at their good fortune. At the very least this took them away from the busy station where it was far more likely that they would be stopped and searched.

Ten miles up the line they leapt from the train as it slowly climbed a steep incline. Then they slipped away into the pine forests. Kostya had a rough idea where they were now and led them through the trees. They had agreed that if they met anyone, they would say they were 'Greens' – the common name for troops who had deserted either from the 'Whites' or the 'Reds' and were just trying to get out of the area. After several hours of wandering Kostya finally led them to a cottage owned by his cousins and it was there that his mother and father were hiding. After as good a meal as Kostya's uncle could provide all three men fell fast asleep.

On the morning of Tuesday, 2 September, Kostya's uncle took them on his horse and cart as far as he dared towards Lake Luban. Then, after a hasty meal among the trees, he left them to make the final stage of their journey.

By that evening they had reached the dunes that bordered the lake. Peter and Paul lay hidden in a thicket, while Kostya left to find a fisherman from whom, so he had been told by his uncle, he might borrow a boat. Kostya had said he would be back in an hour. But after he had been gone for four hours Peter and Paul were beginning to think that they would have to attempt to cross without him. They were only a few hundred metres away from an old windmill which was occupied by a detachment of Red Guards and they had already seen several patrols go past their hiding place. There was a sandbagged machine-gun emplacement at the windmill, positioned so that the gun could sweep both the lake and the shoreline.

Just as they were about to give up hope and move on Kostya appeared, covered in mud. He had been unable to find the fisherman and announced that the area was thick with patrols. The lake was eight to ten miles across so there was no chance of swimming it. They now had no choice but to try and skirt along the shore under cover of darkness.

But there was a problem. The shore of the lake was thick with deep, clinging mud. They sank into it past their knees at every step and it had sapped their strength long before they had forced their way through the first mile. The shoreline was also covered with rolls of rusted barbed wire. In the dark they could not see this clearly and it tore at their clothes and skin until the three of them were ragged and bloody. After an hour Paul estimated that they had travelled less than two miles and they were exhausted. Yet if they were not out of sight of the windmill by the following dawn they would be seen and shot. Any unidentified men out on the lake's shore could only be spies or deserters. The Red Guards would not wait to find out which they were.

So they pushed on. Step by painful step for another hour. And then another. The mud was sometimes waist-deep and it seemed impossible that Paul and Kostya could drag themselves any further through or across it, even with the indomitable strength of Peter to help them.

It was then – not for the first time during his mission – that Paul felt that some sort of divine providence took a hand. It would be nice to think that God was on the side of the British Secret Service, but in any case Peter Sokolov pointed and there, floating at the edge of the lake, was a rowing boat. Hardly daring to believe their luck, the three men hauled their way through the mud towards it. But as they drew closer their hopes began to fade. The boat was clearly a derelict, cast adrift by some fisherman. They could see the gaping holes in the side even as they approached it. At the moment it was resting on a mudbank, but it would never float. When they were able to look inside they found that there were no oars or sails either.

For a moment they were almost prepared to give up, but they knew that it was a choice between the derelict boat and waiting for a bullet in the morning. There was no way they could keep wading through the mud. They were determined to give it one last try. Peter found some rotting boughs which they could use as paddles and they did their best to plug up the worst of the holes with spare clothes. Then the three of them launched the boat out onto the dark waters of the lake. With one man constantly bailing and the other two paddling, they could just about keep her afloat. But if their strength should fail, the water would win and they would find themselves exhausted and miles out in the lake with no hope of rescue. In the darkness they steered by the stars, but they could never be absolutely sure how far from the shore they were. They wondered if patrols along the shore of the lake would hear them and open fire.

By dawn they were about four miles out on the lake, safely beyond the range of the machine-gun post at the windmill. They could hear artillery booming far to the north as the war continued. But despite their exhaustion Kostya and Peter sang as they punted and bailed. They were halfway to safety and they knew that they would make it now.

Paul was not so sure.

He was right to be worried. The boat was the only object on the lake and their approach had been seen by a patrol of Latvian troops. By eight o'clock in the morning, as the little boat crept at last towards the muddy Latvian shoreline, half a dozen soldiers had gathered there, threatening to open fire unless the trio turned back. But Paul, Peter and Kostya were not going to be denied. They clambered out of the boat as it practically fell to pieces around them and then half waded, half staggered through the mud and rushes to the shore. The troops surrounded them, holding them at bayonet point before marching them with their hands on their heads to a nearby village where their headquarters was situated.

In the only brick building in the tiny hamlet the commandant was already the worse for drink despite the earliness of the hour. He swore at them in fluent Russian and said that he was going to have them shot on the spot. In his opinion the only people who would dare to cross the lake were Red spies. The guards were young and nervous. They kept their bayonets levelled at all times and their fingers on the triggers of their guns. Even though they had disarmed the giant Peter Sokolov they were clearly afraid of him.

Paul quickly realised that here, many miles from any sort of authority, the commandant's word was law. Justice along the border was swift, arbitrary and usually fatal. He could very well carry out his threat to shoot them and no one would ever know what had happened. Paul protested that he was English and demanded to see the commandant alone so that he could explain his story. The commandant had enough sense to see that Paul was different, but the other two were clearly Russians and their papers showed that they were in the Red Army. He had very clear orders about people like them. He took Paul into his office. He gave orders for Peter and Kostya to be taken away and shot.

Paul begged, argued and threatened, but the commandant was unmoved. The three packets containing the secret intelligence had quickly been found hidden in Paul's pouch and now the commandant was more certain than ever that he had uncovered a group of spies.

To the sound of rifles being cocked in the street outside, the commandant snatched up one of the packets and thrust a knife under the string that was tied around it. It was then that Paul saw the writing on the packets and remembered that while they had been staying at Kostya's uncle's cottage he had addressed them to the British embassy at Riga in case he was killed and they were later found.

'To the British Commissioner at Riga – you see?' he shouted desperately pointing.

The commandant swore at Paul again, but examined the packets more closely. It certainly did not make sense for Russian spies to have parcels for the British Commissioner. Seizing the chance, Paul suggested that they should be sent under guard to Riga. If he was lying he would be shot anyway. But if the commandant executed them and it later turned out that Paul had been telling the truth, then the commandant would surely hang for his crime.

The commandant sat down heavily behind his desk, still fingering the unopened packet. He began to demand why he had not been informed that British agents would be arriving that morning – and that was when Paul knew that he had him. A few minutes later the commandant sent out the order that the prisoners would be travelling – under guard – to the regional commander at Madon. He did not necessarily believe Paul's story, but he had decided that it would be better if they were someone else's problem. As an afterthought, he ordered that each of the prisoners should be given a bottle of vodka. It was about the only thing the unit had plenty of.

Paul stepped out of the office into the morning sunlight. All around him, village life passed by as if nothing unusual had happened. From the colourful headscarves of the women to the grizzled features of the men, it could have been any village over the border in Russia. Peter and Kostya had been abandoned by their guards and were now slumped half-asleep on a bench against the wooden wall of the hut opposite.

Paul raised his bottle of vodka to his lips and at that moment the adrenalin which had sustained him through all of the last twelve months just simply disappeared. He stood there and felt nothing but utter weariness. He raised a hand to his face and realised that his cheeks were wet with tears. He did not know whether it was relief at his own escape or regret for those he had left behind, but he could not stop it. He thought about Aunt Natalia and Klachonka and Melnikov and Sonia Orlov. He thought about the coffins of the dead children, the old men and women whom he had seen starving in the street. He thought about Russia, a country that he had loved for the past ten years and to which he would probably never return. And he thought about Lieutenant Gus Agar, a brave man who had given everything to try and rescue him and who had ultimately failed.

It was all over.

Five days later Paul was on his way back to London. But until he arrived in Stockholm where he was debriefed by Major Scale, there was one thing Paul Dukes did not know:

Gus Agar was still alive.

The boat they couldn't sink

When Gus Agar opened his eyes after the explosion, the first thing that·struck him was the almost complete silence. No guns were firing, no engine was roaring: there was just the gentle sound of waves washing against the shore. Something also seemed to have gone wrong with the laws of physics because instead of being blinded by the beam of a searchlight he was staring straight up at one as it swung to and fro above him against the night sky.

But wherever he was it wasn't heaven – he was in too much pain for that. It gradually dawned on him that he was lying in a crumpled heap in the footwell of the cockpit. From where he lay he could see into the engine room. Beeley was there, apparently dead, his body slumped lifelessly across the silent engine. Gus tried slowly to disentangle himself from the various pipes and cables at the bottom of the cockpit, trying to work out how badly he was hurt. He had certainly taken a tremendous blow across the forehead because he had a thumping headache. He wondered how long he had been unconscious. As he started to sit up, Beeley too began to move. He looked up, saw Gus and at the same moment seemed to realise that the engines had stopped.

'I'll try to get her going again, sir,' he mumbled weakly and started to haul himself upright.

Gus sat up properly and looked around. It seemed as if the entire crew had been knocked unconscious in some kind of collision. Marshall must have come to his senses first because he was trying to tend to Gefter and Veroline who were both sprawled across the rear of the boat, still out cold.

As he checked himself for cuts and broken bones, it dawned on Gus that CMB7 was immobile – not just not moving forwards, but as motionless as a rock, as though the boat were held in some gigantic vice. He stood up gingerly and looked over the side. In the darkness he could see that they were resting on some sort of under-water obstruction. Looking upwards, he realised that they were almost directly below one of the sea forts. Not far away to star-board was the rocky shore of Kotlin Island. They had run aground on the breakwater that connected the two.

Beeley clambered out of the engine room and sat down gingerly next to his captain.

'No good, sir,' he said. 'The propeller shaft is smashed, the water-tight seams have gone and we've got two massive holes in the hull. Even if we could get her off this breakwater the only place she'd go is straight to the bottom.'

Marshall had roused Gefter and Veroline. The five men gathered in the cockpit and shared a hip flask of rum. Above them the searchlight still swung back and forth. Apart from cuts and bruises, they were all miraculously in one piece. Gus explained their situation. The searchlights must have lost them in the explosions and the confusion when they ran aground. The fact that no patrol boat had arrived to investigate probably meant that the Russians thought they had been sunk. But in the morning it would be a different story. There were right underneath the fort and it was certain that they would be seen. There was a chance that the British sailors and Veroline as a neutral Finn would simply be imprisoned – although there was also a good chance that they would be shot out of hand. But for Gefter, a Russian spy, it would be a different matter. For him a bullet would be a kindness, for if they were arrested and the Cheka got him he would certainly be tortured so that they could find Paul Dukes. Gus asked Gefter what he was going to do. He pointed out that it would only take a few moments for him to swim to shore and that from there he could walk into Kronstadt town, mingle with the locals and probably escape to the mainland. Gefter considered this. He asked what Gus intended to do.

Gus looked around the wreck of CMB7. He did not relish the prospect of waiting to be discovered by the Bolsheviks. He knew that the Cheka had put a price on his head, dead or alive. After the Kronstadt Raid, he suspected that a lot of Bolshevik troops would be quite happy to collect that bounty for 'capturing' him dead.

'I guess we'll try to get her into the water again. See if we can float out on the current. Maybe make it to the Finnish or Estonian coasts.'

But both men knew that was a forlorn hope. Even if CMB7 did float and did not just fall to pieces in the water, there was no way they could get out of range of the sea forts by dawn. As soon as it was daylight they would be spotted and simply blown out of the water. Gus could see from Gefter's bitter smile that he knew this. He had never had much time for Gefter, considering him both arrogant and untrustworthy. But Gefter's next words changed his opinion for good:

'Then I stay also.'

Gefter's courage gave Gus renewed hope. He slapped his knee and winced.

'All right,' he said, 'Richard, get below and start plugging those holes with anything we've got. Use the sea jackets if you have to. The rest of you come with me and we'll see if we can't lever her off this breakwater.'

Veroline, who did not speak much English, realised now what Gus was planning to do. As he had done before he started to panic – noisily. He gabbled in Finnish, but it was clear that he thought they must surrender and throw themselves on the mercy of the occupants of the fortress. Since they were right below the Russians this was a disturbance that was likely to bring the guards right down on them. Gefter, the former prizefighter, ended the argument with a right cross to Veroline's jaw which knocked him onto his back for the second time that evening. Gus, who was about to argue with Veroline, was left open-mouthed. Gefter simply shrugged and clambered out of the boat behind Beeley.

It is no easy thing to move a boat weighing four tons when it is firmly wedged onto a breakwater, but by using sheer physical strength and the boat-hooks as levers Gus and his team persuaded CMB7 to give up her resting place and slide into the water. Marshall had done his best to stuff the holes with clothing and the canvas covers, but the boat immediately began to ship a great deal of water. The only answer was to bail furiously with anything that came to hand.

Gradually they began to drift with the current into the open waters of the Gulf, but it was agonisingly slow going. At this rate they had no hope of being beyond the range of the Russian guns by dawn. Then Beeley had an idea. He took the boat-hooks and from them made a crosspiece which he wedged alongside the firing chamber of the torpedo ram. From the crosspiece he then hung pieces of canvas torn from the deck covering. It made a very small sail, but there was a substantial easterly breeze. Together with the current, Gus estimated that they were now making about two knots. It might just be enough – if they could keep CMB7 facing in the right direction.

The problem was that the rudder assembly had been torn off in the crash. If they held their current direction they would simply sail far out into the Gulf and without a radio or any way of signalling it was very likely that they would die of thirst before they were rescued. Even Beeley was stumped to come up with an answer to the problem, but it was the frantically bailing Gefter who came to their aid. He attached a couple of empty petrol cans to a rope and flung this over the bows. When one of the crew hauled on the rope the petrol cans provided just enough resistance to give a little steerage to the boat. The problem was that they now had fewer items to bail with and CMB7 began to settle increasingly swiftly into the water. Worse still, the faster she settled, the slower she travelled. In desperation, Marshall pulled off his seaboots and began bailing with those. For some reason, the sight of him standing there in his socks and throwing water over the side was so ridiculous that the whole crew forgot their plight and broke out into laughter.

But the moment passed and they all began anxiously watching the eastern horizon beyond the looming bulk of Kronstadt, looking for the first signs of dawn. The dark shapes of the sea forts lay strung out in the water behind them – still far too close for safety.

Yard by yard they drew further away, bailing hard all the time. But the sky was growing steadily lighter and by about three o'clock it was clear to all of them that the sun was going to beat them. They were still within sight of the forts and it was now just a matter of waiting until one of the sentries spotted them and sounded the alarm. Unable to get away, they would then simply be picked off by the eight-inch naval guns on one of the larger fortresses.

One by one they stopped bailing. There really seemed little point now. In fact, the lower they were in the water, the less chance there was of them being spotted. Together they sat in the torpedo trough, sharing a cigarette and waiting for he moment when the disc of the sun would break through the clouds. Gefter solemnly shook hands with each of them and told them what a good try it had been and what an honour it had been to sail with them.

For Gus Agar it was galling to have travelled so far and done so much, only to fail at the very last attempt. He wondered what would happen to Paul Dukes now?

It was then, as Gus was staring out over the sea, that a strange thing happened. Slowly but surely a sea mist began to rise from the water around them. At first he watched it incredulously: it was a phenomenon that he had not seen in these waters before. But then he stood and shouted to the others to start bailing again. He had no idea if the mist would be thick enough to hide them from the binoculars of those in the forts, but he was damned well going to give it a try.

Slowly the mist thickened. It was touch-and-go. At any moment the men expected to hear a boom as one or other of the fortresses opened fire, but the sound never came. The sun rose, the early-morning mist continued to thicken and CMB7 gradually crept to safety. When they were sure that they were far enough away, the five men whooped and cheered and slapped each other on the back. They were safe – if only they could keep the boat afloat a little longer.

The water had risen to the level of CMB7's deck when they heard a small motor chugging away somewhere in the mist. It sounded too slow to be a Soviet patrol boat and anyway the Russians were unlikely to venture this far out beyond the safety of the minefields.

Gefter and Veroline hailed the boat in Russian and Finnish and before long a small Finnish fishing boat slipped through the mist and came to a stop about fifty metres away, just on the edge of visibility in the murk.

Not surprisingly, they were very suspicious and demanded to know what this strange vessel was. Gus ordered Veroline to tell them that they were a Royal Naval vessel from the flotilla at Biorko and that they required a tow to shore. The men would be well rewarded for their help. However, the prospect of a reward was clearly not enough to tempt the fishermen because they immediately started up their engine and began to pull away. Seeing this, Gus nodded to Marshall on the Lewis guns who sent a burst across their bows just to remind them where their duty lay. The fishing boat immediately altered course and pulled alongside. Within minutes CMB7 was being towed back to Terrioki. 'The boat they couldn't sink' had held out to the end.

The mist began to lift as the sun rose and the sea warmed. As they sat there watching the pine forests of the Finnish coast draw nearer,

Gus remarked to Gefter that it was strange to think that they had come all that way just to be saved by a change in the weather conditions.

But Gefter shook his head. Like all Russians he was deeply superstitious. As far as he was concerned, they had not been saved by the weather. They had been saved by God.

Epilogue

Once more Gus Agar, now Lieutenant Commander Augustus Agar VC, DSO, sat in the waiting room outside Cumming's office in Whitehall Gardens where he had waited with Commander Goff just five short months before. In the distance, Big Ben struck eleven o'clock.

He had left Biorko on 17 September, arriving in England on Wednesday, 24 September, just seven days after Paul Dukes. But Gus did not plan to stay in England for long. Although his secret mission was over, he had been given permission by the Admiralty to return and help in the negotiations for the return of the nine officers and men who had been captured at Kronstadt. There would just be time to collect his Victoria Cross and Distinguished Service Order from King George V at Buckingham Palace before he went back.

Before he had left Finland, Gus had learned that Paul Dukes and Peter Sokolov had escaped across the border to Latvia. He was mightily relieved. It was the perfect end to his mission. He had travelled from Helsinki to Stockholm where he had dined with Major John Scale and his wife. Scale had told him that even if the final attempt to get through the forts had not failed, the mission would still have come to an end. With the Soviets having put a large price on his head, the Admiralty had finally decided that it had become too dangerous for Gus to remain in the area. Scale appeared to be very friendly with Gus, but what he did not reveal was that Le May and Hall had finally got their way: Scale had sent a request to Cumming to approach Admiral Cowan. They wanted him to remove Gus from his post on the somewhat bizarre grounds that he was 'very *difficile*'. In other words they had found Gus to be far too much of an independent thinker to work as an agent for MI6. The incompetence and double-dealing of Cumming's organisation had continued to the very end of the mission.

After lunch with Scale, Gus found that he had several hours to spend before his train left for Oslo. He wondered what to do. But as he was walking down the street from Scale's house he stopped to read a tattered poster on a wall and it gave him an idea. That evening, in honour of Peter Sokolov, Gus went to his first ever football match. He watched Sweden play a team from the United States.

As he sat in the waiting room, Gus listened to Dorothy Henslowe and Cumming's two other secretaries typing in the next room. Scale had told him that Paul Dukes was also making his way to England where the British Cabinet were eager to hear his news of the situation in Russia. Unfortunately, many of Paul's views were already known: in Estonia, on his own initiative, he had given private briefings about his mission to the leaders of the White armies in the hope that they would prosecute the war against the Bolsheviks more effectively. Unfortunately, the Whites showed no signs of changing their tactics, but they had leaked these briefings to the press – much to Cumming's disgust. It looked as though Paul Dukes's days as a spy were numbered. Gus wondered if there would be an opportunity to meet before he had to head back again.

The door to Cumming's office opened and a tall, slim, dark-haired man emerged, clutching a black leather briefcase. Gus stood up to enter Cumming's office and in the cramped space the two men both stood aside to let the other pass. There was something about the look in the other man's eye and Gus felt that he knew him. He almost let the moment pass, but then said:

'Excuse me, but your name isn't Dukes, is it?'

Paul Dukes smiled.

'Well, yes, it is.'

Instinctively they shook hands.

'I suppose you know I'm Agar?'

Paul looked incredulous for a moment and then laughed out loud as they continued to shake hands. Cumming was standing at the door of his office, waiting, and Paul had another appointment elsewhere in Whitehall. There was no time to talk now.

'I expect I'll see you again soon,' said Paul and then he was gone.

Within a year, he would be received by the king at Buckingham Palace and become Sir Paul Dukes. To this day he remains the only

MI6 officer ever knighted for his work in the field, an achievement unmatched in one hundred years of the existence of the Service.

Gus went into his final meeting with MI6. Despite the reports from Finland, Cumming offered him a post working for the organisation but Gus refused politely. He had seen more than enough of the duplicitous world of the British Secret Service and he longed for a return to the comparative simplicities of naval life. However, Gus knew that Ed Sindall was very keen to join – as a member of the Royal Naval Reserve he would have been unlikely to be allowed to join the Royal Navy upon his return from Finland. So Gus recommended him to Cumming and Sindall joined MI6 soon after.

As for Gus Agar and Paul Dukes, the two men were to meet many times in the following years – at one stage Paul even took a cruise in the Mediterranean on the warship that Gus commanded. Their careers were never again to match the heights they had achieved in Russia and their personal lives were subject to bitter disappointments. But neither of them ever forgot that summer when they never met in the shadow of the fortress of Kronstadt.

Postscript

What happened afterwards

The Principals:

Paul Dukes

By contacting the British community in Petrograd for funds Paul weakened his organisation. George Gibson advanced 200,000 roubles to Petrovskaya but then the Cheka moved in. Gibson and Petrovskaya were arrested. During his interrogation Gibson was shown coded messages from Dukes which showed that the courier network had been fatally compromised. The networks were broken up, although it is hard to estimate to what extent because of the subsequent weeding of MI6 files. This disaster meant that Paul's espionage work had little long-term effect in Russia.

Paul went on one more mission for MI6 (to Poland), but because of post-war budget cuts and his notoriety he was never taken on as a full-time officer. He left for America where he gave lectures based on his experiences and, in 1922, he wrote a book about them (*Red Dusk and the Morrow*). Paul remained on MI6's books as an 'asset' who could be contacted for particular operations, but his life increasingly centred on two things: a quest for religious truth and the practice of yoga. Paul was largely responsible for introducing yoga to the Western world.

He married twice, the first time in 1922 to Margaret Rutherford, an heiress connected to the Vanderbilt family. The marriage was unhappy and was dissolved in 1929. His second marriage, in 1959, was to his secretary Diana Fitzgerald, who remained his wife until his death. He had no children.

He died on 27 August 1967 in Cape Town, South Africa. It has often been reported that he died from injuries following a motoring accident. What actually happened was that in the winter of 1966 he slipped on icy steps at his home in Bagshot as he was showing an elderly friend to her car. His legs did slide under the car, but it was parked and did not injure him. However, he did suffer some unspecified internal damage and this greatly reduced his mobility. Diana took him to South Africa in the hope that he would revive, but he got steadily worse during the following eight months and really just faded away.

Paul Dukes was referred to in various ways following his exploits – 'The Man They Couldn't Trap', 'The New Scarlet Pimpernel', 'The Man with a Hundred Faces' – and there was of course his unique knighthood. But perhaps one of the greatest tributes came during the Second World War. Enigma decryption material was so heavily protected that it was issued through MI6 as if it was being produced by human agents. Those in Whitehall who were privileged to receive the reports confided to their friends that they knew the identity of the 'super agent' who must be behind it all: it could only be Paul Dukes!

Augustus Agar

He continued to serve with the Royal Navy, including a period on the Royal Yacht. In 1940, he was again charged with conducting a daring raid on an enemy harbour: the plan was to strike at German invasion barges at Boulogne. The operation was dogged by constant problems and when Agar's vessel, the destroyer HMS *Hambledon*, was struck and crippled by a mine in the Channel the project was finally cancelled. Agar went on to command HMS *Dorsetshire*, a heavy cruiser, but after much success she was sunk in the Indian Ocean by Japanese aircraft in April 1942. Agar survived the attack but was badly injured. He was declared unfit for service, but became President of the Royal Naval College in Greenwich from 1943 until 1946.

He never did marry 'Dor'. In 1920 after he had returned to England he was quite a celebrity and in July of that year he married Mary Dent, the nineteenth Baroness Furnivall. The marriage was not happy and they were eventually divorced in 1931. But like Paul Dukes, Agar found love the second time around when he married Ina Lindner shortly afterwards. They remained happily married until his death.

He retired to run a strawberry farm at Alton, Hampshire and he died at Alton on 30 December 1968.

Francis Cromie

He is commemorated on the Archangel Memorial in St Petersburg, but the site of his grave is now lost.

The CMB Team:

Edgar Sindall

He was demobilised in January 1920 and joined MI6 the following month. After a few weeks of training in Paris, he was sent to Stockholm where he worked as Passport Control Officer, the usual MI6 cover role in those days. Agar believed that Sindall wanted to return to the area because he planned to marry a Russian heiress whom he had met at Terrioki. He left Stockholm in March 1924. His movements after that date are unknown.

John Hampsheir

He was sent initially to a nursing home on the Isle of Wight but he never fully recovered from the strains of the mission. He was demobilised in January 1920. He received £768 4s 1d as his share of the prize money from the sinking of the *Oleg*. He married and settled in Moretonhampstead in Devon where he died at the tragically early age of 38 in 1936.

Richard Marshall

His service record appears to be one of those which were destroyed by fire. Nothing is known about his subsequent career.

Hugh Beeley

He returned with the team to England and was demobbed on 21 November 1919. Nothing more is known about him. Members of the Beeley family attended a presentation at the Imperial War Museum in London in the 1970s, but since then contact with them has been lost.

Albert Piper and Richard Pegler

Both men were demobbed on the same day as Beeley and, as with Beeley, nothing more about them is known.

The Kronstadt Crews:

Claude Dobson

He continued to serve in the Royal Navy, rising to the rank of Rear Admiral. He retired in 1935 and died at Chatham in June 1940, aged just 55.

Gordon Steele

He rose to the rank of Commander and served until the Second World War. He retired to Winkleigh in Devon where he died in 1981, aged 88. He is believed to have been the last survivor of the Kronstadt Raid.

William Bremner

He was repatriated in March 1920. After he recovered from his wounds he joined the NID and then MI6. He rose to become Assistant Chief Staff Officer (equivalent to Director level today). In 1940, together with Cuthbert Bowlby, another former CMB officer, he set up the very first MI6 station in Cairo. It is believed that he retired in 1947.

Osman Giddy

At 19 he was one of the youngest men to take part in the Kronstadt Raid. He continued to serve in the Navy, attaining the rank of Commander. He retired in 1946 and died at Worthing, West Sussex in 1980.

David Grahame Donald

He continued to serve in the RAF until his retirement in 1947 as Air Marshall Sir David Grahame Donald KCB, DFC, AFC, MA. He died in Hampshire in 1976.

MI6:

SIS/MI1C/MI6

Thanks largely to the material produced by Paul Dukes, MI6 survived the intelligence review of 1919. It staggered on through the 1920s and 1930s despite budget cuts and numerous intelligence failures and financial scandals, including one suicide. The decline in its reputation was such that by 1939 Winston Churchill wanted to abolish it completely. MI6 tried to bridge the gap during the 1930s by creating the 'Z Organisation' (comprised of MI6 officers under very deep cover) but this was completely blown within days of the start of the Second World War, negating years of careful work. Eventually Churchill was persuaded to run MI6 in parallel with the newly formed Special Operations Executive. This new organisation completely outperformed MI6 during the war, but MI6's reputation was bolstered by Ultra material which, for security reasons, was released as if produced by MI6 agents. When this is stripped out, MI6 contributed comparatively little to the Allied victory. But at the end of the war MI6's political influence in the public-school old-boy network of Whitehall enabled it to absorb SOE – a source of bitterness to many former SOE members. Today, despite its poor performance over the past one hundred years, it is more powerful than ever.

Mansfield Cumming

He continued to lead MI6 until his death in June 1923, although he was often absent due to illness. The myth that he was an intelligence mastermind persists to this day.

Ernest Boyce

The ineffective head of MI6 in Petrograd before Dukes's arrival continued to blunder. He was largely responsible for Sidney Reilly travelling to his death at the hands of OGPU (the successor organisation to the Cheka) in 1925, and in 1927 a major network that he was running in Russia was shown to be comprehensively penetrated. He retired in disgrace in 1928 and worked in Paris for former MI6 officer Stephan Alley. In 1938 he reapplied to MI6 but was told that his services were no longer required.

Raleigh Le May

He is believed to have left MI6 in 1921.

Harold Trevenen Hall

He continued to serve with MI6 in Finland and Estonia where, among other failures, he fell for a ruse and bought documents which appeared to show that the Soviets were funding the IRA. The documents were fairly poor White Russian forgeries and when this hoax was exposed it led to a further fall in the reputation of MI6 in Whitehall.

Victor Jones (ST-35)

He returned to London in December 1919 following the collapse of Paul Dukes's networks. He returned to civilian duties with the Post Office Wireless Department at North Foreland. He was still alive in 1960 when he was Secretary of the Portsmouth Branch of the Royal Naval Association.

The Couriers:

Peter Sokolov

He continued to work on Russian operations for MI6 from his base in Finland. He worked again with Paul Dukes during the Second World War. He eventually retired to Sweden where he lived under the name 'Peter Sahlin' because of the risk of KGB reprisals. He died in 1971.

Gefter

He disappeared after the war, although he did come to England to visit Paul Dukes in 1920. He contributed an article about his work to a book published in Germany in the 1920s, but that is the last reliable trace of him.

Vladimir Constantinov

He became a translator for the BBC and later worked at the Sandhurst Military Academy. He was still alive and living in England at the time of Dukes's death as he wrote a letter of condolence to Lady Dukes.

The Agents:

John Merritt

He and his wife retired to Sussex.

'Klachonka'

Her true identity has never been firmly established and her fate is unknown.

'Aunt Natalia'

She was finally arrested by the Cheka in December 1919. The charges are not known – they might have concerned her connection with Dukes or they might have been to do with someone else she aided. One night in January 1920 she was taken with a group of other prisoners to Irinovka, a town east of Petrograd. She was machine-gunned together with the other prisoners and their bodies were thrown into an unmarked pit.

'Shura Marenko' and 'Sonia Orlov'

Sadly Akulina, Sonia's nanny, wrote later to Paul saying that Sonia had succumbed to famine, illness and the effects of her captivity during the harsh winter of 1919. Shura joined one of the White armies to take revenge on the Bolsheviks who were responsible for the death of his young wife. Whether he succeeded will never be known as he was never heard from again. The story haunted Paul who years later rewrote the entire incident as a short story, but changed their ending to a happy one, with the couple escaping to Finland.

George E. Gibson

He was arrested and imprisoned between November 1919 and October 1920 because of his connection to the Dukes network. At his interrogation the Cheka produced a letter in code which they had intercepted on its way to him (whether by post or secret courier Gibson never knew). Gibson recognised the code as the one that Paul had given him but he refused to acknowledge it. After his release he returned to England. He tried to claim compensation for the enormous amount of money that he had loaned to Paul and to Paul's successor Petrovskaya. MI6 dragged its heels and it was only when Paul threatened to publicly renounce his knighthood and expose their lack of trustworthiness that they finally gave way.

Laura Cade

She was arrested in December 1919 as part of the round-up of Dukes's suspects. But she escaped and hid in Petrograd. She got a message to Paul who sent Peter Sokolov to rescue her. In January 1920 they walked out (although the route is not known). It must have been a hard journey as those who knew her in later life remembered that she still suffered the effects of frostbite. She settled in Littlebury, near Saffron Walden in England. Stories vary: some people remember her as very rich, others only remember her working as a companion to a lady who was very rich. She was in the village until at least the 1950s. She was always accompanied by a young Russian woman who had escaped with her but whose identity is unknown. Her movements after Littlebury are unknown.

The Allies:

Xenophon Kalamatiano

He was finally released and repatriated in 1921 after almost three years of brutal incarceration. However, the US secret service disowned him and he died in 1923 from an infection caused by a hunting accident. In the words of Gordon Brook-Shepherd: 'He was only forty-one, but had packed in twice as much adventure into his few adult years as most people do in a full lifetime.'

The Enemy:

Iakov Peters

In the 1920s he led the operations that captured both Boris Savinkov and Sidney Reilly. He later became first deputy chairman of the Moscow City Soviet, but was apparently arrested and executed during one of Stalin's purges in 1938. However, as befits a man of Peters's reputation there are some doubts about this. Some reports say that he was not executed until 1942, others that he escaped execution altogether.

Royal Navy:

Sir Walter Cowan

He was created 'Baronet of the Baltic' for his work in 1919. He then enjoyed a successful naval career, rising to the rank of admiral. He was placed on the retired list in 1929 but at the outbreak of war in 1939 he applied for re-enlistment even though he was almost seventy. He became liaison officer to 11 Commando, undergoing the same training as the recruits despite his age. He later joined the Indian Armoured Corps in North Africa where he took a full part in the fighting. He was awarded a bar to his DSO for war services and received the unprecedented distinction (for an admiral) of being appointed an honorary colonel for his work with the army. He retired for the second time in 1944 and died in 1956, aged 85.

Captain Wilfred French

He had already left Osea by the time Agar returned from the Baltic, but he was the best man at Agar's wedding in 1920. He enjoyed a successful naval career, becoming Admiral Sir Wilfred French. However, his career ended under something of a cloud when he was blamed for a successful attack by German submarines at Scapa Flow. This was somewhat unjust since French had warned about the very weaknesses that allowed the Germans to attack.

The Vessels:

CMB4

She was displayed at the Motor Boat Exhibition at Olympia in 1920 before being returned to the Thornycroft yard at Platt's Eyot. When the yard closed in the 1960s she was returned to the Navy who stored her at Southampton. She was discovered some years later in a very dilapidated condition and restored by boatbuilding apprentices. She is now part of the Historic Ships Committee's Core Collection of Historic Vessels. She is currently displayed at the Imperial War Museum at Duxford although she is now just a shell, her engine and controls being sadly long gone.

CMB7

She was too badly damaged to be salvaged. When the base at Terrioki was closed down, she was towed out to sea by CMB4 and was sunk with gun-cotton charges.

The CMB Flotilla

Despite the success of the Kronstadt Raid the Admiralty did not really know what to do with the CMBs. Those that had travelled abroad were either destroyed or left to rot. HMS *Osea* was gradually wound down, finally closing in 1921. Some CMBs were transferred to a new base at Haslar, but this was closed in 1925 and the remaining CMBs were either scrapped or used for target practice. Today only CMB4 and one example of a 55ft CMB remain.

The *Gavriil*

Agar and the CMBs had their revenge on the vessel that had inflicted the greatest number of CMB losses. Together with Russell

McBean, Agar laid mines in the cleared channel through the Russian defences. The *Gavriil* ran onto these on 21 October 1919 and sank. There were only two survivors.

Appendix A

The Kronstadt Raid (Personnel)

An extensive search by staff at the National Archives, the National Maritime Museum and the Imperial War Museum failed to discover a full list of the names of personnel who took part in 'Operation R.K.' (The Kronstadt Raid). Many of the relevant documents (including service records) appear to have been destroyed in a fire. It is possible that such a list may yet be found, but in the meantime the following is as complete a list as can be compiled from existing sources.

Royal Navy

Coastal Motor Boats

First team

1. CMB79A (sunk) Lt William 'Bill' H. Bremner RN (wounded and prisoner).
Sub Lt Thomas. R. G. Usborne RN (killed in action).
Chief Motor Mechanic Henry J. Dunkley RNVR MB2714 (wounded and prisoner).
Chief Motor Mechanic Francis E. Stephens RNVR (killed in action).
Able Seaman William G. Smith RN (killed in action).
One torpedo.

2. CMB31 Commander Claude 'Dobbie' C. Dobson RN DSO.
Lt Russell 'Beans' H. McBean RN.
Sub Lt John J. C. Boldero RN.
Chief Motor Mechanic Ernest Yeomans.

Huva – Finnish contraband pilot.
+ one unnamed personnel
Two torpedoes.

3. CMB88BD Lt Archibald 'Mossy' Dayrell-Reed RN DSO (killed in action).
Lt Gordon C. Steele RN.
Sub Lt Norman E. Morley RN.
+ two unnamed personnel
Two torpedoes.

Second team

4. CMB62BD (sunk) Acting Lt Commander Frank Brade RNR (killed in action).
Sub Lt Hector F. Maclean RN (killed in action).
Chief Motor Mechanic Francis L. H. Thatcher RNVR (killed in action).
Stoker Petty Officer Samuel McVeigh RN(wounded and prisoner).
Leading Seaman Sidney D. Holmes RN (killed in action).
Two torpedoes.

5. CMB86 Sub Lt Francis W. Howard RNR.
Sub Lt R. L. Wight RN.
Eng Lt Commander Francis B.Yates.
+ two unnamed personnel
Two torpedoes.

6. CMB72 Sub Lt Edward R. Bodley RNR.
Sub Lt Ronald Hunter-Blair RN.
+ two or three unnamed personnel
One torpedo.

Attack on Gavriil

7. CMB24A (sunk) Lt Laurence E. S. Napier RN (prisoner).
Lt Osman C. H. Giddy RN (wounded [back, shell splinters] + prisoner).
Chief Motor Mechanic Benjamin Reynish RNVR (prisoner).

Chief Motor Mechanic William Eric Whyte
RNVR (prisoner).
Leading Seaman Herbert J. Bowles (prisoner).
Able Seaman Charles A. Harvey (wounded [right
arm, severe] + prisoner).
One torpedo.

Attack on patrol vessels
8. CMB7   Lt Augustus W. S. Agar RN VC DSO.
Sub Lt Edgar R. Sindall RNR.
Midshipman Richard N. O. Marshall RNVR.
Chief Motor Mechanic Hugh Beeley.
'Veroline' – Finnish contraband pilot.
One torpedo.

Royal Air Force
Short Seaplanes (4):
N9056   Major David Grahame Donald.
Pl Off (Obs) Louis James Chandler.

N5049   Fl Lt Colin Boumphrey.
Pl Off (Obs) Lionel James Booth.

N9030   Fl Lt Albert William Fletcher.
Pl Off (Obs) Frank Clifford Jenner.

N9055   Cpt Acland.
Pl Off (Obs)Alexander Rees.

Sopwith Camel (1):
N6638   Cpt Randall.

Sopwith Strutters (2):
N5988   Cpt Williams.
N5997   Fl Off Eric Brewerton.

Sopwith Griffin (1):
N101   Fl Off James MacGregor Fairbrother.
Pl Off (Obs) Samuel Walne.
All aircraft returned safely.

Appendix B

Agar and Erskine Childers

Agar later put the matter of his selection down to his friendship with Captain Wilfred French and this is almost certainly right. But the records of the CMB Flotilla throw up one other tantalising possibility: at one time the intelligence officer for the CMB Flotilla at Osea was Erskine Childers, the same Erskine Childers who had written *The Riddle of the Sands*, the very first modern espionage novel.

During the war Childers served with all three branches of the armed forces – first in the army as an artillery lieutenant, then with the Royal Naval Air Service as an observer, then in the newly formed Royal Air Force as a major. Early in 1917, recently promoted to lieutenant commander, Childers took the first four CMBs across the Channel to their new base at Dunkirk. He served with the Flotilla from 13 December 1916 until 27 July 1917, during which time he participated in thirty-nine CMB missions.

Agar claimed to have known Childers. He described him as a 'very loveable man' and a 'friend'. They were both Irishmen and both airmen. Their fathers had both tried to make their fortunes in Sri Lanka (Ceylon), Agar's as a tea planter, Childers's as a civil servant. They had also both served in the Gallipoli campaign at the same time (Childers as an observer in the RNAS, Agar as an officer aboard HMS *Hibernia*). So there were good grounds for their friendship. But Agar did not join the CMB Flotilla until March 1918, long after Childers had left – so how did they meet? The answer appears to be that when Childers returned from the Irish Convention in April 1918 he became the Intelligence Officer at RAF (RNAS) Felixstowe. But it looks as if he also worked at HMS Osea teaching navigation until September 1918. This must be when he and Agar met.

Mansfield Cumming also knew Childers. They both berthed their yachts at the same harbour, Burlesdon, and although Cumming's official diary only mentions Childers twice it is clear that Cumming knew him. There may even have been an intelligence connection involving the NID and Childers's tours of the German coast in small boats.

Something must have made Cumming decide that the Coastal Motor Boats were the best means to contact ST-25. It could have been a recommendation from another colleague or some department of the Admiralty, it could have been his own interest in fast boats – there was nothing faster than a CMB. We will never know for sure. But just as John Buchan, the creator of Richard Hannay, played an important part in Paul Dukes's life, the connection between Augustus Agar, Erskine Childers and Mansfield Cumming is an intriguing one.

Notes

The following abbreviations are used throughout:

BE – *Baltic Episode* by Captain Augustus Agar;
FITS – *Footprints in the Sea* by Captain Augustus Agar;
RDATM – *Red Dusk and the Morrow* by Sir Paul Dukes;
ST-25 – *The Story of ST-25* by Sir Paul Dukes;
TUQ – *The Unending Quest* by Sir Paul Dukes.

Please see the bibliography for full publishing details of all works cited.

Prologue

Page 1, '*. . . the de facto chief of all British intelligence operations in northern Russia.*' Cromie had served in the Royal Navy since he had joined as a cadet aged sixteen and was considered one of the outstanding officers of his generation. In 1903 he had taken the unusual step of joining the submarine service, but had served with distinction and in November 1915 he had sunk the German cruiser *Undine* whilst on a mission in the Baltic, a feat for which he had received the Distinguished Service Order, the award for valour second only to the Victoria Cross. For their part the Russians had given him their highest award for gallantry, the Order of St. George. After his tour of duty in the Baltic, Cromie had been appointed as Naval Attaché at the British embassy in Petrograd in December 1917. Working directly to Admiral Reginald 'Blinker' Hall of the NID he had soon become, largely through force of personality, the most active and effective of the various intelligence officers based at the Embassy.

Page 1, '*. . . two of the leading British agents in the city whose names were Steckelmann and Sabir.*' This pair had first contacted Cromie at the beginning of August 1918. They had a letter of introduction which they claimed was from Lockhart, the British Agent in Moscow (a diplomatic position, not secret agent – although Lockhart did like to dabble in espionage with his friend Sidney Reilly). Sabir claimed to have been a Russian naval lieutenant before the Revolution who was now serving in the White Guards in Finland as commander of a mining division. Steckelmann also claimed to be a senior White Guards officer with 60,000 White Guards plus 25,000 Lettish troops at his disposal. He also claimed that his contacts in the civil administration could paralyse all railway, telegraph and telephone communication between Finland and Petrograd. *Honoured By Strangers – The Life of Captain Francis Cromie CB DSO RN* by Roy Bainton, p. 245

Page 1, '*. . . and return Russia to Tsarist rule.*' The coup was actually planned for 6 September. *Ace of Spies* by Andrew Cook, p. 167.

Page 1, '*But Cromie knew that the Cheka, the Bolshevik secret police, were closing in on him.*' The Cheka had been created under the command of Felix Dzerzhinsky in December 1917. Cheka stood for '*All Russian Extraordinary Commission for Combating Counter-Revolution and Sabotage*'. It later became the OGPU and then the KGB. In the 1990s, the KGB divided into two new organisations: the FSB (domestic security) and the SVR (foreign intelligence gathering).

Page 1, '*. . . by escaping over the roof in his pyjamas as they came charging up the stairs.*' Bainton, p. 245

Page 2, '*. . . and Cromie was sure that the Cheka had kidnapped him.*' Cromie was correct in his suspicions. Le Page and Consul Woodhouse had been attacked and bundled into a car by the Cheka shortly after midnight just yards from the Embassy as they returned from Woodhouse's flat. Bainton, p. 251

Page 2, '*. . . by a Russian military cadet named Leonid Kanegisser . . .*' Leonid Akimovich Kanegisser (spellings vary), 22, was a student and former artillery academy cadet. He attacked Uritsky in revenge for the execution by the Cheka of his friend Vladimir Borisovich Pereltsveig just a few days before. Pereltsveig was an artillery officer who had been convicted of participating in a conspiracy against the Bolsheviks. Ironically, Uritsky was the only member of the Petrograd Cheka Collegium to vote *against* the death sentence – not because he was merciful, but because he believed that executions for political crimes were counter-productive. Kanegisser shot and mortally wounded Uritsky at 11.15 a.m. on 30 August as he stood waiting for the elevator in the hall of the Commissariat of Internal Affairs in Dvortsovyi Square. Kanegisser, wearing a leather jacket and cap, had arrived earlier and was sitting in an easy chair in the foyer waiting for him. Kanegisser fired once, ran outside and then attempted to flee on a bicycle, but was pursued and cornered in the derelict English Club at 17 Millionnia Street. He ran upstairs, changed his coat and almost escaped in the confusion, but was spotted by Bolshevik troops. In the ensuing gunfight he wounded one soldier, but was eventually overpowered. During his imprisonment he was tortured repeatedly by the Cheka at their headquarters in Gorohovaya Street in an attempt to get him to implicate others, including British and French intelligence officers, but Kanegisser acted alone. He was finally executed on or about 22 October 1918. See *The Cheka* by George Leggett, pp. 105–7

Page 2, '*Gravely wounded, Lenin was thought unlikely to live.*' Fania Kaplan, 28, (usually referred to either as 'Fanny' or 'Dora' which was a name she often used) was a political activist who had a record for political violence which stretched back to 1906 when she was sentenced to perpetual penal servitude for participation in a terrorist act by the Anarchists. She appears to have taken the revolver and launched the attack on Lenin entirely on her own initiative. She broadly supported the aims of the Social Revolutionary Party, but she attacked Lenin because she believed that he had betrayed the Revolution. She was immediately sentenced to death by the Cheka Collegium and was shot in

the courtyard of the Kremlin by the commandant, Pavel Malkov, at 4 p.m. on
3 September 1918. Leggett, p. 107

Page 2, '... *to clear out the "nests of conspirators" in foreign embassies.*'
'When I was questioned by one of the [Cheka], I enquired the reason for our
arrest and received the reply that it was because we had made the Embassy a
nest of conspirators.' George Dobson, *The Times*, 31 October 1918.

Page 3, '... *Cromie pulled a revolver from his pocket.*' Bainton, p. 254. This
was Le Page's revolver. Hall had seen Cromie take it from Le Page's desk
about an hour earlier. Cromie's own gun was found in his flat two days later.

Page 3, '*He had already destroyed any sensitive papers which were held in the
Embassy so he was not worried about that* ...' Bainton, p. 245

Page 3, '*"Remain here and keep the door after me."*' These were his exact
words. Hall's account from his report ADM 223/637, National Archives.

Page 3, '*He wondered if Sabir had actually left to give the Cheka the all-clear
for the raid to go ahead?*' See Hall's account. Neither Steckelmann nor Sabir's
names appeared on the list of those arrested at the embassy. Hall's story is
frustratingly vague. He says that after the first shot both Steckelmann and
Sabir drew pistols and that there was then more shooting, but he does not say
who did this or where he was. He later saw Sabir in the Peter and Paul fortress,
clearly not a prisoner and Sabir had written him some letters in prison which
were probably designed to trap him into damaging admissions. Sabir claimed
that Steckelmann had been shot after the attack, but there is no way of
verifying this. They both appear to have been agents provocateurs, the Cheka
repeating the tactics which had ensnared Robert Bruce Lockhart in Moscow
a few weeks earlier. This involved two different agent provocateurs who
claimed to have been recommended to Lockhart by Cromie. It took some
cheek by the Cheka to pull off the same trick against the same two men twice.
The main aim of the plot seems to have been to capture the White leader
General Yudenich who was in Petrograd at this time. Hall tried to invite him
to the meeting, but he could not be contacted – luckily for him. See also
Bainton, p. 250

Page 4, '*Outside the room a ferocious barrage of shooting began.*' The
description of events in the room is taken from Hall's account. As for events
in the corridor and on the staircase, there are several partial descriptions of
what occurred, but they are contradictory and sometimes do not even agree
on simple facts such as the time of the raid. The following description best fits
the majority of reports, but the truth is that exactly what befell Cromie when
he passed through that door will never be known for certain.

Page 4, '... *the Embassy doors were wide open and the main hall was full of
ten or more Chekist officers.*' *Pravda* later tried to claim that the raid was
carried out with just ten Chekists, but, whilst this may have been strictly true,
it is misleading. George Bucknall senior, a British businessman who had gone
to the embassy to withdraw some money and arrived just moments after the
attack began, said that he saw '*a large number of armed men*' pouring in
through the embassy doors. (Bainton, p. 254). Dobson, the *Times*
correspondent who was inside the embassy, wrote: 'Besides the ten or a dozen
men comprising the Commissioners [Cheka] and their assistants, there was a
strong company of Red Army soldiers for our escort, the crew and marines of
the two torpedo-boat destroyers with their machine guns and any number of
reckless Bolshevist troops in two large barracks not a stone's throw from the
Embassy.' *The Times*, 31 October 1918.

Page 4, '... *a well-known local firebrand called Geller* ...' His name is sometimes given as Heller or Hillier.

Page 5, '... *some Chekists had charged straight up the staircase and were busy looting offices further down the corridor.*' The caretaker of the building interviewed by Roy Bainton in 2001 believed that these were marines who had entered the rear of the embassy building as the Chekists came in at the front, but there is no other record of this. Geller said that he did call for naval troops to seal the embassy, but only after the gunfight with Cromie, so they were at least on standby in the area. A third possibility is that the two men were Sabir and Steckelmann.

Page 5, '... *the bullet lodging in the centre of his forehead.*' Letter from Frances Wagner to the Rev. B. S. Lombard. FO371/4023 National Archives. She was not a witness to the attack, but helped to prepare the body for burial a day later.

Page 6, '... *and, as the echoes of the shooting died away, for a moment there was silence.*' It is hard to be certain now many were killed in the exchange of shots. Sidney Reilly claimed to have seen a row of dead bodies laid outside the embassy shortly after the attack, but this is one of his usual fictions. Robin Bruce Lockhart, son of Robert Bruce Lockhart the British representative in Moscow, claimed that Cromie had descended the staircase firing two Browning automatic pistols (not a revolver) and that he had killed the Commissar. But this account is based on Reilly's stories and is plainly wrong because Geller was not killed in the attack. In London, *The Times* claimed that three Chekists were killed, whereas *Pravda* listed one dead and one wounded. *Krasnaya Gazeta* said that one had been killed and two wounded and named them: Yanson (dead), Bortnovsky (wounded), Shenkman (wounded). Bainton, pp. 262–3. In a Russian work on the Petrograd Cheka, *Vnutri I vne Bol'shogo Doma* by Vasili Berezkhov (1995), it is noted that Geller admitted shooting one of his own men 'by mistake'.

Page 6, '... *but they left a small baby's glove which he had been carrying.*' Account of Frances Wagner. It is possible that this was a keepsake from the birth of his only child, Dolores, who was born in 1907 and was living in England with her mother at this time.

Page 6, '... *but he was clubbed with rifle butts and thrown back into the line.*' There are only three surviving British accounts of what took place in the Embassy that afternoon: Hall's official report written when he returned to London, a statement given by Nathalie Bucknall to the British Consul shortly after the incident and the account of George Bucknall, a former naval officer attached to Cromie's division, now serving in a civilian capacity. George's account was written sixteen years after the event. Each of these witnesses saw only a fraction of what happened and their accounts are in some ways contradictory. There are also several accounts in Russian newspapers but these are necessarily brief and must be regarded cautiously. Only one thing is absolutely certain: Cromie sold his life dearly defending his agents.

Page 6, '... *but there were to be no medals for him.*' In the absence of the award that many thought he deserved, Cromie was made a Companion of the Order of the Bath (Military Division) in September 1918. His widow Gwladys received the award.

Page 6, '... *not just for his single handed defence of the Embassy, but also for his many brave actions in Russia over the preceding ten months.*' For a full account of Cromie's life see *Honoured By Strangers* by Roy Bainton.

Page 6, '... *executed by a Cheka firing squad on suspicion of conspiring against the Revolution.*' Bainton, p. 263

Page 7, '*As one historian has since remarked: it was an open licence for the Cheka to kill.*' Leggett, p. 110

Page 7, '*Other agents made their own way back.*' Such as George Hill and Sidney Reilly.

Page 7, '*There was now no British secret agent left in Bolshevik Russia.*' MI6 did have officers in areas of Russia under White control. For instance, Hill and Reilly went to Odessa and there was an MI6 station in Vladivostock. But Bolshevik Russia remained *terra incognita* to all Western intelligence services. MI6 did try to persuade other individuals, such as the British businessman George Armistead, to travel to Bolshevik areas, but all the indications are that none of these missions ever took place.

Chapter 1: The Man with the Punch-like Chin

Page 8, '*The old man had not even acknowledged his presence yet ...*' Cumming seems to have made a habit of ignoring visitors for the first few minutes of a first meeting in order to unsettle them. Sir Paul Dukes (ST-25, p. 34), Augustus Agar (BE, p. 30) and Compton Mackenzie (*Greek Memories*, p. 309) all record this behaviour.

Page 8, '*... on that morning in May 1919.*' In the very first line of Chapter One of *Baltic Episode* (p. 27) Agar claims this meeting was in February 1919, yet from a host of references in other works, including Cumming's own diary and Agar's personal diary, it is clear that this meeting was in early May. On the other hand, it seems unlikely that Agar could make such a glaring mistake in the first line of his book. It raises the question of whether there was an earlier meeting than historians have supposed. Certainly ST-25 needed rescue by February 1919 and if Cumming really did leave things until May 1919 he was leaving it late.

Page 8, '*... rather like the Mr Punch character in a seaside puppet show.*' Compton Mackenzie, *Greek Memories,* p. 309 'I saw on the other side of the table a pale clean-shaven man, the most striking features of whose face were a Punch-like chin, a small and beautifully fine bow of a mouth, and a pair of very bright eyes'. This impression was similar to that of the Naval Attaché at Athens, Commander W. F. Sells who first met Cumming in March 1916 at a Naval Conference in Malta: 'He's an extraordinary old bird,' Sells told me. 'Obstinate as a mule, with a chin like the cut-water of a battleship.' *Greek Memories,* p. 73

Page 8, '*He remembered being briefly introduced to an elderly naval captain just a few weeks ago by his commanding officer at their base on Osea Island in Essex.*' Although it is often unreliable, a TV proposal written by Agar and contained in his papers at the Imperial War Museum (p. 10) records this visit to Osea as having taken place towards the end of April. This would be consistent with an entry in Cumming's diary in which he applies for permission to use the CMBs on 1 May. See also *Mansfield Cumming: The Search for 'C'* by Alan Judd, p. 434

Page 8, '*... a meeting with a Commander Goff of the Naval Intelligence Department about "Special Service."*' BE, p. 29. Possibly Commander R. S. Goff RN DSO.

Page 9, '... *removed his spectacles and slipped a gold rimmed monocle into his right eye.*' For Cumming's use of spectacles and monocle see Judd, p. 400

Page 9, '"*Sit down, my boy, I think you will do!*"' FITS, p. 88

Page 9, '... *sent away to boarding school in England* ...' Framlingham College near Woodbridge in Suffolk.

Page 9, '... *transformed into reality by the boat builder Sir John Isaac Thornycroft.*' John Isaac Thornycroft was the founder of Thornycroft Shipbuilders. He had been working on skimmer designs for some years before the Royal Navy approached him. He finalised the design of the CMB (adapted from the Thornycroft Crusader) together with his three children: Tom (who designed the engine specially for the CMBs), John (who worked on the design and took over the project once the final design was agreed) and Blanche (who conducted all the trials on propeller design. She eventually became the first ever female member of the Institute of Marine Engineers). The design tests were all carried out in their purpose-built tank at their home on the Isle of Wight.

Page 10, '*They could achieve speeds of up to forty-five knots* ...' *Janes Fighting Ships 1919* only says 'in excess of thirty knots'. Every boat was different (see Chapter Three) but in general the speed of both 40 ft and 55 ft CMBs was 35 knots fully laden and up to 45 knots once the torpedo(es) had been launched. See FITS, pp. 78, 105, 113; ST-25, p. 252. In RDATM (p. 286) Dukes claimed the top speed was over fifty knots, but this is highly unlikely. Forty five knots is equivalent to approximately 52 mph (83 kph), but this seems a great deal faster in a low lying boat on water. By comparison, modern F1 powerboats reach speeds of up to 150 mph in races, but then they don't have to launch torpedoes at the same time ...

Page 10, '... *and generally making things unpleasant for the Germans.*' '... the German naval authorities were in utter dread of them, and never knew when to expect them.' Sir John I. Thornycroft *A Short History of the Revival of the Small Torpedo Boat,* p. 11. This is perhaps a slightly over-optimistic assessment of their performance. The qualities of motor torpedo boats were never properly exploited until World War II. During World War I, although they achieved some notable successes, CMBs were vulnerable to air attack by day and at night their engine noise tended to negate the vital element of surprise. See *The Dover Patrol* by Roy Humphries.

Page 10, '... *the operation to sink blockships in the approaches to Zeebrugge harbour* ...' Operation ZO. The CMBs laid smokescreens to shield larger vessels and two of them entered the harbour and launched torpedoes against a German warship.

Page 10, '*Some CMBs had been sent abroad on other duties* ...' The other operations on which CMBs were deployed at this time were: 1) Eight 55 ft CMBs under Lt Dickinson to Archangel to patrol the River Dvina and assist forces under General Ironside; 2) Eight 55 ft CMBs under Commander Eric Robinson VC to the Caspian Sea to prevent the Baku oil fields falling into Soviet hands; 3) A mixed force of CMBs under Commander the Honourable Patrick Acheson to the Rhine as part of the occupying forces.

Page 11, '... *the organisation which we know today as the Secret Intelligence Service (SIS) or, more commonly, as MI6.*' Cumming's organisation was originally known as the Foreign Section of the Secret Service Bureau. By the outbreak of the First World War it was more simply known as the 'Foreign Service' or the 'Secret Service'. In 1916, the War Office tried to lay claim to the Service by designating it MI1C (MI stood for Military Intelligence), but Cumming refused to accept this. In 1919, the various secret services were re-structured and Cumming's department officially became the Secret Intelligence Service (SIS) which is still its proper name today. Since the name was in a state of flux during the period of this story and because most people know SIS as 'MI6' (a cover name used during the Second World War) that is the title which will be used throughout this book.

Page 11, Agar quote: BE, p. 29

Page 11, '... *built high amongst the rooftops around Whitehall.*' Actually above 2 Whitehall Court. It was a building well known to Cumming for it contained the Royal Automobile Club of which he was a founder member. Today it is the Horse Guards Hotel.

Page 11, '... *gazed across the plane trees of Victoria Embankment to the grey waters of the River Thames.*' *Greek Memories*, p. 309

Page 11, '*(one of Cumming's personal favourites was an invisible ink made from his own semen).*' 'I shall never forget 'C's delight when the Chief Censor, Worthington, came one day with the announcement that one of his staff had found that semen would not respond to iodine vapour [commonly used for developing secret writing], and told the Old Man that he had to remove the discoverer from the office immediately, as his colleagues were making life intolerable by accusations of masturbation. The Old Man at once asked Colney Hatch [research] to send the female equivalent for testing – and the slogan went round 'Every man his own stylo'. We thought we had solved a great problem. Then our man in Copenhagen, Major Holme, evidently stored it in a bottle, for his letters stank to high heaven, and we had to tell him that a fresh operation was necessary for each letter.' Frank Stagg, MI6 officer 1915–17 quoted in Judd, p. 319

Page 11, '... *but we know that one connected him directly to the Director of Naval Intelligence at the Admiralty.*' *Churchill and the Secret Service* by David Stafford, p. 65

Page 12, '*He was always eager to obtain an example of any invention which might be useful for espionage.*' Too many references to mention, but I think that the historian Janet Morgan has summed him up beautifully: '... like Toad in *The Wind in the Willows*, he adored inventions and acceleration. Room could always be found in C's diary for a meeting to set up a new society for the enjoyment of a faster means of locomotion or for an appointment to examine a new technology: electrical gas detection apparatus; metal said to be invisible in sunlight.' *Secrets of the Rue St Roch*, pp. 177/8

Page 12, '... *having been driven across London by Cumming on a terrifying journey.*' FITS, p. 91

Page 12, '*But following a bad fall in which he broke both his arms ...*' Judd, p. 28

Page 12, Cumming quote: Judd, p. 41

Page 12, '... *at the grand old age of fifty-four.*' Judd, p. 47

Page 12, '*He would then extol the virtues of "the female form divine".*' *Around the Room* by Edward Knoblock.

Page 12, '... *just so that he could "have a look at the girls".*' Judd, p. 291

Page 12, '*He selected these young women for their looks ...*' Judd, p. 329

Page 12, '... *those who knew him well described him as "a notorious womaniser."*' '*C*' *A Biography of Sir Maurice Oldfield* by Richard Deacon, p. 7

Page 13, '*A large portrait of Alastair in military uniform dominated one wall of the office.*' *Greek Memories*, p. 310

Page 13, '*. . . there is some evidence that Cumming's wife never forgave him for the loss of her beloved son.*' Various minor points including the fact that Cumming is buried at Burlesdon in Hampshire. His wife May chose to be buried in Scotland.

Page 13, '*. . . on a child's scooter which had been specially imported for him from America.*' Sent by Norman Thwaites from New York station in September 1918. Judd, p. 415

Page 13, '*On one occasion he even used it as a club to attack Vernon Kell, the head of MI5, during an interdepartmental argument.*' *The Red Web* by Tom Bower, p. 13

Page 13, '*At one point it had even seemed possible that the new government might be formed by an MI6 officer . . .*' For details of the coup and Reilly's career see *Ace of Spies* by Andrew Cook.

Page 14, '*. . . until a few months before, had been the capital of Russia.*' The Bolsheviks moved the capital to Moscow on 5 March 1918 because of the threat from the White army under General Yudenich.

Page 15, '*. . . the Cheka, the dreaded Bolshevik secret police, hunted for deserters and infiltrators.*' Interestingly, it was an MI6 officer who claimed to have created the Cheka. George Hill, later the MI6 liaison officer in Moscow during the Second World War, claimed in his memoir *Go Spy the Land* that he had established the 'Bolshevik counter-espionage section' to spy on the Germans in 1918. This is, at the very least, an exaggeration. The Bolsheviks had long suffered under the Tsarist Ohkrana. When they came to power they simply supplanted that organisation, inheriting its premises and many of its personnel as well. See *Secret Service* by Christopher Andrew, p. 215

Page 15, '*. . . the massive island fortress of Kronstadt.*' In fact the proper name of the island is Kotlin Island. Kronstadt was the name of the fortress and town overlooking the main harbour. It was by far the largest and most powerful of a number of fortresses around the circumference of the island and because of this Kotlin Island was often referred to simply as 'Kronstadt'.

Page 16, Cumming quote: BE, p. 31

Page 16, '*. . . any crew member he selected must also be unmarried and without ties of any kind.*' This is what Agar claimed in *Baltic Episode* and we may take him at his word. However, elsewhere he records that it was his commanding officer who suggested that he take only young officers and men because (in view of Agar's youth and lack of experience) they would be easier to command. When he presented the list of team members to Cumming later, Cumming apparently scanned the list and approved of the fact that they were all young and unmarried. This version is possibly more plausible.

Page 17, '*He was in the middle of setting up a flat with "Dor", the woman he planned to marry.*' Agar's diary, although 'Dor's' full name has since been lost.

Page 17, Henslowe quote: BE, p. 32

Chapter 2: The secret 'C' couldn't tell

Page 19, '*. . . he had taken twelve years out of the Navy to be an estate manager in Ireland.*' Cumming retired from the Navy in December 1885 on half-pay, largely because of chronic seasickness (the reason given on his service record). He worked for the Earl of Meath as his private secretary and for an undefined period as his land agent before returning to the Navy in April 1898. Judd, p. 29

Page 19, '... *and he has left us a detailed account of his methods.*' *My Adventures as a Spy* by Sir Robert Baden Powell. First published in 1915, it is now available freely over the Internet on several sites.

Page 20, '... *just next to the Army and Navy stores.*' This was a very poorly chosen site as Cumming was frequently bumping into officers he knew who were calling into the shop next door and having to explain to them what he was doing there miles away from his post in Southampton.

Page 20, Cumming quote: Judd, p. 100

Page 20, Cumming quote: Judd, p. 113

Page 21, '... *and then only if it was a cheap one.*' Judd, p. 125

Page 21, '*Another meeting had to be hastily arranged.*' *M* by Andrew Cook, p. 194; Judd, p. 121

Page 21, '... *a Royal Marines officer, Major Cyrus Regnart ...*' Regnart is most commonly referred to by historians as 'Roy' but in fact his full name was Cyrus Hunter Regnart. See *Royal Marine Spies* by Lt Col D. F. Bittner and Captain J. M. Coleby, Royal Marines Historical Society, 1993, p. 50

Page 21, '*She threw them out into the street and they had to leave hurriedly before the police arrived.*' Judd, p. 250

Page 22, *The TG incident*: Judd, pp. 221–222

Page 22, Cumming quote: Judd p.214

Page 22, '... *it is better to preserve the myth of British intelligence rather than to allow the public (and the organisation's opponents) to know just how bad things are.*' Obviously too large a subject to discuss thoroughly here, but anyone who doubts this simply has to look at MI6's public record: outperformed by every other service in the First World War; racked by so many financial and intelligence scandals between the wars that Churchill wanted to abolish it completely in 1939; lost its entire order of battle and that of the 'Z' organisation to German intelligence at the outbreak of World War Two; outperformed during the war by SOE and only able to justify its existence because Ultra material was disguised as MI6 material; thoroughly penetrated by the KGB after the Second World War (Philby and Blake); the Franks Committee described its intelligence on the Falklands as little better than reading the local newspapers; it armed and trained Muslim extremists in Afghanistan who are now our deadliest enemies; it predicted that Saddam would never invade Kuwait in the First Gulf War (he did) and that Weapons of Mass Destruction would be found in Iraq after the Second Gulf War (they weren't).

Page 23, '... *the former agent Sidney Reilly whose "experiences" are almost complete fiction.*' e.g. *Reilly, Ace of Spies* by Robin Bruce Lockhart.

Page 23, '... *and later rose to be Foreign Secretary.*' Andrew, p. 206

Page 23, Hoare quote: *The Fourth Seal* by Sir Samuel Hoare, Ch 2. See also Andrew, p. 205

Page 23, '*The majority of historians who have studied the period have concluded that Cumming was pretty ineffective ...*' See for instance *The Failure of British Espionage against Germany, 1907–1914* by Nicholas Hiley, Historical Journal, vol. XXVI (1983).

Page 23, '... *Churchill had to admit that the answer was "not much".*' Stafford, p. 55

Page 23, '... *a figure which included four clerks, two typists and two doormen* ...' Judd, p. 288

Page 23, '... *a furniture shop in Brussels.*' At 7 Rue de Garchard. *MI6* by Nigel West, p. 37. Regnart was head of station and his father had been an upholsterer.

Page 23, '... *the newly promoted Captain Cumming* ...' He made the crucial step on 12 January 1915.

Page 23, '*He had also established liaisons with the intelligence departments of every Allied country.*' Judd, p. 350. Headquarters staff was probably just over 40. There were about 30 stations.

Page 23, Cumming quote: This offer was made by General Williamson in March 1913 when the imminence of war was already freeing up funds. The information which had so impressed Williamson and led him to make this generous offer, had actually come from the French Intelligence Service and had simply been 'repackaged' by Cumming. Judd, p. 255

Page 24, '... *Cumming had not had a good war.*' Another broad subject and it can be hard to quantify performance, but as one guide it is estimated that during the war 235 allied agents had been convicted by the Germans, of which only 55 were believed to have worked for MI6. This might mean that Cumming's organisation was better, but the reality is that the other services were more active. West p.42

Page 24, '*The War Office had run over 6,000 agents* ...' Morgan, p. 338

Page 24, '... *an extremely accurate picture of the movement of German forces behind the Front.*' Train-watching networks consisted of groups of civilians in occupied countries, often no more than little old ladies who sat and watched as trains went past the bottom of their gardens. They would record each type of wagon by shelling peas into different bowls or inserting different stitches into a row of knitting. Signalmen and other railway workers noted insignia on troops' uniforms as they boarded trains. This information was used to build up a detailed picture of the position of all German units and their movements. Several major offensives were foiled in this way as the Allies knew exactly when and where to expect the attacks. The War Office Secret Service ran networks under such code names as '*Sacre Coeur*' and '*Frankignoul*'.

Page 25, *MI8:* Interception and interpretation of communications.

Page 25, *MI9:* Assistance in the escape and evasion by Allied POWs.

Page 25, '*Winston Churchill was among a number of influential figures who supported the idea of an amalgamated intelligence service.*' Stafford, p. 108

Chapter 3: Froggy chooses Sinbad

Page 26, '... *which connected the 600-acre island with the mainland twice a day at low tide.*' FITS, p. 83

Page 26, '... *but it was still a working farm* ...' Bunting Brothers Farm, FITS, p. 82. Today it is a private estate, but the concrete traverser pit and the slipway are still there.

Page 29, '*He and Gus were firm friends.*' 'I went over the list of young Subs in my mind and decided to tackle one Hampsheir whom I knew and liked. He was a quiet sort of youngster, but knew his job and did it efficiently.' Agar TV proposal.

Page 29, '... *and then pounded repeatedly by forces of several tons as the*

CMBs *bounced across the waves.*' 'The conditions under which the motors have to work in these boats are undoubtedly more severe than in any type of aeroplane ...' Thornycroft, p. 11

Page 29, '... *they were allowed only the light of one tiny electric bulb per boat.*' A curtain across the far end of the engine compartment stopped this light being seen through the forward observation hatch.

Page 29, '*CMB motor mechanics were considered the very best in the Royal Navy.*' 'It is quite certain that there is no other motor mechanic's job which is comparable in risk and severity of the work which they have to perform.' Thornycroft, p. 11

Page 29, '*Trained at the elite Rolls-Royce engineering works ...*' Agar TV proposal, p. 16

Page 29, '... *and his ability to get the best out of any machine.*' 'I knew him well. In temperament he was rather like Hampsheir in that he was reserved, spoke little, looked rather doleful with a perpetual worry, but actually in character a wonderful man and dedicated to his job.' Agar TV proposal, p. 16

Page 30, French quote: Agar TV proposal, p. 15

Page 30, '*His nickname in the CMB Flotilla was "Sinbad" because of his buccaneering attitude.*' Letter Sindall to Agar 11-3-20. Agar papers, IWM.

Page 30, Agar quote: Agar TV proposal, p. 17

Page 30, '... *Captain French agreed and they selected 20-year-old Richard Pegler.*' Pegler's participation is a bit of a mystery. His name does not appear in either of Agar's books, his service record shows no record of travel to the Baltic and he did not receive a medal as the other team members did. His name first turned up in the papers of John Hampsheir as someone who accompanied them from Osea to London. However, Agar's personal diary and other papers make it clear that Pegler was a full member of the team and travelled with them to Helsinki where he remained for the duration of their stay. Sadly the reason why Agar chose to exclude him from the public record must now remain a mystery. It may simply be that Agar thought there were already enough names for his readers to handle but, if so, it seems a little harsh. A signal recorded in the Koivisto airfield log as sent to Agar's base at Terrioki concerns someone who had gone AWOL. Was this Pegler? There is no other evidence, so the idea must remain pure speculation.

Page 30, Agar quote: BE, p. 39

Page 32, '*Motor torpedo boats had been in existence for many years ...*' Thornycroft had built his first one for the Royal Navy in 1877.

Page 34, '... *and sent it racing forwards much faster than the CMB could travel.*' Torpedoes varied, but their speed was usually in the region of fifty knots.

Page 34, '*The boats were built at the Thornycroft yard at Platt's Eyot (pronounced "eight") on the River Thames ...*' Those who value the past may be interested to know that the shed in which the CMBs were constructed was until very recently (and may still be) standing, although in a dilapidated condition, at Platt's Eyot. There is a photograph on the Internet at: http://www.marketingreinforcements.pwp.blueyonder.co.uk/index_plattseyot.html

Page 35, '... *great jets of smoke and flame from its exhaust ...*' This fault in the design was later turned to advantage by fitting a device to the CMB exhausts which allowed them to lay smokescreens to shield the movement of other vessels.

Page 36, '*In total, the Admiralty was to order more than one hundred CMBs.*' In total 117 were built: 40 ft: 39, 55 ft: 73, 70 ft: 5.

Page 37, Agar quote: BE, p. 184

Page 37, '*On 8 April 1917 ...*' Humphreys, p. 109. Humphreys records the date as 4 May, but from other sources 8 April appears to be the correct date.

Page 37, '*... a hunting pack comprising CMBs 5,6 and 9.*' The CMBs often used to hunt in packs of four to increase their effectiveness.

Page 37, '*The CMBs raced away into the safety of the darkness using their ability to skim over the Germans' own minefield to prevent a pursuit.*' One of the two skippers whose torpedo found its mark was Lieutenant 'Mossy' Dayrell-Reed in CMB9, two years before he was to figure so prominently in the Kronstadt Raid (see Chapter 12). He was awarded the DSO for his bravery in this action, but Beckett only received the DSC.

Page 39, CMB7 account: *Dangerous Waters* by Leonard Piper, pp.181–2

Page 40, '*... a cheque for 1,000 guineas made out to "bearer".*' In both *Baltic Episode* and *Footprints in the Sea*, Agar stated that the sum was a thousand pounds, but the receipt which he signed and is now preserved amongst his papers at the Imperial War Museum is clearly for £1,100 i.e. 1,000 guineas. It is possible that an extra £100 was advanced later in the mission, but there is no suggestion of this in any of the surviving papers. The bank appears to be Partridge and Cooper Ltd, 191–192 Fleet Street, London.

Page 40, Cumming quote: BE, p. 36

Page 42, '*... and cables were attached to CMBs 4 and 7 which were as ready as Beeley and his team could make them.*' John Hampsheir's log, Imperial War Museum.

Page 42, '*... and were a little put out that MI6 had only booked them third-class tickets!*' Agar TV proposal, p. 20

Page 43, '*He conducted them to the nearby Railway Hotel where the SNTO had booked rooms for them.*' Hampsheir's log.

Page 43, '*... the Fennia was not rated to carry passengers.*' BE, p. 40

Page 43, '*... and Finland had introduced prohibition at the same time she became independent.*' Prohibition was continued in Finland until 1932.

Chapter 4: Very special measures

Page 47, *Accounts of Cheka torture:* Leggett, p. 198

Page 47, '*He was the third of five children – four boys and a girl.*' Ashley b. 1885, Irene Catherine b. 1887, Paul Henry b. 1889, Cuthbert Esquire b. 1890, Marcus Braden b. 1893. Considering the obscurity into which they were born, they were an amazing family: Ashley became a highly successful playwright and one of the founders of the National Theatre. He married the ballerina Marie Rambert and helped her to establish her world-famous dance company. Cuthbert became one of the country's leading oncologists. He was awarded the OBE and the Dukes system for classifying cancerous tumours of the bowel is still in use today. Of the other two, Marcus died in his forties while working as a government officer in Malaysia and Irene, an academically gifted woman like her mother, died after a life dogged by serious illness.

Page 47, '*... the minister of the local Congregationalist church.*' The Congregational Chapel in Bridgwater stood at 19 Fore Street although the family lived in North Field. The chapel had been founded in 1864. It was demolished in 1964 and in 1966 what remained of the congregation merged with that of nearby Westfield.

Page 47, Cuthbert Dukes quote: Memoirs of Cuthbert Dukes in the Dukes Papers, Hoover Institution Archives.

Page 48, *'taking first place among all the women graduates in England.'* Memoirs of Cuthbert Dukes.

Page 48, '*. . . he always proudly referred to her as "Edith Pope BA."'*. See for instance his various entries in *Who's Who*.

Page 48, '*. . . whom he described as "infinitely kind" . . .'* TUQ, p. 9

Page 48, Moses Turner account: TUQ, p. 9

Page 49, *'It was Paul's great misfortune to be sent to the Congregationalist Boys' School at Caterham in Surrey.'* TUQ, p. 13

Page 49, '*. . . making sure that the two of them spent plenty of time alone together.'* TUQ, p. 13

Page 50, *'an awkward man to get on with'* Cuthbert's words.

Page 50, '*. . . he also seemed to associate his father's marriage to a woman twenty years his junior with some failure to control his sexual urges.'* 'Even Victorian and Edwardian divines were in the last analysis human, and my father, being made willy-nilly in God's image like the rest of us, had promptings at about sixty which caused his once again to covet a wife.' TUQ, p. 14

Page 51, '*. . . giving lessons in the town of Enschede, on the border with Germany.'* TUQ, p. 15

Page 51, *'He bought a rail ticket to St Petersburg.'* TUQ, p. 35

Page 51, '*. . . Anna Essipova, the school's principal professor of piano who also trained Sergei Prokofiev and Alexander Borovsky.'* TUQ, p. 38

Page 51, *'Instead he continued to play at occasional concerts . . .'* TUQ, p. 47

Page 51, '*. . . a friendship which was to last for the rest of their lives.'* Coates remained at the Mariinsky after the Russian Revolution and he may even have been one of Dukes's contacts during his mission. He refused to be cowed by the Bolsheviks. There is a rather touching story that Zinoviev, leader of the Petrograd Soviet, stormed into a rehearsal at the Mariinsky which Coates was leading and demanded that only music of 'political significance' should be played during the upcoming first anniversary of the Revolution. Coates calmly informed the firebrand that he could demand 'political music' whenever he, in return, decided to provide musical politics – but not before.

Page 52, *'They were known locally as "Big Boy Albert" and "Dukelet".'* ST-25 p. 15. This might raise questions in some quarters about their sexuality, especially in light of Dukes's living arrangements with Gibbes. But Coates was (apparently) happily married, Dukes conducted a long and tempestuous affair with an (unhappily) married Russian noblewoman throughout this period (given the pseudonym 'Vera' in his books) and there is no suggestion that Gibbes was ever homosexual. So, whilst all things are possible, the evidence is strongly against it.

Page 52, *'In 1916 he resigned from the Mariinsky to work for the Commission full-time.'* ST-25, p. 15

Page 52, *'There was some crossover between the work of the Bureau and the work of the various military intelligence agencies working out of the British embassy . . .'* For an analysis of the Bureau's work and its connections with the world of intelligence see *Joy Rides? British Intelligence and Propaganda in Russia 1914–17*, Historical Journal, vol. XXIV (1981).

Page 52, *'During this period, Paul became close friends with the novelist Arthur Ransome who was then the Russian correspondent for the Daily Chronicle.'* ST-25, p. 22

Page 52, '. . . *and on some occasions Paul even wrote Ransome's column for the newspaper.*' ST-25, p. 22

Page 52, '*When the first Russian Revolution broke out in March 1917 . . .*' February by the Russian calendar.

Page 53, '*He witnessed the street fighting at close hand and saw the rampaging mobs throw police agents from the roofs of buildings where they had been hiding.*' ST-25, p. 20

Page 53, '*Paul was at the Finland Station to witness Lenin's arrival from Switzerland.*' ST-25, p. 22. This was 16 April.

Page 53, '*In July, he was sent back to London as special liaison officer between the Anglo-Russian Bureau and the Foreign Office.*' ST-25, p. 22

Page 54, '*He was sent to the Front in Flanders where he produced intelligence reports about the state of the armed forces.*' Some believe that Dukes was already working for MI6 at this time. This is unlikely and Dukes denied it saying of his recruitment almost a year later: '. . . the Secret Service was to me an utterly unknown quantity . . .' (ST-25, p. 27.) There is no obvious reason for him to lie about this.

Page 54, Dukes quote: ST-25 p.25

Page 54, '*Paul agonised over the issue for several days and finally went to Buchan personally and begged for his help.*' ST-25, p. 25: 'I must go back . . . I said so to my superiors – and saw a gleam in the eye of the author of Greenmantle.'

Page 54, '*He suffered from a digestive problem which had completely undermined his health . . .*' He spent the first three months of the war bedridden with this ailment. *Memory Hold the Door* by John Buchan, p. 164

Page 55, '. . . *and even the Boy Scout movement.*' He knew a lot about the latter from his youngest brother Marcus who was awarded the Silver Wolf for his services to the organisation. As for the YMCA, this may sound odd to modern ears but, in the days before the United Nations or even the League of Nations, the YMCA was very active in providing humanitarian relief in disaster areas.

Page 55, '*Paul boarded the sleeper to London arrived at Kings Cross station early the following morning and found a chauffeur-driven car waiting for him.*' This was almost certainly Ernest Bailey. He had been Cumming's personal driver since at least 1914. Cumming left Bailey £100 in his will and he served for several years under Cumming's successor Admiral Sinclair. Judd, pp. 288, 344, 345, 472. West, p. 74

Page 56, '*This man was Lieutenant Colonel "Freddie" Browning, second in command of MI6.*' Frederick Henry Browning 1870–1929.

Page 56, Hoare quote: Andrew, pp. 204/5

Page 56, '*We have no use for the "usual channels" – except in the early morning!*' MI6 officer Frank Stagg quoted in Judd, p. 326

Page 56, '*Browning told Paul to go away and return at 4.30 p.m. the following day for a further briefing.*' ST-25, pp. 28–29; RDATM, p. 6

Page 57, Dukes quote: ST-25, p. 31

Page 57, '. . . *but upon the outbreak of war he had joined the Indian Political Intelligence department, tracking Indian nationalists who were working with the Germans.*' The reason that so many Indian intelligence officers played such an important role in the early development of the British Secret Services was that, prior to the twentieth century, India and Ireland were the only places in the British Empire where it was thought that organised counter-espionage was necessary – because of the strength of nationalist feeling. Elsewhere in the Empire a combination of occasional sources reporting through the Foreign Office and the military were thought sufficient.

Page 57, '*He had then joined MI6 and served on the New York station before taking up this new post.*' Robert Nathan was knighted in 1920 and died in 1921. In RDATM, Dukes did not mention Nathan at all and ascribed all his work to Browning. However, in ST-25 Dukes quoted a few lines from Nathan's obituary in *The Times*, knowing that he had been dead almost twenty years and that it would be almost impossible to trace it. Today a computer search of the electronic record is quite straightforward. Nathan's role as head of the Political Section was revealed in Cumming's diary and this also ties in with incidental comments in ST-25.

Page 57, Nathan quote: ST-25, p. 31

Page 57, '*As to the means whereby you gain access to the country, under what cover you will live there, and how you will send out reports, we shall leave it to you, being best informed as to conditions, to make suggestions.*' RDATM, p. 7

Page 57, '*. . . his memoirs are stuffed full of the frustrations of dealing with "fools in London" . . .*' For instance *Extremes Meet*, p. 21, where Mackenzie laments the fact that he cannot get a commission for his extremely capable assistant Tucker: 'He was better entitled to a commission than many of those fellows in Queen Anne's Mansions [Whitehall Court], who would never hear any report more alarming than some of those he had written home. They could swagger across St James Park in uniform, looking more like park keepers than [Intelligence Officers]; but they would have thought twice about landing on the Anatolian shore at night to take off a messenger.'

Page 57, '*. . . the character Colonel Nutting represents all the pompous inadequacies of the typical MI6 staff officer.*' See, for instance, *Greek Memories*.

Page 58, '*. . . he was sent abroad the very next day without any training whatsoever.*' All's Fair, pp. 41–43

Page 58, '*Paul consistently told a rather odd story about this moment.*' ST-25, p. 33

Page 58, '*He either marked the notecase or observed her secretly because when he returned he knew that she had not touched it.*' Judd, pp. 208–9

Page 58, '*. . . he did not learn Cumming's real name for another eighteen months.*' ST-25, p. 35

Page 59, Cumming quote: RDATM, p. 11

Page 59, '*. . . Cumming did not have a collection of guns in his office and Reilly did not meet Paul until after Paul's return from Russia.*' For the claim that Reilly was present see *Ace of Spies* by Lockhart, p. 131

Page 60, '*Two weeks later Paul was told that it was time for him to set out again.*' ST-25, p. 37

Page 60, '*His cover was as a diplomatic courier under the alias "Captain McNeil".*' *Gentlemen Spies* by John Fisher, p. 20

Page 60, *Details of Thornhill's career*: Andrew, pp. 204/5

Page 60, '*Paul was told that he could also call on Commander Andrew Maclaren of the NID who had served on the naval staff of the embassy in Petrograd and much later was to be MI6 station chief in Warsaw.*' ST-25, p. 39

Page 60, '*The question remained of what his cover would be and by what route he would travel. It was 600 miles to Petrograd ...'* RDATM, p. 11

Page 60, Thornhill quote: ST-25, p. 39

Page 61, *'Major John Scale'* Scale had formerly been on the MI6 station in Petrograd.

Page 61, *'In 1918, the MI6 station in Stockholm consisted principally of two officers ...'* A third man at the embassy, Wyatt, may also have been a member of the MI6 station. It was he who first approached Ransome to spy against Bolshevik Russia, but he may have been straight Foreign Office. Support staff and secretaries have not been included in this total. At this stage in MI6's development it is possible there were none. Most officers did their own clerical and secretarial work for reasons of secrecy.

Page 61, *'Clifford Sharp'* It may seem strange that the editor of a leading left-wing magazine had become an intelligence officer on the borders of Bolshevik Russia, but Sharp had been appointed editor by Beatrice and Sidney Webb for his editorial skills rather than his politics. It is fascinating to speculate about the connections which led Sharp from London's literary circles to the British Secret Service in Sweden, but if the clues exist somewhere in official documents those papers have yet to be released. His war service ended a few weeks after Dukes passed through Stockholm and he returned to the helm of the *New Statesman*, a post he was to occupy until 1931.

Page 61, *'... the novelist Arthur Ransome had arrived in Stockholm on 5 August ...'* The Life of Arthur Ransome by Hugh Brogan, p. 205

Page 61, *'She had been one of Trotsky's secretaries in Petrograd ...'* Brogan, p. 153

Page 61, *'... and was now personal assistant to V.V. Vorovsky, the Bolshevik ambassador to Sweden.'* Brogan, p. 204

Page 61, *'Intelligence reports stated that Ransome was a Bolshevik agent and he was widely regarded as a traitor.'* Brogan, p. 204

Page 61, Knox quote: Brogan, p. 162

Page 61, *'... the Foreign Office was considering whether to prosecute Ransome under the terms of the Defence of the Realm Act, possibly even for high treason.'* Brogan, p. 207

Page 61, *'Arthur and Evgenia had set themselves up in a cabin at Igelboda ...'* Brogan, p. 215

Page 61, *'Those who did visit him included members of the MI6 station ...'* For instance, he lunched with Sharp. Ransome had written for the *New Statesman* before the War. Brogan, p. 220

Page 61, *'... turned out years afterwards to have been less friendly than they pretended.'* Arthur Ransome, *Autobiography*, p. 262

Page 62, *'Paul planned to visit Russia in secret ...'* Arthur Ransome, *Autobiography*, p. 262

Page 62, Dukes quote: ST-25, p. 40

Page 62, *'... six months later he was arrested as a Bolshevik spy ...'* On 30 January 1919 Ransome was expelled from Sweden, along with Evgenia and other Bolshevik personnel and sent back to Moscow. From there he returned to England and was arrested upon his arrival at Kings Cross on 25 March 1919. He was interrogated by Sir Basil Thomson, head of the intelligence unit at Scotland Yard – (*Signalling from Mars – the letters of Arthur Ransome*, edited by Hugh Brogan, p. 85. Also Brogan, p. 234)

Page 62, *'So at the beginning of November Paul boarded a steamer for Helsinki.'* ST-25, p. 40

Page 63, '*He was now Sergei Ilitch, a Serbian commercial traveller.*' ST-25, p. 40

Page 63, Dukes quote: ST-25, p. 41

Page 63, '*After several weeks, one of Paul's contacts in Helsinki came up with a name, Melnikov.*' A pseudonym, but in both ST-25 (p. 141) and RDATM (p. 151) Dukes cites Melnikov's real name as Nicholas Nicholaievitch Melnitsky. This is barely different from 'Melnikov' and yet there was no need to continue to protect his identity as the Cheka knew all about him.

Page 63, '*One account is that the name was given to him by White Russians in Helsinki.*' ST-25, p. 41

Page 63, '*Another is that he was introduced to an American secret service agent who had just escaped from Russia who provided him with a letter of introduction to Melnikov.*' RDATM, p. 12

Page 63, '*But Melnikov had been one of Cromie's agents ...*' RDATM, p. 12

Page 63, Dukes quote: RDATM, p. 13

Page 64, '*I had some papers referring to the insurrection at Yaroslavl ...*' Yaroslavl is a city on the Volga river about 250 kms north-east of Moscow. From 6–21 July 1918, counter-revolutionaries of Savinkov's organisation rose up against the Bolsheviks as part of a planned national uprising. Red army forces surrounded the city and subjected it to a prolonged artillery bombardment, which included poison gas. Hundreds were killed in the shelling or drowned in the Volga trying to escape. In the weeks after the revolt was put down, the Cheka executed more than 350 opponents.

Page 64, Melnikov's account: RDATM, p. 13

Page 64, '*... good-quality alcohol was better than hard cash and Paul had brought a considerable amount of it with him.*' Several months later Agar encountered some emaciated refugees from Petrograd hiding out in an old fishing boat. Having listened at length to how they and everyone else in the city was starving, Agar was astonished when he offered to supply them with anything they wanted – the one thing they wanted was whisky!

Page 64, '*... not realising that Paul had managed to preserve one last store of the valuable liquid which he kept hidden in a medicine bottle.*' ST-25, p. 42

Page 64, '*Since one of Paul's main tasks was to resurrect Cromie's organisation this contact could prove vital – if Melnikov could find him.*' Merritt's first connection with intelligence appears to have been in 1918 when he prepared a survey of the state of Russian industry. This may have been when he came in contact with Cromie and/or Boyce. BECOS later sought reimbursement for seven months of his salary because of his work for the British government. As with others who became involved in intelligence matters (see later references to George Gibson) they had a devil of a time getting the money.

Page 65, Melnikov's departure: ST-25, p. 43

Page 65, '*On Sunday, 24 November ...*' This is the date given in ST-25, p. 43. Dukes' diary records the crossing as Friday 15 November, but because the difference in old and new Russian calendars this is almost certainly wrong.

Page 66, Border guard's quote: ST-25, p. 46

Page 69, '*... pulling on the medicine bottle of whisky in order to keep warm.*' The brand was Johnnie Walker Red label! ST-25, p. 114

Chapter 5: Peter Sokolov

Page 73, '... *pausing only to show their Finnish visas at the Immigration Office* ...' Hampsheir's passport was date stamped by the Finnish immigration authorities.

Page 75, '... *spent the rest of the day having breakfast and lunch ("at ruinous prices") and playing cards.*' Agar's diary

Page 75, *Raleigh Le May*: He sometimes appears as 'Riley' Le May, but Raleigh is the spelling in the Foreign Office lists.

Page 75, '*Major John Scale, the head of the MI6 station at Stockholm and also in overall charge of all MI6 operations in northern Russia, had also travelled to Helsinki for the meeting.*' Although in *Baltic Episode* Le May is described as 'ST-30', notes on the back of photographs taken at the time record him as 'ST-23'. Scale has been referred to by other authors as ST-0 because he was in charge of the area, but in his notes Gus refers to him as 'ST-29'. This is possible if, as appears to be the case, ST numbers were awarded chronologically. There is a photograph of Broadbent annotated 'ST-32'. Sidney Reilly was ST-1.

Page 76, '*Equally, it was essential that Admiral Walter Cowan commanding British naval forces in the Baltic, should be briefed on the mission.*' Agar's diary.

Page 76, '... *Reval, the capital of Estonia* ...' Now Tallinn.

Page 76, '... *he was sending a destroyer and Gus would be taken to meet him on the following day.*' In almost every other account Agar claims that it was his idea, inspired by seeing a British destroyer, to see Cowan. But his diary is clear that he was told when he arrived that there would have to be a meeting. Given the delicate political situation throughout the Baltic, this is surely right.

Page 76, *Peter Sokolov*: ST-25, p. 231: '... he was a former NCO and a student of law. He was tall and muscular, round shouldered, with thick fair hair and a good-humoured but somewhat shy impression'.

Page 76, '... *and he had won four caps, playing for Russia at the 1912 Olympics.*' Peter Sokolov played five times for Russia:

22/8/1911(no cap)	v England Amateurs (Friendly) Lost 11–0.
30/6/1912	v Finland (Olympics, Sweden) Lost 2–1 (England beat Denmark 4–2 in the final).
1/7/1912	v Germany (Olympic 'Consolation tournament') Lost 16–0! Gottfried Fuchs, German centre forward scored ten goals, a record for an international match which stood until 2001.
5/7/1912	v Norway Lost 2–1.
14/7/1912	Captained Russia against Hungary in a friendly in Moscow. Lost 12-0.

Page 77, '... *played as a central defender.*' The Russian team appears to have played a 2–3–5 formation – which probably explains why they always lost!

Page 77, '*Although Peter spoke very little English, Gus could speak some Russian and soon warmed to him.*' 'He had a superb physique and in addition was full of guts and courage, I took a liking to him immediately, and although I knew little Russian and he no English at all, we managed to understand each other and never had any differences. We became close friends ...' BE, p. 45

Page 77, '*Peter suggested the tiny harbour of Terrioki.*' Spellings vary. It is now the Russian town of Zelenogorsk, but the little harbour is still there.

Page 77, '... *Cowan's flagship, the cruiser HMS Cleopatra* ...' HMS

Cleopatra was Cowan's flagship until 28 June when he transferred his flag to *HMS Delhi.*

Page 78, '*Rivett-Carnac didn't fall for this story for a second and continued to watch Gus curiously as he hung around the ship waiting for the return of the Admiral.*' BE, p. 46 – In an earlier version on this story in FITS, p. 95, Gus had tried the even more preposterous story that he was a previously unmentioned twin brother!

Page 78, '*It was 7.30 p.m. before the Admiral finally returned.*' Agar's diary

Page 78, Agar quote: BE, p. 47

Page 78, '*Cowan was known to arrange his numerous campaign medals in an order which showed off their colours most pleasingly rather than in the official order.*' *Freeing the Baltic* by Geofffrey Bennett, p. 65

Page 78, '*. . . he was known throughout the Royal Navy as "The Little Man" or simply "Titch".*' BE, p. 47

Page 78, '*. . . Little would simply say "Aye, Sir" and then do nothing, knowing that by the following day Cowan would have forgotten or thought better of it.*' Bennett, pp. 66–69

Page 78, '*. . . the British government had simply said that British forces were on "a summer cruise."*' Bennett, p. 111

Page 79, '*. . . but if they ever ventured forth and were well-handled, they could blow his force out of the water.*' This was a very real threat: on 17 January 1919 Trotsky had announced that to create a fighting fleet, Tsarist officers must be re-instated and ships' Soviets must be abolished. The reforms which were soon to produce victory for the Red army on the battlefield threatened to have the same effect at sea. (Bennett, p. 82) By 29 May, Cowan was impressed by the *Petropavlovsk*'s 'heavy and well-disciplined fire' although she was not yet confident enough to advance beyond the protection of the minefields. (Bennett, p.117)

Page 79, '*. . . naval personnel in uniform, not young officers masquerading as civilians.*' BE, p. 49

Page 79, '*. . . said that in his opinion the plan was outlandish if not impossible.*' FITS, p. 90

Page 79, '*Mines represented the greatest daily threat to Cowan's squadron throughout the mission and were to account for the loss of several British ships.*' The light cruiser *Cassandra* (sunk, 5 Dec 1918). NB. Rear Admiral Alexander-Sinclair was in command of the Squadron at this time; Cowan's then flagship the light cruiser *Curacao* (damaged 13 May 1919 and forced to return to England); the oiler *War Export* damaged c.23 May; mine sweepers *Gentian* and *Myrtle* sunk 16 July; destroyer *Verulam* sunk 4 September (she actually struck a British mine).

Page 79, '*It does not appear to have occurred to him before this meeting to use CMBs to counter that threat.*' The Admiralty did not receive a request for CMBs until later in June. See Bennett, p. 121

Page 79, '*. . . he had once captured an enemy submarine during a naval exercise by having his men lasso its periscope from the deck of his destroyer – and was reprimanded for the damage he caused! . . .*' It was considered 'unsporting'. Bennett, p. 58

Page 80, '*Gus wondered if Cowan would issue them with torpedoes?*' In early accounts, Gus claimed that this was Cowan's idea, but all his later accounts are consistent in recording this as his request and this is certainly more logical.

Page 80, '*Still not entirely convinced, Cowan said that he would give the matter further thought.*' Agar audio tape, Imperial War Museum.

Page 81, '*Meanwhile Consul Bell and Vice-Consul Le May were negotiating with the Finns for permission to use the boats in Finnish waters.*' Agar's diary.

Page 81, '*Gus ordered the mechanics to repaint the boats in their light grey camouflage colour immediately.*' Agar's diary. He is quite specific about this and it shows how much the plan had changed since his departure from London. Elsewhere he claims that this was not done until the boats arrived at Biorko.

Page 81, *General Hubert Gough*: General Sir Hubert de la Poer Gough, 1870–1963.

Page 82, '*Commander C. G. Stuart, captain of the Voyager*' BE, p. 53

Page 83, '*They stripped the engines as far as possible and tried to repair the damage that the sea water had caused.*' Once again *Baltic Episode* is completely at odds with Gus's personal diary. Whilst the diary records all the problems detailed here, in *Baltic Episode* Gus simply says: 'Our CMBs in tow of the *Voyager* stood the long journey from Abo very well'. It also conflicts with Hampsheir's diary which reads: 'Very rough trip. Tow parted twice on No7 and once on No 4'. One possible explanation is that Gus did not want to seem to be blaming Commander Stuart for the delay in the rescue mission which now occurred.

Page 83, '*. . . and two great wings of spray, the trade mark of a fast-moving CMB at full power, flew high to either side in her wake.*' The following account by the secret agent Gefter is one of the few surviving records of what it was like to travel in a CMB: 'As it gathered speed its prow rose higher and higher above the surface of the water. The boat did not float, but skimmed over the surface of the water, sometimes almost rising above it. In rough weather it seemed that the boat would be destroyed by its own speed . . . The motor was running at half speed which was a good thirty-five kilometres an hour. Behind the stern, the wash of the boat formed a deep pit in the water, whilst at the sides two bow waves formed like high glass walls. The whole boat trembled with a shiver as if making a monstrous effort.' *Reminiscences of a Courier* by A. Gefter.

Chapter 6: The Zorinsky Enigma

Page 86, '*. . . his first thought had been to find the apartment belonging to John Merritt.*' In RDATM Dukes referred to Merritt as 'Mr Marsh' and in ST-25 as 'John Johnovich' (p. 68). The spelling of his name varies between documents. George Gibson who knew him well spelt it 'Merritt', but he appears in other documents as 'Merrett'.

Page 86, '*. . . a twenty rouble note . . .*' About ten shillings then (ST-25, p. 73) approximately £50 today.

Page 86, '*Thank you,*' he mumbled, '*but what is the good of money? Where shall I get bread?*' RDATM, p. 30. In ST-25 he places this meeting later in the day.

Page 86, '*. . . Paul then shoved all of the bread into the man's outstretched hands.*' ST-25, p. 58

Page 88, '*They decided to bring him in, hoping that he would betray the rest of his network.*' *Vnutri I vne Bol'shogo Doma* by Vasilli Berezkhov.

Page 88, '... *he walked four miles across the city to the hospital in a street called Kamenostrovsky Prospekt.*' RDATM p.32

Page 88, '*Then he hired one of the very few remaining horse-drawn cabs and headed back to the Finland station where he had arrived that morning.*' RDATM, p. 34

Page 88, '... *and the faded red bunting which still hung across the streets from the celebration of the anniversary of the Revolution a few weeks earlier only emphasised the desolation.*' RDATM, p. 30

Page 88, '*It was run by a mother and daughter in a top floor apartment ...*' ST-25, p. 62

Page 89, '*Paul was particularly struck by his slightly crooked mouth, perhaps the legacy of some injury.*' RDATM, p. 37

Page 90, '*There were forty flats in Ivan Sergeivitch's apartment building near the Kazanskaya.*' RDATM, p. 43

Page 90, '*Her name was Stepanova and she was staying there with two other people, her nephew Dmitri and Varia, the family nanny.*' These were all pseudonyms used by Dukes to protect their identities

Page 91, '*The snow was now falling steadily and there was a biting wind.*' ST-25, p. 64

Page 91, '... *the woman in charge told him that he could eat there every day as long as he had money and as long as they didn't get raided.*' RDATM, p. 45; ST-25, p. 66

Page 91, '*At first he had been panicked, living as he said later: "from minute to minute and hour to hour."* ' RDATM, p. 46

Page 92, '*The doorbell in the flat rang loudly and Paul awoke with a start.*' ST-25, p. 67

Page 92, '... *and she had even found him an old pair of Ivan's pyjamas.*' RDATM, p. 47

Page 92, '... *stood a giant of a man with ginger hair ...*' ST-25, p. 85

Page 93, '*Merritt explained that he had managed to evade capture by shaving off his beard; few people seemed to recognise him without it ...*' RDATM, p. 49

Page 93, '... *Merritt had knocked him out with one punch ...*' Not surprising since Merritt was a powerful man, well over six feet tall. One of the pseudonyms Dukes used for him was 'Ilya Murometz' after the giant legendary Russian hero.

Page 93, '... *one or two of them still occupied positions at the Russian Admiralty and Ministry of War.*' ST-25, p. 69

Page 94, '... *said that Paul could use it as a safe house describing it as "... one of the safest places in town".*' RDATM, p. 53

Page 94, '*The Policeman smiled quietly and said that it could possibly be done – for thirty thousand roubles.*' Comparisons are very difficult because of the passage of time and the effect of the conditions in Petrograd, but this amount would be in the region of £70,000 today.

Page 94, '*Apparently he had already given the informant ten thousand roubles and Merritt promised the final ten on the day his wife was released.*' ST-25, p. 75; RDATM, p. 58

Page 95, '... *encircled by the militia and Soviet sailors who often provided the muscle for Cheka raids.*' As they had done during the attack on the British embassy and the killing of Captain Cromie.

Page 95, '*Still, not sure of whether to trust Zorinsky, but reluctant to turn down any possible lead, Paul agreed.*' ST-25, p. 78; RDATM, p. 66

Page 97, '*He did not arrive there until 11 a.m . . .*' RDATM, p. 73

Page 98, '*Paul spent much of the rest of the day writing his first CX report for MI6 . . .*' To this day all MI6 intelligence reports are called CX reports. The exact reason has been lost over time, but it is believed that it originally meant 'From C exclusively'.

Page 98, '*He was carrying the identity papers of his former coachman. He hoped that these would be good enough for him to travel north from the city by rail from the Okhta station.*' ST-25, p. 86

Page 98, '*. . . burrowing deeply into the heaving mass of desperate passengers inside in the hope of avoiding discovery.*' This turned out to be a smart move: at a small station halfway through the journey the train was subject to a surprise search by Red Guards, but as they fought through the press of people to board the train from the platform, Merritt and one of his contacts who was also on the train were able to slip away on the other side of the train and escape into the forest. ST-25, p. 87

Page 99, '*. . . a wave of depression swept over Paul.*' '. . . as I slowly retraced my steps into town an aching sense of emptiness pervaded everything, and the future seemed nothing but impenetrable night.' RDATM, p. 78

Page 99, '*. . . but some of them listened and slowly he began to reconstruct the intelligence networks.*' ST-25, p. 90

Page 99, '*. . . she hid all his reports in the flat while he was waiting for someone who could take them out of the country.*' ST-25, p. 97; RDATM, p. 95

Page 99, '*. . . he also had the opportunity to see Bolshevik leaders such as Trotsky, Zinoviev and Lunarcharsky at close quarters.*' RDATM, p. 79

Page 99, '*. . . if Paul would only hand over 100,000 roubles "for expenses".*' RDATM, p. 88

Page 100, '*Meanwhile, Zorinsky wanted 60,000 roubles to bribe the investigator handling Melnikov's case . . .*' Bearing in mind the problems of accurately translating these figures into modern currency, 60,000 roubles would be somewhere in the region of £150,000 today.

Page 100, '*Zorinsky recommended paying 30,000 roubles up front and the rest when Melnikov was released.*' ST-25, p. 98

Page 101, '*A few days later he told Zorinsky that he had abandoned his plans to travel to Finland, but would be going to Moscow for a few weeks instead to make contact with agents there.*' RDATM, p. 99; ST-25, p. 100

Page 101, '*If she had been English there would have been some hope, but she had been born in Russia . . .*' ST-25, p. 101

Page 103, '*It was now a quarter to five . . .*' RDATM, p. 104

Page 104, '*He hailed another sleigh and they made their way as quickly as possible to Maria's flat.*' RDATM ps 103–5. For some reason all the details of the escape are omitted from the later work ST-25 including 'Mrs Marsh's' forename 'Lydia'.

Page 106, '*Far from the mile which the guide had predicted it soon became clear that the distance to the border was more like ten or twelve.*' RDATM, p. 113

Page 107, '*She certainly handled the journey with greater fortitude than any of the other women.*' At one point Paul had to use his own body to make a bridge across a snow-filled ditch so that the party could cross. The princesses might have been happy to walk across his back, but they didn't pay very much attention to him otherwise. In their own account of the journey they remembered him as Swedish.

Chapter 7: The Commandant of Terrioki

Page 108, '*To remove the engine of a CMB meant taking out most of the deck first and then disconnecting and lifting out a solid block of metal weighing over half a ton.*' BE, p. 59

Page 109, '*. . . although John Hampsheir would stand by and give whatever assistance he could.*' In FITS (p. 99) Agar says that the mechanics from the *Francol* assisted and at the end of the work he offered them a reward out of Cumming's money which they refused. This story isn't repeated in *Baltic Episode* and Agar's diary makes it clear that Beeley and Hampsheir were the only two who worked on the engine.

Page 109, '*He told Admiral Cowan of his plight and Cowan immediately dispatched the destroyer HMS Versatile to Helsinki to collect the spare engine and Pegler.*' In BE (p. 59) Agar claims that CMB4 was fixed in just twenty-four hours, using the spare parts they had brought to Biorko in the boats. This absolutely conflicts with the account in his diary written at the time and also with Hampsheir's diary which confirms that a new engine had to be sent for from Helsinki and that it took 'the next few days' to fit it. His diary is then blank until Sunday 15 June when it reads 'Boat ready' This tallies with Agar's diary in that the full refit took a week.

Page 109, '*. . . where there was a submarine depot ship, HMS Maidstone, which had the facilities to completely strip and repair it.*' FITS, p. 99

Page 109, '*Gus dispatched Peter to Terrioki on horseback through the dense Finnish pine forests to try and make contact with the local smugglers and finalise the deal for a pilot.*' FITS p.100. This agrees with Agar's diary (although it says simply 'by road' rather than horseback). On the other hand BE (pp. 59–60) Agar says that Peter travelled with him by CMB on Tuesday 10 but mentions no earlier trip overland.

Page 111, '*Gus offered the captain and mechanics of the Francol some of Cumming's thousand guineas in recognition of their assistance, but they refused.*' FITS, p. 99. In this version, the assistance rendered by the *Francol*'s mechanics throughout the refit is considerable. This is entirely possible, but seeing as in this version they are working on the seized engine, not a new one – which conflicts with Agar's detailed diary entries – I have chosen to follow the latter narrative.

Page 113, '*Gus pulled him off the repair duties and insisted that he rest for a few days. Richard Marshall and Bert Piper took over.*' Agar's diary entry 11/6/1919

Page 114, '*. . . and then, having gathered Sindall, Marshall, Peter Sokolov and Hall, he set off immediately in CMB7.*' In BE (p. 59) Agar says that he made this journey on Tuesday 10 in CMB4 with Beeley and Peter in complete secrecy. He omits all reference to Hall or to any emergency. This conflicts with all the entries in his diary for this period. FITS, p. 103 implies that the journey was made on Saturday 7 June which is far too early if details given elsewhere are correct. Hampsheir's diary confirms that CMB4 would not have been able to make this trip as it was still under repair. As elsewhere, I have followed Agar's diary which was written at the time. In his books, his tendency is to change details to protect the reputation of others.

Page 114, '*But Gus did not want to risk CMB7's engine figuring that it was better to arrive at a steady pace than not at all.*' Agar's diary states that they set out at 2100. BE (p. 60) claims they arrived at 2 a.m. Over a distance of just fifty miles these accounts are impossible to reconcile.

Page 114, '*He calculated that this added another twenty miles to the journey.*' FITS, p. 100

Page 114, '*... and asking him to go down to the water's edge and signal with a torch every five minutes between midnight and 3 a.m.*' BE, p. 59. FITS, p. 100 claimed that it was Peter who was asked to make a signal with a torch between 0100 and 0130.

Page 114, '*They arrived off the mouth of tiny Terrioki harbour not long after 2 a.m.*' FITS, p. 100 says 0100.

Page 115, '*... and relations between Gus and Hall, already tense, became a little bit worse.*' Agar diary entry 12/6/1919

Page 115, '*The harbour was barely fifty metres wide, just about enough room to moor a dozen yachts.*' FITS, p. 93; BE, p. 60

Page 115, '*He had Finnish sentries with him and told the crew where they should moor the small rowing boat they had brought with them.*' This was called a 'pram'. It was a little like an open canoe. Agar had purchased this in Finland as a way of landing the couriers from the CMBs.

Page 116, '*... Broadbent understood that this meant Peter and called that it was best to leave him on the boat as the sentries tended to treat any Russian who arrived as a possible Bolshevik spy.*' According to FITS, pp.100/1 Peter and a smuggler were waiting on the jetty. There is no mention of Broadbent or the guards at all. This is very unlikely to be correct.

Page 118, '*... which Cumming had dreamed up and which he later described as "a cock and bull yarn".*' BE, p. 61

Page 119, '*Could, he wondered, Gus and his boat undertake a small reconnaissance expedition to see if these vessels had sailed from Kronstadt harbour?*' BE, p. 64; FITS, p. 103

Page 120, '*... provided a local fisherman and smuggler called Veroline ...*' Probable spelling. Agar's handwriting is hard to read at this point and judging by the accuracy of the other names he gives this was almost certainly a phonetic spelling.

Page 121, '*As Peter had predicted Gus also had to hand over two bottles from his dwindling supplies of Royal Navy rum.*' FITS, p.104 and Agar's diary. In *Baltic Episode* Agar rather disingenuously says that he does not remember how much he paid Veroline but that it was 'at least £10'! He may have been slightly embarrassed at the astronomical sum he had to pay. (According to FITS, p.104 the price also included two bottles of rum.) In this version of the story, Agar also attributes the recruitment of Veroline to Commandant Sarin. This is possible, but a) in Agar's diary it is clear that Sokolov was always the one who expected to provide the smuggler pilot and even in *Baltic Episode* Agar admits that the two men had worked together before; b) if the smuggler was Sarin's man he would have been quite likely to tell Sarin what Agar was up to and Agar could not allow this; c) Sarin only asked Agar to sail out to Tolboukin lighthouse, not to go through the line of forts – so why would Sarin need to provide a smuggler pilot anyway?

Page 121, '*At 10.30 p.m. just as the twilight was darkening ...*' This is the time entered in the diary which is usually an hour different from times recorded elsewhere. BE and FITS says 10 p.m. Darkness at this date was approximately 10.30 p.m. to 1.30 a.m.

Page 121, '*Sindall and Marshall were left behind on the jetty with Hall.*' BE, p. 68

Page 121, '*But Gus ordered him only to drop an agent on the Estonian coast – not to try and penetrate the line of forts again.*' FITS, p. 105

Page 122, Agar quote: BE, p. 68

Page 123, '*He was close enough to see barges tied up at the northern mouth of the Neva river on which Petrograd was situated.*' The river ends in a delta and has several outlets to the sea.

Page 126, '*If any of them had seen CMB7's approach and turned to attack now, the British boat would be defenceless.*' Agar's diary entry 13/6/1919. He never acknowledged making this failed attack in the body of any of his books possibly because he was annoyed that he let temptation get the better of him. If he had failed to return, Sindall would have been left in a very difficult position, not knowing if the passage through the forts was safe or not. However, he did include this attack in his official report to the Admiralty which is reprinted in the Appendix to *Baltic Episode*.

Page 127, '*Sarin introduced Gus to the old priest who tended the church and said that he should be allowed to use the tower for observations whenever he wished.*' FITS, p. 106

Page 127, '*He had a friend, Mr Fountovsky . . .*' Possible spelling. Agar wrote in pencil and the writing has become rather blurred at this point. MI6 did have a Finnish agent – Mr Lapäas – living nearby. Agar acknowledges that he assisted during the mission, but his name never appears in the diary. Lapäas later became the local mayor, but was executed by the Russians during the Russo-Finnish war in 1940.

Page 128, '*. . . paused briefly for dinner at the Fountovsky's villa at Oasikivoka . . .*' Again a possible spelling. I haven't been able to find it on any maps, but many names in the area have changed since 1919.

Page 128, '*Captain F.A. "Figgy" Marten took some convincing.*' BE, p. 90. For narrative reasons Agar moved this incident to another date. See Chapter 9.

Page 129, '*It was the first time he had slept in a bed for at least four nights.*' In BE, Agar is forced to place this journey after the sinking of the *Oleg* because he had not mentioned that CMB4 was under repair. He does not mention the car nor his subsequent collapse, merely describing the journey as 'tiring'!

Page 129, '*Their names were Turner and Young . . .*' Possibly from the cruiser HMS *Dragon* where Agar had lunch that day, but this is not certain.

Page 130, '*Once the city would have been a blaze of light at night, but now there was only electric power for a few hours each evening.*' ST-25, p. 71

Page 131, '*Even so Gus whispered to Hampsheir that if there was the sound of shots or any sign that Peter and ST-25 were in trouble he was going to take CMB4 in close to give them covering fire.*' FITS, p. 108

Page 131, '*A light rain squall passed over.*' ST-25, p.263 confirms this.

Chapter 8: Melnikov's Marvellous Uncle

Page 134, '*Why, you and Mrs Merritt of course.*' ST-25, p. 118

Page 134, '*In Stockholm he had spent Christmas week staying with the head of the MI6 station, Major John Scale, and his wife.*' In RDATM (p.114) published in 1922, Dukes claimed that he spent the time in hiding at a flat in Helsinki and saw no one, but in ST-25 published in 1938 (p.113), Dukes corrects this to Stockholm and 'Major S.' who is of course Scale.

Page 135, Cumming quote: ST-25, p. 113

Page 135, '*He also hoped that Melnikov would become his senior agent in the new network that he was establishing.*' ST-25, p. 125. Dukes seems to have forgotten Melnikov's loose tongue at this point.

Page 136, '*Zorinsky said he did not think so and to Paul his answer seemed honest.*' RDATM p.119. The forenames of the Policeman are given as Alexei Fomitch. This incident is completely missing from ST-25, which makes it all the more interesting as most of Duke's omissions from this later version of the story were made for operational security reasons.

Page 137, '*Despite the risk of working in front of Zorinsky he set about copying it there and then. He could check whether it was genuine later.*' ST-25, p. 120; RDATM, p. 121

Page 137, '*Once again Zorinsky appeared to have pulled off a miracle.*' 'I began to think Zorinsky a genius – an evil genius, but still a genius!' ST-25, p. 121; RDATM, p. 122

Page 138, '*Paul later confessed that he suddenly felt "an intense and overpowering repugnance" for this man who was controlling him so easily.*' ST-25, p. 122; RDATM, p. 123

Page 138, '*He noted the reason for the medical exemption with bitter amusement: "incurable heart trouble" – exactly the diagnosis that had prevented him from serving in the British army in 1914.*' ST-25, p. 125

Page 138, '*But that requirement was a very recent regulation and Paul's passport did not have it. Disappointed, Zorinsky handed it back.*' This is another incident which has been removed from the 1938 version of the tale. The reason why is unclear.

Page 139, '*. . . Paul knew that he dared not start asking questions about another of Cromie's former contacts.*' RDATM, p. 127

Page 139, '*If he really was trying to squeeze Paul dry then he could easily have asked for ten times what he was actually getting for the intelligence he was providing.*' RDATM, p. 136

Page 140, '*Three weeks later, at 10.30 a.m. on Sunday, 25 January 1919 . . .*' At RDATM pp.131 & 136, Dukes says that the meeting occurred on 'a cold Sunday in January' and that they had just heard that Rosa Luxemburg had been murdered. Since she was killed on 15 January, Sunday 18 January is possible, but since Dukes sees the uncle three weeks after his meeting with Zorinsky in 'early January' and it is early February 'some days later' when he collects his new passport, 25 January is more likely. This description has been removed completely from ST-25.

Page 141, '*He decided that he would have to use the Policeman to find out what was really happening to Melnikov.*' RDATM, p. 151

Page 141, '*It was in the name of Alexander Vasilievitch Markov, who was a 33-year-old clerical assistant at the main Post and Telegraph Office in Petrograd.*' RDATM, p. 144

Page 143, '*He never saw Varia or Stepanova again.*' RDATM, p. 160; ST-25, p. 140

Page 143, '*She was a pretty, young English governess, Laura Ann Cade.*' Also known as Laura Anne Cade, Laura Anna Cade or just Anna Cade.

Page 143, '*The Guild organised parties and staged plays and reviews.*' He also knew her from sharing rooms with Sydney Gibbes, a fellow Englishman who had become tutor to the Tsarevitch. Gibbes had also known Laura Cade for several years – at least as early as 1911 when she apparently wrote and performed a little skit entitiled 'Only Me' for the St Petersburg Guild of English Teachers of which Gibbes was Vice-President. In 1916 they purchased and ran 'Pritchard's English School for Modern Languages' together. The partnership had been forcibly dissolved in August 1917 when Gibbes left for internal exile with the Tsar's family in Tobolsk, Siberia. Gibbes only narrowly escaped being murdered along with the Tsar's family at Ekaterinburg and later returned to England. See *The Romanovs and Mr Gibbes* by Frances Welch.

Page 143, '... *together with a rather fat female servant known to one and all as "the Elephant".*' ST-25, p. 136

Page 144, '... *whoever had enciphered the message in Helsinki had made a mistake and the message from MI6 was undecipherable.*' RDATM, p. 169

Page 144, '*So Paul asked Peter to return again that very night.*' RDATM, p. 170

Page 145, '*But then, on 10 February came the greatest blow of all.*' Approximate date. Dukes records it as almost three weeks from the date of Melnikov's execution. ST-25, p. 141

Page 146, '*The smuggler, who was actually Finnish, had just smuggled a load of butter into the city,*' RDATM, p. 163

Page 147, '*Ten thousand marks if we escape!*' bellowed Paul into his ear ...' Finnish Marks rather than roubles of course as this was a Finnish smuggler.

Page 150, '*He was marched at bayonet point to the nearest coastguard station where he was stripped of all his belongings and thrown into a cell.*' RDATM, p. 167

Page 150, '*As soon as Henry Bell heard that Paul was held at Terrioki, he arranged for him to be transferred to the British Consulate immediately.*' *Land of the Lakes* by H. M. Bell, p. 91. This was not the only time that Bell had to deal with strange visitors arriving mysteriously from Russia. In December 1918 an Englishman named 'Marx' appeared in Helsinki, claiming that he had escaped from Petrograd over the land border into Finland. He wanted to be given a visa to get to England. But Marx had no documents other than a warrant issued by the Swiss Legation in Petrograd. Bell was highly suspicious and felt sure that Marx must be some kind of Russian agent. But the Foreign Office gave him the 'all clear' and Bell sent him on his way. He encountered this man in London some time later and he spun Bell a cock and bull story about being chased out of Finland purely because his name was 'Marx' and the Finnish authorities thought that he must therefore be a Bolshevik. Infuriatingly, Bell does not say more (which, sadly, is all too typical of his memoirs). There is no trace of 'Marx' or anyone who might be him in published intelligence sources.

Page 151, '*Even today, intelligence-service analysts acknowledge that these reports were better than any intelligence MI6 had ever produced before.*' 'In subject matter, details, authority and highest-level sourcing these were a spymaster's dream and quite probably superior to anything that had landed on C's desk throughout the four years of war against Germany.' – *Ironmaze* by Gordon Brook-Shepherd, p. 133. Brook Shepherd was given access to MI6's secret archives through his government connections so he knew what he was talking about.

Chapter 9: Too late the hero

Page 153, '... *so cold and exhausted that the crew had let him rest during the journey back from Petrograd.*' BE, p. 77

Page 153, '... *from where he could take another look at the battlecruisers shelling Krasnaya Gorka* ...' BE, p. 77 The name Krasnaya Gorka means 'Little Red Hill'.

Page 155, '*He followed Paul to a secluded and enclosed part of the gardens where he found Paul slumped on a stone bench.*' Dukes claimed that this meeting took place on 12 June (ST-25, p. 254), but that would have been impossible given the timing of Gus's journey to Finland. From both Gus's and Hampsheir's papers it is clear that this meeting took place on Saturday 14 June. Dukes omits this meeting completely from RDATM.

Page 155, '*Peter described it as being like "a monstrous bird."*' ST-25, p. 252

Page 156, '... *which listed three dates in late July when the mystery machine would be able to pick him up.*' ST-25, p. 254

Page 157, '*As a base of secret operations, the Villa Sakharov was quite lively.*' The Agar papers have numerous photographs of life at the Villa Sakharov including Dinah, numerous tennis matches, sunbathing parties and various Russian families – many of whom seem to have had very eligible daughters.

Page 157, '*To top it all, on that very first day, the French military attaché from Helsinki called to see the operation.*' Agar's diary. The attaché reappeared for a formal dinner at the team's dacha on 30 June. The pilot Reichel and Commandant Sarin were amongst the guests. Apparently the attaché (Le Gondalache?) became very drunk and made a speech lasting an hour.

Page 157, '*Sarin apologised profusely and promised that he would sort it out.*' Agar diary entry 16/6/1919.

Page 157, '... *Gus using his favourite telescope, Sarin a pair of binoculars.*' One of Agar's telescopes is on display at the Imperial War Museum in London.

Page 158, '*After a lull, the bombardment had recommenced at eleven o'clock that morning.*' BE, p. 82

Page 158, '*Sarin explained that the garrison of the fort were not Russians, but Ingrians.*' Often referred to as 'Ingermanlanders'.

Page 158, '*These people were not just fighting the Bolsheviks, they were fighting for their independence.*' It was later discovered that the Krasnaya Gorka had risen before the general revolt was ready because the commandant of the fortress had come under suspicion and a Commissar had arrived to arrest him. ST-25, p. 268

Page 158, '*The leaders of the White armies, aristocrats and Tsarist snobs to a man, wanted the old Russia back and for them this meant the Russian empire complete with all its subject peoples.*' 'There is no Estonia. It is a piece of Russian soil, a Russian province.' – General Yudenich. See Bennett, p. 105

Page 159, '"*TAKE NO OFFENSIVE WITHOUT DIRECT INSTRUCTIONS FROM SNO BALTIC STOP*" This is telegram MC 470 from C. Agar papers, IWM. In BE (p. 82) Gus amalgamates MC 470 and MC 479 into one telegram. In FITS (p. 110) Gus has the fateful telegram received in Admiral Cowan's cabin with the Admiral looking on. From all the other evidence this must surely be a fiction created by Gus to sum up his dilemma in the limited space available to him in that book.

Page 160, '*Broadbent did not express an opinion* ...' At least, not one which has been recorded anywhere.

Page 160, '*ADMIRALTY DOES NOT APPROVE . . .*' This is telegram MC 479 from London. Agar papers. IWM. Based on the version in *Baltic Episode*, some authors have tried to suggest that Cumming skilfully left Agar an opening by specifying '. . . *without direct instruction for SNO Baltic*'. This telegram makes it clear that there was absolutely no doubt at all about Cumming's position.

Page 160, '*As soon as Gus said those words the pressure lifted.*' 'Once the decision was made I felt tremendously relieved in my mind.' BE p.82

Page 160, '*Shortly before 11 p.m . . .*' Again there is a slight but significant difference between Gus's diary (2230) and his books. In *Baltic Episode* (p.83) he says departure was 'just before midnight'. The distance he had to travel and the timing of the attack make a departure between 1030 and 1100 most likely.

Page 161, '. . . *but Gus decided he could maximise that chance if they concentrated both torpedoes on the Petropavlovsk, she was the more heavily armed of the two.*' BE, p. 83

Page 162, '. . . *and was armed with 12 six-inch guns . . .*' For comparison, this is the same calibre of armament as that of *HMS Belfast* moored on the Thames.

Page 162, '*Other than the two battlecruisers she was largest warship in the Russian fleet.*' Her captain was N. Milashevich (Bennett, p. 125).

Page 163, '*She had shelled Krasnaya Gorka for about four hours and had then ceased fire some time before 7 p.m.*' Agar audio tape IWM. Shelling ceased at some point between 1800 and 1900 hours.

Page 163, '*Soon all three men were soaked to the skin.*' Agar's diary.

Page 163, '*The destroyers drew closer until they were only two hundred metres away on either side.*' BE, p. 86.

Page 164, '*It had almost taken his hand off and now there was no way of launching the torpedo.*' In BE (p. 86) Gus says that Hampsheir had injured his hand. Hampsheir does not mention this in his diary and in a photograph taken just hours after the attack his hands are quite visible – there is no sign of an injury, but Hampsheir was greatly distressed by the explosion.

Page 164, '*If he had any sense they would make a run for it now while they still had a chance.*' *Baltic Episode* places this incident at shortly before 1 a.m. Hampsheir's diary places it one hour earlier and this is consistent with Gus's diary.

Page 164, '"*You hold her steady sir. I'll help Mr Hampsheir,*" *said Beeley clambering into the cockpit.*' FITS, p. 112 makes it clear that it was Beeley alone who carried out the repair.

Page 165, '*Using the pliers Beeley tightened the nut. The rest of the mechanism felt as if it was OK.*' The mechanical detail is from John Hampsheir's log.

Page 165, '. . . *but for Gus, standing in the cockpit with nothing to do but watch the silhouettes of Russian warships all around him, this brief delay seemed to last an eternity.*' In Agar's official VC citation in the *London Gazette* it says that he was in the vicinity of the enemy for 20 minutes while the torpedo was being repaired. This has been interpreted by some authors as meaning that it took twenty minutes to repair the torpedo-launching system. In fact, Hampsheir's diary and Agar's audio tape at the Imperial War Museum Sound Archive make it clear that the *total time* they were among the Russian fleet was twenty minutes. The actual repair took about five. It then took another ten minutes to get CMB4 into the correct firing position. Hampsheir's times are very precise.

Page 165, 'For another ten minutes they continued to creep forward until Gus decided this was about as close as they could expect to get.' In Baltic Episode Gus begins the attack run as soon as the charge is replaced, but this does not tally with the careful timings of Hampsheir in his diary.

Page 166, 'At this point they were about nine hundred metres from the Oleg ...' BE, p. 87, although in his version Gus said that he launched at 500 yards. In his audio tape at the IWM Gus says it was 'between 500 and 1,000 yards'. In his diary Hampsheir estimated that they were between 900 and 1,000 yards from the Oleg when they fired.

Page 166, '... it seemed to Gus that every vessel in the Soviet Baltic fleet was firing at them as they raced for a gap between two of the destroyers.' Agar's audio tape, IWM.

Page 167, 'Although he could not hear anything, both Beeley and Hampsheir were standing alongside him in the cockpit, laughing and cheering as they were thrown about.' 'Everybody opened fire on us ... We leave going full speed 1125 rpm and shot falling all around us. Two big shells missed my stern by 5–10 yards ... Spray and sea drenching us to the skin, but we were merry and bright and gave three cheers although we couldn't hear each other because of the engine.' Agar's diary.

Page 168, 'Minutes later he was asleep.' Such was the secrecy surrounding the mission that until the 1960s and the publication of Baltic Episode there was a great deal of confusion about what actually happened. Gus's VC citation stated that CMB4 was damaged by enemy fire and had to be repaired before the attack whilst moored amongst the enemy ships. Paul Dukes, who knew Gus personally and had discussed the attack with him, thought that CMB4 had been damaged by a mine the day before (this was clearly CMB7) and that the boat had to be repaired before making the successful attack the next night.

Page 169, 'He demanded to know what was going on.' Elsewhere the secret of the CMBs remained intact for a little while longer: for instance, on 21 June, based on Soviet information, the New York Times reported that the Oleg had been sunk by a British submarine.

Page 169, 'Since CMB7 needed to be towed to Biorko for repairs anyway, Gus was quite happy to agree.' At this point in Baltic Episode Gus inserts the journey by land to Biorko and the interview with the Captain of HMS Dragon which actually occurred on 13 June. He also says that he travelled in a truck provided by Sarin rather than the car of one of the local MI6 agents. This also means that subsequent events are placed in a slightly different order in that book – which in turn is different from the order in Footprints in the Sea (!)

Page 170, 'Gus didn't know whether his gamble had paid off or not.' FITS, p. 115

Page 170, 'In all his time in the Royal Navy he had never seen such a reception.' Agar's diary entry.

Page 170, 'That evening Gus was invited to dine with Admiral Cowan on the flagship HMS Cleopatra.' Agar's diary entry.

Page 170, '... he, Cowan, would tell them that the attack had had his full support right from the outset (even if he hadn't known about it, he added with a twinkle in his eye).' BE, p. 93

Page 170, '... claiming that they had been attacked by the entire British fleet which had been forced to retreat before the Bolshevik navy's heroic defence and the sacrifice of the valiant Oleg.' ST-25, p. 269

Page 171, '*He remained deeply grateful to Cowan for the rest of his life.*' *Baltic Episode* was dedicated to him.

Page 171, '*The next day, Friday 20 June, CMB4 returned to Terrioki with Hampsheir and Beeley, under the command of Ed Sindall.*' John Hampsheir's diary.

Page 171, '*Gus spent the rest of the day making arrangements with the Finnish naval liaison officer, Lieutenant Foch . . .*' FITS, p. 119

Page 172, '*Arrangements had been made for him to take a flight to inspect the site of the attack on the Oleg and confirm her fate.*' In *Baltic Episode* Gus says that Sarin arranged this, which is possible, but it would have been more logical for the Finnish liaison officer to have organised it and this may be a device to assist with his re-arrangement of events in this book.

Page 172, '*Gus's pilot was actually a Swede, Arthur Reichel.*' BE, p. 91; FITS, p. 116

Page 172, '*Gus climbed into the front seat of the aircraft . . .*' It is not clear which type of aircraft this was. Gus called it both 'a Junkers' (FITS, p.115) and 'an Aviatik' (TV proposal). The Junkers CL1 did see service in Finland at this time, yet Gus is also clear in his diary that it was a seaplane. There was a Junkers CLS1 seaplane variant with twin floats, but only three were ever built. An Aviatik is highly unlikely.

Page 172, '*. . . and, together with another seaplane flying as escort, they set off south for the Oleg's last known position.*' In *Baltic Episode* Gus describes taking this flight in one aircraft from an airfield inland at Fort Ino. In his diary it is a seaplane and there are two of them.

Page 172, Agar quote: BE, p. 92; FITS, p. 116

Page 172, '*. . . his first reaction was not one of triumph, but of revulsion that he had caused the death of so many men.*' In fact, although the *Oleg* had sunk in only twelve minutes, only five men were lost. (Bennett, p. 126)

Page 172, '*Gus was later told how the survivors, including the women and children, were lined up in pits and machine gunned. Many of them were not killed by the Bolshevik bullets but were buried alive.*' Worse still, the Estonians responded to the disaster by disarming the remainder of the Ingrian forces on the grounds that they were secretly planning to set up their own republic. The Estonians were under such pressure that they had to re-arm them about a month later. (Bennett, pp. 128 & 135)

Page 172, '*It was every bit as horrific as he had imagined.*' Although this is what Gus believed at the time some doubt has been cast on this version of events since. Another version was that the Ingrians murdered their prisoners, over 1,000 people escaped and only the commandant Nikolai Neklyudov (whom Gus consistently misnames as 'Nedlukov') was executed. It was Stalin who gave the orders to bombard the fortress from the sea and who formed the Coastal Army Group at Oranienbaum for the assault. Stalin never forgot the resistance of the Ingrians. During his time as ruler of the Soviet Union 97% of Ingrians were either executed or deported to Siberia. There are only 20,000 of them living in the region today.

There was one other effect of the Krasnaya Gorka revolt. On 14 June the patrol vessel *Kitoboi* hoisted a white flag and sailed over to Finland. Her captain joined the Estonians and was captured by the Bolsheviks in September. They crucified him – literally. (Bennett, p. 129)

Page 173, '*Reichel stayed with his aircraft and waited for a boat to come and tow him to shore where they would make repairs.*' Agar's diary.

Page 174, '*1 BOAT OUT OF ACTION STOP 3 WEEKS TO REPAIR ...*'
Copy in Agar papers IWM.

Page 174, '*He also met Raleigh Le May's new and enthusiastic young assistant whose surname, he thought, was "Card".*' Agar's diary. This must surely be MI6 officer Harry Lambton Carr. He had just been recruited by Raleigh Le May in London for 'passport control duties' and later, in the 1930s, became the MI6 head of station in Helsinki. *The Red Web* by Tom Bower, p. 13

Page 174, '*... and for the first time encountered the professional jealousy which Victoria Cross winners sometimes have to endure.*' The classic example would be Lieutenants Chard and Bromhead who both won the Victoria Cross for conducting the defence of the mission station at Rorke's Drift during the Zulu Wars. Jealousy within the Army dogged their subsequent careers.

Page 176, *The Bruton argument:* Agar's diary entry. The astonishing thing about this interview is that Gus recorded it in such detail, almost word for word across several pages. He never allowed any of this criticism into any of his later accounts, following the unwritten rule of the Royal Navy at that time that officers should never speak ill of each other in public. It may seem like poor form to make such things public now, when those involved can't speak in their own defence, but Agar carefully preserved this record and it is important to show that even heroes don't necessarily have an easy ride – they are subject to the same petty problems and back-biting as the rest of us.

Page 176, '*... and Gus now began to worry about what was happening at Terrioki during his absence.*' Agar was also frustrated by the delay in returning to Terrioki. It seems that Captain Bruton had an unfortunate tendency to upset people: he told the captain of HMS *Vanity*, Commander Rawlings, that he must remain in Reval as he (Bruton) had promised General Gough that HMS *Vanity* would remain at his disposal for the immediate future. Rawlings had to wait in port whilst he sent an urgent message to Admiral Cowan who told him to ignore any such instruction. The delay meant that it was one o'clock the following morning before HMS *Vanity* finally left port.

Page 176, '*Apparently Raleigh Le May had arrived at Terrioki on Saturday 21 June.*' Date confirmed by flimsy of telegram sent by Agar on 28 June (Agar papers IWM).

Page 178, '*... but after twelve minutes the gunfire finally ceased. CMB4 had disappeared into the night-time murk.*' Details are from John Hampsheir's diary.

Chapter 10: Failure to communicate

Page 180, '*... their incompetence had almost reduced Paul Dukes to tears.*' ST-25, p. 280

Page 181, '*... but in fact Paul had lied. He had other ideas.*' RDATM, p. 172

Page 181, '*... Paul asked for his help in finding a guide.*' ST-25, p. 152

Page 182, '*He was also carrying large bundles of cash.*' Sometimes MI6 sent agents with diamonds instead of money as they were easier to carry and easy to convert, but there is no record that Paul was given any. For instance see Judd p.429: Sidney Reilly was sent to Russia with £500 in notes and £750 in diamonds. The diamonds might have had more to do with Reilly conning the gullible Cumming than with operational efficiency.

Page 184, '*Finally, after thrashing around for ten minutes . . .*' RDATM, p. 179

Page 185, '*A few minutes later, an old man in his mid-fifties entered.*' RDATM, p. 182

Page 187, '*They arrived at nine o'clock and immediately there was a great scrum to leave the train.*' RDATM, p. 189

Page 188, '*. . . but the Cheka officers had given an exact description of Paul including the fact that he had a front tooth missing.*' ST-25, p. 167

Page 189, '*That was the warning signal: "Stay away!"*' ST-25, p. 170

Page 189, '*He heard the Russian word for "lock pick" and a sound as though keys had been passed from one person to another.*' RDATM, p. 198

Page 190, '*This time it was that a large box would be placed in a certain window where it was visible from the street.*' RDATM, p. 200. This is one of the many small details missing from ST-25. The reason is not clear.

Page 191, '*Paul's plan was to adopt a new identity and make the Cheka think that another British agent had arrived in Petrograd.*' ST-25, p. 227

Page 191, '*With his radically different appearance, almost all his former agents believed that he was a different man when they first saw him.*' ST-25, p. 228

Page 192, '*There was also a pair of wire framed spectacles which made Paul look like "a pale intellectual".*' And quite a bit like John Lennon! RDATM, p. 224 (photo).

Page 192, '*Zorinsky had arrived in Terrioki only a day or so after Paul had left.*' RDATM, p. 206; ST-25, p. 174

Page 193, '*The genuine intelligence Zorinsky had provided must have been bait to lure Paul into providing as much information about British intelligence operations in the city as possible . . .*' ST-25, p. 173

Page 194, '*He had first met her in February 1919 through one of his other contacts who had suggested that her flat could be used for a meeting.*' In order to preserve the anonymity of his agents Paul never revealed which contact.

Page 194, *Aunt Natalia's description*: ST-25, p. 218

Page 194, '*It says something about Paul that he found this an endearing trait rather than a sign of advancing senility . . .*' ST-25, p. 222

Page 195, '*By the middle of March disturbances in Petrograd factories had become so severe that Lenin himself planned to visit the city.*' The Cheka later claimed that Paul was behind these disturbances. ST-25, p. 179

Page 195, '*As Paul and his new friend approached the People's Palace . . .*' A former sports centre paid for by the Tsar.

Page 196, '*Paul noted wryly that Zinoviev, the leader of the Bolsheviks in Petrograd, who only two years before had been a stick-thin agitator now weighed almost twenty stone.*' Stalin had him executed in 1936.

Page 196, '*While the people of Petrograd lived in famine conditions, he was housed in luxury at the former Astoria Hotel.*' ST-25, p. 242

Page 197, '*. . . the mysterious "Shura" who had provided Paul with his Markovitch passport and some of his best intelligence leads.*' Although not stated in the text this is confirmed in the index of ST-25.

Page 199, '*Two thousand roubles which he had stuffed into his pocket during the raid were enough to pay for everything for the next few months.*' ST-25, p. 213

Page 199, '*Serge, his own brother, had betrayed the gang to the Cheka.*' ST-25, p. 210. At least that was what Paul Dukes believed. No other explanation was ever found.

Page 199, Sonia's description: ST-25, p. 199

Page 201, 'Strunseva's description: ST-25, p. 211

Page 201, '*This close shave was yet another reminder to Paul that he must never lower his guard even for an instant and increased the strain on his nerves even more.*' Paul claimed that this was the only serious error he ever made as a secret agent (ST-25, p. 221). The reader may feel that this is not quite true . . .

Page 202, '*He had even managed to recruit a source right inside Trotsky's "Revolutionary Council of the North" and was able to copy the minutes of their meetings.*' Brook Shepherd, p. 325

Page 202, '*All that the conspirators were waiting for was a sign from the British that they would come to their aid.*' ST-25, p. 237

Page 202, '*With these officers in place and discipline restored, the Bolsheviks might really be able to beat the Whites.*' ST-25, p. 238

Page 202, '*On 31 May Pravda printed a now infamous statement from Lenin and Felix Dzerzhinsky headed "Death to Spies!"*' 'Smersh Spionam!' Smersh is the Russian word for death. It became the colloquial name for Soviet Military Counter-Intelligence in the Second World War and this gave the former naval intelligence officer Ian Fleming the idea for the name of the villainous organisation in his James Bond novels.

Page 202, '*Where was MI6?*' ST-25, p. 231: 'I was completely isolated from the outside world during these months, for although I found couriers to carry my despatches out, none returned to me and I was ignorant as to whether my messages were being delivered'.

Page 203, '*. . . but the longer Cumming's silence continued the more he became convinced that it would have to be done.*' ST-25, p. 240

Page 203, '*The tanks had been sabotaged by officers of the White army.*' ST-25, p. 242

Page 203, '*When the revolution failed, he was brutally tortured and then imprisoned for eighteen months.*' He once showed British diplomat Robert Bruce Lockhart the mangled ends of his fingers where his nails had been torn out. Lockhart did not believe he was the monster he was purported to be. *Memoirs of a British Agent* by Robert Bruce Lockhart, p. 328

Page 204, '*To the British Press he was known as "the Red Terrorist".*' e.g. *Daily Express* 16 August 1919. There is some doubt about whether all that was said about him was true. He certainly denied that anything like the number of deaths alleged had occurred. In the chaos of Revolutionary Russia under the Terror it is almost impossible now to determine the truth, but his reputation at the time is certain.

Page 204, *Xenophon Kalamatiano:* He had been caught on the evening of 18 September 1918 trying to climb over a wall to the safety of the American consulate in Moscow. The Americans had abandoned the Consulate a few days earlier and the perimeter was heavily guarded by Soviet troops, but the Consulate was still under the protection of the Norwegian delegation and he would have been safe if only he could have got in. He was actually climbing the wall when he was hauled down by the gatekeeper who had spotted him and cried for help. He would probably have made it if only he had not tried to protect the walking stick containing all his operational papers. Kalamatiano's remains one of the great unsung tales in the history of espionage and hopefully one day his story will be given the attention it deserves. See Brook Shepherd, p. 232

Page 205, '*In one of his CX reports, Dukes was soon describing the terror measures introduced by Peters as "exceeding everything previously known."*' Brook Shepherd, p. 141

Page 205, '*A conspiracy was uncovered in the Red VIIth Army and anyone connected with it was ruthlessly dealt with.*' Bennett, p. 119

Page 205, '*But they were due to expire in a little over a week and Paul noticed that the Chekist who examined them made a careful note of the expiry date in his notebook.*' ST-25, p. 241

Page 208, '*. . . there was nowhere else to go and only a few minutes left before curfew, but the officer slammed the door.*' Less than a year later, this officer was executed when the Yudenich network was rounded up by the Cheka.

Chapter 11: Gefter

Page 210, '*He could hear the deep boom of naval gunfire somewhere out in the Gulf.*' ST-25, p. 264

Page 210, '*. . . he decided that he would continue to operate in Petrograd, but would travel more frequently to Moscow.*' Paul already had agents in Moscow on a regular salary by 12 June (ST-25, p. 282)

Page 211, '*It was here that he had the most contacts and here that his chances of survival were greatest.*' ST-25, p. 228

Page 211, '*Peter Sokolov had said that Paul could stay at his student flat.*' Peter Sokolov said that he knew the flat had not been searched by the Cheka because of the thick layer of dust over everything. ST-25, p. 265

Page 211, '*The search became an excuse for general looting, rape and murder.*' See Leggett, p. 284

Page 211, '*He became Alexander Bankau, a draughtsman working at one of the factories in Petrograd.*' It is possible that these papers were provided by MI6, but highly unlikely. The only contact had been through Peter Sokolov and although he could have brought them in MI6 would not have known which seals and signatures to use.

Page 212, '*There were dozens of families clustered outside waiting for their turn.*' ST-25, p. 224

Page 213, '*He stuck to his decision not to use the flat any more.*' ST-25, p. 266

Page 213, '*. . . his senior officer arranged for Paul to be sent around the country to find petrol, tyres or motor spares which gave him a perfect cover story for travelling to Moscow and elsewhere.*' ST-25, p. 288

Page 214, '*It was shortly after joining the Red Army . . .*' Paul's Red Army papers were backdated to 25 May 1919, but he joined in June.

Page 214, '*He was running a large network and every single agent required money – for food, for bribes and simply to survive.*' 'There was not a person who did either regular work for me or performed incidental services of one sort or another but who had to have assistance, in some cases a fixed salary, in others with occasional financial help supplemented with food. This last was the highest and most desired form of recompense.' ST-25, p. 282

Page 214, '*This was known as the "Committee for the Relief of the British Colony in Petrograd."*' *The Times* 3 December 1919.

Page 214, '*. . . Mr Gerngross, had been arrested just a few days before . . .*' On 2 June.

Page 214, '... *on suspicion of espionage.*' Statement given by George Gibson to the Foreign Office in December 1920. National Archives.

Page 214, '*Yet, despite the risk, Paul now turned to the secretary of the Committee, George E. Gibson, a British businessman who worked for the United Shipping Company in Petrograd.*' In ST-25, Dukes gives Gibson the pseudonym 'Mr George'. The reason is unclear. The Cheka knew all about him by then and seeing that George was his first name anyway it was hardly much protection. But this weak pseudonym is consistent with describing John Merritt as 'John Johnovitch'.

Page 214, '*John Merritt had introduced Paul to Gibson just before he escaped from Russia.*' Statement given by Gibson to the Foreign Office in December 1920. National Archives.

Page 215, '*Paul asked for approximately 100,000 roubles.*' This estimate is based on the fact that Paul made three visits to Gibson during July and August (ST-25, p. 286) and borrowed a total of 375,000 roubles. (Correspondence between Gibson and the Foreign Office held at the National Archives.) It would be about £250,000 today, which shows both how large Paul's network was and just how expensive espionage can be.

Page 215, '... *and gave Gibson a receipt signed "Captain McNeill", his MI6 cover name.*' Gibson quickly destroyed this receipt which was just as well considering that the Cheka arrested him again just a few months later. (ST-25, p. 286) He seems to have borrowed much of this money from a Jewish moneylender named Ernest Lapin.

Page 215, '*In reality, Gibson had a terrible time trying to get MI6 to refund the money.*' Statement from Gibson to the Foreign Office. Dukes described this as '*a convenient way for Gibson to get money out of the country*'! (ST-25, p. 285) Considering the difficulty Gibson had in getting MI6 to cough up this was a bit of a cheek.

Page 215, '*In Petrograd alone, Party membership was reduced from more than one million people to little more than four thousand.*' ST-25, p. 271

Page 216, '... *Paul later referred to July and early August as the quietest period of his mission.*' ST-25, p. 292

Page 217, '*He was always tired and woke shaking in fright at the slightest sound in the night.*' ST-25, p. 293

Page 217, '*Strong swimmer though he was, he doubted that he would make it.*' ST-25, p. 301

Page 217, '*He turned out to be a former Russian midshipman named Gefter.*' It was claimed that this was a pseudonym, but Paul Dukes's diaries record meetings in the 1920s with A. Gefter who is presumably the same person and a photograph in the Agar papers is annotated with the same name. According to Agar's diary, Sindall had landed Gefter on the evening of Friday, 8 August.

Page 217, '*In his time he claimed to have been a prizefighter, an artist and an actor.*' BE, p. 109

Page 217, *Gefter description:* ST-25, p. 303

Page 217, '*Paul should make arrangements to be ready.*' In fact it was Paul who had to help Gefter. He was already attracting attention from the famine stricken citizens of Petrograd. Several people had pointed him out in the street and said that he must have come from over the border because he was obviously well-fed. Furthermore, the identification documents MI6 had provided Gefter with were very poor and Paul had to provide him with a complete new set. Gefter relates how impressed he was with the quality of these new forgeries and that he finally felt safe. *Reminiscences of a Courier* by A. Gefter.

Page 218, '*By August 1919 Sonia had been in prison for four months* . . .' ST-25, p. 212

Page 218, '*Both men were armed with revolvers.*' ST-25, p. 214

Page 218, '*Paul claims that neither he nor Shura had any idea how the escape was to be effected* . . .'ST-25, p. 214

Page 219, '*. . . met the Red Cross nurse in the courtyard and had walked through the main gates with the other visitors.*' The fact that this escape attempt involved the assistance of a Red Cross nurse was a very serious breach of the integrity of that organisation. Although she appears in RDATM, she is missing from ST-25 in 1938. Paul might have been advised by the censor that the British Government could not be seen to have condoned such a breach.

Page 220, '*. . . but it later turned out to have been a fire in the dockyards.*' ST-25, p. 306

Page 221, '*He peered out at the horizon and tried to get his bearings from the Elagin lightship which marked the Eastern end of Kotlin Island.*' Unlike the Tolboukin lighthouse, the lightship was withdrawn every winter when the Gulf iced over.

Page 221, '*Eventually, Gefter shouted that they would have to turn for shore.*' Gefter's English was not very good. According to his own account he shouted: 'I am compelled to renounce the plan of conducting you to your destination.' One presumes that Paul's reply was a little more direct . . .

Page 222, '*He used one of the oars to help him float* . . .' Typically, in his account of the escape attempt, Gefter claimed that he had no trouble swimming, but had to give Dukes one of the oars because he was in trouble.

Chapter 12: The Kronstadt Raid

It is hard to ascertain the exact details of what happened that night. Many of the eyewitness accounts do not agree on the sequence of events. Even the simplest facts have become confused – for instance, Bill Bremner was certain that no British aircraft attacked during the raid, despite all the evidence of every other eyewitness, including the pilots themselves. Paul Dukes, (who had a personal briefing from Gus Agar), thought that there had been eleven CMBs on the raid not eight (ST-25, p. 319)

Page 224, '*He had seen General Yudenich and his bunch of cronies at first hand, resting in luxury in their Helsinki hotels, and he was not impressed by them.*' Yudenich and his staff were based at the Societenhusen, the best hotel in Helsinki. Agar spent several days there in July and enjoyed considerable attention as the man who sank the *Oleg* (Agar's diary).

Page 224, '*Unfortunately Scale tried to get clearance for this scheme from the difficult Captain Bruton so the plan came to nought.*' Agar's diary 3/7/1919: He tried to see General Gough, but Bruton said he had to be there and that Agar had to tell him what it is about first. 'I swallowed this nasty piece of medicine and told him as much as I thought he could digest.' They then went to see Gough together. Gough admitted that he had not yet even sent an officer to reconnoitre. Bruton then told Gough that if he wanted boats in support then that would be entirely a matter for the military mission, not for Agar, and anyway *he had already ordered 12 boats from England* (!) Agar was dumbstruck at this complete nonsense. He finally decided to leave Bruton to 'stew in his own grease'.

Page 225, '*Her propeller shaft and engine mountings were badly damaged.*' Agar wrote: 'This practically puts the boat out of commission and is too much to bear. Am very glad he [the pilot] couldn't understand what I said about him.' In *Baltic Episode* Agar omits this episode and claims (p. 151) that the damage was caused by a collision with the breakwater at Terrioki after the failure to collect Dukes on 14 August.

Page 225, '*The newly repaired CMB7 would have to be the mainstay of the courier service from now on.*' This trip is also recorded in Hampsheir's log – more evidence that he was not sent home as Agar always claimed, although it does not mean that he actually went on this mission.

Page 225, '*On the same day as the attack he received a telegram from Admiral Cowan informing him that he had been awarded the Victoria Cross for his sinking of the Oleg.*' Agar's diary.

Page 225, '*. . . Gus was referred to in the press as "the mystery VC".*' BE, p. 153

Page 226, '*. . . the Finns had sent six couriers in two weeks and not one had returned.*' Telegram flimsy, Agar papers IWM.

Page 226, '*Instead he remained at Terrioki as an interpreter and camp helper.*' Agar's diary: 'Constantinoff (sic) returned with a bullet in him – failed to get through – am afraid he is not the right type. Too much like a girl and lacks guts . . . Guide led him straight into the midst of Bolshevik soldiers and he was lucky to get away.' BE p.118 paints a rather less condemnatory picture of him, probably because he was still alive at the time of writing.

Page 226, '*. . . and MI6 assumed that he had been either killed or captured.*' Agar's diary entry 1/8/1919

Page 226, '*He thought that Peter had run away to join the White forces in Estonia preferring to fight openly instead of having to deal with ". . . all the messing about he got from the people at Helsingfors . . .".(i.e. Hall and Le May)*' Agar's diary entry 3/8/1919

Page 226, '*These were Victor Jones (ST-35) and John Busby (ST-36).*' BE, p. 123. Agar says that 'Vic Jones' and 'John Bush' were assumed names, but a letter from Jones to Agar in 1960 confirms that this was his real name. As for 'John Bush', photographs of 'the two wireless men' annotated by Agar give his name as Busby and correctly name Jones.

Page 226, '*. . . Jones was a former RNVR Chief Petty Officer who had been demobbed and was working for the Post Office Wireless Department.*' Letter Jones to Agar dated 28 April 1960. There is also a photograph of the two men with the note 'These were the two wireless people trying to communicate with Petrograd'.

Page 227, '*Gus was stunned by Hall's ignorance. Very slowly and carefully he replied: '"All of them."'* Agar's diary entry 5/8/1919

Page 227, '*Hall breezily replied: "Oh that doesn't matter." Gus looked at him coldly and then left the dacha without saying another word.*' Agar was careful to record Hall's exact words.

Page 227, '*This may be the end of our whole show . . .*'Agar's diary entry 5/8/1919

Page 228, *It was Muir who first referred to Gus as "the mystery VC".* Daily Express 31/7/1919

Page 228, '*Even The Times correspondent was only granted one very brief interview with Admiral Cowan.*' BE, p. 155

Page 229, '. . . *on 4 July when the British Cabinet had finally decided that, whilst they would not formally declare war on Soviet Russia, it should now be considered that "a state of war" existed between the two nations.*' Leggett, p. 286

Page 229, '*Furthermore, the harbour gun crews might still be in their shelters when the CMBs arrived.*' Although torpedo-carrying aircraft were available at this date, air-launched torpedoes could not be used in Kronstadt harbour as it was too shallow.

Page 229, '*HMS Vindictive arrived in Biorko Sound on 20 July.*' Eric Brewerton's log, Imperial War Museum. The *Vindictive* had sailed from the Firth of Forth on 2 July.

Page 230, '. . . *thanks to a freak high tide, three tugs and the efforts of hundreds of sailors jumping up and down on her deck to shake her clear.*' Brewerton's logbook and other notes.

Page 230, '*It was a job which Gus and other officers quite frankly thought could not be done . . .*' Agar said as much in *Baltic Episode*.

Page 230, '. . . *only eight of these were to eventually assist in the attack due to maintenance and other problems.*' *Vindictive* carried 12 aircraft (two Camels, three Strutters, three Griffins and four Short seaplanes), but several of these were unavailable for the mission. One Griffin crash-landed in the sea on 13 August – it was salvaged but unusable. One Strutter's engine failed on take-off. Cowan's flagship supposedly carried one Sopwith Camel, but this is never mentioned in the reports. The Bolsheviks also had twelve aircraft operating in the area, but the two sides never met in combat. The greatest danger was in taking off and landing. The only aerial victory recorded by the British was the downing of Krasnaya Gorka's observation balloon. (Bennett, p. 135).

Page 230, '. . . *and carried either four small fragmentation bombs or a single 50lb (23kg) high explosive bomb.*' The armament of Camels could vary – these figures are from Brewerton's notes on the Camel that was assigned to *Vindictive*.

Page 231, *RNAS Mess song:* Liddle, *Men of Gallipoli*, p. 242

Page 231, '*Major David Grahame Donald .*' Although the RNAS had officially merged with the RFC to form the RAF the Royal Air Force on 1 April 1918 and although Agar refers to him as Squadron Leader, Donald had not yet been awarded this rank. Brewerton papers IWM. See also Bennett, p.130.

Page 231, '*A former Scottish rugby international . . .*' Two caps as a prop for Scotland: v Wales 7/2/1914 and v Ireland 28/2/1914.

Page 231, '*The seaplanes were moored on the shore at Sidinsari within sight of Cowan's squadron.*' Bennett, p. 131

Page 231, '. . . *the dour Scotsman neatly summed up the feelings of all his young pilots: "Jesus Christ!"*' 'The aerodrome from which the land machines had to rise in the dark was a month before a wilderness of trees and rocks and in size was quite inadequate.' – Walter Cowan's official report of the raid. However, the drop to the sea did have some advantages: Brewerton, who was then a young pilot in one of the Strutters, later remembered how on his first flight from the airstrip he took off only to find out that his plane's trim had been incorrectly set and he immediately plummeted towards the sea. Thanks to the drop he was able to grab the trim wheel and pull out of the dive in time. Brewerton papers IWM.

Page 232, See Thornycroft, p. 33. '*Eight mechanics bravely answered the call.*'

Once the boats were prepared, it is not clear how many of these men actually travelled to Finland and took part in the raid. At least two and possibly as many as six did.

Page 232, '*On Friday, 25 July, the first CMB arrived.*' Agar's diary.

Page 232, '*In the early morning of 30 July, Major Donald took nine aircraft on the first bombing raid over Kronstadt harbour.*' Operation 'DB' named after Admiral David Beatty. Three more aircraft later made a second attack.

Page 232, '*Since the airfield was not ready, they took off from the deck of the Vindictive.*' The signal log for Koivisto airfield opens on 5 August 1919. See also article in *Flight* magazine 15 April 1920.

Page 232, '*. . . Donald's planes first encountered anti-aircraft fire when they were still four miles from their target.*' From Fort Alexander on the northern shore. (Bennett, p. 134)

Page 232, '*Donald described the anti-aircraft as "very effective throughout" and they were lucky to escape without any losses.*' Bennett, p. 134

Page 233, *Ed Sindall's attack on the Russian motor boat:* Agar's diary. Altogether Marshall expended 700 rounds during the attack – Hampsheir's log.

Page 234, '*On 9 August the remaining CMBs arrived.*' Dobson's report. Agar's diary says 10 August but he is sometimes a day out.

Page 234, '*On 12 August, Bremner and Dobson were taken on a reconnaissance flight over Kronstadt and had a look at the defences.*' Brewerton's log. He flew Dobson in the Strutter (the ballast was removed for this of course). Bremner's memory was that he took a flight several days before Dobson's arrival and did not accompany Dobson on this flight, but his memory has been shown to be fallible in other important aspects of the mission, so it is impossible to be certain.

Page 235, '*Her captain, V. Sevastyanov, was a former Tsarist officer and he had already taken his ship into several encounters with Cowan's squadron.*' For instance, on 4 June the *Gavriil* had sunk the British submarine *L55* with the loss of all hands. Bennett, p. 119

Page 235, '*That afternoon, Cowan called the CMB officers together for a briefing.*' Agar's diary.

Page 235, '*. . . the most important were the two giant battlecruisers the Andrei Pervozvanni and the Petropavlovsk.*' The *Andrei Pervozvanni* was commanded by L. M. Galler who later rose to become Commander-in-Chief of the Soviet Navy in the Second World War. Bennett, p. 125.

Page 235, '*The next target was the submarine depot ship Pamiat Azova.*' She was an old pre-war (1890) cruiser which had been converted to submarine support duties and is sometimes referred to as the '*Dvina*'.

Page 235, '*Reconnaissance photographs showed that this depot ship currently had two submarines berthed alongside, preparing to go to sea.*' BE, p. 160

Page 236, '*The fifth target was the caisson of the dry dock . . .*' The gates which sealed the dry dock from the harbour.

Page 237, '*He clearly liked this man a lot more than Gefter whom he described as "bombastic" and someone who "might give the whole game away to save his skin."*' Agar's diary. This view seems to have been shared by Le May and Hall. Agar notes that they refused to let Gefter have Paul Dukes's contact address until the very last moment in case he disappeared.

Page 237, '*Everything depended on Hugh Beeley and his tending of the engine, but once again he triumphed.*' BE, p. 151. Agar claims to have dropped Peter Sokolov during this trip, but his diary does not record this. Furthermore, he attributes the damage caused to CMB4's propeller on 26 July to this trip, so it may have been a matter of narrative convenience.

Page 237, '*... John Hampsheir's nerves were finally gone. He was never to make another trip in a CMB.*' Agar's diary: 'Finally struggled into Terrioki 0145 ... This is the worst trip I have done. I really did not expect to get back in our little boat through those seas. I took Hampsheir and Beeley with me this time and poor old Hampsheir just about caved in. His nerves I'm afraid are practically gone.'

Page 238, '*The other was a Finn named "Huva" ...*' Dobson's report.

Page 238, '*... could speak fairly good English so Gus suggested that he travel in Dobson's boat in case the flotilla ran into enemy fire and became separated.*' Agar's diary.

Page 238, '*However, the promise of double pay and two quarts of British navy rum each finally convinced them.*' BE, p. 164, although in this version Agar says it was Veroline who travelled with Dobson.

Page 238, '*That afternoon, Friday, 15 August, the crews held their one and only rehearsal for the Kronstadt attack.*' Agar's diary.

Page 239, '*The storm then continued for another day and a half and at one stage was so bad that the CMBs were forced away from the Vindictive to seek shelter in a small inlet off the main bay.*' Letter of Sub Lt Francis Howard, 2 September 1919.

Page 239, '*Zero hour, the moment when the CMBs would pass through the forts to begin their attack run, was set for 0045 on Monday, 18 August 1919.*' Copy of the operational plan contained in the Brewerton papers. This was issued by Donald and headed 'Opn V 11'.

Page 240, '*The starboard engine of CMB86 was giving particular cause for concern. It was only firing on six cylinders despite frantic last-minute work to repair it.*' Letter of Sub Lt Francis Howard, 2 September 1919.

Page 240, '*Another officer who had not expected to be part of the attack was Lieutenant Commander Frank Brade ...*' Referred to by Agar in *Baltic Episode* as 'John Brade'.

Page 240, '*It must have occurred to the crews for the Kronstadt attack that this plan was disturbingly similar – except in this case they were going right into the harbour, the very heart of the enemy defences.*' *Ace's Twilight* by Robert Jackson, p. 123.

Page 241, '*Dobson chose to follow the smuggler's advice and veered away. The rest of the flotilla followed him.*' There was no way that the formation could be restored since none of the 55-foot CMBs were carrying their wireless sets and signalling had been forbidden in case it gave away their position. Dobson later claimed that Agar's boat separated from the main group 'according to plan' – this was news to Agar! (See Dobson's account in *The Times* 19 October 1919).

Page 242, '*Yates told Howard that he would see what could be done and disappeared back into the engine compartment with the other mechanic.*' Letter of Sub Lt Francis Howard, 2 September 1919. Knowing of CMB86's problem engine, Dobson had told Howard that if he could not reach the harbour, CMB86 should patrol the line of forts and engage any patrol craft which tried to intercept the CMBs on the return journey. Howard did his best to comply with this order.

Page 242, '*Even so, the air attack by Donald and his men had not yet started.*'

This is according to Dobson's report and certainly seems consistent with Major Donald's report. However, Agar believed that the bombing raid had already started when the CMBs arrived. Bremner remained convinced that the bombing attack was over before the CMBs arrived and always quoted a Russian seaman who said: 'Why did you send your planes to wake us up so that we were ready to fire at your boats?' But Bremner was definitely wrong.

Page 242, '*They had experienced considerable difficulty getting airborne and they were very late.*' An absence of surface wind meant that the seaplanes struggled to get into the air with their bomb load. One seaplane managed to carry two bombs, one carried one, but the other two had to unload and go without any bombs at all. The engine of one of the Strutters failed on take-off and it had to be scrubbed from the mission. (Donald's report included in the Giddy papers, National Maritime Museum.)

Page 244, '*He headed straight on for the alternative "waiting berth" at the hospital ship.*' Debrief of Bremner, 8 February 1920.

Page 244, '*Giddy later estimated that there were at least ten different shore batteries firing at CMB24 at this time.*' BE, p. 174 quoting Giddy's own account 'Our Russian Interlude' from *Blackwood's Magazine* 1930.

Page 244, '*Afraid of hitting her, he broke off the attack and put CMB24 into a wide turn to buy some time.*' Napier's debrief. This CMB was never identified because of the confusion during the attack. It might have been Steele, but Napier thought it was Bodley, which would place his attack on the *Gavriil* much later.

Page 244, '*Either Sevastyanov's men were incredibly accurate or they were unbelievably lucky.*' In his official report Dobson said that he believed CMB24 had been blown up by her own torpedo striking the bottom. This would be consistent with Giddy's account that they had fired as soon as they came out of the turn – surely their speed was not high enough to avoid 'a death dive' which usually required a long straight run? But it is hard to believe that Napier made such a beginner's mistake, Giddy claimed there were three shells which sank the boat and in the official Soviet communiqué they repeated the story that the *Gavriil* had hit with her first shot. (see Bennett, p. 155)

Page 244, '*He felt a searing pain in the small of the back and knew that he had been hit by shell splinters.*' Giddy was taken to Kronstadt hospital after the attack where these were removed by the surgeon. His injuries were not life-threatening.

Page 245, '*"Well, that's sugared it".*' These are the words quoted in Giddy's published account for a discerning public, but one suspects that his actual words might have been a good deal earthier.

Page 245, '*He was about to go below and see what could be done to get the engines going again when first one and then another shell landed on either side of the boat, knocking him off his feet again ...*'Osman Giddy in interview given to the *Surrey Comet* 19 May 1920.

Page 245, '*... Harvey fell back with his right arm shattered at the elbow.*' Official debrief of Napier 16 April 1920.

Page 245, '*Either way, the remaining boats were now at the mercy of the Soviet destroyer which would have a clear shot at any CMBs entering or leaving the harbour.*' It was some weeks before the fate of Napier's boat was known. Confused reports after the raid said that he had been sunk by sea forts south of Kronstadt as he tried to fight his way out through the main navigation channel. E.g. Dobson's official report.

Page 245, '*For the moment the Gavriil was occupied with machine-gunning the survivors of CMB24 as they floated in the water . . .*' BE, p. 175

Page 246, '*As they roared towards the rapidly listing Pamiat Azova, Mossy Reed brought one engine to a stop . . .*' CMB engines had no reverse gear.

Page 247, '*Above him the sky was lit up by the beams of searchlights and the twinkling streams of tracer fire from the British aircraft.*' Normally British aircraft would use one tracer bullet to every three rounds of .303 ammunition, but for the night attack the mixture was one tracer to two normal rounds so that the pilots had a better chance of hitting the Russian gun emplacements.

Page 249, '*He was amazed at how the little boats had been able to survive the storm of fire that had been directed at them, noting that even the anti-aircraft pom-pom guns were now depressed to their minimum elevation so that they could join in the defence.*' Brewerton's logbook.

Page 249, '*One bullet or shell splinter had pierced the carburettor, reducing her speed, and then another struck the launching gear, jamming it completely.*' See Thornycroft, p. 35. In a letter to Agar, Bodley confirmed this. He was having trouble with both his engine and steering gear even as he approached the harbour entrance. He believed that a shell splinter had damaged or cut a steering rope as he was passing through the forts. Even so, he tried to continue with the attack. The final damage was to the pipe from the explosion bottle which meant that the ram could not be fired. With no way to launch his torpedo there was nothing more he could do. Bodley confirmed that he broke off his attack *before* entering the harbour which is contrary to the belief of some writers e.g. Thornycroft. Dobson claimed that Bodley's torpedo jammed as he was attacking a second destroyer which was coming to the aid of the *Gavriil*, but this is wrong. [Dobson's official report quoted in *The Times* 11 October 1919].

Page 249, '*He veered away to starboard and headed for home.*' The map of the attack included in *Baltic Episode* shows Bodley well inside the harbour and attacking the dry dock when his firing gear was hit. However the original in the Agar papers at the IWM is annotated asking for this to be corrected to show that Bodley did not reach the harbour. For some reason this was not done and the map is incorrect.

Page 249, '*Enemy fire had put one of Bremner's two engines out of action and he had fallen far behind Dobson and Steele.*' Bremner's debrief.

Page 250, '*The explosion was so fierce that Gus later reported that it must have been the Gavriil which had been hit and successfully sunk.*' FITS, p. 136

Page 250, '*. . . moments later Brade fell dead at the wheel as bullets pierced the canopy of the little cockpit.*' Papers in the Agar collection at the IWM confirm that Brade was killed after leaving the harbour but before he could attack the *Gavriil*. According to Bremner he was hit in the face.

Page 251, '*The Gavriil was only two hundred yards away . . .*' Bremner said that he fired the torpedoes at 250 and 200 yards range, although in one much later account, Bremner said that it was Brade who fired the torpedoes.

Page 251, '*The forts opened fire at considerable range, but were very accurate.*' '. . . heavily fired at with machine and rifle fire and guns of various calibres' – Dobson's official report.

Page 252, '*A lesser man might have run straight for home, but Randall was an experienced pilot and as he blipped the engine, he felt sure that it would keep running this time.*' The events of Randall's flight are confirmed by several sources including Brewerton and Dobson.

Page 252, '... *Dobson using the smoke apparatus fitted to the exhausts of his boat to create cover for Steele.*' Some CMBs carried adaptations to their exhaust systems so that they could lay smokescreens for larger vessels. Fortunately CMB31 was one of them.

Page 253, '... *where he landed on the beach about fifteen minutes later.*' At 0406 according to the Koivisto airfield signal log, but most other aircraft had landed long before this (for instance, Brewerton was down at 0245, Lieutenant Fairbrother at 0300), so this may be the time that his fate became known rather than the time he landed. He was spotted by aircraft sent to assess the damage caused by the attack. His Camel could not be repaired on site. It had to be dismantled on the beach and returned to Koivisto in a lighter.

Page 253, '*Yates had managed to get one bank of the starboard engines restarted and they were limping back towards the line of forts at a speed of about seven knots.*' Brewerton papers IWM.

Page 253, Fairbrother quote: Fairbrother Papers, RAF Museum Hendon, AC 1998/46/1–3. (In several respects Fairbrother's account of the raid is wrong – just as several of the sailors' accounts differ – which shows how even eyewitnesses to a historic event can be mistaken.)

Page 253, Howard quote: Letter of Sub Lt Francis Howard, 2 September 1919.

Page 254, '*Bodley reattached the tow and the two boats headed for Biorko Sound.*' Some books have described Bodley towing Howard through the forts under fire, but it is clear from the original sources that the attempt failed. HMS *Wessex* was waiting at the edge of the Russian minefield, took over the tow of CMB86 from Bodley and they finally arrived back at Biorko at 0745.

Page 254, '*Gus wrote later that he was in no doubt that Fletcher had saved their lives.*' FITS, p. 137. Agar later wrote of the airmen in a personal letter to French: 'Without them I don't think any of us would have got back'. (Letter dated 18 August 1919, Agar papers, IWM).

Page 255, '*They had not sunk the Gavriil as Gus Agar had believed, but the Petropavlovsk, Andrei Pervosvanni and Pamiat Azova were all either sunk or badly damaged.*' There is some confusion about the immediate effects of the raid. According to Russian reports, the *Andrei Pervozvanni* was hit once and the *Petropavlovsk* twice, which is odd since the *Petropavlovsk* was the harder target. (Agar believed that one of the hits on the *Petropavlovsk* was actually on the thick steel cable securing it to the harbour wall rather than on the ship itself. It is not clear if this was correct.) There is also the question of whose torpedo missed. It would be natural to assume that this was Steele because he was under such pressure, but he was so close he could hardly miss and was sure that his torpedoes had struck home. Bremner was certain that he saw one of Dobson's torpedoes explode prematurely and was amazed that it didn't take Dobson's boat with it. But Dobson never mentioned this and Bremner was wrong about other significant details of the raid. All of the Russian vessels were later repaired because the water in the harbour was too shallow for them to sink. The *Andrei Pervozvanni* was kept afloat and was in the dry dock undergoing repairs by the following morning. But the raid had achieved its purpose – the repairs took a very long time, the Russian Baltic Fleet was crippled and nothing larger than a destroyer emerged from Kronstadt harbour for the remainder of the conflict.

Page 255, '*Although eight men had lost their lives on the mission ...*' Lt A. Dayrell-Reed (CMB88), Lt Commander F. Brade (CMB62), Sub Lieutenant

H. F. Maclean (CMB62), Leading Seaman S. D. Holmes (CMB62), Chief Motor Mechanic F. L. H. Thatcher (CMB62), Sub Lt T. R. G. Usborne (CMB79), Able Seaman W. Smith (CMB79), Chief Motor Mechanic Francis E. Stephens (CMB79).

Page 255, '... *nine of those missing had survived and were being held prisoner.*' Lt W. H. Bremner (CMB79, wounded), Lt O. Giddy (CMB24, wounded), Chief Motor Mechanic H. J. Dunkley (CMB79, wounded), Chief Motor Mechanic B.Reynish (CMB unknown), Chief Motor Mechanic W. E. Whyte (CMB24), Stoker Petty Officer S. McVeigh (CMB62), Leading Seaman H. J. Bowles (CMB24), Able Seaman J. A. Harvey (CMB24), Lieutenant L. E. S. Napier (CMB24).

Page 255, '*As soon as they heard those words everyone knew that it could only be one man: Bill Bremner.*' Letter V. H. Jones to Agar 28 April 1960.

Page 255, '*Along with the other eight prisoners he would survive to be repatriated in March 1920.*' The British prisoners were in the water for about an hour. They were treated well by the crew of the *Gavriil* who gave them tea and cigarettes. After being transferred from Kronstadt to the mainland, they were taken to Gorohovaya by the Cheka for questioning. Although not tortured, the officers were held in solitary confinement and were treated quite roughly. For a while it seemed as though they were going to be shot as spies. But after several weeks all the men were transferred to Schpalernaya Prison and eventually to the former Andronievsky Monastery in Moscow. Conditions were severe and food was scarce. White Russians offered to smuggle food in to the prison twice a week to prevent starvation and were paid 4,800 roubles a month by MI6. But as Giddy remarked upon his return to England: '*Balls! We never got it.*'

Page 255, '... *although when all the facts became known most agreed that he deserved the higher award.*' e.g. Agar who wrote when summarising the events of that night: '*I think Bill's was the most outstanding feat of all.*' FITS, p. 138

Page 256, '*He was buried on 19 August ...*' Date is from Brewerton's logbook.

Page 256, Cowan quote: Cowan to Brewerton giving a summary of his report to the Admiralty. Brewerton papers IWM.

Chapter 13: Lucky Number Thirteen

Page 257, '*He had managed to find a route overland through the fighting in Estonia.*' At least that was what he said. But in his 1924 account of the journey, the details appear to be copied almost word for word from Dukes's account published just two years earlier. Paul Dukes annotated a copy of this account for Gus Agar and he too seemed to find this story odd. We will probably never know exactly how Gefter got back to Finland.

Page 257, '*The reality of this observation was emphasised on the morning of 20 August. Two Soviet aircraft flew over Terrioki and dropped seven bombs.*' That same day, Bolshevik agents tried to sabotage the aircraft on the landing strip at Koivisto. At 11.15 that morning, sentries chased and fired at a man who was seen trying to get into one of the hangars. (Koivisto Signals Log). There was another attempt and more shots were fired on 2 September (Brewerton's logbook).

Page 258, '... *but someone clearly wanted them out of the area and would probably try again.*' BE, p. 139

Page 258, '*Since Gefter and Peter were accounted for, Gus wondered if the courier Kroslov had been intercepted and had talked under torture. There was no way of knowing.*' Agar's diary.

Page 259, '*Those who knew Gus Agar remember that one characteristic about him stood out: like Horatio Nelson, the hero of Trafalgar, he believed that the most important calling in life was to do his duty.*' Many references, but his nephew's wife who knew him fairly well towards the end of his life, summed up his character when she said in an interview with the author: 'He was the last of the Edwardian gentlemen. If he said that a thing would be done, then it would be done.'

Page 260, '*He shook Marshall by the hand and told him to go and help Beeley prepare CMB7 for sea.*' Agar's diary.

Page 260, '*They were not carrying a torpedo.*' When not carried in the CMBs, the torpedoes were simply pushed out of the troughs and floated in the water next to the fishing boat in Terrioki harbour. They were so low in the water that they were invisible to the Finnish troops on shore. Agar TV proposal IWM.

Chapter 14: Run For Home

Page 264, '... *but the waters at the edge of the Gulf were very shallow for some distance and now that there were more patrols he was sure he would be seen.*' ST-25, p. 322

Page 264, '*But a few days later Peter Sokolov reappeared.*' ST-25, p. 323

Page 264, '*Besides that, his army unit was moving up to the Latvian Front and that would end the most effective part of his cover story.*' ST-25, p. 323

Page 265, '*Within a few days, the Cheka had also picked up V. N. Rozanov, a leader of the Union for the Regeneration of Russia ...*' Soyuz Vorozhdeniia Rossii

Page 265, '*In his hiding place Peters found detailed lists of all National Centre members and intelligence contacts.*' Leggett, p. 286

Page 266, '*So his contacts in the Army provided him with the papers of a soldier recently killed at the Front. Paul became "Private Vladimir Piotrovsky."*' ST-25, p. 326

Page 266, '*Paul's commander also provided the newly resurrected Private Piotrovsky with an order to report to an artillery regiment on the Latvian front near Dvinsk.*' RDATM, p. 287

Page 266, '*Kostya had worked for Paul as a runner carrying messages around the city and doing small jobs for the network.*' RDATM, p. 287

Page 266, '*Since Kostya was happy to desert from the army, Paul decided to take him along.*' ST-25, p. 325

Page 267, '*It all served to emphasise to him that it was time to leave.*' RDATM, p. 207

Page 268, '... *Paul, Peter Sokolov and young Kostya set out for the last time on the evening of Saturday, 30 August 1919.*' RDATM p.287. Dukes says that they left on 'a Sunday evening'. ST-25, p. 324 says that it was 'one day in early September'. The only day which fits both of these descriptions is Sunday, 7 September. However Dukes's diary makes it clear that he left Petrograd at 6 p.m. on Saturday, 30 August.

Page 268, '. . . *despite the protests of the occupants – which tended to die down as they realised just how big Peter was.*' RDATM, p. 288
Page 268, '*They travelled for eleven hours . . .*' RDATM, p. 288
Page 268, '*He was clearly a member of the grandly named "Committee for Combating Desertion."*' RDATM, p. 288
Page 269, '. . . *Peter said that one of the search teams was already in the next compartment and they were searching everything, even the seat cushions.*' RDATM, p. 289
Page 269, '*In desperation, he pulled out the packets and thrust them under his seat.*' RDATM, p. 289
Page 270, '*He put a reassuring hand on his arm and murmured to him to keep his chin up.*' ST-25, p. 330
Page 271, '*There was a sandbagged machine-gun emplacement at the windmill, positioned so that the gun could sweep both the lake and the shoreline.*' ST-25, p. 334
Page 271, '*In the dark, they could not see this clearly and it tore at their clothes and skin until the three of them were ragged and bloody.*' ST-25, p. 334
Page 272, '*By eight o'clock in the morning . . .*' ST-25, p. 335
Page 274, '*He did not necessarily believe Paul's story, but he had decided that it would be better if they were someone else's problem.*' According to Dukes's diary, they were taken to Madon the following day (3 September). At 8 p.m. on Thursday, 4 September, they were taken to the British Consulate at Riga where they stayed for twenty-four hours. They arrived at Reval on Sunday, 7 September. Dukes then travelled back to London via Helsinki, Stockholm, Oslo (Christiana) and Bergen, arriving in Newcastle at 8 a.m. on Wednesday, 17 September.

Chapter 15: The boat they couldn't sink

Page 278, '"*Then I stay also.*"' BE, p. 187
Page 278, '*As he had done before he started to panic – noisily.*' FITS, p. 142
Page 279, '. . . *the petrol cans provided just enough resistance to give a little steerage to the boat.*' FITS, p. 143
Page 281, '*They had been saved by God.*' And Gus was forced to agree: 'Was it a "miracle" like Dunkirk, or perhaps an answer to a prayer? I am sure it was both. *Thy will be done.*' FITS, p. 143

Epilogue

Page 282, '*Once more Gus Agar, now Lieutenant Commander Augustus Agar VC, DSO.*' He had been promoted at the end of July.
Page 282, '*In the distance, Big Ben struck eleven o'clock.*' The date of this meeting is not recorded in the diaries of Agar, Dukes or Cumming. It must have been between 24 September when Agar arrived back in the country and 4 October when Dukes left London to go on leave. Cumming's diary entries for this period are a good illustration of how that book must be treated with caution. He records Dukes's return on the 17 September, Dukes's meeting with Churchill on the 18 September and with Lord Curzon on the 20

September – although the dates are correct, he places them all in November. (Judd, p. 435).

Page 282, '*He had left Biorko on 17 September, arriving in England on Wednesday, 24 September, just seven days after Paul Dukes.*' Agar's diary.

Page 282, '*He had travelled from Helsinki to Stockholm where he had dined with Major John Scale and his wife.*' Saturday, 20 September (Agar's diary).

Page 282, '*In other words they had found Gus to be far too much of an independent thinker to work as an agent for MI6.*' Cumming received notification of this request from Scale on 28 August so the decision must have been taken just before Agar's last mission. Given Cowan's very high opinion of Agar, if Cumming forwarded the request, he no doubt treated the request with the contempt it deserved. Judd, p. 435.

Page 283, '*After lunch with Scale, Gus found that he had several hours to spend before his train left for Oslo.*' At 2130. Oslo was then known as Christiana.

Page 283, '*He watched Sweden play a team from the United States.*' In his diary Agar records this as 'USA v Sweden', but the US national team was not playing at this time. Bethlehem Steel, the US champions, were touring Sweden and they beat a 'Select Swedish XI' 3–2 in Stockholm. However, according to official records this was on 21 September not the 20. This just may be a matter of Agar's occasionally inaccurate record-keeping.

Page 284, '*So Gus recommended him to Cumming and Sindall joined MI6 soon after.*' In a letter dated 11 March 1920, Sindall specifically thanks Agar for recommending him to Cumming (Agar papers, IWM).

Select Bibliography

Dukes, Sir Paul, *Red Dusk and the Morrow* (Williams and Norgate 1922)
    The Story of ST-25 (Cassell 1938)
    The Unending Quest (Cassell 1950)
Agar, Augustus, *Footprints in the Sea* (Evans Brothers 1959)
    Baltic Episode (Hodder and Stoughton 1963)

Dukes's books have been out of print for sixty years and rarely appear on the second-hand market. Agar's books are also out of print, but are slightly easier to find.

In 1967 Agar recorded an interview for the Imperial War Museum Sound Archive. Sadly it only covers the period up to his sinking of the *Oleg*. At the time of writing, those with Internet access can hear the complete interview at the website of his old school: www.oldframlinghamian.com/images/articles/AgarVC.mp3

Andrew, Christopher, *Secret Service* (Heinemann 1985)
Arthur, Max, *Symbol of Courage* (Pan Macmillan 2005)
Bainton, Roy, *Honoured By Strangers – The Life of Captain Francis Cromie CB DSO RN* (Airlife Publishing 2002)
Bell, Henry M., *Land of the Lakes* (Robert Hale, London 1950).
Bennett, Geoffrey, *Freeing The Baltic* (Birlinn 2002)
Bittner, Lt Col D. F. and Coleby, Captain J. M., *Royal Marine Spies* (Royal Marines Historical Society 1993)
Bowen, Tom, *The Red Web* (Aurum Press 1989)
Brogan, Hugh, *The Life of Arthur Ransome* (Jonathan Cape 1984)
    Signalling from Mars: The Letters of Arthur Ransome (Jonathan Cape 1997)

Bruce-Lockhart, R. H., *Memoirs of a British Agent* (Pan Macmillan 2002)

Calder, Robert, *Willie, the Life of W. Somerset Maugham* (William Heinemann 1989)

Cook, Andrew, *Ace of Spies* (Tempus Publishing 2002)
    M: MI5's First Spymaster (Tempus Publishing 2004)

Dawson, Lionel, *Sound of the Guns: The Story of Sir Walter Cowan* (Pen in Han 1949)

Deacon, Richard, *A History of the Russian Secret Service* (Frederick Muller Ltd 1972)

Fisher, John, *Gentleman Spies* (Sutton Publishing 2002)

Gade, John A., *All My Born Days – Experiences of a Naval Intelligence Officer in Europe* (Charles Scribner's Sons, New York, 1942)

Gefter, A., *Reminiscences of a Courier – Archives of the Russian Revolution*, Vol. X, pp. 149–164. (Slovo Publishers, Berlin 1924)

Hart-Davis, Rupert, *The Life of Hugh Walpole* (Macmillan and Co 1952)

Humphries, Roy, *The Dover Patrol 1914–1918* (Sutton Publishing 1998)

Ireland, Bernard, *War at Sea* (Cassell, 2002)

Jackson, Robert, *Aces' Twilight* (Sphere Books 1988)

Judd, Alan, *The Quest for 'C' – Mansfield Cumming and the founding of the Secret Service* (Harper Collins 1999)

Knightley, Phillip, *The Second Oldest Profession* (Pimlico 2003)

Landau, Henry, *All's Fair* (Blue Ribbon Books 1934)

Leggett, George, *The Cheka* (Clarendon Press, 1981)

Linklater, Andro, *Compton Mackenzie: A Life* (The Hogarth Press 1992)

Morgan, Janet, *The Secrets of the Rue St Roch* (Allen Lane 2004)

Munson, Kenneth, *Fighters 1914–18* (Blandford Press 1968)
    Bombers 1914–18 (Blandford Press 1968)

Piper, Leonard, *Dangerous Waters – The Life and Death of Erskine Childers* (Hambledon and London 2003)

Radcliffe, Maud, *A Baltic Story* (Published privately, London 1993)

Ransome, Arthur, *Autobiography* (Jonathan Cape 1976)

Thornycroft, Sir John I., *A Short History of the Revival of the Small Torpedo Boat* (privately published 1920)

Walpole, Hugh, *The Secret City* (Sutton Publishing 1997)

Welch, Frances, *The Romanovs and Mr Gibbes* (Short Books 2002)

West, Nigel, *MI6* (Weidenfeld & Nicolson 1983)

Reference Works
Who's Who
Janes Fighting Ships 1919

Other sources
Captain Stephen R. New, Unpublished MA Dissertation: 'The Development and Operational Use of Coastal Motor Boats 1904–1919'.

Imperial War Museum:
The personal diary and papers of Captain Augustus Agar
The papers of Sub-lieutenant John White Hampsheir
The papers of Squadron Leader Eric Brewerton

National Maritime Museum:
The papers of Admiral Sir Walter Cowan
The papers of Captain Osman Giddy
Memoir of Sub-lieutenant Francis Howard RNR by Captain Vincent Howard RN

National Archives:
Foreign and Colonial Office Lists
Royal Navy, Royal Naval Reserve and Royal Naval Volunteer Reserve records

RAF Museum, Hendon:
The papers of James MacGregor Fairbrother

British Library Newspaper Archive at Colindale:
The Times
Daily Express
The Daily Telegraph

Hoover Institution Archives at Stanford University:
The personal diaries and papers of Sir Paul Dukes

Maps

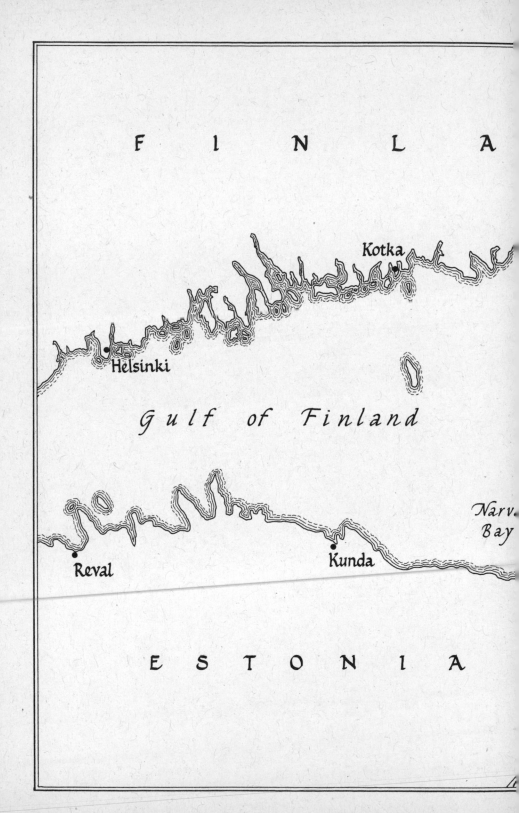

F I N L A

Kotka

Helsinki

Gulf of Finland

Narv.
Bay

Reval

Kunda

E S T O N I A

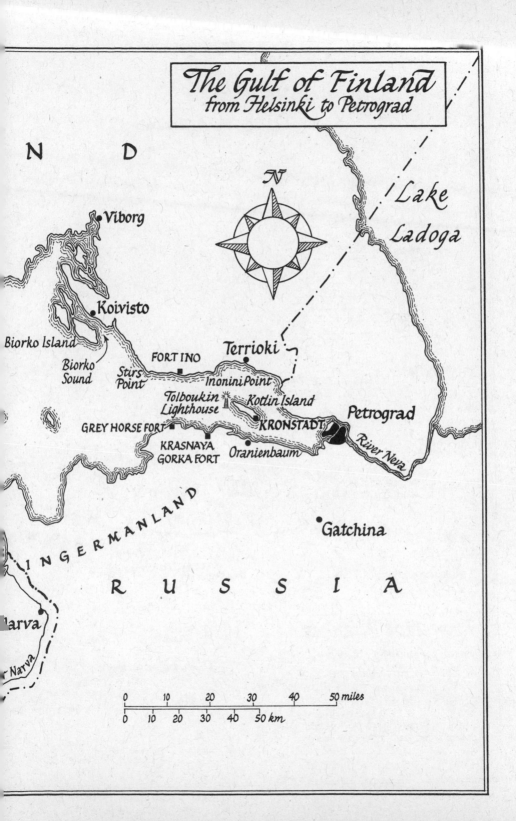

The Gulf of Finland
from Helsinki to Petrograd

N D

N

Lake Ladoga

• Viborg

• Koivisto

Biorko Island

Biorko Sound

FORT INO

Stirs Point

Terrioki

Inonini Point

Tolboukin Lighthouse

Kotlin Island

GREY HORSE FORT

KRONSTADT

Petrograd

KRASNAYA GORKA FORT

Oranienbaum

River Neva

• Gatchina

I N G E R M A N L A N D

R U S S I A

Narva

R. Narva

0   10   20   30   40   50 miles

0   10 20 30 40 50 km

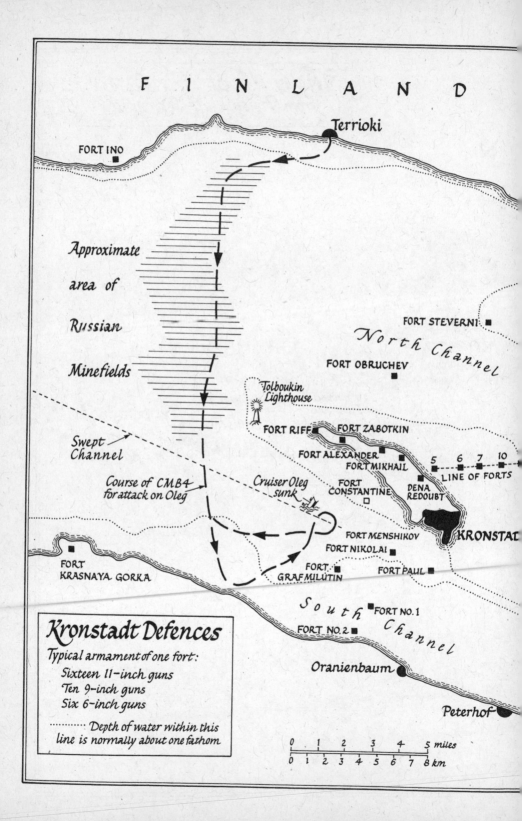

F I N L A N D

Terrioki

FORT INO

Approximate

area of

Russian

Minefields

FORT STEVERNI

North Channel

FORT OBRUCHEV

Tolboukin
Lighthouse

*Swept
Channel*

FORT RIFF   FORT ZABOTKIN

FORT ALEXANDER

FORT MIKHAIL

5   6 7   10

LINE OF FORTS

*Course of CMB4
for attack on Oleg*

Cruiser Oleg
sunk

FORT
CONSTANTINE

DENA
REDOUBT

KRONSTAD

FORT MENSHIKOV

FORT
KRASNAYA GORKA

FORT NIKOLAI

FORT
GRAFMILUTIN

FORT PAUL

South FORT NO.1

Channel

FORT NO.2

Oranienbaum

Peterhof

Kronstadt Defences

Typical armament of one fort:

  Sixteen 11-inch guns
  Ten 9-inch guns
  Six 6-inch guns

.... *Depth of water within this
line is normally about one fathom*

0 1 2 3 4 5 miles
0 1 2 3 4 5 6 7 8 km

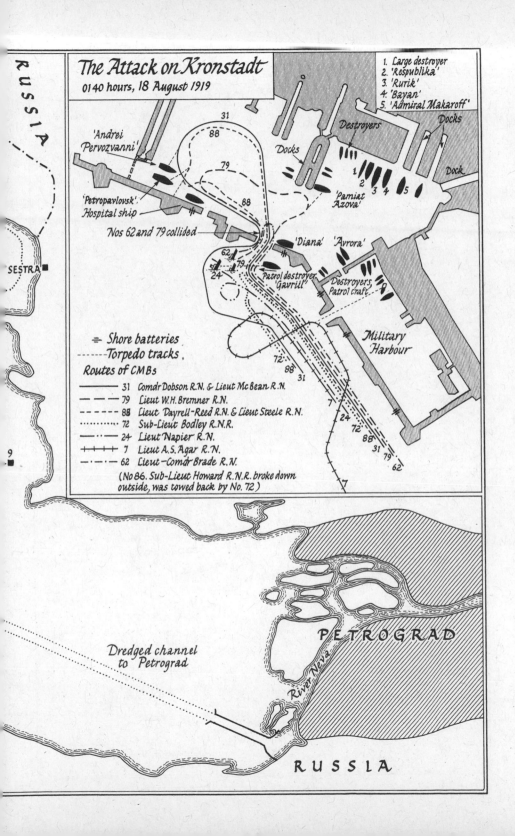

The Attack on Kronstadt
0140 hours, 18 August 1919

1. Large destroyer
2. 'Respublika'
3. 'Rurik'
4. 'Bayan'
5. 'Admiral Makaroff'

RUSSIA

'Andrei Pervozvanni'

'Petropavlovsk'
Hospital ship

Nos 62 and 79 collided

Docks

Docks

Docks

Dock

Destroyers

'Pamiat Azova'

'Diana'   'Avrora'

Patrol destroyer 'Gavriil'

Destroyers, Patrol craft

Military Harbour

SESTRA

⚊ Shore batteries
┈┈ Torpedo tracks
Routes of CMBs

──── 31 Comdr Dobson R.N. & Lieut McBean R.N.
─ ─ ─ 79 Lieut W.H. Bremner R.N.
- - - 88 Lieut Dayrell-Reed R.N. & Lieut Steele R.N.
········ 72 Sub-Lieut Bodley R.N.R.
─┼─┼─ 24 Lieut Napier R.N.
┼┼┼┼ 7 Lieut A.S. Agar R.N.
─·─·─ 62 Lieut-Comdr Brade R.N.

(No 86. Sub-Lieut Howard R.N.R. broke down outside, was towed back by No. 72.)

Dredged channel to Petrograd

PETROGRAD

River Neva

RUSSIA

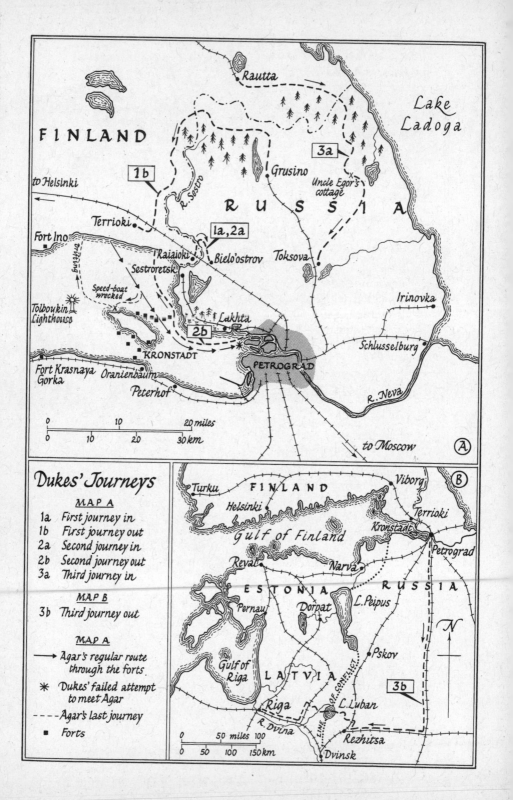

FINLAND

to Helsinki

Fort Ino

Terrioki

Raiaioki

Sestroretsk

Tolboukin
Lighthouse

Speed-boat
wrecked

KRONSTADT

Fort Krasnaya
Gorka

Oranienbaum

Peterhof

1b

1a, 2a

Bielo'ostrov

Lakhta

2b

PETROGRAD

R. Sestro

R U S S I A

Rautta

Grusino

3a

Uncle Egor's
cottage

Toksova

Irinovka

Schlusselburg

R. Neva

Lake
Ladoga

to Moscow

0   10   20 miles
0   10   20   30 km

A

Dukes' Journeys

MAP A

1a First journey in
1b First journey out
2a Second journey in
2b Second journey out
3a Third journey in

MAP B

3b Third journey out

MAP A

→ Agar's regular route
through the forts

✳ Dukes' failed attempt
to meet Agar

- - - Agar's last journey

■ Forts

FINLAND

Turku

Helsinki

Gulf of Finland

Reval

Viborg

Terrioki

Kronstadt

Petrograd

Narva

ESTONIA

RUSSIA

Pernau

Dorpat

L. Peipus

Gulf of
Riga

LATVIA

Pskov

Riga

R. Dvina

L. Luban

Rezhitsa

Dvinsk

3b

N

B

0   50 miles 100
0   50   100 150 km

Index